NEW DIRECTIONS IN ARCHAEOLOGY

CENTRE AND PERIPHERY IN THE ANCIENT WORLD

CENTRE AND PERIPHERY IN THE ANCIENT WORLD

EDITED BY MICHAEL ROWLANDS,
MOGENS LARSEN AND
KRISTIAN KRISTIANSEN

The right of the
University of Cambridge
to print and sell
all manner of books
was granted by
Henry VIII in 1534.
The University has printed
and published continuously
since 1584.

CAMBRIDGE UNIVERSITY PRESS

CAMBRIDGE

LONDON   NEW YORK   NEW ROCHELLE

MELBOURNE   SYDNEY

Published by the Press Syndicate of the University of Cambridge
The Pitt Building, Trumpington Street, Cambridge CB2 1RP
32 East 57th Street, New York, NY 10022, USA
10 Stamford Road, Oakleigh, Melbourne 3166, Australia

First published 1987

Printed in Great Britain at the University Press, Cambridge

British Library cataloguing in publication data

Centre and periphery in the ancient world. –
(New directions in archaeology)
1. Social history – To 500
I. Rowlands, Michael   II. Larsen, Mogens
III. Kristiansen, Kristian   IV. Series
930   HN9

Library of Congress cataloguing in publication data

Centre and periphery in the ancient world.
(New directions in archaeology)
Bibliography.
Includes index.
1. Mediterranean Region – Civilization.
2. Mediterranean Region – Commerce.
I. Rowlands, M. J.   II. Larsen, Mogens Trolle.
III. Kristiansen, Kristian, 1948–.   IV. Series.
DE60.C46 1987   930′.09′1822   87-26401

ISBN 0 521 25103 6

AN

CONTENTS

CONTRIBUTORS

Professor Phil Kohl, Department of Anthropology, Wellesley College, Wellesley, Massachusetts 02181, USA.

Professor Leon Marfoe, The Oriental Institute, University of Chicago, Chicago, Illinois 60637, USA.

Dr P. R. S. Moorey, Department of Antiquities, Ashmolean Museum, Oxford OX1 2PH.

Dr Mogens Larsen, Carl Niebuhr Institute of Near Eastern Studies, 2 Kejsergade , DK 1155, Copenhagen K, Denmark.

Professor M. Liverani, Instituto di Paletnologia, Universita di Roma, Italy.

Professor C. Zaccagnini, Lingotineri, Mellini 7, 1-00193, Roma, Italy.

Dr Daphne Nash, Ashmolean Museum, Oxford OX1 2PH.

Dr Colin Haselgrove, Department of Archaeology, 46 Saddler St., Durham, DH1 3NU.

Dr Lotte Hedeager, Stoltenberjsgade 3, 1576 Copenhagen-K, Denmark.

Dr Kristian Kristiansen, Ministry of the Environment, Amaliegade 13, DK-1256, Copenhagen-K, Denmark.

Dr Michael Rowlands, Department of Anthropology, University College London, London W1E 6BT.

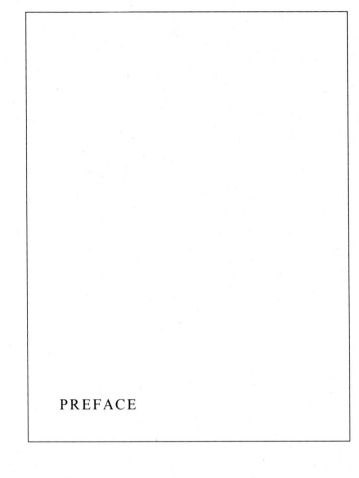

PREFACE

Many of the papers in this volume were first given at a conference entitled 'Relations between the Near East, the Mediterranean World and Europe – 3rd to 1st millennium BC' which was held at Aarhus in 1980. This was also the occasion when a number of the problems and ideas which are the concern of this volume were first discussed. One of these is characterising forms of fluid and open-ended networks of social relations, usually subsumed in archaeological and historical terminologies by such shorthand phrases as 'exchange', 'interrelations', 'interractions' (either hierarchical or egalitarian systems), 'dependency' or, as here, by borrowing from Immanuel Wallerstein the notion of centre and periphery. All of these terms offend in one way or another and may be said to imply a Eurocentric bias. But this is something from which we are unlikely to escape and our only defence must lie in being clear as to the problem we wish the term to address and help us to understand.

In this volume, we take this to be the nature of exploitation and its manifestations on a regional scale. Wallerstein's concept of centre and periphery has the advantage of asking how exploitation functions in social contexts that are not the products of modern states with their nationalised economies and class structures. It challenges us instead to conceive of local communities as ideologically formed to resist the conditions that promote inequalities and domination. This raises the question of the relation between power and cosmology and how the pursuit of self interest should ideally conform to the maintenance of universal order. This has of course long been recognised, although not without disagreement as to how one inscribes itself on the other. Even so, an emphasis on transcendent moral authority denies any simple imposition of a rationalist model of conscious power struggles and legitimation in the analysis of premodern (and modern!) forms of domination. In particular, it would disagree with such modernist categories as structure/agency and the consequent tendency to limit culture to the symbolic as the negotiation of meaning and the strategising of power (e.g. Hodder 1982; Miller and Tilley 1984).

Another problem is whether exploitation necessarily depends on coercion. In periods of crisis, this is undoubtedly the case. But in more stable circumstances, repression may be more securely based through establishing a hegemony of shared interests and beliefs in the benefits of maintaining the established order. What are the conditions which promote the recognition of crisis and desire for change in contrast to the desireability of reproducing the same? Narrative prehistories are often structured around such opposing views of stagnation and dynamism.

It also tends to be assumed that different forms of exploitation are contained within 'societies' or 'ethnic groups' which are accepted, rather unproblematically, to be bounded units. Yet modern nation states, as political units, have been unusually successful in developing controls over the material and social resources within their boundaries. Unique developments in state bureaucracies, military organisation, surveillance, transport and communication are crucial factors in explaining their success in contrast to premodern societies. By making complete social boundedness an unusual occurrence whose evolution needs to be explained, we might also account for the fact that the archaeological unit of analysis has become more intractable and difficult to define with increasing sophistication in measuring variation in the material culture record.

This certainly affects any literal use of Wallerstein's centre–periphery model in prehistory since it is axiomatic to his definition of exploitation that the relationship should be one of unequal exchange between sovereign units. Yet the unitary models of social stratification on which this relies are not the most helpful for understanding premodern forms of inequality. The idea that widely dispersed elites could recognise themselves as a community forming a network of shared power and meaning precisely to help each other control local hierarchies from which they attempt to be culturally remote and yet upon which they may be quite fragilely imposed, is not so rare a feature even in modern European history.

Finally the original geographical definition of the conference has been retained in order to allow for patterns of exploitation in social and political relations that may not correspond to contemporary culture area definitions. This pursuit of the particular is justified by the assurance that understanding the interplay of the abstract and the particular will lead us to useful propositions about the diversity of human societies.

Our thanks are due to all the scholars who contributed to the original conference as well as to the Danish Research Council for the Humanities and to Aarhus University for their financial support. We are also grateful to our editors at Cambridge University Press: Kate Owen and Peter Richards.

Michael Rowlands
Mogens Larsen
Kristian Kristiansen

Part one

Theoretical perspectives

Chapter 1

**Centre and periphery:
a review of a concept**

Michael Rowlands

Introduction

One of the great strengths of marxism as a critical doctrine has been its claim to expose purportedly complete explanations as in fact partial and ideologically biased. As Lukacs put it, 'it is not the primacy of economic motives in historical explanation that constitutes the decisive difference between marxism and bourgeois thought but the point of view of totality' (Lukacs 1968:27). In the mid twentieth century, the dominant theory of development in the core countries of the capitalist world economy had added little to nineteenth century theories of social change. Societies changed due to the logic of their internal historical development and either because of historical accident or indigenous advantages, some were simply more advanced than others. In other words, the framework was historicist and fixed firmly in categories of thought that anticipated all societies moving through objectively similar stages of growth and development. Moreover each society was moved along in this process by a constant examination of its own origins and an assessment of its rate of progress. This subjective evaluation of an objective past formed the ontological basis on which future growth was deemed to depend. It is more than a coincidence that physical excavation of past fragments and their being brought into order through interpretation and publication should also have developed as the dominant archaeological method by which this process of self identification would be achieved.

In *Emile*, Rousseau urges his heroine to preserve authenticity against all the dissolving influences of modernity and recommends 'First of all, you must build a wall around your child's soul. Behind the protective enclosure of education the underground work of excavation could go on to recover the buried roots of the human spirit on which true liberation depended' (cit. Berman 1970:171). It is perhaps symptomatic of twentieth-century pessimism that this attitude to the benefits of digging deep had already soured by the time of Freud. 'The destruction of Pompeii was only beginning now that it had been dug up' he says in his description of the Rat Man (Freud 1909:153). This Nietzschean theme that the products of human life (spontaneity) become corroded when brought into the light of day (conscious reason) has generated a rich discourse much of which is probably irrelevant for most practising archaeologists. Yet in the decline from Enlightenment optimism to *fin-de-siècle* pessimism, excavation retained a privileged if transformed role. The royal road to archaeological knowledge betrays its own origins in an objectivity/subjectivity dualism that quite unquestioningly accorded privilege to the means of constituting a long and enduring narrative of its own past. Rousseau's advice betrays a related theme that is equally constant. Self-identity can only be constituted through the prior existence of a sense of boundedness. This thoroughly modern virtue assumes that awareness of historical development is a conscious process and is restricted to motivated actors living within the bounds of their mutually accepted limits of self-identity. In this respect there is little difference between historicist, evolutionist or diffusionist doctrines since for them, the autonomy of the cultural unit is never in doubt, only its capacity for creativity. Yet boundedness requires a definition of 'otherness', an excluded category of the incomprehensible or the undesirable against which the certainty and familiarity of habitual and traditional action can constantly be reaffirmed. Censorship functions as a strategy of exclusion to place such aberrations into the space of the alien, the primitive or the unconscious. Whatever their form, all share common properties in their unpredictability, irrationality or uncontrollable nature in contrast to stable self identity being the product of belonging to bounded social units embedded in traditional ways of life.

The categories of objectivity and subjectivity have been largely shaped by this peculiarly western experience to the extent that they have been constituted in constant antagonism to each other (Rowlands 1984b). In archaeology, 'digging deep' in order to reconstruct the particular history of a unique historical community has for long been opposed to a tradition of skeptical disbelief that values an outsider point of view. Whilst the former privileges the search for identity through authenticity, the latter emphasises truth usually by claiming that historical processes exist that operate outside of human conscious knowledge altogether. Moreover subjectivity was attacked as being not only Eurocentric and mystifying but intentionally concerned with denying its own real conditions of objective existence. The total assault on subjectivity in the post World War II era is understandable given that some of the most barbaric acts of twentieth-century history were perpetrated as a justification of the view that objective and subjective conditions of existence were only to be experienced within the same socially defined unit. Various nationalisms, fascisms and the 'gulag' have been pursued in the belief that a subjective definition of wholeness, as a product of historical or racial purity, should physically dominate and control all the objective material conditions which affect it. Given that this has been a constant recipe for militaristic expansion as well as the baleful consequences of a 'hunger for wholeness' which placed all those outside the bounds of pure identity as inferior and non-human, it is scarcely surprising that all attempts to rationalise or integrate subjective and objective approaches in the post-war era have resulted in failure. Even so, their antagonism is quite misguided and perpetuates a pathology of the western intellectual tradition. Those who adhere to a scientific, objectivist stance can never cope with the real emotional forces that shape people's perceptions of their own past and the role it plays in the present. And those that espouse a dogged subjectivism espouse a relatavism that can make nothing of the ironies and unintended consequences of the history that impinge upon sentient human action. Moreover, those that adopt the psychotic solution of jumbling the two stances together become confused or worse. By the early 60s in a range of different fields, a solution had been arrived at which recognised the distinctiveness of the two stances and yet which also recognised their complementarity. Both were seen as necessary aspects of the same cognitive process which may be carried on in different contexts without it necessarily arousing conflict between them (cf. Jay 1977). It is to this tradition that attempts by writers such as Braudel, Frank and Wallerstein to revise modern European theories of social change belong and against which their claims have to be judged.

Development and underdevelopment

In the late 40s and 50s, the dominant view of world history stressed the independent development of the West, which had now reached a peak of economic and political power, and a world role for the USA in the management of international politics and development. Comparative sociology had demonstrated conclusively that the precocious rise of the West was due to a unique combination of material and cultural factors that were not to be found elsewhere. Through the transmission of technological and managerial skills, economic aid and education, it was envisaged that the developed West could intervene to break the conditions of historical underdevelopment in the rest of the world. These ideals passed from political science into anthropology to generate a distinctive body of fieldwork and publication in this period (see Wolf 1982) and also into archaeology through the impact of neo-evolutionist doctrines in America and Britain (cf. Binford 1962; Renfrew 1972).

As a perspective on modern development, these views were most trenchantly criticised by André Gunder Frank (1966, 1969) and Immanuel Wallerstein (1974, 1979a); for the precapitalist eras by Ekholm (1977) and Ekholm and Friedman (1979, 1980) and more cautiously by Jane Schneider (1977); and for the ethnographic non-capitalist world by Eric Wolf (1982). Frank articulated the then heretical position that capitalism had been expansionist since the sixteenth century and wherever it penetrated had turned other areas into underdeveloped dependent satellites (Wallerstein's peripheries) in order to extract surpluses to meet the requirements of at first mercantile and subsequently industrial metropoles (Wallerstein's centres). Both Frank's and Wallerstein's theses are strongly circulationist in arguing that the expansion of a world market has created an international division of labour as a precondition for exploitation to take place. The underdevelopment of peripheral areas was not a result of their archaic social structures but a product of their historical relations with the developed world, ever renewed and intensified by the transfer of surplus and their dependence on manufactured goods and technological innovation from industrialised core areas.

The general argument has not gone unscathed and the literature on the debate is now so enormous as to be impossible to summarise here (cf. Goodman and Redclift 1982: Chapter 2). Some of the most astringent criticisms have come from orthodox Marxists who have criticised the emphasis on unequal exchange and the failure to analyse internal class relations within core and peripheral social formations. They have objected also to the functionalism of the argument which denies peripheral formations their own histories of development and resistances to exploitation (Laclau 1971; Brenner, 1977). A theory which claims that conscious identity with local social units, whether nation states, ethnic groups, or religious movements, is shaped and formed by outside forces is unlikely to appeal to those advocating political action as a means of equalising the world order. Neither Frank nor Wallerstein (or their critics) have been particularly interested in the precapitalist era. To exaggerate slightly, it might be said that they chose to reproduce the modern/premodern division of world history and saw a 'world system', imperialism and a 'world economy' as uniquely modern phenomena. Prior to the sixteenth century, they argued, history had been the product of expanding polities (world empires) that related to each other through conquest, militarism and tribute (Wallerstein 1974: Intro.). In this respect, Wallerstein can be placed firmly in the substantivist camp. By contrast, Ekholm and Friedman have stressed the long-term continuity which exists between precapitalist and capitalist world economies and noted that the transition to the modern world economy was itself the product of the dissolution of a previously unified medieval European/Mediterranean world economy (Ekholm and Friedman 1979; 1980, also Schneider 1977). In many respects, and in particular the emphasis on the longevity of capital accumulation, their thesis is part of the long-standing primitivist/modernist debate on the characterisation of the ancient economy (cf. Will 1954; Finley 1973). It needs emphasising therefore that it is the scale of interaction, rather than the significance of 'trade' or the existence of primitive or archaic forms of capitalism, that has most appealed to some archaeologists and historians working in earlier time periods. World Systems/Dependency theory has had greater impact on rethinking the significance of large-scale spatial/temporal shifts in geopolitical centres; on the correlation of expanding peripheral formations with political decentralisation in far-away core areas and on the theorisation of irreversible social change (e.g. Kohl 1978; Frankenstein and Rowlands 1978; Gledhill 1979; Kristian-

sen 1982; Upham 1982). In addition, more interest has been shown in how it helps to understand cyclical development in early states and empires, on modes of incorporation and resistance to incorporation by peripheral social formations and the effects of both on their internal development (Kohl 1977; Hedeager 1978b; Haselgrove 1982). Questions which previously had floundered in the vaguer language of interaction and diffusion or had never been raised because the subject matters were deemed to belong to separate, specialist disciplines.

However, as some of the chapters in this volume demonstrate, a simple projection of such ideas into the past has not proceeded without difficulty (cf. Kohl, Larsen). Kohl summarises the position for the Ancient Near East in the following manner: 'the model of a world system, which Wallerstein defined for the modern era only imperfectly, describes structured interactions in antiquity... the development of underdevelopment in the Bronze Age was sharply constrained or itself underdeveloped' (this volume p. 22). The reasons for this, he summarises, were that technologies were neither as specialised nor as controlled in the same way; transport systems limited large-scale interregional economic integration and the capacity of cores to control and dominate their peripheries for long periods of time were more constrained (Kohl, this volume p. 23). In fact, similar criticisms have been levelled at Wallerstein's characterisation that the modern world has been 'capitalist' in the above sense, since the sixteenth century and it has been argued instead that most of these features are true only for the post World War II (see Wolf 1982). So, whether this constitutes a real capitalist/precapitalist empirical contrast is open to doubt. Nevertheless, as Kohl further remarks, 'models that fail also instruct and consideration of the economic and political linkages among disparate social formations is essential to advance beyond the theoretically simple minded and empirically innocent alternatives proveded by neo-evolutionism' (Kohl this volume, p. 24). It has to be the purpose of this introductory chapter to suggest ways in which such theories, used heuristically, can help us to do so.

Systems of social reproduction

Theorists of markedly different positions have chosen to agree that the analysis of social units is distinct from interpreting interactions between them. The reasons for this are complex and rooted in the conditions leading to the development of modern nation states and the promotion of international trade as their optimum means of interaction. The result is a received wisdom which polarises the categories of production and exchange and privileges the first as occurring within a bounded social unit and determines that the latter exists between them. Moreover, the internal circulation of goods within a social unit is assumed to take on a different form from foreign trade and to be influenced by social factors which might otherwise be considered as market imperfections.

Such ideas are characteristic of many general analyses which have interpreted modern social development through posing dualistic evolutionary models of exchange relations. This includes the general influence of Marx, Weber and Polanyi, who, although varying in specific content, tended to dichotomise between capitalist and precapitalist, rational and non-rational, embedded and disembedded economies and thus temporalise what was in origin experienced spatially. Marx's well-known assertion that the exchange of objects precedes historically the exchange of labour and that it took place initially on the boundaries of or between productive communities, whilst internal distribution took the form of an exchange of use values, guides the work of Meillassoux (1971), Sahlins (1974), Godelier (1977) and Gregory (1982). Much the same ethos underlies Mauss's distinction between gift exchange (or reciprocity) as the foundation of social relationships, and commerce as the seeking of profits through trade bringing about social dissolution (Mauss 1954). Polanyi's work was based on a strong political conviction that the function of the economy should be to strengthen social relationships and to eliminate conflict in the allocation of wealth which should conform to the values of each society (Humphreys 1969:203). The subordination of economic means to social ends had been for Polanyi a feature of all previous societies and in this sense he agreed with Weber that the unleashing of a pure economic rationality was the distinctive feature of modern capitalism and, for this reason, it was impossible to use its categories to understand the premodern. Weber's notion that status dominated in the ancient world and 'trading for gain' was of negligible importance and severely constrained is thus still central to debates on the characterisation of the ancient economy (Weber 1976; Finley 1973; Garnsey, Hopkins and Whittaker 1983; D'Arms 1981; Larsen, this volume).

In contrast to much of this orthodoxy, Wallerstein has always stressed that capitalism did not emerge in one particular bounded territorial unit but within what he terms a multi-state system (Wallerstein 1979a). His thesis therefore poses state-economy problems that are not singular but plural. The real value of this insight may have been obscured by his overestimating the international aspects of capitalism and his insistence that the 'world economy' has been capitalist since the sixteenth century AD. This tended to distract him and others from inquiring into the unevenness of the process and in particular that a 'capitalist core' in Europe was not formed 'all of a piece' but developed through the formation of increasingly antagonistic and self-contained nation states. Yet, in the sixteenth century, early modern Europe formed an emerging core which shared a certain unity within which relatively weak states held insecure control over their respective economic systems (Tilly 1977). Even the absolutist regimes of Spain and Portugal were unable to control the flow of bullion and treasure from the New World to the Netherlands and England to fund mercantile development there rather than within their own territories. What shaped this unity is unclear. It certainly was not Christianity, as in the Medieval world, nor was there a strongly idealised cultural–historical unity. Ties of diplomacy, court exchange, intermarriage of royals, foreign alliances and treaties of mutual support and defence were their overt manifestation.

The point to stress, therefore, is that the multi-state systems of early modern Europe, depending as they did on military strength and international treaties, were neither strongly articulated with the workings of the international economy nor with their own civil societies. A fully developed 'organic state' in which economy, social classes, culture and religion were 'nationalised' and limited to increasingly antagonistic nation states is a post eighteenth century phenomenon. Only then does it make sense to describe production as internal and trade as external or the state – paraphrasing Marx – as an executive committee managing the common affairs of the ruling classes. Moreover, only then can one say that a set of capitalist economic relations had been tamed and possessed by a nation state holding a monopoly of military force and able to regulate their self-contained economic interests within what were to become separate imperial domains.

It would be unrealistic to expect a similar set of contingencies to operate in earlier historical periods, although the incentives to regulate would certainly exist (cf. papers by Liverani and Zaccagnini, this volume). Hence, the stress on systems of social reproduction denies the necessary existence of bounded and self-contained geo-political units as a starting point to study interaction. This means more than simply taking 'trade' into account and might imply, for instance, the existence of extensive networks of political alliances imposed horizontally upon local and discrete populations (cf. Howard and Skinner 1984). In such cases, defining inside/outside divisions in social activity may be of less significance than recognising different scales and hierarchies of relations operating at different levels of geo-political resolution.

Centre – periphery
The pair of opposites, centre (or core) and periphery, has been extensively used to refer to the structure of integrated regional economic systems. In a modern context, these terms were first used in work concerned with understanding deterioration in the 'terms of trade' for agricultural and mineral products in relation to manufactured products in international trade. These two poles were taken as given and attention was focussed on what accounted for the deteriorating terms, given that it contradicted Ricardo's rule which states that partners in international trade should benefit equally by specialising in the production of commodities in which they held a comparative advantage in labour and other costs of production. Subsequently, attention turned to the formation of the division of labour through which respective patterns of export specialisation had formed. Centres came to be defined, therefore, as those areas which controlled more developed technological skills and production processes, forms of labour organisation (e.g. wage labour) and a strong state-ideological apparatus to defend its interests.

Peripheries were said to lack these attributes and to have been modified to meet external demands for raw materials. The functionalism which assumes that the periphery can simply be 'read off' by the role it plays to reproduce far-away centres has, understandably, been a most vigorous source of disagreement, particularly amongst third-world theorists (cf. Laclau 1971; Brenner 1977).

A number of difficulties exist in operationalising the content of this scheme – as it stands – to Old and New World areas of 'civilisation'. In fact to do so would present an array of empirical sequences. In the Ancient World, as has been pointed out, trade in bulk commodities over long distances may have been minimal (Adams 1974); land transport costs were high (Adams 1979; but see Hopkins 1983); technologies simple and easily dispersed (Kohl this volume); and resources more likely to be 'luxuries' (cf. Larsen this volume; Schneider 1977). Even Mesopotamia's chronic shortage of raw materials would not in itself imply dependency and a need to ensure regular supplies unless we knew why stone for temples or metals for internal circulation were critical to the reproduction of city states. But this may only be as much as saying that the Ancient World does not measure up to the complexity of the modern – which would not be surprising. What we should look for instead are the general axioms underpinning the scheme that may then be operationalised in several distinct empirical settings.

Centres

The definition requires that groups of polities and in particular their ruling elites become net consumers of resources (however culturally defined) from other polities by a variety of relations of exploitation. What is consumed is less important than how it is consumed, i.e. the circuits of consumption–production have to be traced to assess their importance for reproducing the whole. Such systems are rarely single polities although competition and the achievement of core hegemony may produce this situation. Usually we find groups of polities of roughly similar size, enmeshed in dynastic ties and treaties to regulate relations with each other in order to minimise conflicts of interest. (Examples may be Sumer, Larsen 1979; Valley of Mexico, Brumfiel n.d.; Maya, Marcus 1984.) It may be the network of alliances and its density and topological form that best define a centre, or those sub-centres that are in conflict for core hegemony. Struggles between rival core polities and tendencies toward core expansion are the likely result of competition for diminishing resources or loss of control over resources.

Peripheries

This requires the identification of polities and elites that are constrained to meet demands for surplus product. The actual transaction may involve transfers between different rulings elites to the perceived advantage of both. Hence peripheral incorporation may not involve devolution but quite the reverse. Yet, it has to be assumed that the costs of meeting these demands in terms of rates of exploitation in the periphery are greater than those at the centre. It also has to be assumed that peripheral elites have less choice in exchange partners and become increasingly dependent on such alliances in order to sustain local domination and stave off attacks on their status orders. Peripheries locked into political cul-de-sacs endure greater exploitation than those enjoying choice as a means of resistance. Hence, it is to the advantage of core polities to agree amongst themselves to limit competition over access to their respective peripheries in order to increase rates of exploitation. By reducing the capacity of their peripheries to resist, core elites potentially risk the survival of their peripheral

partners: a calculation that is likely to depend on awareness as well as the availability of alternative options.

To define a social formation as peripheral requires therefore that it be possible to show that (a) however defined, the conditions which reproduce and extend social inequality are dependent on the network of alliances to which local elites belong; (b) that the costs of maintaining such a position are unequally distributed, both in terms of the relative rate of exploitation of local populations and the costs to local elites to participate in external alliance. Moreover, accepting the stress on specific forms of capitalist exploitation in the Frank/Wallerstein model, the most likely difference when compared with precapitalist cases is likely to be that the form of exchange is more politically motivated and directed towards control over persons rather than the direct intervention in the technological conditions of production and commodity exchange. Hence, quantitative measures of the degree of dependence and exploitation are likely to be misleading without a prior assessment of what kind of influence is being exercised over what kinds of social activity.

Structures of exploitation

World Systems theory promise a unified explanation of the development of 'complex societies' and 'tribal groups', the absence of which has long been problematic in unilinear evolutionary models. If the two categories are linked as parts of a single spatio-temporal process, rather than forming an evolutionary sequence, the central question raised is what constitutes the relationship between them? Moreover, it could be argued that the relationship is primary and constitutes the overt categories of centre and periphery.

Unequal exchange

The relation of unequal exchange is given priority in Frank and Wallerstein's theory of capitalist expansion (Emmanuel 1972). This states that the location of different production processes, labour forms and wage levels determines the transfer of surplus from peripheral primary producers to core producers of manufactured goods. The process of accumulation operates throughout the system to relocate production and capital investment wherever profitability is highest. That this may require the use of violence at times or involve other forms of direct intervention would – in their view – still be selected for by this basic economic calculus.

However, this is specific to the development of industrial capitalism and presumably cannot be generalised to earlier periods. A modified argument has been made which relates to mercantile activity either in the contemporary third world (Kay 1975) or for earlier periods (Wolf 1982: 183). This argues that different forms of production, existing as historical givens, are brought into exchange with each other through the entrepreneurial role of specialist traders. Profits accruing through the exploitation of price differences distributed in space are gained by those agents capable of organising trading expeditions and by the power holders of the societies they belong to. It is further argued that for merchants to maintain, if not expand, differentials in rates of exchange, it is necessary that they exclude rivals from their sphere of influence since competition would lower exchange rates to the benefit of the producers. Excluding others from competition may be achieved in a number of different ways, e.g., benefits accrue to strong states that could intervene to preserve monopoly mercantile interests by force if necessary; or by the development of transport technologies over that of rivals (a feature particularly important in European mercantile expansion but also in Phoenician and Greek trade as well (Frankenstein 1979).

In order to exclude competitors, merchants have to depend on alliances with indigenous power holders to develop their interests. Yet it has also to be in the interest of the latter to harness mercantile activity to meet their needs. As has often been observed the relationship between state and merchant has therefore rarely been a harmonious one. The relationship of mercantile accumulation to state power has understandably gained a considerable literature which cannot possibly be summarised here (see Curtin 1984). Yet a central theme is the form of domination linking merchant capital to state power. This may involve power holders acting as discrete providers of trading capital, or wielding a monopoly in the supply of specialist products as well as controlling the means of violence and exerting forms of symbolic domination.

Until recently, far less attention had been paid to how 'complex societies' were able to penetrate and dominate internal circuits of exchange in peripheral societies. In such situations the term 'exchange' has consistently been used to refer to those situations where neither profit nor satisfaction of needs was supposedly a dominant motive for the circulation of goods. What had been discovered instead were various forms of exchange where evaluation of objects takes place within some morally defined hierarchy of value (Firth 1939:44). The study of exchange became the study of idealised relations based on the assumption that giving in the absence of alienation (or in the certain knowledge of a return) engenders social relationships. Once this basic assumption was accepted, the argument narrowed to specifying that different forms of exchange would exist in the same society, one of which would dominate and articulate all the others. Where for Marx, persons and objects became commodities in a system of relationships he called capital, so for Lévi-Strauss, Godelier and others, persons and valuables become gifts in a system of relationships called kinship (cf. Damon 1980). The transition from gift exchange to commodity sale is therefore, in essence, a theory of transition whereby dominance over the circulation of persons is replaced by control over the distribution of things. Normally this in envisaged as an historical transition in evolutionary terms (Mauss 1954:35, 68). Yet if we accept the argument for the coexistence of both forms in some societies over long periods of time, then the question is rather, how did kinship function to dominate and distort incipient forms of capital accumulation? Moreover, on what basis can it be said that kinship functions as a dominant social relationship in non-capitalist societies and how does it determine a particular mode of (gift) exchange? (Godelier 1972).

These are important questions to answer in the context of current interest in prestige good systems and their role as peri-

pheries to more complex centres of state/mercantile development (Ekholm 1977, Frankenstein and Rowlands 1978, Gledhill 1979, Kristiansen 1978, 1982, Weigend *et al.* 1977). Yet, a simple kin-based periphery versus non kin/class-based centre model is unhelpful. Claims to common genealogies and to ancestry, expressed in the exchange of appropriate gifts, are a dominant political practice in most early states and empires (cf. Liverani and Zaccagnini this volume). Commerce was subordinated in such societies precisely because local and international power relations were recognised and legitimised through gift exchange. We shall return to the question of their articulation later but more immediately the question to answer is what do we mean by prestige goods and how does the circulation of such gifts relate to the distribution of inalienable rank in kin-ordered societies of such varying complexity?

Hierarchy and exchange

Mauss claimed that for exchange to take place, culturally defined objects had to be produced as things (Mauss 1954). Yet, that it was a gross assumption to assume that in being given, such objects were alienated, i.e. lost, to the original owner. Inalienable wealth takes on important priorities since the act of 'keeping while giving' (to use Weiner's term 1985) implies not only that it or an equivalent must be returned but that being able to enforce this is, in itself, a means of domination. To lose a valuable is thus to expose oneself and one's group to social diminishment. Now there appears to be nothing in the act of exchange itself to prevent this occurring but when the object in the act of exchange is given prominence, attention is drawn instead to the quality of ownership of a shared property. Mauss's well-known discussion of the nature of the gift focused precisely on how prestige items were embodied with a 'spiritual matter. . . part of one's nature and substance' that created the obligation to give, to receive and to repay (Mauss 1954:10). He provided a wide range of examples of valuables which circulated but whose possession he described as 'immeuble' or inalienable (Mauss 1954:7, 167–7). For instance Maori nephrite adzes and cloaks were distributed at rituals marking births, marriages and deaths because:

> Each treasure (ta'onga) was a fixed point in the tribal network of names, histories and relationships. They belonged to particular ancestors, were passed down particular descent lines, held their own stories and were exchanged on various memorable occasions. Ta'onga captured history and showed it to the living and they echoed patterns of the past from the first creation to the present. (Cited in Weiner 1985:220)

The emphasis in this and other comparable cases is on the circulation of objects that are endowed with a common spiritual substance and which people possess temporarily as members of a 'community of shared memory'. An equation is postulated between persons and things which denies the possibility of their loss or separation without doing violence to personal or group identity. For Mauss, this contrasted explicitly with the logic of capitalist commodity exchange where goods engender a symbolic detachability of persons from things in order that their value be kept distinct from the objective conditions of their production. Such a statement cannot apply to all capitalist social relations, no more than Mauss's notion of the gift can apply to all non-capitalist relations but the contrast does evoke the notion of dominance of exchange relations alluded to earlier.

Yet, for wealth to be inalienable implies both the power to keep while giving and the power to exclude others from the right of temporary possession. In other words, the term suggests property relations, certainly different from capitalist notions of ownership, but none the less a definition of persons and social relations in terms of possession of things. Marilyn Strathern has recently defined a broad category of societies as 'bridewealth systems' where things come to stand for persons or parts of persons and their circulation to stand for their possession (Strathern 1985:196). The circulation of bridewealth objects can substitute for persons or parts of persons (e.g. their labour) in such a way that their possession will bind people into relations of clientship and obligation.

It should be possible therefore to establish connections between the circulation of inalienable prestige objects, the control over persons or their attributes and the distribution of inalienable rank. One possibility, as in the case of the Maori, would be for things to come to stand for qualities possessed by some and not others. Friedman's analysis of the Kachin demonstrates how control over persons and the appropriation of their surplus is linked to control over communal deities which ensure general prosperity (Friedman 1975). Political ritual offices are defined by the right to perform these functions for the community as a whole. The distribution of inalienable wealth is in this case analogous to that of the Maori. It does not in itself define rank but functions to demarcate relative access to the source of power which underlies it. Hierarchy is defined therefore by not having to give and achieves this by closing off access to circulation through rules of endogamy (marriage prescriptions), rules of succession (creating exclusive roles and offices) and by rules of exclusion (creating categories of non-persons). Many West African societies contrast with this general situation in their concern with the jural definition of status (Goody 1962). Here, persons are invested with offices which may be endowed with rights to wealth, knowledge and property. Kinship roles are defined as a certain kind of inheritable estate separate from the persons who hold them. This yields a hierarchy of positions rather than persons, based on the inheritence of offices (and regalia) as well as excluded categories of non-office holders (junior males and women are defined as jural minors). The detachability of persons from things in this context is more complete in the sense that eligibility to office is a matter of defining a position rather than directly exercising control over persons. This in turn can be contrasted with recent generalisations about the nature of exchange in Melanesia where a more direct relation between control of persons and the circulation of prestige objects has been observed (Strathern 1982). Here, it is the person who is the prime form of moveable property and is circulated rather than any material property which s/he owns and others inherit.

The argument so far has demonstrated variability within a category of exchange which shares a common concern with how inalienability engenders certain types of social relations and defines different categories of persons. To paraphrase Marilyn Strathern:

> things can indeed behave as gifts. They may stand for whole persons or for part persons and their disposable attributes. Persons are thus constructed as bundles of assets to be distributed among others (thus making relationships).
> (Strathern 1985:202)

Not only does this constitute a system of control over the disposal of persons and their attributes through control over the circulation of things, but it also allows the relationship to be mystified. In capitalist commodity relations, this takes the extreme form of denying that any relation between them exists at all. By contrast, in bridewealth systems there is a general tendency for both persons and things to be explained as supernaturally caused and to figure prominently in the kinds of cosmologies which Bloch and Parry have recently described as 'the systematic attempt to transform death into rebirth or a regeneration of either the group or the cosmos' (Bloch and Parry 1982:42). Any direct connection between the control of persons through the control of things is thus denied in favour of stressing their common derivation from a supernatural origin. To analyse these systems, a distinction is needed between 'power from' which has an ideologically constructed source in sacred origin and tradition and 'power over' which describes control over persons and attributes through manipulating the production and circulation of things (see Merquior 1979: Chapter 1 for this distinction). A dynamic for social change lies in the conditions that promote discordance in the relation between these structures over time.

Weiner argues that the circulation of Maori valuables at certain ritual occasions served to re-establish or extend exchange (hence social) relations between the members of dispersed descent groups claiming a common ancestry. The fact that no single line of descent could claim to control the conditions of their social reproduction required that each should be represented and be seen to share in the circulation of the spiritual substance that each held as common to all. Hence the highest-ranked valuables formed a set which no descent line possessed completely but all elements of which had been possessed once and would be again. Such networks formed totalities and the circulation of valuables exactly replicated the limits of a sense of wholeness justified by a belief in a common ancestry. Simply excluding members from circulation could not be the basis for domination since it served only to create a category of non-persons with whom social relations could not be established. However, by making claims to superior ancestry, existing claims could be devalued in the overall hierarchy of social value. Hegemony was established through the continuous expansion of alliances with other more prestigious centres and legitimised through claims to common origin to which those of inferior origin within a totality were unable to lay claim. By this logic, Weiner is able to explain the bewilderment of Maori notables confronted with Europeans whose main concern was to establish alienable rights to property (mainly land) and remove themselves from further exchange obligations. The sorry story of European contact and the dissolution of local hierarchy is a familiar theme and need not detain us here (cf. Ekholm 1977; Sahlins 1981; Wolf 1982). A more relevant and equally widely recognised theme is the identification of centres in kinship-ordered societies as 'ceremonial' in the sense that they hold a monopoly of sacred origin. The cosmological ordering of the Mayan realm is a particularly clear example of how the spatial organisation of ceremonial centres is concerned with symbolic closure such that nothing is left outside (Marcus 1984). The theme is widely replicated and it suggests that a pervasive feature of such forms of closure is the capacity to maintain strict hierarchical equivalence in the relation between persons and things.

What may originally have been a dispersed pattern of circulation becomes 'centralised' in the sense that a single claim to represent the totality of those of common descent has been successfully achieved. This claim constitutes a denial of exchange due to the fact that gifts which represent the essence of wholeness are never given out but become the monopoly of particular lines of descent. When Polynesian chiefs, for example, were described as imbued with the sanctity of mana and the sacred powers of divine ancestry, this served to separate them physically from non ritual exchange within their communities. Even indirect contact was dangerous. Tahitian chiefs were carried around so that their feet should not touch the ground and endanger its fertility. Kwakiutl chiefs were constituted as privileged bestowers and commoners as obligatory receivers (and givers) according to Goldman. Here, in his phrase, 'the donor is simultaneously benefactor and destroyer and the receivers are reciprocally the benefited and the destroyed, presumably on the model of the hunter and his animal game' (Goldman 1984:128). In both cases, giving is a privilege derived from superior access to ancestral and supernatural powers. Moreover, the relation between the first beginning (sacred origin) and the present is also expressed through men, more specifically chiefs, acting as universal donors of timeless substance to those of low rank acting as universal receivers, who could respond only with alienable gifts of surplus product.

The social and ideological realities of such systems are thus rooted in the ontology of self. Exploitation stems from the impossibility of envisaging oneself to be outside the claim to wholeness and yet no longer participating directly in the conditions of its reproduction. Such servile status is reinforced further by the fact that what may be received as the inalienable possession of those of high status requires a return in alienable surplus product from those of low rank. Hence, bridewealth or labour given as local surplus is lost from possession as a return for the maintenance of the inalienable conditions of social reproduction. It could be argued that some notion of self-exploitation is more appropriate in this situation yet objectively we are dealing with a notion of 'sacrifice' in which absolute surplus is alienated in return for maintaining the ontological conditions of reproducing the self.

It follows that in all cases where prestige objects circulate as rights, we should find other subordinated systems of production and exchange where goods are categorised as alienable products.

A number of authors have argued recently for the co-presence of a number of different forms of production and circulation that may be entwined in different patterns in distinct social settings (Adams 1974; Hopkins 1983; Wheatley 1975; Yoffee 1981). This replicates Polanyi's more subtle point that whilst different forms of exchange may be present, one would form the dominant mode of allocation which all the others would ultimately serve (Polanyi 1957). In addition, this raised the issue argued most cogently by Jane Schneider in her review of Wallerstein (Schneider 1977), that distinguishing different 'economic forms' rests on the misplaced acceptance of a utility luxury dichotomy in the analysis of the circulation of goods. As Larsen (this volume) points out, few of the goods circulating in the elaborate Mesopotamian commercial networks he describes were intended to satisfy biological or utilitarian needs. If attention is turned to the 'commodities' themselves, we find a more confused pattern in which items that clearly embody various kinds of ontological statement about the definition of the person, power and its origins are imbued, in certain contexts, with commercial (trading for gain) connotations. Nor is this only a feature of so called 'complex systems'. Strathern, in his comparison of Melanesian exchange systems, has emphasised that the circulation of valuables is used quite unproblematically for personal gain through the attachment of side increments (Strathern 1971). The supposed universal antagonism between commerce and reciprocity may thus be overgeneralised due to the importance of this theme in the Graeco-Roman world and its European heritage (cf. Parry 1986).

Cosmology and exploitation

The terms centre and periphery are highly specific to a sense of identity developed in the West. Wallerstein, for instance, has been accused of reproducing a typically Eurocentric evolutionist view of recent world history in which an active and progressive centre subordinates and transforms a passive and backward (i.e. primitive) periphery (Goodman and Redclift 1983:47). Nineteenth-century evolutionism was part of an ideological mode of thought which justified a radical break between civilised centre and savage periphery to legitimise exploitation without responsibility. This contrasts strangely with many premodern definitions of the alien which strove to assimilate a savage, wild 'other' as a necessary part of sustaining a cosmic order. Even Renaissance and Enlightenment views of the naked and threatening savage required debate as to whether the latter could be or already was human and could be incorporated into a Judaeo-Christian world view. Such contrasts in the way centres and peripheries are culturally constructed also have to be viewed as the product of long transformational processes that are rooted in a common ontological problem of constituting identity through either the eradication or the creation of difference.

Lévi-Strauss has argued that primitive classifications strive to collapse time into space through a form of cosmic closure which establishes a continuum between culture and nature (Lévi-Strauss 1966). The world as a closed and bounded cosmological order is threatened by the eruption of chaotic material outside of its control. This suggests a timeless, concentric model in which culture as a gift of nature (i.e. the supernatural) spreads out to assimilate and order a chaotic world (cf. Friedman 1982:42). The constitution of modern society as an analytic unit is, by contrast, a product of separation and alienation and required the development of science to replace cosmological ordering as its source of existential security. Presenting this as a rupture between a modern, scientific and techno-rational centre opposed to a primitive, prelogical and mystical periphery which should be either civilised or preserved is thus a contemporary myth.

In a premodern sense, a rupture between centre and periphery is denied or at least never considered irreparable. Liverani's discussion of the ideology of the neo-Assyrian empire shows how they viewed their own periphery as a failed cosmos; one not yet realised but one that could be eventually. This 'difficult path' could only be overcome by a king's virtue whose duty it was to extend a cosmic order as an embodiment of himself to an unruly periphery which was sterile and blocked until his presence would cause towns and palaces to be built, arid land to be irrigated and a great cycle of creation and rebirth to be extended as a defence against cultural decay (Liverani 1979d). Once incorporated (and it is significant that war for an Assyrian king should be like a hunting expedition), the function of a periphery is to serve its cosmological centre to ensure its proper functioning. Periphery to centre is constituted as a relationship in much the same way as that of the identity of the individual to the whole. In other words, the relation between centre and periphery is organic in contrast to the mechanistic view of modern ideologies. The Assyrian view is of course a common theme and forms a debateable area in Eliade's work (Eliade 1959). Yet Geertz on Negara, Marcus on the Maya or Wheatley on Shang China all stress the arrangement of centres to enclose an ordered whole and the aestheticisation of an expanding cosmological realm (Geertz 1982, Marcus 1976, Wheatley 1971). Hopkins's discussion of Roman emperor worship is much nearer our modern perception (Hopkins 1978). The difficulties presented to a man who becomes divine in order to create a unified political order has a distinctive twentieth-century ring to it.

Evolutionary and devolutionary cycles

It has often not been sufficiently appreciated that dependency and world systems theories were intended as dynamic models of modern world history. Wallerstein, for instance, accepted the established view that capitalism operates in cyclical rhythms. Short-term or business cycles were already well-known consequences of equalising supply and demand vectors, but the existence of longer term cycles covering fifty years or more was less certain (first proposed by Kondratieff, cf. Wallerstein 1979c). Work by historians on price formation from the end of the Middle Ages to the eighteenth century had suggested that even longer cycles of growth and decay govern periods of 150 years or more (cf. Braudel and Spooner 1967). François Simiand had already independently suggested that world economic history was characterised by long periods of growth and expansion (A phases) followed by periods of crisis (B phases) which could only be resolved by further expansion (Simiand 1932). For Marx, such crises were specific to the capitalist mode of production possessing

a tendency towards overproduction, whilst Luxemburg would argue later that such crises could be resolved only by the global expansion of commodity markets as a means of continued production and capital accumulation (Luxemburg 1951). Others would now stress a greater variety of causes (e.g. Mandel 1978) but would still accept that historically capitalism has tended to expand in search of markets and raw materials and that such systems have experienced significant crises resolved by renewed expansion.

More complex models have been developed to relate shorter and longer term cycles into a single expansionist dynamic. Perhaps the most well known is Braudel's model of the *longue durée* (Braudel 1978) which combines short-term cycles of discontinuous change within longer cycles of continuous process. Attempts at a more rigorous synthesis of short- and long-term cycles (given that for many the existence of the latter is still highly debateable, see special issue of *Review* Wallerstein 1979c) can be found in Kula (1976) and Wallerstein (1980).

It is hardly surprising that a notion of short-term and long-term cycles nesting in a single dynamic should appeal heuristically to those working in earlier time periods. The specification of long-term cycles was sufficiently vague to encourage thinking that this was not a phenomenon limited to the rise of industrial capitalism. Braudel's early work on the history of the Mediterranean world as the product of short-term cycles of expansion and decay of states and empires underlain by a long-term stability of constraining factors was particularly influential (Braudel 1949). Friedman modified this argument in an ethnographic context by asserting that a long cycle would predict evolutionary or devolutionary stages depending on the material conditions of social reproduction (Friedman 1975). Short cycles are due to 'the variation that occurs owing to political and economic constraints operating within the technological limits defined by the long cycle' (Friedman 1975:187). The fact that short-term cycles should ultimately be determined by the techno-ecological limits on production has been widely criticised (e.g. O'Laughlan 1975; see Friedman 1979:15–16 for a defence of his argument). Nevertheless he adheres to the primacy of the long term in a later article where he states that short cycles of political growth and collapse are embedded in longer evolutionary cycles determined by the conditions of agricultural production (Friedman 1982). In effect, the question is more whether long-term cycles exist at all as autonomous determinants (and if so whether they are the products of biological imperatives rather than a social dynamic) rather than being formed from a coalescence of shorter cycles of political expansion and decay. In answer to this, a number of different views have been produced as to what constitutes long-term cycles. An early precocious attempt is Steward's discussion of cyclical conquests (Steward 1949). The argument is set in the short term, with each era marked by different conditions of expansion and decline, although population pressure and competition for resources is a constant theme. Friedman uses the limits on intensification of agricultural production and an increasing trade density model to explain short-term cycles of chiefdom formation and devolution in Oceania (Friedman and Rowlands 1977; Friedman

1982) and the idea has been used to interpret the European Bronze Age by Rowlands (1984a). Kristiansen uses the intensification of agricultural production model in his analyses of local production cycles in the Scandinavian Bronze Age and argues that they are in turn linked to changes in the regional exchange system (Kristiansen 1979; 1982). Parker Pearson's interpretation of the Danish Iron Age distinguishes only short cycles of differential wealth accumulation leading to an inflationary spiral which, he argues, results in a crisis of major proportions in the long term of a millennium of development (Parker Pearson 1984). Miller, in an analysis of the ideological structures of the Harappan civilisation, suggests that this represented the beginning of an irreversible oscillation between the principles of Harappan/Buddhism versus Vedic Hinduism/modern Hinduism that characterises much of later South Asian history (Miller 1985:62–3).

It should be emphasised that most of these cases deal with cyclical change in peripheral formations and so far few attempts have been made to theorise similar kinds of trajectories for more 'complex' states and empires (cf. Friedman and Rowlands 1977; Gledhill and Larsen 1982). Moreover, in contrast to those theorising modern capitalism, archaeologists have had no reason to dismiss previous periods of expansion and contraction as irrelevant, and taking these into account has often meant setting highly contingent and arbitrary conditions on the periods that authors have chosen to study. Outside of the Braudelean theme of understanding what maintains the constancy of culture despite change, the discovery of a single dynamic operating over long periods of time, appears hard to find. Hence, whether long-term cycles exist and if so what their relation is to the empirically surer short-term cycles remains problematic.

It has not been sufficiently appreciated that a theory of cyclical change also includes a theory of shifts of centres in space. In other words, expansion and contraction processes have rarely been geographically stable. In the case of shorter cycles, this may involve intra-regional shifts in influence between competing centres within a single core area, as for example in a competitive city state phase or, in more modern terms, nation state competition in nineteenth-century Europe. However, it has been frequently claimed that these oscillations in intra-core hegemony are interspersed by much larger scale shifts in the arrangements of centres and their peripheries (called either logistics or secular trends: Cameron 1973; Wallerstein 1979c). In modern history, it is argued that the rise of capitalism in the West cannot be separated from a decline of the earlier Arab domination of the Mediterranean, and the expansion of industrial capitalism in northwest Europe cannot be separated from the decline of the Spanish and Portuguese empires in the seventeenth and eighteenth centuries (Wallerstein 1974). More recently, the 'kapitallogik school' has argued that the current world economic recession is more than another cyclical downturn but represents a significant loss of competitive advantage by the older western industrialised core and the rise of new centres of imperialist accumulation (Frobel 1980; not all would agree cf. Klapinsky 1984). Centre–periphery as a relationship does not therefore predict a fixed and immutable position but implies that constituent groups will move through different statuses as a necessary feature of maintaining the relationship.

It is perhaps the historical experience of capitalism that a decline of an old centre should be necessary for the expansion of the whole system (the post World War II shift from Europe to the USA for instance) which has prompted the frequent observation that similar events occurred in the Ancient World. The shift of centres of imperium from southern to northern Mesopotamia in the third to first millennia BC; the east to west relocation of political centres in the development of the Mediterranean world; the re-emergence of Middle Eastern imperialism in late Roman times has been the stuff of grand narrative world history for many years. With a decline of the West scenario literally in mind, such narratives were clearly serving as contemporary warnings. Max Weber had the fate of Wilhemine Germany in mind when he claimed that a corrupt bureaucracy conspiring with large landowners to avoid taxes promoted the expansion of a feudalised 'natural exonomy' in the late Roman Empire in the west (Weber 1976). This thinly veiled attack on the evils of socialism and state bureaucracy has spawned some sophisticated variants on the general theme that excessive state control can transform cores into parasitic consumers which eventually undermine their own revenue base. This is broadly the A. H. M. Jones and Brunt position on the decline of the western Roman Empire which has recently been given a more sophisticated revision by Hopkins (1980) and Whittaker (1983). Hopkins argues that there was an inner circle of tax-exporting provinces in the early Roman Empire which also exported surplus product to gain the money to pay taxes. These 'exports' were consumed in the Italian heartland and in an outer ring of militarised frontier provinces. This stimulated long-distance trade and a vast expansion of goods in circulation through an integrated monetary economy but also decentralised manufacturing to the outer provinces and created a consumption centre that relied increasingly on tax and tribute to be maintained. The crises of the third century AD, necessitating a shift to tax in kind to ensure supplies to the army and the state bureaucracy, made it possible for local army commanders to control taxation directly and establish themselves as rival governments to an increasingly dispensable imperial centre in Rome. The feudalising tendency of the late Empire is explained in this revised Weberian model by the linkage between different forms of tax and their effects on production and trade. Polanyi also believed that strong states stifle mercantile activity because otherwise they would set up competing centres of wealth accumulation. It was Polanyi's contention that ports of trade not market places were growth points in the ancient economy (Polanyi 1978:246). The model of 'stagnant' bureaucratic states surrounded by expanding mercantile 'city states' in which the latter would eventually overcome the former has for long been held as a justification of modern European expansion and its historical destiny. Yet, it has received some empirical support. Oppenheim once argued that southern Mesopotamia produced a corona of merchant city states to serve as intermediaries or buffers in long-distance trade but which soon outgrew the parent centres and absorbed them into empires (cited by Larsen 1979:99).

In all these arguments, it is ultimately the temporal that is seen to dominate over the spatial shifts in the waxing and waning of particular centres. This is generally true of all the long cycle theories. In Wallerstein's model, for instance, peripheries evolve to semi-peripheral status and new peripheries are formed because of crises and breakdown in their respective cores (Wallerstein 1979a). Whether it is Luxemburg's version of the expansion of commodity markets or Hopkins on frontier provinces gaining from taxation and trade, it is crisis at the centre which promotes growth in the periphery. This could suggest too smooth an expansion/contraction model which more detailed work may well contradict. As Kohl has stressed (this volume), the degree of integration between centres and peripheries is often less systematic than might be assumed and often required direct intervention and coercion to achieve conditions of political and economic dependency. In general therefore systematic integration and linkage cannot be assumed and has to be demonstrated. Resistance to incorporation may well be militate against the operation of a simple expansion model.

Conclusion

The purpose of this introduction has been to provide a general survey of those aspects of dependency and world systems theory that either have or are likely to stimulate thinking in archaeological and historical research. An uncritical acceptance of the arguments made by earlier proponents of these traditions can be avoided by stressing the heuristic value of engaging in debate over these issues as well as justifying their applicability in contexts far removed from those originally envisaged. The fact that, in the process, many of the problems that beset archaeological theory may be seen instead as the products of the era that such theories purport to explain is equally a salutary lesson in archaeological objectivity. If a general point can be made it is that no certainty exists in extrapolating from the more well known (because it is the present) to the less known (because it is the past).

The chapters in this volume all relate to the Ancient Near East, the Mediterranean and Europe from the development of early states to the expansion of the Roman Empire. The papers in part two are all concerned with political developments in the Ancient Near East and in particular, the notion of a regional system as a framework of analysis. In part three, the papers are concerned with pointing out the problems in conceptualising 'local societies' as discrete centres of historical action separate from the wider regional system. The area includes both the Near East and Europe during the second millennium including the 'crisis' at the end of this period. Finally, part four is a comprehensive study of the Roman Empire as a single system including core, semi- peripheries, peripheries and external areas, and shows how they relate to each other in often uneven and contradictory ways.

Part two

Regional systems and the genesis of dependency

Chapter 2

The ancient economy, transferable technologies and the Bronze Age world-system: a view from the northeastern frontier of the Ancient Near East

Phil Kohl

Scholarly reaction to the publication of I. Wallerstein's initial volume (1974) on the modern world system was surprisingly strong. Initial enthusiastic responses were elicited from historians of the *Annales* school and from historians and anthropologists working within a more critical or Marxist tradition. Opponents represented an equally broad spectrum of political and academic traditions with criticisms extending from empirical inaccuracies to theoretical objections over Wallerstein's view of history or, more specifically, over the teleological determinism implicit in his reified concept of a supra-historical world system (e.g. Brenner 1977; Hunt 1978; for a balanced but critical assessment Wolf 1982: 21–3). The work clearly was related to the writings of dependency theorists, such as Amin (1974) and Frank (1976), but was distinguished by its longer and more detailed historical perspective.

Ancient and medieval historians were less drawn into the creative furor stimulated by the study for the simple reason that Wallerstein was interested in the formation of the modern world system, which he viewed as a process that began in the sixteenth century and which he considered qualitatively distinct from earlier large-scale developments. Ancient empires, which encompassed 'worlds' of their day, functioned and were structured differently from the unique system that ushered in the modern era:

> Empires were a constant feature of the world scene for 5,000 years. There were continuously several such empires in various parts of the world at any given point of time. The political centralization of an empire was at one and the

same time its strength and weakness. . . . Political empires
are a primitive means of economic domination. It is the
social achievement of the modern world, if you will, to have
invented the *technology that makes it possible* to increase
the flow of the surplus from the lower strata to the upper
strata, from the periphery to the center, from the majority
to the minority by eliminating the 'waste' of too cumber-
some a political structure. (1974, 15–16, emphasis added)

The modern world system is distinguished by primarily economic
as opposed to political, cultural, or presumably even ideological
linkages among its constituent parts. Political diversity, primacy
of the economic sphere, and control and development of a technology capable of supporting and expanding such a system are the
critical variables, according to Wallerstein, that distinguish the
modern era from ancient and medieval times. The modern world
system also is characterized by a highly complex global division of
labor which results in major regional differences: some areas
become exporters of primary resources, while others produce and
successfully market industrial products. The exchange uniting
different regions is not symmetrical but structurally weighted or
tipped in favor of the politically more powerful and technologi-
cally advanced core states of the West. The exchange relations
which develop are thus beneficial to the core areas and detrimen-
tal to the peripheries which essentially are exploited or 'underdeveloped' by these relations. Wallerstein's model becomes even
more complex when he shows how specific nation-states' core
status shifts over time and how certain countries, termed semi-
peripheries, provide a built-in flexibility to the world system.

The question naturally arises as to whether or not Wallerstein is correct in his insistence that such a system only emerged
during the beginnings of the modern era in the sixteenth century
AD. One intelligent and generally laudatory review of Wallerstein's original study criticizes the book precisely for its perpetua-
tion of this great divide between modern and ancient/medieval
times:

From the point of view of social science, Wallerstein's most
significant contribution is the suggestion that processes of
interaction and unequal exchange might explain events not
only in Third World areas transformed by European hegemony in the nineteenth and twentieth centuries, but in
earlier periods within Europe itself. This establishes a unity
of theory between Western and non-Western peoples, the
absence of which has long been problematic in unilineal
models of change whose ethnocentrisms are consistent with
their inability to account for the disparity between Europe's
precocious advances and other people's 'lag'. . . . *The
Modern World-System* suffers from too narrow an application of its own theory. For, although Wallerstein admires
Owen Lattimore's description of the differentiation process
according to which ancient Chinese civilization 'gave birth
to barbarism', . . . he does not view the pre-capitalist world
as systematically integrated through the operations of
world economic forces. (Schneider 1977:20)

According to the reviewer, Wallerstein too easily dismisses the

external economic linkages forged by non-Western political
empires, denigrates the effects and importance of earlier long-
distance trade in luxury goods, and, consequently, fails to adequately explain or understand the motivations and stimuli which
led to the Great Discoveries and the beginnings of the modern
era. The book suffers, in short, from an unnecessary, self-limiting
ethnocentrism which bestows special status upon modern European development.

Thus, through their insistence upon the unique features
of the modern capitalist world system, Wallerstein and his disci-
ples join the ranks of the 'substantivists' in economic anthropology and the 'primitivists' in ancient history who qualitatively
distinguish ancient from modern economies and who argue
against the applicability of contemporary economic theory to primitive and ancient social formations. Perhaps the most celebrated
theorist of this school, Karl Polanyi, set his Great Transformation
in the nineteenth, not the sixteenth, century and emphasized different factors, such as the relative lack of alienation, commercial
exchange, and formal marketplaces in precapitalist societies.
Wallerstein's view of earlier times is less developed but also far
less utopian: a politically non-unified world-economy never
emerged in ancient times for the technology necessary 'to increase
the flow of surplus' sufficient to maintain it was never developed.

This chapter cannot review, much less settle, this hallowed,
perhaps irresoluble debate (cf. Pearson 1957 for a now dated over
view but cf. now Hall 1985) over qualitative or only quantitative
differences between modern and precapitalist societies. Application of Wallerstein's model of a world system to earlier periods
does not imply a rejection of the substantivist argument for essential differences or incomparabilities, a position which grapples
with other issues besides the articulation of separate societies in
external networks of exchange. The important problem is to
determine the degree to which the world system's model can
be employed to elucidate the development of precapitalist
societies. Points of non-correspondence may be as instructive as
similarities, or, in other words, the utility of the model can only be
assessed by attempting to apply it to earlier social formations.
This chapter will selectively review archaeological materials from
early class societies in the ancient Near East that illustrate external exchange relations over widely separate areas.

Political empires and intercultural exchange in the ancient Near East

Wallerstein's characterization and dismissal of earlier
world-empires must be examined in greater detail. According to
Wallerstein, empires are political units; they expand by incorporating new territories and obtain necessary resources and
materials through the coercive imposition of tributes and taxes.
Goods flow to the political center and – in classic Polanyi-like
fashion – are redistributed by the State according to its own specific rules of allocation. Earlier 'world-economies' may have existed, but they always were transformed into political empires. The
argument for the unique character of modern times again seems
to emphasize differences in the forces of production or have a
technological base:

The modern world-economy might have gone in that same direction [towards empire] – indeed it has sporadically seemed as though it would – except that the techniques of modern capitalism and the technology of modern science, the two being somewhat linked as we know, enabled this world-economy to thrive, produce, and expand without the emergence of a unified political structure. (1974:16)

Certainly, ancient political empires levied tributes on conquered areas and imposed taxes, either of labor services of goods, on its subjected citizenry. Some early civilizations may have expanded politically, as Wallerstein suggests, to incorporate areas from which they obtained essential resources. Although known almost exclusively from archaeological data, the Harappan or Indus Valley civilization may have expanded in precisely this fashion. Unlike the Old Assyrian settlement at Kanesh (cf. below) where traders adopted the local material culture, entire Harappan colonies, containing exclusively Harapan materials, have been discovered well beyond the confines of the Indus Valley. The Harappan settlements at Shortughai on the Ai Khanoum plain of northeastern Afghanistan provide the most striking illustration of this difference (cf. Francfort and Pottier 1978). J. Shaffer (1982: 44–5) has suggested that the distributional evidence from Harappan sites indicates that foreign trade was unimportant to this early civilization for Harappans built their complex social order through elaborate *internal* exchange networks that redistributed local resources throughout their vast domains; even more intriguingly, Lamberg–Karlovsky (n.d.) recently has proposed that the striking uniformity of Harappan remains and other evidence peculiar to this early civilization may indicate that their society was structured by some incipient *caste* principles which require separate tasks to be performed by specific endogamous groups.

Regardless of whether or not these interpretations are correct, Harappan materials always have been considered enigmatic, if not unique, and its pattern of expansion is not shared by the best-documented early civilization: Mesopotamia. Indeed, consideration of the development of early Mesopotamian civilization reveals that, at least, two features of Wallerstein's analysis are incorrect: (a) 'world-economies' and political empires were not always commensurate with one another; and (b) there existed no irreversible trend for the former to transform itself into the latter. Mesopotamian civilization developed over the course of roughly three millennia: political empires and periods of expansion alternated with periods of breakdown, nomadic or semi-nomadic incursions, and times of intense competition and struggle between local, culturally related, but politically autonomous city-states. Individual cities remained the basic building blocks of state formation in Mesopotamia at least through the third and into the second millennia BC. The well-documented example of the old Assyrian trading network in the early second millennium BC (cf. Larsen, this volume) clearly demonstrates how the economic life and prosperity of a city, Assur, depended upon its middleman role in the long distance exchange primarily of silver and gold from Anatolia for tin and textiles from regions to the east and south. This profit-motivated trade extended far beyond the political borders of any state and linked into a single world system

areas stretching from the Anatolian plateau to southern Mesopotamia east across the Iranian plateau possibly to western Afghanistan (Cleuziou and Berthoud 1982). Similarly, the earlier royal archives from Ebla in northern Syria unequivocally demonstrate that even when cities expanded into kingdoms of considerable size they still engaged in essential 'international' exchange, transporting raw materials, luxury goods, textiles, and even livestock and agricultural products, such as olive oil, across recognized political boundaries (Pettinato 1981: chapter VII).

An even earlier reliance on intercultural exchange can be reconstructed from archaeological materials dated to Early Dynastic times. Sumerian civilization, of course, developed on an alluvial plain that was noteworthy for lacking most essential natural resources besides clay and possibly salt (Potts n.d.). The trade that developed partly as a result of this deficiency cannot be dismissed as the relatively unimportant luxury exchange of status markers among participating elites. As Schneider (1977: 23) correctly has emphasized, Wallerstein's distinction between luxury and staple exchanges is misleading and discredits the political importance of the former:

> The relationship of trade to social stratification was not just a matter of an elevated group distinguishing itself through the careful application of sumptuary laws and a monopoly on symbols of status; it further involved the direct and self-conscious manipulation of various semiperipheral and middle level groups through patronage, bestowals, and the calculated distribution of exotic and valued goods.

Moreover, since trade was one means by which the competing city-states of Early Dynastic Sumer obtained non-indigenous resources, it was essential for them to produce commodities that could be exchanged. Textual and archaeological evidence (cf. Adams 1981: 147–51) together confirm that they succeeded primarily by engaging in the surplus production of woollen textiles or a production for exchange that was intimately related to the internal structure of Sumerian society. Analyses of the distribution of archaeological materials in the mid-third millennium have demonstrated that finished commodities, as well as raw materials, were imported into Sumer (Kohl 1978; 1979). In other words, the intercultural trade which developed between resource-poor Mesopotamia and the resource-rich highland areas of Anatolia and Iran necessarily transformed the productive activities of all the societies participating in the exchange network without the development of an overarching polity or empire. For example, a specialized center for the production of elaborately carved soft stone vessels has been excavated at the small, non-urban settlement of Tepe Yahya in southeastern Iran. There is no evidence to suggest that this centre was incorporated into a larger political unit encompassing the urban centers that imported its vessels.

It also has been proposed that Sumerian and other lowland cities held a competitive advantage in this exchange at least insofar as that they could obtain commodities and natural resources from multiple, isolated, and autonomous communities, such as Tepe Yahya, while the highland communities came to rely exclusively upon the goods – textiles and possible foodstuffs – that they received from Mesopotamia and Khuzestan (Kohl 1978: 471–2); the highland settlements became locked into unequal exchange relationships for both internal and external reasons. Needs and demands, of course, were artificially created, but, more importantly, the small communities that engaged in the production of highly crafted commodities were themselves internally transformed. Emergent elites who directed these productive activities came to depend upon the continuance of the trade to maintain their newly acquired privileged positions within society. If correct, this pattern seems to resemble Wallerstein's model of the modern world system and leads us to question his reasons for rejecting comparisons between ancient and modern times.

Multiple cores, unequal exchange, and underdevelopment in the Bronze Age

However, the nature of this unequal exchange and the problem of detecting structurally induced underdevelopment and dependency demand closer scrutiny. Cultural evolution throughout the greater Middle East during the third and second millennia BC was not exclusively nor even dominantly related to developments within Mesopotamia. Reference already has been made to the geographically more extensive and culturally more uniform Harappan civilization, and any complete discussion must consider Egypt and, as shall be examined below, southern Central Asia. There were multiple core areas which co-existed and intermittently came into direct or indirect contact with one another. Each 'core' manipulated an adjacent hinterland which at times it may have attempted to control. Egypt's relations with Nubia, the Levantine coast, and the Sinai peninsula provide a striking illustration of such a regionalized 'world system'. Meluhhan or Indus villagers may have resided in Mesopotamia (Parpola, Parpola, and Brunswig 1977), and now direct archaeological evidence suggests that the Harappans, like the Sumerians, were interested in the copper resources of Oman (Weisgerber n.d.; 1981). Southern Central Asia or what has been termed the Namazga civilization (cf. Kohl 1981) exchanged some materials with Harappan centers as is evident from the discoveries of Indus seals, ivory sticks, and etched carnelian beads at Altyn-Depe in southern Turkmenistan (Masson 1981). Sites along the piedmont strip of southern Turkmenistan and in the lowland plains of Bactria and Margiana contain numerous objects made from materials, such as lapis lazuli, turquoise, and various metals, which were not available locally but which existed in adjacent regions and which must have been procured through some regularized intercultural exchange network. In short, the Bronze Age world system of the late third and early second millennia BC was characterized not by a single dominant core region economically linked to less developed peripheral zones, but by a patchwork of overlapping, geographically disparate core regions or foci of cultural development, each of which primarily exploited its own immediate hinterland.

The existence of such multiple cores in sporadic contact with one another is not a peculiar anomaly of the Bronze Age world system but points to a basic disconformity between this system and that postulated by Wallerstein for the modern era. Specifically, peripheries situated between cores were far from helpless

in dictating the terms of exchange; they could develop or terminate relations depending upon whether or not these relations were perceived to be in their best interest. For example, recent archaeological excavations in the United Arab Emirates and Oman at sites such as Hili (Cleuziou n.d.; 1980), Bat (Frifelt 1976), and Maysar (Weisgerber 1981) have revealed the existence of a fairly uniform late third–early second millennia culture characterized by distinctive architecture, ceramics, and mortuary practices which, at least at Maysar, was engaged in the large-scale production of copper for exchange. Evidence also suggests that many more mining and copper refining sites of this period once existed throughout the mountainous interior of Oman but subsequently were destroyed by later Islamic sites exploiting the same deposits. The archaeological data are consistent with cuneiform documents recording extensive trade with Makkan, a region which exported copper and diorite to Mesopotamia, but ceramics, ingot forms, and an excavated triangular-shaped seal from Maysar also indicate metallurgical relations with South Asa (Weisgerber 1980: 106, fig. 77; n.d.). Although it is still too early to determine whether or not this prehistoric Omani culture maintained exchange relations simultaneously or successively with Sumer and Harappa, it seems impossible to refer to the systematic underdevelopment of this autonomous culture. If anything, prehistoric Oman appears to have prospered or been sustained at a more complex level of cultural development than would have been possible in the absence of these exchange relations. While circumstantial, this evidence seems to contradict a model of exchange so unequal as to foster 'the development of underdevelopment'.

There is little reason to doubt that patterns of dependency or, perhaps better, interdependency were established as a result of intercultural exchange in the Bronze Age world system. Less developed peripheral societies probably were more strongly affected by participation in this exchange than were the more densely populated, internally differentiated civilizations which emerged on lowland alluvial plains. Dependency could lead to exploitation, and, if later myths, such as Enmerkar and the Lord of Aratta, are a guide (cf. Kohl 1978: 472 and criticisms pp. 476–84), it is possible that in exceptional circumstances – during a drought or famine – the more powerful urban societies could dictate the terms of the exchange. But the relations between ancient cores and peripheries were not structurally analogous to those which underdevelopment theorists postulate are characteristic of First–Third World relations today. Unless conquered (i.e., incorporated into a larger polity), ancient peripheries could have followed one of several options ranging from withdrawal from the exchange network to substitution of one core partner for another. Archaeological and historical evidence converge to suggest that most intercultural exchange systems in antiquity were fragile, lasting at most a few generations before collapsing. This inherent instability is related to the relative weakness of the bonds of dependency that existed between core and peripheral partners.

Transferable technologies: the case of Central Asia

Peripheral societies of the Bronze Age not only had more options available to them, but they also did not necessarily suffer

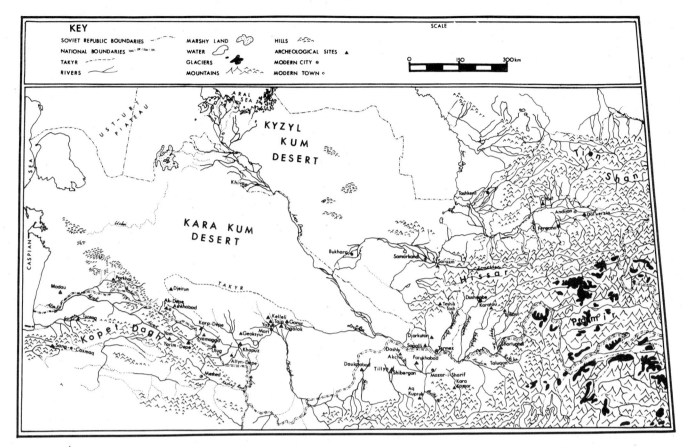

Fig. 2.1. Western Turkestan: major prehistoric archaeological sites

from a technological gap which doomed them to politically and militarily inferior positions *vis-à-vis* civilized cores. That is, consideration of the technological base of these early Bronze Age civilizations also reveals a fundamental structural discrepancy between ancient and modern world systems. It is not that the scale of intercultural trade in the late third–early second millennia BC was a fraction of that which united the world in the sixteenth century AD, nor that the speed, reliability, and capability of transportation and communication systems in the Bronze Age were greatly circumscribed relative to the systems which developed at the beginning of the modern era. These are relative phenomena. Rather, a qualitative difference exists because critical technologies, such as metal working and later horse breeding, were not controlled by core areas alone. Bronze Age technologies could not be monopolized but quickly diffused from one area to another or, in this sense, were transferable. Moreover, important technologies often initially developed or were further refined in peripheral areas close to the natural sources of the necessary resources.

The uses to which transferable technologies could be put varied from society to society depending upon their needs and internal structure. In his final summary of the Bronze Age Childe contrasted progressive barbarian Europe with the stultified, despotic societies of the ancient Near East:

Yet the relations of production that thus made possible the establishment of a metallurgical industry, fettered its development. So the types of tools and weapons and the technical methods for their production, established by 3000 B.C., persisted in Egypt and Hither Asia with hardly any progressive change for the next two millennia. The reasons for such stagnation are not far to seek. The urban revolution in the Orient liberated craftsmen and specialists from the necessity of procuring their own food, but only at the cost of complete dependence on a court or a temple. It gave them leisure to perfect their skills but no encouragement to do so along progressive lines; for the last thing to interest a divine king or high priest would be labour-saving devices. ... The more progressive character of Aegean industry and craftsmanship is legitimately explicable by reference to the social and economic structures within which they functioned. Craftsmen had not been reduced, as in the Orient, to an exploited lower class because no class division had as yet cleft Aegean societies. Their patrons were themselves practical men who would appreciate the efficiency of tools and weapons. (Childe 1957: 8–9)

Childe's analysis, of course, is dated, and his insistence on Europe's progressive and the Orient's despotic character – questionable and embarrassingly ethnocentric. Childe consistently underestimated the potential surpluses that could have been generated by Neolithic economies (Kohl and Wright 1977) and thus incorrectly asserted that the first 'regular use of metal' had to have occurred within the highly productive river valleys which spawned the earliest civilizations of the Old World. Though based on the evidence available at the time, Childe's model neglected to consider the potential of peripheral areas for internal technological innovation or for their adoption of easily transferable technologies due to their own internally generated needs; smiths or 'immigrant specialists' simply ventured forth from cores to ply their skills and wares under less repressive social conditions. The model was mechanical and highly diffusionary or core-focused. However, it nicely linked technological development to social structure and, if properly modified, can be used to illustrate another fundamental discrepancy between ancient and modern core–peripheral relations; viz., major technological innovations which made possible new forms of social organization and which could alter existing balances of power often appeared in peripheries or along the frontiers of civilized society. Peripheral societies not only exercised a considerable range of options in dealing with more powerful trade partners but, in certain times and places, also developed new techniques or applied nearly universal skills in a broadly 'progressive' fashion that ultimately had far-reaching social and political consequences. The remainder of this chapter will illustrate the potential for innovation characteristic of ancient peripheries through consideration of Late Bronze developments in Central Asia.

Western Turkestan, an area that has been referred to as the northeastern frontier of the ancient Near East (Tosi 1973–4) stretches from the Caspian Sea in the west to the Fergana valley in the east and from the Aral Sea in the north to the Hindu Kush and Atrek valley of northeastern Iran in the south. It can be defined as the vast area of interior drainage formed by the streams draining the Kopet Dagh and northern Hindu Kush mountains and by the Atrek, Tedjen, Murghab, Amu Darya, Zeravshan, and Syr Darya rivers and their tributaries (Fig. 2.1). Today, it is divided among three nation-states: Iran; Afghanistan; and the republics of Turkmenistan, Uzbekistan, Tadjikistan, and part of Kirghizia in the Soviet Union. The boundaries of prehistoric culture areas and modern political borders rarely coincide, but the existence of the latter usually implies a different history of archaeological investigation for regions separated by the borders, and this fact strongly affects current understanding. Specifically, most of the data presented below has been gathered by Soviet archaeologists working along the fertile *atak* or piedmont strip of southern Turkmenistan and on the lowland plains of Margiana (lower Murghab) and Bactria (southern Uzbekistan–northwestern Afghanistan).

Western Turkestan consists of largely uninhabited deserts (Kara Kum and Kyzyl Kum, in particular), rugged mountain ranges, lowland alluvial plains, watered piedmont zones, and intermontane valleys. Important rivers, such as the Amu Darya and Zeravshan, that rise in the high eastern mountain ranges are fed largely by melting snows, while those in the west, such as the Murghab, Tedjen, or numerous streams of the Kopet Dagh, rely more on rainfall or, in some cases, tap groundwater sources (Dolukhanov 1981). Southern Central Asia is a landlocked basin with a sharply continental climate and is very arid, particularly

throughout its low-lying plains. While Soviet specialists disagree on the extent of environmental change during the Holocene (Contrast Lisitsina 1978: 189–93 with Vinogradov and Mamedov 1975: 234–55), a longer term pattern of general desiccation is clear. Neolithic archaeological remains deep in the Kyzyl Kum and Bronze Age settlements far to the north of the area currently watered by the lower Murghab suggest, at least, that waters flowed much farther into the deserts as recently as the early second millennium BC.

Systematic prehistoric investigations in Central Asia began with the work of R. Pumpelly at Anau in 1904, but this initial work only was refined and extended on a large scale by Soviet archaeologists after World War II. Soviet scholars, such as B. A. Kuftin (1956) and V. M. Masson (1956), documented a rich prehistoric sequence along the northern foothills of the Kopet Dagh in southern Turkmenistan which extended from Neolithic through Iron Age times and which related to developments on the Iranian plateau. Soundings at the major urban site of Namazga-Depe (50 ha.) yielded a basic six-period sequence (NMG I–VI) which has been confirmed and further refined by subsequent work, particularly at Altyn-Depe (c. 26 ha.; cf. Masson 1981). While regional differences were detected in specific periods, most scholars were impressed with the uniformity of the Namazga or southern Turkmenistan culture which stretched nearly the entire 600 km. length of the piedmont strip and emphasized that developments in this area led to the appearance of socially differentiated urban societies (Masson 1968). Moreover, ties between southern Turkmenistan and southern areas, like Pakistani Baluchistan, particularly the Quetta valley, and Iranian Seistan, were recognized and even led to speculations of colonization or movements from southern Turkmenistan south as early as the Late Aeneolithic of NMG III period (late fourth millennium) that may have been partly responsible for the emergence of such large centers as Shahr-i Sokhta in eastern Iran (Tosi 1973). In other words, in our terms, southern Turkmenistan was recognized early as its own core area, not perhaps as spectacular or as densely populated as the better known cores of the Tigris–Euphrates, Nile, and Indus valleys, but one which developed a distinctive, internally complex culture that occasionally seemed to have significantly influenced developments in adjacent peripheral areas.

According to Soviet investigators, the NMG-related settlements in southern Turkmenistan continued to expand through the Middle Bronze NMG V (end of third millennium BC) or so-called urban period, but during the subsequent Late Bronze NMG VI period large settlements along the piedmont strip, like Namazga and Altyn, either were abandoned or only continued to be occupied on a sharply reduced scale. Several interpretations – none of which is mutually exclusive – have been advanced to explain this decline, including: (a) environmental degradation due both to natural causes and to human overexploitation of the environment (Dolukhanov 1981); (b) 'barbarian' invasions from the northern steppes, possibly representing the arrival of Indo-Aryan groups (a theory first proposed by E. F. Schmidt at Anau but later accepted by many Soviet investigators, such as A. A. Marushchenko and A. M. Mandel'shtam); (c) a shift from primarily overland to maritime long-distance trade in the late third millennium BC leading to the decline of settlements not only in southern Turkmenistan but in the Gorgan plain (Tureng Tepe, Shah Tepe), the Iranian plateau (Hissar), and Seistan (Shahi-i Sokhta); this shift may have been associated with the consolidation and southern expansion of the Harappan civilization (Dales 1977); (d) an ingenious thesis of overurbanization (Biscoine 1977), which is based upon an analysis of known settlement size, postulates that too great a percentage of the total population lived in the cities and towns of southern Turkmenistan creating an artificial situation that could not sustain itself; and (e) a theory of colonization or emigration from southern Turkmenistan to the recently discovered and clearly related Bronze Age settlements in **Margiana and Bactria** (cf. Sarianidi 1981). Reasons for such a colonization need to be established; and determination of when such a movement actually began, how suddenly it occurred, and whether or not it proceeded only from west to east constitute some of the unresolved difficulties with this last explanation.

We cannot review the merits and demerits of each theory; some, like Dales' provocative hypothesis of a shift from overland to maritime trade, are extremely difficult, if not impossible, to establish conclusively on the basis of archaeological evidence. In a very real sense, however, the discoveries of numerous Bronze Age settlements in Margiana and Bactria suggest that a false problem has been posed; a crisis in urbanization or social devolution in southern Central Asia (and by extension throughout areas farther to the south) never occurred. Urban life did not collapse, but settlements shifted in Central Asia to the lowland plain formed by the lower Murghab and to the southern and northern Bactrian plains. These settlements were clearly related in terms of their material features to the earlier settlements in southern Turkmenistan, but they also were different. Sites were obviously planned and fortified; burial practices changed; and more numerous and advanced metal tools and weapons were produced on the Margiana and Bactrian sites. Known area of occupation in Margiana alone during its so-called Gonur or second stage of development (cf. Sarianidi 1981) is roughly double that documented in southern Turkmenistan or the core area during its period of urban florescence (NMG V). If southern and northern Bactria also are considered, the estimated area of *expansion*, not contraction or collapse, doubles once more. That is, present evidence suggests that settled life minimally was four times as extensive in Bactria and Margiana during the Bronze Age than in southern Turkmenistan (cf. Kohl 1983: chaps. 11, 13, 14, 15 for these estimates). While chronological correlations between the different regions need further clarification, it is obvious that the development of settled life in Bactria and Margiana cannot be accounted for solely or even primarily on the basis of emigration from southern Turkmenistan. In addition, hundreds of archaeological sites or stations, comprised chiefly of lithic remains, have been documented north of Margiana in the Kyzyl Kum desert (Vinogradov and Mamedov 1975) and immediately north of the Bronze Age sites in southern Bactria (Vinogradov 1979). It is likely that the relatively sudden appearance of planned Bronze Age sites on these lowland plains also involved the incorporation of these less technologi-

cally advanced peoples (cf. Kohl 1983: chap. 5 for a discussion of the Kyzyl Kum sequence and its apparent shift in orientation roughly at this time). The known core area of southern Turkmenistan was replaced by new centers in Bactria and Margiana at the end of the third and beginning of the second millennium. The cultures which developed in these newly settled areas clearly were related to the earlier cultures that evolved over several millennia in southern Turkmenistan but also exhibited new features, perhaps reflecting their mixed origins. We will briefly review materials from two Bactrian sites: Sapalli and Dashly 3.

The most informative and supposedly earliest North Bactrian site is Sapalli-Tepe in southwestern Surkhandarya province (Uzbekistan), a *c.* 4 ha. settlement with a central fortified area (82 × 82 m.) which was totally excavated by A. Askarov from 1969 to 1973 (Fig. 2.2; Askarov 1973; 1977). The excavated structures at this obviously planned site were fortified from the outset and consisted of eight separate multi-roomed complexes, termed 'patriarchal households' by the excavator (cf. Askarov 1973: 136–9 for an interesting, if speculative, comparison and contrast of Sapalli's social organization, as reconstructed from its architecture, with that recorded in the *Avesta*), grouped around a central open area and separated from one another by streets and alleys. These quarters seem to be generally self-sufficient, each containing several domestic hearths and evidence for pottery production. Thirty such hearths, possibly representing as many individual families, were found in the earliest period. While pottery-making was attested for each quarter through the discovery of two-tiered, two-chambered, and one chambered-combined kilns, conditions for production must have been terribly cramped with some kilns having only a *c.* one sq. m. section. Despite the general picture of independence and self-sufficiency for each quarter, there is some evidence for specialization: bread ovens occur only in certain quarters; quarter 1 has a craft shop for the production of bone and antler tools; quarter 6 has a particularly elaborate potters' workshop; and quarter 3 has a shop for preparing bronzes.

138 graves were excavated under the houses and in the walls at Sapalli, and the preservation was excellent with remains including figured metal pins, shaft-hole axe-adzes (which also can be paralleled on southern Bactrian tombs, at Hissar IIIC, and in the Mehrgarh VIII cemetery and site of Sibri in Pakistani Baluchistan), drilled bead seal-amulets, and food offerings and textiles, including the remains of silk clothing in four cases and caches of wheat and millet seeds. The graves included 125 individual and 13 collective burials or a contrast with the slightly earlier graves from Altyn where roughly 2/3 of the adult burials occurred in collective graves. The richest tombs contain only *c.* 50 objects, primarily pottery vessels, and female burials in general were richer than those of males. The number of goods in the graves seemed to depend upon the age of the deceased with infant and children's graves containing fewer gifts, possibly suggesting that status was achieved, not ascribed nor inherited. In general, little social differentiation beyond that of sex and age was evident in the Sapalli graves despite the high craftmanship and sophistication of the grave goods, particularly the metals.

Sites from southern Bactria or northwestern Afghanistan

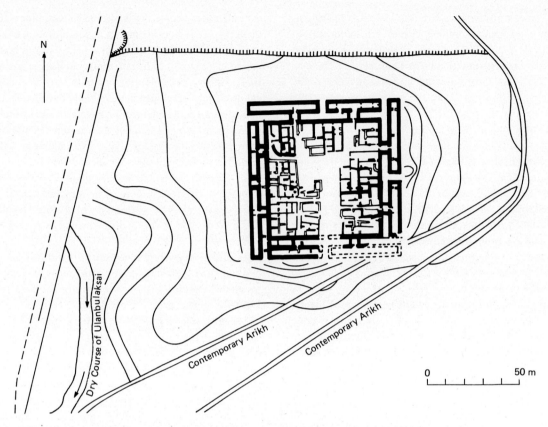

Fig. 2.2. Sapalli-Tepe: central compound and surrounding area, northern Bactria (southern Uzbekistan)

were discovered and excavated by the Soviet–Afghan archaeological expedition from 1969–1979. At least sixty-four Bronze Age sites were recorded in four separate oases along the dried-up extensions of streams, such as the Balkh-ab, flowing down from the western Hindu Kush. Dating of the sites is problematic: a sequence of some duration, probably extending back towards the middle of the third millennium is suggested, though it is also clear that most of the materials should be contemporaneous with the North Bactrian and Margiana settlements which can be dated to the end of the third through the first half of the second millennium BC. Sites include small planned fortified settlements, such as Dashly 1 (110 × 90 m.), reminiscent of Sapalli; industrial or craft production sites of uncertain dimensions marked by extensive scatters of debitage, including slag and wasters of lapis lazuli and turquoise; and very large settlements, like the c. 90 ha. site of Farukhabad 1.

The site of Dashly 3 contained two interesting groups of structures: a complex centered around a circular building or 'temple' (Fig. 2.3; Sarianidi 1977: 34–40); and a fortified compound or 'palace' similar to those excavated at Sapalli and Dashly 1 (Fig. 2.4; Sarianidi 1977: 41–50). The circular building, which was enclosed within a rectangular wall 130–150 m. to a side, was formed by a double row of walls encircling an area c. 40 m. in diameter. While the interpretation of the site as a temple is speculative, the central building complex contained several enigmatic features, such as hearths built on brick platforms, which were filled with white ash, and pits, which contained

lightly burned animal bones, suggesting some possibly non-utilitarian activity associated with the use of fire. Three rings of domestic structures outside the building but within the wall were thought to represent the residences of the separate temple community, though no direct evidence supports this problematic interpretation.

As at Sapalli, the Dashly 3 'palace' appeared to have been built largely at one time. It consisted of a symmetrical, rectangular walled area (84 × 88 m.) with an inner central court (38 × 40 m.) and had several false entrances and narrow T-shaped corridors. Access to the compound was deliberately restricted. After the original buildings were abandoned, new structures were built within the former central court and older rooms were reused, one of which functioned as a place for casting metal. In this room (no. 51) a two-part kiln was situated together with a clay mold for casting an axe-adze and copper ingots. More evidence for metallurgical production was discovered during the final or fourth period of occupation when the original planned architecture had further decayed and poorly built rooms were constructed.

The mortuary evidence from southern Bactria consists of roughly 100 properly excavated burials from Dashly 1 and Dashly 3 and thousands of illegally plundered tombs. In several highly specific respects the former excavated burials closely resemble those from Sapalli and other sites in northern Bactria and suggest relatively little social differentiation. It is more difficult to interpret the plundered tombs since their context has been

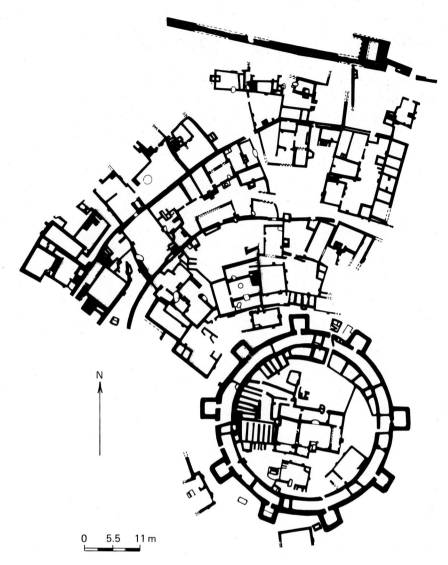

N

0   5.5   11 m

Fig. 2.3. Circular building at Dashly 3: southern Bactria (northwestern Afghanistan)

destroyed. Some of the objects, particularly the metals, from these tombs are truly spectacular (cf. Sarianidi 1977; Amiet 1977, 1978; and the systematic catalogue of objects from the Kabul bazaar by Pottier (1981) offers striking parallels to excavated materials from sites farther south in Baluchistan and southeastern Iran. Some Bactrian seals, for example, appear to have been cast from the same mold as those found in the rich cemetery at Shah-dad on the western edge of the Dasht-i Lut in southern Iran (compare Sarianidi 1977: 94, Fig. 48, no. 12 with Hakemi 1972: pl. XXIB.). In fact, the plundered Bactrian materials necessitate a re-evaluation of assemblages earlier collected by Stein and other scholars throughout Baluchistan (Jarrige 1982); seemingly incongrous and unexpected discoveries, such as a limestone column and shaft-hole axe from Shahi Tump (Stein 1931: 90–4), can be related to the Bactrian materials, suggesting some intensive trade or, more likely, north to south movements of peoples among the regions. Unfortunately, it is impossible to assess properly the significance of the plundered materials, and, until an undisturbed cemetery is scientifically excavated, one can only assume that the same rela-

tive similarity of grave lots recorded at Sapalli, other North Bactrian sites, Dashly 1, and Dashly 3 characterized all tombs – even those containing highly crafted objects. That is, despite the beauty and obvious craftsmanship of the Bactrian materials, there are no known royal or disproportionally wealthy tombs; present mortuary evidence suggests relatively little stratification within the society that produced them, an interpretation consistent with the relatively sudden appearance and mixed character of these settlements.

Analysis of these Central Asian materials is not illuminated by a simple reference to Wallerstein's world system's model. Rather, significant discrepancies emerge: an older core (southern Turkmenistan) appears to have been quickly superseded immediately subsequent to its florescence through a large-scale expansion onto formerly uncultivated, naturally fertile plains; the new settlements appear to have been remarkably self-sufficient and well-organized, though less internally differentiated than the earlier urban centers of southern Turkmenistan; at the same time, metallurgical technology, in particular, and the scale of subsistence and

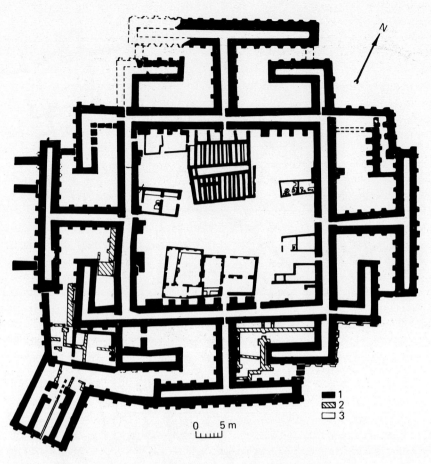

Fig. 2.4. Dashly 3 'palace' or planned compound: southern Bactria (northwestern Afghanistan)

craft-related productive activities seem to have increased substantially. Peripheral frontier areas were transformed into cores which were both more and less developed than the societies that they replaced. In addition, the recorded shifts in settlements appear to have been accompanied by significant changes in methods of transportation related to the introduction of the horse and utilization of the spoked wheel.

Horse bones are found at Kelleli 1 and/or Taip (Kuzmina 1980: 27, 33) and at the later Takhirbai 3 site in Margiana and at Tekkem-Depe and Namazga-Depe in the piedmont strip. The horse initially was domesticated on the south Russian steppe from the Don to the Volga in the fourth millennium and was introduced into Central Asia on a significant scale during the Late Bronze period (ibid.). Such an introduction or contact might be suggested by the presence of diagnostic incised 'steppe' ceramics on many of the sites in the lower Murghab and at Tekkem-Depe; in addition, a clay model head of a horse was found at Namazga-Depe. Although one cannot confidently speak of the advent of mounted pastoral nomadism or the extent of true horsemanship at this time, it seems likely from what is known of immediately succeeding periods (e.g. at Pirak to the south, Jarrige and Santoni 1979) that riding skills were developing at the end of the third and the beginning of the second millennia and that these must have profoundly affected the entire area of southern Central Asia. The evidence for spoked, as opposed to solid, wheels consists of a

model wheel with four brown painted spokes and an emphasized hub from Namazga, a wheel with six red painted spokes from Tekkem, and another spoked wheel from El'ken-Depe (Kuzmina 1980: 27). The significance of this development is unclear, though it presumably led to increased mobility and ease of wheeled transport for hauling goods and/or also for military purposes.

The new settled societies in Bactria and Margiana, some of whom may have moved farther south into Baluchistan and eastern Iran, adopted pre-existing, easily transferable technologies in strikingly innovative and politically significant ways. This adoption, possibly analogous to that postulated by Childe for his 'progressive' European barbarians, resulted in the abandonment of an older core area and indeed may have been partly responsible for the collapse of early urban civilization in south Asia (cf. Allchin and Allchin 1982: 298–308). Core areas, in short, were not terribly stable, and critically important technologies, capable of transforming or being transformed by political relations among interacting areas, were readily transferable to less developed regions, some of which were situated closer to natural source deposits or breeding plains for live resources, such as horses. Technologies, of course, did not diffuse automatically, and their importance, even use, differed from one social context to the next. But the model of a world system, which Wallerstein defined for the modern era, only imperfectly describes structured interactions in antiquity. *Economic* development and dependency were not linked phenomena during the Bronze Age in the manner postulated by contemporary critical theory for – to paraphrase their terminology – the development of underdevelopment in the Bronze Age was sharply constrained or itself underdeveloped. Critical technologies, such as metal working, could diffuse relatively easily and new means of transportation and sources of power, such as horses, could be raised in peripheral zones and radically restructure this ancient world system. Technological gaps, which dependency theorists argue pervade First–Third World relations today, simply did not exist in the Bronze Age in a manner that signified permanent political dominance or subjugation. Gatherer-hunter and nomadic stockbreeding populations on the Central Asian steppes or on the previously uncultivated plains of Margiana and Bactria rapidly adopted and transformed technologies that developed elsewhere, and these innovations made it possible – not inevitable – for them to alter established methods of interaction and political relations throughout many disparate regions of the greater Middle East.

Central Asia clearly interacted with South Asia and Iran in the late third millennium, but it was neither a core, periphery, or semi-periphery in terms of economic exchange with any of these areas. Contact was at best indirect and sporadic with Mesopotamia and non-existent with the eastern Mediterranean. A stray chlorite weight carved in an immediately recongizable 'Intercultural Style' (cf. Brentjes 1971) or the discovery of etched carnelian beads in Thailand and Southeast Asian spices in second millennium Mesopotamian contexts do not demonstrate the existence of a unified world system in any meaningful economic sense; materials and ideas simply could have diffused throughout Eurasia in a variety of ways. For Wallerstein's model to apply one must demonstrate economic dependency, and this one can do for only separate, relatively restricted areas of Eurasia during the third and early second millennia BC.

The neo-evolutionary models of regional autonomous development, which can be legitimately criticized for ignoring history or, in Braudelian terms, the conjuncture(s) of different structures, remain popular precisely for this reason. Prehistoric materials from the Balkans may bear some resemblance to those from western Turkey but to link them in turn to the Caucasus or, worse yet, Iran and points farther east is to invite ridicule. There was not a single Bronze Age world system but, if you will, overlapping world systems which constantly shifted and modified their boundaries due to unpredictable historical events, technological changes, or the formation and dissolution of larger political units and alliances. Thus, in the early to mid-third millennium southern Iran, extending the length of the Zagros, was united into a world system dominated by Khuzestan and possibly south-central Iran at the site of Anshan. The Namazga civilization of southern Central Asia formed part of another world system, perhaps spatially resembling that defined by Biscoine and Tosi as prehistoric Turan (1979). Relations with South Asia and its Harappan-dominated world system changed during the latter part of the third millennium, possibly related to the previously mentioned hypothesis of a shift from overland to maritime long-distance exchange and to the development of metallurgy, particularly the production of weapons, and the introduction of horses.

The Bronze Age world systems lacked an equivalent – if we follow Wallerstein – to western Europe in the late fifteenth and sixteenth centuries. There was no direct contact from one end of these Bronze Age world systems to the other. There was no single core, but a patchwork of core areas which succeeded only fleetingly in dominating their peripheral neighbors. The relative impermanence of core and peripheral areas was one of the major distinguishing features of Bronze Age world systems; means of communication and transportation simply were not sufficiently advanced to allow core areas to control and dominate their peripheries for long periods of time. Successful, long-lived political empires only emerged later, and they were explicitly distinguished by their politically imposed unity from the world system of modern times. Moreover, developments that occurred in peripheral zones soon transformed these backward societies, as on the plains of Bactria and Margiana and, perhaps, at Shah-dad in southeastern Iran, into core areas of their own. Expansion and colonization during the Bronze Age into largely unsettled areas continuously stimulated development and were structurally similar to the Greek overseas ventures of the seventh and sixth centuries BC, if not to the much later discovery and conquest of the New World and Australia. However, the Bronze Age colonies, as in Bactria, soon became more advanced than their homelands for they quickly achieved, if they did not originally possess, political autonomy and could develop relatively freely of limiting historical and social constraints.

The currently fashionable regional ecosystemic perspectives on the development of Bronze Age societies represent an advance over earlier diffusionary theories for they compel us to consider long-term structural phenomena, but they are still inadequate because they refuse to acknowledge the importance of historical events and the coming together of different cultural systems. Although it is notoriously difficult to assess the scale of the exchange of materials and ideas between prehistoric societies, archaeological data unequivocally demonstrate that contact occurred, and it is reasonable to assume that in many cases its effects were substantial. Utilization of Wallerstein's concept of a world system has the singular advantage of emphasizing that such contacts were based on fundamental economic considerations that were not necessarily to every society's adaptive advantage but were the products of stronger societies or elites within those societies attempting to impose their will and desire for material gain upon less developed areas.

However, the correspondence between a Bronze Age (or ancient) and modern world system is far from exact for precisely the reason that the control exercised by core areas was circumscribed and dependent upon relatively egalitarian or transferable technologies and primitive means of transportation and communication. Thus, for example, the advent of mounted warriors and effective chariots transformed interregional relations throughout the ancient Near East during the second millennium BC, ushering in various Dark Ages in older core areas and the emergence of new power centers, as in central Anatolia. For reasons of control and the complexity of the technology upon which this control is based, it is difficult to believe that a structurally similar rapid shift in the balance of power will occur to alter relations between underdeveloped and advanced countries today – at least without the prior internal transformation of the latter.

Cynics might argue that the Wallerstein model, questionable at best for the modern era, is so inapplicable to earlier periods as to make reference to it misleading or meaningless. Models that fail, however, also instruct, and consideration of the economic and political linkages among disparate societies is essential to advance beyond the theoretically simple-minded and empirically inaccurate alternative provided by neo-evolutionism. For both modern *and* ancient times Wallerstein's model of an interacting world system raises the essential, though often overlooked, problem of determining the most appropriate spatial and temporal unit of analysis. One cannot deny the open-ended

nature of social systems in the past any more than one can ignore the interconnections among societies in the modern era (Wolf 1982). Moreover, because such interconnections have intensified during modern times, it is obvious that cultural evolution primarily must be reconstructed from archaeological, not ethnological, evidence. That Wallerstein's model cannot be applied literally to the Bronze Age does not mean that the search for interconnections and structured interaction is unproductive. Rather, the task now is to determine how and why interactions at different, archaeologically attested stages of cultural development both resembled and differed from those of today. The model cannot be applied literally to earlier social formation, but its necessary alteration may help us better understand the development and character of pre- and early State societies and, perhaps more hopefully, gain insights into the nature of the contemporary world.

Chapter 3

Cedar forest to silver mountain: social change and the development of long-distance trade in early Near Eastern societies

Leon Marfoe

During a short span of time around 3000 BC, apparently sophisticated, complex systems that exhibited many of the attributes of urbanism and possibly state structures appeared across an area stretching from the Nile and Aegean in the west to central Asia in the east. It is not impossible that these regional developments may represent a loosely integrated and related series of changes (cf. Kohl, this volume). However, my purpose here is not to attempt such a major undertaking, but to focus on narrower regional changes within this broader context. Recent research has shed light on two remarkable phenomena occurring just prior to 3000 BC. During these few centuries, an emergent Egyptian state established a significant presence on the southwestern tip of Asia; to the east, a movement of south Mesopotamian origins across a broad front sent ripples deep into the foothills and montane valleys of the eastern Taurus mountains. In this penumbral arc between the two 'nuclear' areas of Egypt and Mesopotamia, a number of urbanized polities appeared shortly thereafter, from the Mediterranean littoral to southeastern Turkey. The concern of this chapter is to discuss the potential cross-efforts of these three regional developments, and particularly the role played by the two external phenomena in the development of local institutions in the Levant and Syro-Anatolia.

Rather than attempt a chronological, descriptive account, the details of which are already known to specialists, my objective is to sketch an interpretive history around these details. This sketch is a departure from some studies in that it views regional developments not from the perspective of self-contained, local systems moving along a largely internally generated, evolutionary trajectory[1], but as part of larger, systematically interrelated social changes occurring coevally. It thus views local changes as both cause and consequence of external linkages within a wider 'international' system of differentiated components with as yet ill-defined boundaries. This approach obviously converges with a now pervasive line of thought rooted in the ideas of dependency theory, world systems and internal colonialism[2]. Basic to such a wider view is the concept of 'cores' and 'peripheries', the primary characteristic of which is a hierarchical relationship between a dominant core and a subordinate periphery. Both as a metaphor and as a model, this concept clearly lends itself to the long and frequently noted fact that of all the potential 'cores' in the Near East, the 'pristine' regions of Egypt and Mesopotamia were striking not only for their early, prodigious and enduring civilizations and economic base, but also for their remarkable deficiency in raw resources (cf. Larsen 1979). They were, in short, the most successful in achieving the widest margins of new growth – at least as regional entities.

In this chapter, I wish to explore the potentialities of just such a wider view and the underlying concept of a 'primitive accumulation of capital' in the core–peirphery model. But insofar as the principal purpose here is to discuss the effects of 'core' linkages in one of these 'peripheries', my interest in the hierarchical/ dependency character of this model, lies in the notion that there

may be systematic interrelationships between local systems that
provide a context for social change. In the following pages, then,
I will focus on two long-distance linkages, between Egypt and
the Levant and between Mesopotamia and Syro-Anatolia, and in
the examination of the nature of these linkages, attempt to assess
localized social changes as a product of interrelationships among
early Near Eastern societies. In view of the paucity of documentation that can be brought to bear on this approach, any conclusion must be hypothetical. It must therefore be considered only a
tentative probe that leaves much unanswered.

The development of long distance trade
The pattern of Egyptian interaction with the Levant

One linkage that has become prominent in recent research
is the nature of Egyptian interaction with the Levant. Unfortunately, any attempt to define discrete 'patterns' of contact is of
course confronted with immense difficulties, not the least of which
is that the mainly archaeological evidence represents a more idiosyncratic and cumulative view of whatever 'real' patterns actually
existed.

Prior to late Naqada II, Egypt maintained an extensive
but low level of contacts with the Levant, the majority of which
were probably overland with Palestine, where many of the basic
resources were available. Copper came from the wadi Arabah and
possibly the Sinai, turquoise from the latter, and various coniferous woods, grapes and olives were available in the highland interior (Lucas and Harris 1962). Limited quantities of these materials
found in Egypt attest to a sporadic trickling of items through an
as yet unknown, but probably loose form of multiple, down-the-
line exchange (Baumgartel 1947/60; Kantor 1965).

Such contacts were probably relatively slow and laborious
ventures that extended from the Sinai to northern settlements like
Merimde and Maadi and then to villages farther south. To cross
140 kms overland from Qantara to el Arish may have required
four days on foot. And whether treks farther inland were needed
or relay links were provided by exchange points in southwestern
Palestine, the burden of any bulky traffic would have been difficult with or without pack animals. Journeys to the Syrian coast
by sailing craft may not have been any easier. Certainly, Egyptian
vessels existed in Naqada II times, but these were constructed
without a keel from local wood for the considerably easier river
traffic, where the prevailing north winds would have facilitated
upstream trips. On the Mediterranean, an outbound trip up the
coast would have required four days of coastal hugging to reach
Carmel, six or more to Byblos, and twelve to Ras Shamra, even
with the aid of favorable westerly winds and sea currents. With
countervailing winds and currents on the return, eight to ten days
would have been needed for an inbound coastal hugger from
Carmel. Particularly considering the seasonal and risky constraints on seaborne travel, then, there were few advantages
for a maritime traffic with limited cargo space over the land
route.

Sociopolitical developments within Egypt may have led to
substantial changes in these arrangements. Although 3150 BC is
generally accepted as the date for the establishment of a unified

entity in Egypt, it is becoming apparent that by late Naqada I or
II times, a number of towns may have crystallized from clusters of
earlier villages to form the successive capitals of an Upper Egyptian polity (Kemp 1977). Certainly by Naqada III, the spread of a
middle Egyptian assemblage to the delta suggests that at least one
of these polities may have extended its sway over the northern
settlements to result in the traditional 'unification' of Upper and
Lower Egypt (Kaiser 1964). The existence of these Predynastic
polities is of significance not only because they provide a context
for foreign contracts in this period, but because the later rise of a
unified Egyptian state ran concurrently with the accelerating
tempo of these activities. The aggressive expansion of an Upper
Egyptian polity resulted in intensified foreign ventures roughly at
the time of unification.

A burst of activity is readily seen in the Nubian Group A
remains, where contacts with high-status Nubians were made
(Trigger 1976). The growth of Asiatic connections in this phase,
however, is more impressive. Beginning with the last rulers of
Dynasty 'O' and accelerating with the initial kings of Dynasty I,
large, probably more frequent and organized state-sponsored
expeditions were sent into southwestern Palestine. Supported by
minor stations on the north Sinai coast, small trading stations,
way-camps and possibly colonies and outposts were established.
These two areas of intense activity sent ripples into the coastal
plain and inland valleys.[3]

In Egypt, a monopoly of this lucrative link – particularly in
copper – may have contributed to the further centralization of the
state between Dynasties I and III, if not earlier. Impressionistic-
ally, at least, there seems to be a significant rise in copper found in
Egyptian contexts from Naqada III onwards. In a tomb dating to
the reign of Djer (Dynasty I; Emery 1949), 700 copper objects
(including 75 'ingots') were found. By Dynasty II, a smaller but
similar cache was deposited in the tomb of Kha^{c}sekhemwi,
suggesting perhaps that a control over this strategic resource was
a royal and/or elite prerogative. By Dynasty V, copper was sufficiently common to be used for a long drainpipe in Sahure^c's
funerary complex, indicating that the deployment of wealth that
surely preceded the Old Kingdom was laid mainly in the late Predynastic and Early Dynastic periods.

At some point, in Dynasty II, this phase of Palestinian
contact appears to have tapered off, perhaps because of the internal problems thought to have begun with the reign of Peribsen
(Edwards 1971), as well as the emergence of urban polities in
Palestine by that time. Although the procurement of turquoise,
copper and bitumen may have been maintained (Gardiner and
Peet 1955), subsequent contact during the Old Kingdom is poorly
attested, possibly due to the problems arising from rearrange-
ments in control, production and distribution ensuing from fluctuating political conditions. The narrative of Weni (Dynasty VI)
suggests that 'punitive', booty-gathering expeditions may have
persisted, possibly alongside of a considerably restructured commercial arrangement (Pritchard 1969: 227–8), but there is as yet
little evidence for whatever rearrangement might have taken
place.

The first signs of a vastly different pattern emerged up the coast at Byblos, under Khaᶜsekhemwi and his successors. This shift to a third phase of maritime traffic was probably not a disjunctive one, since some form of infrequent, maritime exchange may have existed to some degree as far north as the Amuq in earlier times. But it is not until late EB II that an abundance of imported Egyptian or Egyptian-influenced objects attest to direct and presumably strong links between possibly state-commissioned Egyptian personnel and Byblite personages of high rank (Montet 1928; Jidedjian 1971).

Finer trends in this shift are discernible in quantitative comparisons of Levantine vessels found in dated Egyptian tombs of nobles or court officials and Egyptian inscriptions. The inscriptions suggest an escalation of activities from the end of Dynasty II to Dynasty IV, a plateau in Dynasty V, and a peak in Dynasty VI (Chehab 1969). The vessels confirm this trend, and indicate further that there was a general change from small jugs to large storage jars during this period (Helck 1971; Marfoe 1978).

Were there, then, underlying factors for this northward shift in the main thrust of Egyptian relations with Asia? One possibility is that the construction of larger, sea-going ships may have led to easier, faster and cheaper transportation compared to the overland traffic. In contrast to animal and human porterage, a shipborne journey could have carried a larger cargo in half the time, even excluding the ease of immediate delivery on the coast compared to the extra efforts needed for the Palestinian interior. Such ships, made of coniferous wood, first appear in Dynasty IV, but later in the Old Kingdom, there are specific references to 'Byblos' (*kbn*) ships – presumably because they were capable of making the voyage to Byblos – some of which were intended to fetch timber for ship construction (Faulkner 1940). The building of these ships, therefore, may have been related to a second factor, the superior and wider range of timber products on the Syro-Lebanese littoral. To be sure, conifers are already attested in Predynastic and Early Dynastic contexts (Lucas and Harris 1962), but sufficient quantities were necessary before such large ships could be built, and these in turn were needed for large shipments. The greater scale of later traffic thus may have been in part a product of this spiralling interdependence between timber procurement, ship construction and carrying capacity.

Another factor might have involved cost-efficiency in the scale of imported commodities. Grape and olive occur over most of the Levant, but by the Old Kingdom, the successful transplantation of the grape to Egypt is attested by references to vineyards, winepresses and grape processing scenes (Dynasty IV and later; e.g., Göedecken 1976). In contrast, olive – which is attested by well-developed strains by possibly Installation III at Byblos – was probably not transplanted until the New Kingdom (Lucas and Harris 1962). Since it has been suggested that the earlier importation of small jugs may have represented a traffic in wine (Stager n.d.), while the later, large storage jars may have been more suitable for seaborne traffic (Hennessy 1967), the change in imported vessels mentioned above may indicate a change in emphasis from grape to olive oil and resinated products. It seems possible, therefore, that changes in the relative costs of transportation due to a decline in the demand for foreign

wine (because of local Egyptian production) coupled with the decreasing cost of shipborne oil may have been instrumental in influencing consumption in Egypt, and in tipping the balance in favor of the Syro-Lebanese littoral, where timber was also in demand.

A further, though as yet unsupportable, factor may have included a demand for silver from northern sources, where an early transhipment center for this resource may have been Byblos (Prag 1978). The role of this early precious metal may have lain in ceremonial contexts. But it is at least possible that with the supplies of copper increasing during the Old Kingdom, the perceived devaluation of copper may have enhanced the perceived value of silver. In this context, the enormous differential in the gold–silver ratio between Egypt and western Asia[4] may have provided a powerful stimulus for an exchange of Egyptian gold for Asiatic silver. Considering their early roles in the display of conspicuous consumption, this may have been another compelling reason for the realignment in the volume and direction of Egyptian contracts.

If the low level of trade climbed from a slow start in Dynasty III toward a peak in Dynasty IV – a point also hinted at by Dynasty VI biographical inscriptions – what was the impact of this commerce upon Egypt? Such a line of investigation into a structure hitherto viewed as a static, monolithic state and temple economy cannot be sustained by existing documentation as yet, but a few highly tentative suggestions may still open up a realm of inquiry into the early centralization and later destabilizing forces that resulted in the disintegration of the Old Kingdom. While an intangible ideological motivation may have affected any accounting, one possibility is the gradual democratization of the use of credit within the economy. A unit of value, perhaps based on a metal standard, was in use in a house sale by the Old Kingdom, so that an indirect effect of this process may have been the appearance of *de facto* land ownership and property sales in this period (Peet 1935–8; Janssen 1975). It is still another conceptual leap to consider that the growth of a titled nobility/bureaucracy and private landownership perhaps not insignificantly paralleled the rising trend in overseas ventures during Dynasties V and VI. That the nobility also played a role in this state monopoly and took part in the consumption of imported products seems clear (Newberry 1938; Kanawati 1977; Helck 1971). Therefore, it is possible that a *partial*, possibly small contribution of any 'capital' accretion that might have occurred, fed by an inflow of foreign resources, may have led to the sort of land fragmentation, state immunities and perpetual cult endowments which coalesced with the proliferation of official titles and hereditary transfers in the later Old Kingdom (Baer 1960). In short, it is perhaps within the context of a slightly more dynamic, expanding economy that the accumulation of wealth and a rising nobility and state bureaucracy may perhaps be partially understood. Indeed, this later diffusion and usurpation of royal prerogatives by the nobility perhaps converges with the birth of a new literary genre in the First Intermediate Period, a form of 'wisdom literature' (Pritchard 1969: 412–25). With its emphasis on 'self-made' men and personal initiative, there is a striking parallelism with the ethical changes and mental transformations of a later capitalistic age, early modern Europe.

Thus, one might discern two possible strands in the pattern of Egyptian–Levantine contacts. First, whether it served ideological motives or not, Egyptian foreign ventures may have partly followed a degree of 'maximizing' principles, although such 'strategies' were probably only sluggish responses to the socially and culturally constrained consumption habits of an insulated elite. Although there is insufficient information on how this elite emerged in Predynastic times, it seems possible that its later development was influenced by the opportunities that arose within from personalities in some way connected with that structure.

A second possibility, however, is that state-building also went hand-in-hand with the creation of this elite and the forging of opportunities in part through extra-regional linkages. A state monopoly of an inflow of goods – especially metals – can be a factor in a state's capability to mobilize human energy, a phenomenon that was spectacularly successful in the Egyptian case. As durable, reputable, quality controllable resources with a degree of scarcity, metals have possessed a substantial potential for binding allegiances in later times (cf. Schneider 1977; Richards and Mazzaoui n.d.). At least as an extended hypothesis, then, the early centralization of the state structure may have been in part achieved by the deployment of capital through proscribed yet 'legitimate' channels that restricted the range of alternate modes of acquisition. In this regard, the apparent erosion of royal prerogatives in the latter part of the Old Kingdom may suggest that group and individual interests began to diverge from the goals of the state. Such a theme at least is worthy of further exploration.

The pattern of Mesopotamian interaction with Syro-Anatolia

A second linkage of equal importance developed overland between Mesopotamia and Syro-Anatolia at roughly the same time, but a succinct outline of this pattern is far more difficult to draw. Among the hurdles to be faced are the largely unsystematic data that reduce analyses to an impressionistic assessment of ceramic distributions along crude typological lines. Another effect is the rudimentary temporal control of fluid synchronisms and relative chronologies. A further difficulty arises in the terms 'Mesopotamia' and 'Syro-Anatolia', which imply regional units of analysis with defined boundaries and sharp cultural discontinuities. Neither was true by historic times, and perhaps a more appropriate framework would be a web of overlapping, interlocking but discrete, individual links of enmeshed local systems, forming a highly variegated fabric of connections that range in strength or access and permeability or porosity.

As early as the eighth millennium BC, the broad distribution of obsidian suggests that a 'Mesopotamian' awareness of resources and routes extended well beyond the alluvium. But it is not until the middle Halaf period that a coherent pattern of ceramic distribution encompassed a broad cross-section of ecological zones. Formed in the piedmont rainfall farming zones, the Halaf assemblage never appeared in the drier southern Mesopotamian region, but extended onto the highland massif along the major waterways and stretches of intermontane valleys (Mellaart 1975).

In this scheme, the spread of later Ubaid 'contacts' can thus be seen to be the linking up of two hitherto separate 'networks', one based on the south Mesopotamian alluvium oriented toward the south and east, and the other based on the northern steppe aligned toward the high-land arc (Oates *et al.* 1977). In other words, while early Ubaid linkages by the Hajji Muhammad phase had extended to the Arabian coast and western Iran, roughly contemporary with middle/late Halaf, later 'northern' Ubaid – our understanding of which remains at a rudimentary, ceramic level – generally followed the middle Halaf pattern. Although the limited archaeological evidence weighs against direct, habitual exchanges and at most for a series of interlocked segments of routes, the significance of this trade need not have been negligible. These distances closely approximated the limits of later Mesopotamian interaction in the historical periods, when by Akkadian and Ur III times, the borders of most ventures were at least conceptually circumscribed by the 'Cedar Forest' and 'Silver Mountain' of the highland ring. The even later Emar itinerary indicates that a direct roundtrip of 2,350 kms between the shorter route from Larsa to Emar via the northern steppe/piedmont route required a march of 194 days, while from the northern center of Assur, it meant 1,290 kms in over a hundred days (Hallo 1964). The roughly contemporary Cappadocian trade indicates that by then such trips were habitual, although Yahdunlim of Mari found an even lesser trip by the Euphrates route an unusual event. Thus, whether by foot or donkey, the farthest distances that were regularly frequented required perhaps a half-year roundtrip at about 30 kms/day, while the river routes may have been slightly faster (downstream). These horizons were first opened up in the later Ubaid period.

This linkage is perhaps significant because it occurs within the context of the appearance of the first substantial towns in southern Mesopotamia. As such, it provides a setting for urban development in Early–Middle Uruk Mesopotamia, and particularly for the next discernible phase, when there was an extraordinary shift toward urban concentrations at Uruk in the late Uruk period.

Perhaps what is even more remarkable about this next phase is the extension of direct and indirect linkages onto the Iranian plateau (Weiss and Young 1975), to Egypt (Moorey, this vol.), and into Syro-Anatolia. Although finer chronological subdivisions will undoubtedly unravel the complexities of this latter phenomenon, which took place over a period of time, a number of features are now more discernible. Rather than an amorphous spread of isolated artifacts across the Syrian steppe and Taurus piedmont, one such feature is the directional character, which shows discontinuities and a fading of frequencies away from the riverine nexus along the Euphrates and the Khabur. At least in an early stage of this phase, the massive, intense character of Habuba Kabira/Quannas/Jebel Aruda suggests a direct transplantation of colonists and Mesopotamian urban features (Strommenger 1980b; van Driel and van Driel-Murray 1979), with an element of self-conscious calculation in an aggressive program. Away from the mid-Euphrates complex and the Khabur, where Brak may yet prove to be another center (Fielden 1981), a trail of related settlements and possible way-stations proceed well into the highland arc and the west (Esin in METU 1970–9), where the transformation of local assemblage attests to the pervasive effect of this contact. At an apparent later stage, the appearance of local variants (Palmieri 1981) may reflect bursts of activities at intervals and in different forms. These features may suggest that the routes of contacts proceeded up the main waterways, from which secondary linkages emanated out into a periphery.

Just what sort of organization and transactions underlay this varied pattern is elusive, but it seems not improbable that for the first time Mesopotamia was directly exploiting the highland resources. If cities like Uruk were undergoing rapid expansion, with immense construction projects and conspicuous ceremonial displays, they must also have concentrated a stratified demand for finished products and sustained production with an inward flow of resources and an outward flow of finished products (Adams 1981). What sort of commodities and resources were entailed? Silver is still rare, but copper is more prominent than before and is even more abundant by Early Dynastic I times (e.g., Burney 1980; van Driel and van Driel-Murray 1979; Palmieri 1981). In bulk, the most important upland resource may have been timber, the demand for which may have been increased enormously by construction and manufacturing (Rowton 1967; Willcox 1974). Perishable essences, oils and wine are suggested by later texts (Leemans 1960). For outflows, the export of bitumen (van Driel and van Driel-Murray 1979), and the massive manufacturing industries of later times are possibilities (Lambert 1953; Jacobsen 1970; Limet 1960), along with indications of animal husbandry in the archaic texts.

Whether or not this superficial resemblance with the Egypto-Levantine case implies state building in Mesopotamia is still uncertain, but the inflow of essentially 'luxury' items in contrast to the outflow of mainly manufactured commodities points to elite demands and an organized production system highly suggestive of centralizing social formations in Mesopotamia. And as Moorey so cogently argues in his accompanying paper, the implied connections overland to Egypt in the Naqada II–III period may well have sent ripples across most of Syria.

How this phase ends and gives way to a vastly different pattern by Early Dynastic III is unclear, but there are indications that a critical shift had transpired by around Jemdet Nasr/Early Dynastic I times. The first indication is that an apparent decline in Uruk-related remains may suggest a restructuring of the earlier exchange mechanisms. The second indication is the apparent formation of local urban polities in the highland arc, where substantial centers had emerged even prior to the partial association with the Early Transcaucasian Culture (Esin, Hauptmann in METU 1970–9; Whallon 1979). Third, an initial trickle of Syrian mass-produced wares that reaches significant proportions by the mid-third millennium hints at a rising Syrian interchange with the highlands as early a EB I (Esin in METU 1970–9). Fourth, breaks or declines in occupation at a number of sites on the periphery point to a slightly later disruption in highland/piedmont political configurations (van Loon 1978; Palmieri 1973). Fifth, the appearance of the domesticated ass between the late fourth and early third millennium (Zarins 1978; Gilbert 1982) may represent a greater emphasis on the northern steppe route away from the major waterways. And last, changing political configurations on the lowlands indicate that a new balance of power had arisen. In south Mesopotamia, the Late Uruk pattern fragmented into a mosaic of competitive centers. In north Mesopotamia and Syria, a fragmentation of regional assemblages from Ninevite V to the Amuq are an indication that strong urban polities had emerged to challenge each other and erect a formidable buffer to Mesopotamian aspirations on the northern steppe.

To examine these themes further, we must turn to the more erratic, episodic pattern discernible for the first time by ED III. These seem to cast doubt on the slow, cumulative process drawn so far for the preceding phases, but if both are viewed as no more than two contrastive time phases – one stable and long term, the other dynamic and conjunctural – that are superpositiond in the historical process, this pattern probably extended far backwards beyond the mid-third millennium.

One characteristic of this pattern may have been the movement and role of metals. Copper was already established as a unit of measure in the early third millennium, but a few centuries later, its relative abundance may have resulted in a shift to silver as the preferred medium of exchange (Lambert 1953; Limet 1960; 1972). By the early second millennium, silver was the international means of payment, although it was replaced briefly by gold (Leemans 1960; Brinkman 1972). Thus, although it was rare enough in the Ur III period to be merely a basis for establishing equivalents (Curtis and Hallo 1959), the increasing role of silver in part defines the existence of this phase.

The directional movements of silver are difficult to discern in broad, spatial patterns, but a few general observations can be made. Anatolia was only one of several sources that provided silver for Mesopotamia, but in view of the presence of silver in east Anatolian and Syro-Mesopotamian contexts as early as the Uruk-Jemdet Nasr period, and in large amounts by the mid-third millennium (Pettinato 1979), it seems likely that Anatolia was a main source for much of the third millennium (Moorey 1982). By the early second millennium, a north to south flow was more prominent, and after entering south Mesopotamia, may have moved farther south (e.g., Sasson 1966; Leemans 1960). In this regard, both the Old Assyrian and Ur trade may indeed epitomize the strategy of resource-deficient Mesopotamia: to procure raw supplies and precious metals through the payment of transhipped goods and locally manufactured items like textiles (Larsen 1976; Oppenheim 1954). But since by the mid-third millennium similar strategies may have been practised by the strong Syrian states, involving large quantities of stockpiled silver, any net accumulation in Mesopotamia in aggregate would probably have been attracted by more cost-efficient or desirable products (e.g., Crawford 1973). To be sure, foreign demand for Mesopotamian products possibly included a significant element of intangible tastes, perhaps influenced by Mesopotamian cultural values in the Uruk-Jemdet Nasr period (see below), but any comparison of the large Early Dynastic Mesopotamian city-states with the diminutive polities of the source-bearing regions must confront a dramatic contrast in factors of scale[5]. Thus, if production was fed by inflows of raw materials and capital outlay, any superior export capacity that might have existed should trace its origins not only to superior organizational skills and pervasive cultural values, but also to an earlier disposition towards long-range resource acquisition, a remarkable discrepancy in agricultural land and hence capital base, and larger, stronger state systems. Such a 'headstart' may have been established in the Ubaid period, when the two 'networks' were linked.

For these arguments and postulations to have any validity, a number of implications must follow. One is that silver might have moved at a higher velocity and in greater bulk on an inter-regional level since silver payments formed part of the international trade transactions as early as Pre-Sargonic times. At a regional level, however, one might perceive silver as moving in a relatively tight, virtually closed sphere, the main stocks retained partly in hoarded form by state and other public institutions, while only small amounts changed hands (Limet 1960). Another and perhaps more important implication follows from the change after the Late Uruk period to indirect modes of resource procurement, in which the alteration of trading arrangements may be discerned as a series of sequential responses to shifting political alignments and routes first in the highlands (EB I), then in south Mesopotamia (ED I), and finally on the Syrian steppe (mid-third millennium). If the linkages between regional systems became fully articulated and interlocked at this time, they formed a transportation and communications web in which transactions may have been segmented by political or cost–distance factors. In other words, new, constantly changing points of equilibrium in balancing gain against loss, that were imposed by the variables confronting each consignment, meant that Mesopotamian relationships with the resource areas were no longer asymmetrical in either a sociopolitical or commercial sense.

It is this theme of a 'headstart' followed by a siphoning off, curtailment or merely a change in equilibrium of flows that provides a significant setting for the turbulent politics on the Mesopotamian social landscape in subsequent periods[6]. The inter-city conflicts of the ED city-states, with their propensity for escalating local disputes into mass warfare, may have been not only a by-product of fragmentation, but also a continual need to retain or attain basic advantages along common routes and in common resource areas. The final battle between Lagash and Umma may thus be an illustration of the opportunities to gain 'windfall' booty by capturing stockpiled silver.

In this light, the Akkadian empire was less an aberration or an apogee in an evolutionary development than merely an extreme reached in a constantly oscillating pattern of peaks and lows. The transformation of the alluvium into a coherent sociopolitical entity, like later experiments, may have altered some of the cost–distance factors toward more favorable terms, and may have spurred the reorganization of the economy into greater productive scale. But campaigns by a state that could exact tribute were probably brief flurries in a fluctuating hegemony, and territorial expansion as a viable strategy had its attendant costs. A larger and differentiated bureaucratic infrastructure required greater surpluses, labor inputs and resources, which inevitably led to a spiral of further expansion, resources, and costs, ultimately leading to decentralization (cf. Yoffee 1979). Internal develop-

ment towards sociopolitical integration as a reflex of new, external political factors held its own point of equilibrium, and given its inherent fragility, was only one of several possible responses. As later ages of far less expansive capabilities attest, far-reaching trade may have persisted under even minimal conditions of integration, because economies of scale may have served a similar purpose.

Herein lies a further implication for the maintenance of Mesopotamia's economic edge. If a private, albeit limited, commercial role existed well before its firm textual attestation (Foster and Powell in Hawkins 1977), one might see its later expansion as a consequence of several converging developments. One would be the increasing supply of precious metals, which would have facilitated the conversion of accumulated, perishable wealth to investments. A second may be the private holding of land, which might have encouraged investment into and from land (Gelb 1969). While these factors may have provided only a capability for investment, a third factor might be the new variables of access to distant regions, that imposed limitations on the possibilities of direct exploitation or conquest. In this newly opened niche, the opportunities stemming from the need to procure resources from more risk-laden, costly ventures abroad may have provided enough incentive by the later third millennium for the tentative investment into trading expeditions, a point that is suggested by later contract stipulations underlining the precarious balance between risks and profits (Oppenheim 1954). In this niche, it is the *interstitial* role of the public or private trader, weaving his way between capricious kings, bandits, customs, delays and dissatisfied customers, that provides a vehicle by which the role of precious metals might have mobilized the circulation of capital between private, state and temple lands, depositories and commercial ventures.

The significance of the foregoing sketches can now be summarized briefly. Beneath the broad disparities that characterized early Egypt and Mesopotamia, there may be a degree of subtle similarity possibly symptomatic of an undercurrent of common processes, at least between the late fourth and late third millennia. There has been a tendency to view Egypt and Mesopotamia as self-contained systems whose developments were shaped by forces intrinsic to these areas. If my arguments are valid, however, such tendencies should be modified to consider changes that may in part be attributable to an interplay between local and external forces. In this regard, one possible effect of their outcome may have been a 'primitive accumulation of capital' and its role as a force for change. Such a conclusion would include a measure of 'market forces' in these periods. Since there is now little controversy over some 'pressures' by as early as the late third millennium, at least in Mesopotamia, one might consider the relative effect of such forces, and in particular, the relative degrees to which responses were 'embedded', or the 'scalarity between ceremoniality and the usage of silver as a theoretic measure (Liverani 1979a)'.

Without turning towards a facile formalism, my suggestion is that perhaps studies based mainly on the late third/second millennia have blinkered us to the possibility of constantly fluctuating, perhaps even increasing degrees of structural constraints in these early societies, under varying sociopolitical conditions and over centuries, rather than the more common notion of a lineal evolution from embedded to market systems (cf. Adams 1974). Viewed as units of analyses, both Egypt and Mesopotamia appear to display a degree of 'maximizing rationality' at least in their macro-relations with other regions. By the mid-third millennium, it may be possible to discern beneath these relations a degree of differentiated groups, perhaps working within the constraints of the local political economy towards divergent ends. But the actual outcome of Egyptian and Mesopotamian foreign relations appears in aggregate and over the long term to be attributable to the behavior of a small elite core that emerges with the centralization of the state. Structured undoubtedly by certain ideational frameworks, the basic course of external economic behavior was apparently determined by the wants of this core, which in its aggregate behavior may not have been too dissimilar in its operation to a 'firm' or 'firms'.

In differentiating between the aggregate and its component behaviors, it may well be that on a microeconomic scale, individual actions may be seen as the result of short term objectives reflecting 'class' or 'group' values, and expressd as parity exchanges or tribute surplus transactions. But over centuries, such cultural values may well have persisted for generations, and may thus be reducible to a long-term constant. If this is so, then even if such cultural constraints are poorly understood, variations in macro-economic relations may be indicative of tendencies masked in the short term. And this is far more probable in 'external' relationships, where transactions beyond the sector defined by kinship and ideological ties provided the broadest opportunities for gain. Over a fairly long period of time, then, degrees of elasticity in response to any 'market pressures' or accumulated imbalances in exchange would have been a function of long-term tendencies, which in turn would have been dependent on the relative ease in the transmission of pressures, and of the liquidity of the economy.

The effective transmission of 'pressures' is related to the ability to communicate them rapidly, and their magnitude is associated with the knowledge, arrangements and communications that are facilitated by the transportation, handling and social connections of the linkages. In turn, these depend on progressive refinements in the levels of commercial know-how, transportation techniques and interpersonal relationships, all of which may have changed between the fourth and third millennia. Such refinements may have eased changes in the relative levels of operation and their impact over the long term.

In regard to liquidity, the central features of a more dynamic economy would be reduced to two elements. One may have been a culturally conditioned, entrepreneurial awareness that might have operated for various motives, at public or private levels, within a generally widespread 'embeddedness'. The second element would have lain in the ability to invest in productive means. Over the long term, this would have hinged on the relative degree of liquidity in assets, and in particular, on the velocity or rate at which capital could have been circulated and transferred from surplus to investments and then into production and sur-

plus, gradually accumulating to a 'critical mass'. Insofar as investment entails a degree of risk, the relative convenience of 'hedging' or 'spillover' would have been a critical factor in the decision to invest (however unconscious this 'decision' may have been), and this in turn would have been immensely aided by suitable instruments of investment and ventures to invest into. The former would have depended particularly on the availability of a 'universal' medium of exchange. Thus, however sluggishly supplies may have responded to demands (hoarding and conspicuous display may have been 'dampeners'), the concept of a 'primitive accumulation of capital' as a force for change may have pivoted around the role of precious metals as such a medium of exchange, that in a pre-monetary economic system would *suddenly* grease the wheels (so to speak) of a ponderous market mechanism of 'pressures'. In this perspective, the motive for the acquisition of metals may well have lain originally in intangible or utilitarian reasons, but its role would have hinged on its negotiability. In other words, given the variety of structural constraints in any partially 'embedded' ancient economy, the crucial variables with the potential for a long term, *relative* impact on 'pressures' leading to social change were refinements in the social and technical aspects of commercial transactions, and the availability of a 'universal' medium of exchange.

The Levant and Syro-Anatolia in interregional perspective
The implications of the above discussion are that if the early 'cores' responded to an interplay between local and external forces in the slightly more dynamic manner suggested, then an examination of the effects and cross-effects of the two sequences of interaction described above may be instructive for understanding the development of local systems within the contexts of long-distance relationships. Unfortunately, the broad regional variations and largely uneven and unsystematic data are such that only idiosyncratic rather than paradigmatic views are possible at present.

There is no reason to discern significant, enduring differentiation in social structures among the early farming villages that were established throughout the Near East. Basic changes in social groupings do not seem to appear until around 5500 BC, along with possibly wider and thicker webs of exchanges that have facilitated scheduling and the balancing of local inequities. Despite the broadening of these overlapping exchange networks, however, none appears to have been a sustained success. Considering the lack of incentives for investment, increased labor inputs, the accumulation of goods beyond the need for balancing local inequities and the levelling of variable incomes, or indeed the relative inability to store and transfer 'wealth', local systems may have stabilized or collapsed once a certain level of production had been reached. As in the Halaf, one of the more successful cases, the existence of a set of exchange networks and vertical differentiation in the fifth and fourth millennia were perhaps necessary but hardly sufficient reasons for the intensification of linkages beyond a certain level, and as such, provided only a context for growth.

With varying degrees of impact during the late fourth and

early third millennia, the crystallization of new urbanized, socio-political structures in the Levant and Syro-Anatolia may have been triggered by the Egyptian contact from the Naqada III onwards, and the Mesopotamian thrust into Syro-Anatolia in the Uruk-Jemdt Nasr period onwards. In the brief timespan following the initial establishment of these intensified linkages – and depending on finer synchronisms, perhaps less than a century in some cases – true town sites had emerged, accompanied by a general overall increase in settlements in many cases (Amiran 1970; Kempinski 1978; Whallon 1979; Marfoe 1979). By the mid-third millennium, large, expansive city-states are known (e.g., Matthiae 1981). And with this disjunctive leap was a profound, so far qualitative change in the degrees of social distinctions, the division of labor, concepts of world order and the rise of militarism.

How, during the course of the fourth millennium, a number of factors may have combined with existing structures to impel at least in part the existing societies toward an upward curve of production and surplus accumulation may indeed call for a range of regional differences. Here, I wish to focus on only selected aspects of the long-distance relationships and their impact, that may have been a fairly common element among these differences. One such, possibly essential, element of these relationships can best be seen at Byblos, although the impact of cross-traffic here is probably unusual in that it magnifies effects that may have been more subtle elsewhere. The roots of urban formation at Byblos can, of course, be indistinctly traced back to the Late Chalcolithic period (Installation II), when signs of social ranking (see below), a traffic in silver and other resources, as well as a genetically well developed horticultural emphasis on orchard crops like olive may have already existed (Dunand 1973: 330). In the late fourth millennium, the 'Proto-Urban' village (III) became transformed into an urban installation (IV), although the precise synchronisms between this development and the phases of Egyptian and Mesopotamian contact are still unclear (Dunand 1950; Jidedjian 1971). In any case, it seems to be no earlier than the Jemdet Nasr period, and no later than Dynasty II in Egypt, and thus somehow closely related to the rising tempo of cross-traffic between the burgeoning shipping lanes from Egypt and the possibly overland trade with Syria (cf. Moorey this volume).

What is most significant about the urbanizing process at Byblos is the degree to which cultural perceptions and ideational frameworks were altered. The scale and intensity of Egyptian contact and Syrian cultural assimilation there points to a cultural transformation of sweeping proportions and enduring qualities (Monet 1928; Jidedjian 1971). Epitomized by the personification of the Egyptian goddess Hathor as the patron goddess Baalat-Gebal of Byblos, the close connections between the long tradition of Byblian kingship and theocratic institutions with Egyptian business transactions persisted for over 2,000 years. Expressed at the Byblian end by the association of royalty with Egyptian symbols, and at the Egyptian end by the identification of Byblos as an unparalleled resource area, this long relationship clearly traces the origins of Byblian statecraft to an Egyptian encounter of grave ideological significance, at least in the perception of its rulers.

What is significant, too, as later traditions and contemporary sources indicate, is that the role of kingship can in part be traced to a nodal, intermediary position in this foreign trade, although at the time of the Wen-Amun narrative, the relationships between Byblites and Egyptians were being reassessed (Pritchard 1969: 25–9). How these nodal positions originally emerged is at present uncertain, but Prag's (1978) suggestion of a transhipment center in silver may be at least a partial explanation. In any case, if the Late Chalcolithic Byblos tombs are any indication, possibly 2.5 per cent of the population may have belonged to such groups, if the presence of silver and small amounts of gold were indeed markers. By later times, a long though poorly documented record of elite consumption – in one case, an inscription attesting to the commodities (not just preciosites) included in offerings; in other cases, 'Egyptian' objects in royal tombs; in a third case, an association of 'Abydos' vessels and Jemdet Nasr-type seals with a major building – points to the centrality of the elite in the procurement, consumption and exchange process. In this light, the institutionalization of an Egyptian-oriented Byblian cult becomes understandable; as a guide and as a rationalization, facets of Egyptian civilization were translated into local idioms that became the cultural and ideological framework of a Byblian polity and the legitimizing prerogative of its elite. Thus, while the detailed Byblian case draws its substance in part from anachronistic documentation, it seems not unwarranted to postulate from the weight of circumstantial evidence that the intensification of Egypt linkages with the littoral allowed the far-reaching tentacles of inland trade with central Syria to be focused at one or a few nodal points, of which Byblos was unquestionably one. Within this settlement, groups or individuals with perhaps a long-standing position central to the earlier traffic were able to control most of the redistributive functions associated with imports, exports and transhipments, and through this role, were able to emerge as a ruling – not merely ranking – elite.

Although the lack of a firm chronology makes it difficult to discern finer details in this process, the Byblian case at least focuses attention on the existence of a self-conscious, possibly self-aggrandizing group, whose wants may have provided the main stimulus for political centralization and urban development. By at least the Early Dynastic period, Stager (n.d.) has recently pointed out that Egyptian demand from the Levant had been possibly restructured by an emergent elite to include not only raw materials but also processed products like wine and oil. At least as a viable hypothesis, then, it is possible to suggest that in order to maintain their central positions, a Byblian connection would have had to reorganize the means of producing a surplus. Already well advanced in olive cultivation by this time, but possibly mainly for subsistence purposes, the insertion of a foreign demand may have shifted production toward an emphasis on labor-intensive modes, requiring a degree of time-frozen investments, changes in the form of land ownership, and new means of organizing labor, as well as procurements and distribution. Such a scheme at least draws scrutiny to the restructuring of social patterns into new, expansive forms of production as a process of surplus extraction, in which the accelerated rise of a new local elite with its own concept of conspicuous consumption – especially if associated with new cultural values – may have led to different kinds of labor mobilization and a sustained chain of self-generating investment and production by at least Old Kingdom times.

The roles thus sketched for the cross-traffic impact on Byblos – as a cultural and political transformation centered around an elite group – are weighted toward the Egyptian linkage, and form only suggestive clues for understanding the far more ambiguous transformations in other regions. It may apply, for instance, in a modified form to Arad, where a complex of public, secular and religious structures arose in association with a town located on the early 'copper road' to Egypt. (There, at least, an association with the accoutrements of new cultural perceptions and social groups – seals, copper implements and fine 'Abydos' vessels – may suggest a roughly similar transformation) (Amiran 1978; 1980; Marfoe 1980).

Yet, a clear distinction in archaeological assemblages exists between the Levant, where the Egyptian impact may have been more profound, and central Syria and northern Fertile Crescent, where a more ambiguous, though similar and parallel transformation took place. Much farther north of Byblos and Arad, Braidwood's (Braidwood and Braidwood 1960) assertion that phase F in the Amuq constitutes the most radical change from the preceding phases remains essentially correct. The establishment of a highly organized, religiously focused community at Habuba Kaira/Qannas/Jebel Aruda (possibly among others) may have had wide-ranging disequilibrating effects on local communities on both the northern steppe and highlands. To be sure, the timespan in which Late Uruk/Jemdet Nasr relationships are evinced at a number of sites undoubtedly encompassed a greater chronological range than the relatively short-lived settlements associated with Habuba Kabira. But a least at various stages of these early Mesopotamian activities, however indistinguishable they may be at present, ripples may have been felt as far afield as Cilicia, the Orontes valley, perhaps the Hawran, and probably the Syro-Lebanese littoral, where it may have linked up directly with the Egyptian traffic either directly or indirectly at Judeidah, Byblos and possibly Hama, to result partially in the Egyptian impact discussed by Moorey.

By slightly later times, and particularly in areas near silver (Keban, Amanus), copper (Ergani) and timber sources, local centers had emerged in the areas of Late Uruk/Jemdet Nasr contacts (Palmieri 1981; Burney 1980), amidst a cultural and political transformation as profound and as permeative as at Byblos and Arad. As Whallon (Whallon and Kantmann 1967: 130) points out: 'the Early Bronze Age in the area [the Keban] witnessed the rapid development of a strikingly large population with a pattern of settlements strongly suggestive of a complex, centralized organization'. How such centers were organized is still unknown, and may have to await the full publication of sites like Norşuntepe and Tepecik (Esin and Hauptmann in METU 1970–9), but at Malatya, the best example to date, the close association of copper weapons, seals and seal impressions along with vessels related to Mesopotamian varieties within major buildings in VIA may be indicative of a new elite operating at the nexus of exchange and procurements systems, with values permeated by

Mesopotamian concepts translated into local idioms (Palmieri 1981).

Here, then, we have a variant of the Byblian theme, in which, if Burney (1980) is correct, there is a more direct impact from the Mesopotamian quest for metals. Although hammered copper objects occur on rare occasions in earlier times, a fairly uniform, and certainly widescale operation in the mining, smelting, manufacturing and distribution of copper was in existence by the Late Chalcolithic period. Evidence for mining and processing comes from the presence of ores, lumps or caches and individual items at a number of sites (Tepecik, Malatya VII, Amuq F) across a broad area, quite apart from the extensive networks around the Dead Sea and Sinai (Muhly 1976). At roughly the same time, small amounts of silver are also to be found – in one case, in clear association with copper and seals in elite burials (van Loon 1978). For both these metals, therefore, the crucial role lay in their characteristics as comparatively scarce resources with highly restricted sources, distribution and processing procedures. Their controllability, and mobilizative and accumulative properties may thus have become a major factor for destabilizing access to resources and for the concentration of social and economic power. As part of a widespread network of flows in precious metals, the rise of a nodal elite group undergoing a major cultural transformation is at least a partial explanation for the rise of local centers.

But only partial. For the impact of the introduction of precious metals may have had longer term consequences. Precious metals are also highly portable, divisible resources that can be relatively easily standardized. As such, they provide a far more liquid means of converting, circulating and accumulating wealth. Given a fairly high demand, and a motive for raising production as a means of surplus extraction, the greater ease of converting wealth into investment-oriented, labor-intensive forms of production may have overcome any blockages in decisions to make long-term investments. The great shift in emphasis on horticultural crops requiring time and labor may be in part a product of this new ability in the third millennium (Stager n.d.). Such a hypothesis cannot be documented as yet, and considering the embedded character of the economies at the time, it may be fair to ask whether such early centers or their institutions could have indeed operated in part as a 'firm', even over a fairly long period of time. Yet, a few centuries later, such a description may well be adequate for the new city-states on the Syrian steppe.

It shoud be recalled that the origins of the new polities on the Syrian steppe, away from these source areas, remain obscure, and possibly did not follow the pattern so far discerned. There is, in fact, a period between the early and middle third millennium for which we have little evidence. By the mid-third millennium, however, a secular ruling group had emerged at Mardikh, at the core of a highly elaborate bureaucratic state machinery participating in a large system of resource procurement, mobilization and production, and perhaps drawing directly upon Mesopotamian concepts of world order for its cultural framework (Pettinato and Matthiae 1976; Matthiae 1981; Petinnato 1981). Similar elements appear to be present at a number of other sites on the steppe

(Margueron 1980; Moortgat 1957–78). Of particular significance at Mardikh is the fact that accounts documenting the inflows and outflows of the palace for the first time reveal a large-scale production of textiles and agricultural products, and particularly substantial movements and stockpiles of silver and some gold (Pettinato 1979).

Two elements in this picture are striking. Although perhaps acquired originally for ceremonial or other intangible motives, the use of silver as a standardized unit of measure by this time would indicate that it (perhaps quickly) became an effective way of tangibly expressing new relationships in cumulative units of wealth. Possibly in contrast to its earlier Late Chalcolithic role as a decorative device, it is conceivable that a role as a medium of exchange emerged as new political relationships were renegotiated in both local and external contexts. Such new realignments are faintly discernible. After the Egyptian emphasis shifted toward a maritime route to the Syro-Lebanese littoral (and Dynasty IV and VI objects have been found at Mardikh), excavated sites in Palestine reveal that some sites (e.g., Arad) were abandoned by the end of EB II, and that a number of fairly large nucleations, particularly in the north, had replaced the more numerous scattering of smaller EB II centers by the mid-third millennium (Kempinski 1978). In the northern highland resource areas, the spread of the Early Transcaucasian culture and the slightly later reduction or abandonment of major sites like Malatya and Korucutepe may signify that basic political realignments had taken place (Paleieri 1973; van Loon 1978). When resettled or reorganized, the predominant foreign imports are no longer of Mesopotamian origin or inspiration, but are essentially Syrian. On the steppe, a few genuinely Anatolian items are to be found in mid-third millennium contexts, along with strong evidence of Mesopotamian connections. In this flux of realignments, from which arose the Syrian economies of scale, a standardized unit of exchange with widespread demand would have been a logical outcome of the earlier cultural transformations, and a guarantee against unstable partnerships. So as metals gained a wider common acceptance between new partners, so too did the exchange undergo changes in meaning.

But the major reorientations in trading relationships outlined above may have had other consequences, and here emerges the second element in the picture. The rise of Syrian economies of scale may have significant bearing on both the northward shift of Egyptian maritime interests and the Mesopotamian reorientation to indirect links with the resource-bearing highlands. For if Syria now became the principal partner with the highlands as a result of political realignments, as the ceramic evidence suggests, it may also have become in part a channel for Egyptian gold and northern silver. In this position as the central hub between at least an eastern, western and northern spoke, the intensified cross-effects of such interactions may have been a significant factor for Syrian urban development and local production, even though the details of this process are not yet clear. With this shift in the balance of power, what may have been essentially a Mesopotamian thoroughfare for expeditions to the silver mountains and cedar forests now became major commercial brokers. While Palestine, like the

Spanish West Indies in the seventeenth century, became a 'ghost arena'.

In summary, the above sketch does suggest how the early urban polities in the Levant and Syro-Anatolia became a sustained success. The most important element seems to have been the formation of a strong elite core endowed with cultural values translated from foreign idioms. In this perspective, the maintenance of these roles may have depended on the acquisition of specific imported goods, in exchange for locally produced or transhipped products. It is perhaps in satisfying these demands that the spur for sustained investment and production might have occurred, oil in the case of Byblos and textiles in the case of Mardikh. By later times, such motives need not have been conscious ones, but an infrastructure of specific consumption and production patterns had been formed.

Conclusions

The system that emerged by the mid-third millennium was a wide but poorly articulated landscape of heterogeneous groups and political units interconnected by fluctuating linkages between mainly elite groups. Insofar as my examination has been largely descriptive and hardly rigorous, it should be evident that my data base is largely unsystematic. We are now aware of extensive exchange networks, intensive traffic and substantial volumes of goods traversing the Levant and Syro-Anatolia. However, we are largely ignorant of how this operated or emerged, apart from hints in the late fourth millennium. Here, then, I have suggested a hypothetical framework that would at least encompass the diverse and unsystematic information. This framework postulates that between the late fourth and third millennia, a faint, highly buffered 'market mechanism' may have operated for different periods of time and in different regions along these networks, with a number of systems. This mechanism may have emerged out of the needs of newly formed elite groups in Egypt and Mesopotamia, whose early attempts at the direct acquisition of 'luxury' goods were altered by changing foreign political circumstances, that were in part a product of these attempts. The assumption here is that the opportunities for gain in any partially 'embedded' society lie primarily outside the sectors defined by kinship ties or institutional relationships, and particularly in long-distance trade, where political relationships are more subject to renegotiation under changing circumstances.

It is this restructuring in the barely discerned early third millennium that may have given rise to 'firm-like' behavior by elite groups, who then probably dominated virtually all foreign trade. It is perhaps doubtful that there was much linkage between foreign exchange and domestic production for most of the third millennium. But my suggestion is that elite structured demands required the import of certain goods that could only be acquired through the production of certain other goods. These, in the main, may have consisted of a variety of finished and raw precious metals, textiles and processed agricultural products. In the context of new political relationships, the terms of exchange may have altered or extended to obtaining items on the best terms. Exchange rates may have become increasingly mediated by standardized values, which acted as one reassurance in changing face-to-face relationships, and in manipulating a series of conversions. In this respect, certain precious metals may have taken on a new role. It is a matter of conjecture, of course, as to whether an abstract concept of 'capital' then developed, but considering the large-scale production that emerged in a variety of 'industries', such a development is not inconceivable. In any case, the quantum leap in the production of certain goods is suggestive of 'firm-like' behavior and a substantial reorganization and mobilization of labor.

Where 'exchange rates' may have remained stable in certain linkages over a long period of time, increasing productive efficiency may have led to a form of 'economic rent', obviously in a number of factors, possibly resulting in structural differentiation and more atomistic action. At least among major states, such interstitial roles may have exploited a widening niche, providing a more direct linkage between the internal and external sectors of the economy. In any case, although structured around the wants and responses of a small core, such relationships were hardly static, and in the course of fluctuating interactions, resources may have been 'freed' to result in more potentially divergent, entrepreneurial activities. This, however, may have been more of a fluctuating rather than evolving situation, dependent on specific opportunities.

The above hypothetical framework was probably limited to only a small sector of the respective economies, and to highly varying degrees. Hence, its operation may be discernible only over the long term. But an interesting consequence of these arguments, then, is that the continuous changing balance of power in the 'world order' of the third and possibly second millennia meant that regions constantly sought to enlarge their apportionment at the expense of others. Because these relationships between regions were fluctuating, there were never 'cores' and 'peripheries' in the *strict* sense of dependency theory, but only more or less successful 'firms'. In Mesopotamia and Egypt, strong state systems with vigorous local economies may have taken on some of the character of 'cores', but periodic attempts at conquest are indications that advantageous relationships and terms of exchanges were ephemeral situations. Regionally defined 'peripheries' are also elusive, and the rise of Syrian economies of scale in the mid-third millennium is an illustration of the shifts in the balance of power that could re-alter relationships. Relationships may have been systematic in that certain nodal areas were always the channel for specific goods, but the political arrangements of these relationships were highly variable.

Acknowledgements

Earlier versions of this paper were read by participants at the Aarhus conference, as well as R. Adams, M. Gibson, L. Stager and H. Wright. I wish to thank these readers and the editors for most helpful comments, and absolve them of any responsibility for the contents of the paper.

Notes
1 For a summary of such views, see Redman 1978.
2 Derived in part from Frank (1969) and Braudel (1972), these views are best seen in Wallerstein (1974) and Hechter (1975).
3 The main lines of recent work are seen in Amiran 1973, 1974, 1980; Gophna 1976; Oren 1973; Rothenberg 1972a; Yeivin 1960.
4 Silver was valued at 1:2–3.5 to gold in Pharaonic times (Černy 1954), but at 10:1 in Ur III Mesopotamia (Limet 1960), where gold appears as early as the Ubaid period. Intermediate between these two ratios is the 5:1 rate at Mardikh (Pettinato 1979).
5 A rough indication of this contrast can be obtained in comparing the EB settlements in Whallon (1979) and Adams (1981). In general, the Early Dynastic centers vary between 40–100 ha., with Kish at 80 ha. among the largest. It would be fairly safe to say the EB centers in the Levant, the Syrian littoral and the Taurus piedmont seldom exceeded 20 ha.
6 The arguments expressed here are similar to Ekholm and Friedman (1979) and Larsen (1979). However, I stress the oscillatory rather than evolutionary aspects of this process.

Chapter 4

**On tracking cultural transfers in prehistory:
the case of Egypt and lower Mesopotamia[1] in
the fourth millennium BC**

P. R. S. Moorey

But most cultural transfers were the work of anonymous carriers.
So many were they, some moving quickly, others so slowly, that it
is almost impossible to find one's way through this immense
baggage hall in perpetual confusion. For every piece of cultural
baggage recognized, a thousand are untraceable: identification
labels are missing and sometimes the contents or their wrappings
have vanished too.

F. Braudel, *The Mediterranean and the Mediterranean
World in the Age of Philip II* (London, 1973), p. 761.

It is now thirty years since the late Henri Frankfort published his
Patten Foundation Lectures on *The Birth of Civilization in the
Near East* in which he sought to demonstrate that during the
fourth millennium BC, as complex societies emerged in Egypt and
Mesopotamia, a highly individual pattern of culture was already
apparent in each region, containing the essential features which
were to distinguish them throughout their subsequent development. In doing so he returned to a topic to which he had made
distinguished contributions over the previous twenty-five years
and which had preoccupied students of the region in one form or
another since the pioneering days of Egyptology and Assyriology
in the middle of the nineteenth century. At the heart of it lay a
complex question of cultural interaction, for by the end of the
nineteenth century it was already clear to scholars that Egypt and
Lower Mesopotamia had been in contact with one another at the
most formative stage of their development.

The direction of this contact, and its impact on the recipient, was hotly contested from the outset. For the early champions
of each civilization the idea that it might have been stimulated,
or might even have borrowed, from the other, was derogatory.
Before 1914 it was customary to explain changes in Egypt and
Mesopotamia in terms of migration or conquest by peoples from
some hypothetical, then unidentified, region peripheral to both.
Fieldwork between 1918 and 1939 revealed the fallacy of this
model. As knowledge of prehistoric Mesopotamia in particular
increased spectacularly in those years, the individuality of the
early societies in both areas became apparent, whilst the case for
some kind of initial contact became steadily stronger. It polarized
interpretations even more markedly, as some now argued force-
fully for the autonomy and self-contained character of these two
'pristine states', whilst others appealed to an invasion or migration from Lower Mesopotamia, round Arabia, up the Red Sea
and along Wadi Hammamat, to explain the emergence of the
Dynastic state in Egypt. In 1951 Frankfort assumed a central
position, arguing that though the time of this contact might be
established, how, and where, it was made were questions without
answers. His magisterial summing up forms an admirable departure point for this paper. 'We observe', he wrote, 'that Egypt, in
a period of intensified creativity, became acquainted with the
achievements in Mesopotamia; that it was stimulated; and that
it adapted to its own development such elements as seemed compatible with its efforts. It mostly transformed what it borrowed
and after a time rejected even these modifications' (Frankfort
1951: 110).

In this chapter I have taken the fact of interaction for granted, as, to a greater or lesser extent, it is now generaly accepted. My purpose here is threefold: to describe the present pattern of archaeological evidence for this contact; to establish as far as possible its character; and to attempt an explanation of its social and political impact, if any, both on the primary participants and on the peripheral areas through which it passed. Before doing so I should perhaps say that this paper was written at the invitation of the Editors after the Aarhus Conference, which I did not attend. I did not therefore benefit from critical discussions on that occasion, nor was I in a position to assimilate the main conclusions then reached in debate.

The pattern of the archaeological evidence in 1980
(see Fig. 4.1)

The earliest objects of distinctively Mesopotamian type to appear in predynastic Egypt are small stone cylinder seals. They had begun to arrive there by the middle of the Gerzean period (Naqada IIb–c; Sequence Dates 46–50). (See the chronological note on p. 46). Only six are so far known from controlled excavations in Egypt (Boehmer 1974, nos 1–6). These early cylinder seals are simply engraved with combinations of 'eyes', fishes and linear patterns. When Frankfort published his lectures in 1951 they were believed to date from the later Protoliterate period (Uruk III: Jamdat Nasr) in Mesopotamia. Excavations since then at Susa and Choga Mish in ancient Elam (modern Khuzistan in Iran), and at Habuba Kabira on the Euphrates in northern Syria, have shown them to be contemporary in origin with the more finely worked and elaborately decorated seals long taken to be the oldest cylinder seals at Uruk and Susa, dated to the earlier Protoliterate period (Uruk IV/Susa 18–17) (Amiet 1971:221, Fig. 43:10; 1972:110–11; Kantor 1972; Topperwein 1973; Le Brun 1978). Previous to this only stamp seals were used in the Near East, though no native examples are yet known from Egypt. These new chronological synchronisms have indicated that the earlier Gerzean period in Egypt was approximately contemporary with Uruk IV in Mesopotamia and that the first contact between the two regions was somewhat earlier than Frankfort had supposed. This is endorsed by the only distinctively south Mesopotamian stamp seal yet to have been found in an archaeological context in Egypt, where it appears in grave 7501 at Naga ed-Deir, dated to the earliest phase of the Gerzean period (Nagada IIa). A parallel may be cited from level 17 at Susa, contemporary there with fish designs on cylinders (Amiet 1971: Fig. 44:7; for Naga ed-Deir, Lythoe and Dunham 1965:318ff). A stamp seal in a middle to late Gerzean (Naqada IId) grave at Harageh appears by contrast to be of North Syrian origin or inspiration (Engelbach 1923:14, pl.LV – grave 470; Buchanan's identification).

These scattered indicators tentatively mark out the primary frame for a network of contact extending from Khuzistan, up the line of the river valley into Syria and thence to Egypt, excluding Palestine and Sinai. No object of Egyptian manufacture, it should immediately be noted, has yet been found in Protoliterate Mesopotamia or Elam. An even more elusive, if complementary, distribution pattern is provided by ceramics of Mesopotamian type.

Distinctive jars, for liquids not solids, with broad shoulders and three or four triangular shoulder handles, joined by a band of incised decoration (Kantor 1965:10, Fig. 4), are very occasionally found in Egypt. They are alien to the local ceramic tradition, but have an ancestry which may now be traced back through pottery found at Habuba Kabira in Syria to southern Mesopotamia (including Elam) (Sürenhagen 1974–5; Delougaz 1952: pl. 164). But here again isolated vessels from Egypt are much closer in form, fabric and decoration to these prototypes than to anything yet recognized in southern Syria, Lebanon, Palestine or Sinai. In Egypt only one such vessel, and it is already departing from the canonical 'Uruk IV' Mesopotamian type, has a closed archaeological context in a grave at Matmar, dated SD 58 (Brunton 1948: pl. 12:G5112). In view of its increasing importance in defining the primary peripheral zone of 'Uruk IV' penetration, it needs to be said categorically that the bevelled rim bowl is not yet known in Egypt, nor in Palestine or Sinai (Kantor 1965:35); comparisons to the contrary are inexact (Baumgartel 1947/60 I, 93). Jars with drooping spouts, another 'Uruk' type, are common both in Gerzean Egypt and in Palestine during the same period; but erect spouts, common in Palestine, are relatively rare in Egypt (Hennessy 1967:30–1). As body forms and fabrics vary markedly, the relationship here lies in a common ancestry usually sought in the Mesopotamian 'Uruk IV' repertory as represented at Habuba Kabira (Surenhagen 1974–5: pls 4–5, etc.). There is at least one such vessel from Egypt, in tomb 1759 at Naqada, dated SD 41, that in form and fabric falls into the 'Uruk IV' category and might be a direct import (Petrie and Quibell 1896:pl. XXXVI D92).

Mesopotamian finished goods were then reaching Egypt, albeit only in a trickle trade, by the earliest phase of the Gerzean period. Although the pots are small liquid containers and dispensers, nothing is known of what was traded in them, if anything, and no chemical or geological analyses have yet been done of the relevant fabrics for comparative purposes; all judgements are still those of the eye. Lapis lazuli is the only commodity found in Gerzean Egypt that may confidently be recognized as an import ultimately coming from a source east of the Tigris. Until conclusive geological evidence is forthcoming for a natural source of this mineral closer to Egypt than the mines at Badakhshan in modern Afghanistan, about 5,000 kilometres away, they are accepted as the source of all lapis lazuli in Gerzean Egypt (contra Nibbi 1981; cf. Herrmann 1968; Payne 1968). Lapis is not known there before the Gerzean period. The earliest dated grave group in which it has so far been found is Matmar 3005, SD 40–3. Thereafter it is recorded in almost every excavated cemetery from Gerzeh south to the First Cataract, though it is by no means common. Only eleven of the recorded 2000 graves at Naqada, for instance, contained it. It is used either for beads or pendants, very rarely for lapis and gold tubes; in every known case the manufactured lapis lazuli objects are of local type and normally appear in the more richly equipped graves (Payne 1968). Lapis lazuli has been found at Djebel Aruda in Syria at this time, but not yet in sound archaeological contexts in Anatolia, southern Syria, Lebanon (not even apparently at Byblos), Palestine or Sinai. Lapis beads reported from the Nahal

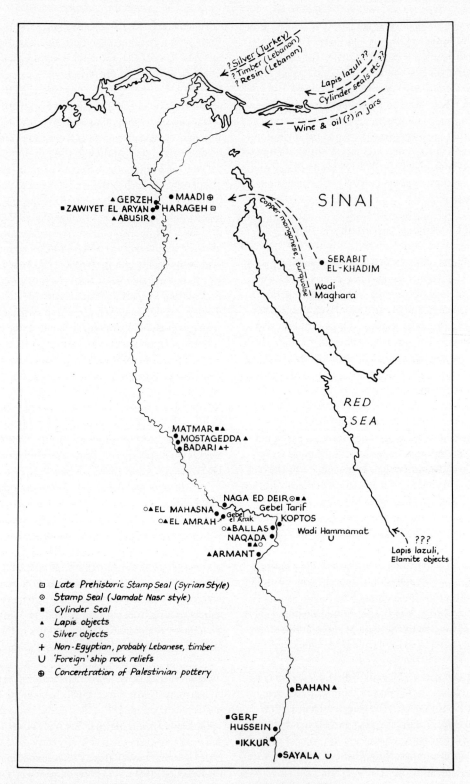

Fig. 4.1. Map of Egypt to illustrate the main imports from the Near East in Predynastic Times.

Mishmar cave are of uncertain date (Bar-Adon 1980:150). Small objects of lapis lazuli first appear in Northern Mesopotamia by the end of the Ubaid period there, but are not regularly found in the south until the later Protoliterate period, by which time the occurrence of lapis in the north may have been more restricted.

This has been taken to indicate a change in trading mechanisms within Iran, where Elamite expansion onto the plateau took control of trade along the 'Great Khorasan Route' from north-east Iran into Mesopotamia (Herrmann 1968:52; Weiss and Cuyler Young, Jnr. 1975). On the chronological synchronisms used here, it would have been during this 'Northern control' that lapis lazuli first reached Egypt, correlating well with the seal and ceramic traces of cultural contact already discussed. There was to be a break in the arrival of lapis in Egypt, from after the reign of Djer in Dynasty I through dynasties II and III, that matches a similar disruption in Mesopotamia according to present interpretations of the data there (Herrmann 1968; Payne 1968).

Before passing from imported finished objects and raw materials of eastern origin in predynastic Egypt to a consideration of 'Mesopotamian' motifs and traits in Gerzean art, some attention may usefully be given to a potential vehicle for transmission which, though still absent in the Egyptian archaeological record, is now evident elsewhere along the exchange routes of the period and may be postulated as one of Braudel's missing 'baggages'. The earliest written documents from the Near East, both in the 'Uruk IVa' horizon of Mesopotamia and Syria, and the slightly later 'Proto-Elamite' phase in Iran, are of two broad categories: hollow clay balls, some bearing numerical signs, that contain tiny clay spheres, cones, etc. ('calculi'), (Lieberman 1980; Schmandt-Besserat 1980) and small clay tablets, the earliest impressed only with marks denoting numerals (Susa 18–17), then with linear signs of recognisably pictographic character. Both often bear impressions made with elaborately carved cylinder seals of a type not yet reported from Egypt. These archaic accounting and record devices are now known at Uruk, and up the line of the Euphrates and its tributaries to Habuba Kabira and Brak, and also right across Iran to the frontiers with Central Asia (Schmandt-Besserat 1980: Fig. 3). There is every indication that they were a necessary part of the development of long-distance trade in the middle of the fourth millennium BC. The Mesopotamian and Elamite motifs recognized in Gerzean art are commonly found elsewhere on broken sealings from bales and jars and on such tablets and bullae. None of these has yet been found in Egypt. Whether tablets and bullae travelled is an open question. If they were primarily legal documents to provide the possibility of verifying the accuracy of a transaction, they would presumably have been stored at the place of transaction for reference back (Lieberman 1980:325). For the moment seals, and sealings on commodity packages, seem to be the most likely travelling vehicles of transmission in this case.

It has long been acknowledged that certain motifs in the art of later Gerzean Egypt are of Western Asiatic origin. Five have been particularly studied in this respect: the winged griffin; the serpent-necked feline; entwined snakes framing rosettes; a human hero flanked by lions; and animals in human attitudes. They appear on luxury objects, some certainly of ceremonial use. With a growing body of evidence from Iranian sources, particularly, in recent years it has become clear that many of these motifs were probably of Elamite rather than of Sumerian origin, though this distinction has to be drawn with caution for this early date (Amiet 1957, 1980:202; Boehmer 1974b). In Egypt they have survived most conspicuously on the carved ivory and embossed sheet-gold handles of a restricted number of serially flanked flint knives, whose chronology, in the absence of good evidence from controlled excavations, is still insecure. As the handles were made for

a very distinctive type of flint blade, for which there is still no compelling evidence of manufacture after the Gerzean period, they all predate the First Dynasty, and may extend well back into the Gerzean period (Kantor 1944:119ff; Baumgartel 1947/60, II, 79ff; Needler 1980). Oriental motifs and stylistic traits are much less evident on the better known series of large carved slate palettes, which are again without controlled archaeological contexts. They are generally agreed to concentrate towards the end of the predynastic period, culminating in the greater Hierakonpolis palette bearing the name of Narmer (Kantor 1944:134; Baumgartel 1947/60, II, 89ff). Frankfort argued that a transfer of foreign Mesopotamian information was indicated as much by stylistic traits as by motifs, singling out for particular emphasis two examples (1951: 102ff). In Dynastic Egypt, he pointed out, animals and human figures are never used to produce purely decorative designs as they are in Mesopotamia and, significantly, in predynastic Egyptian art. Then again he saw it as the 'Egyptian manner' to represent the hunter's prey in flight, whereas it was the Mesopotamian practice to render his prey as unaffected by attack, as also in some archaic Egyptian representations.

No single 'foreign' element in predynastic Egyptian art has played so prominent a role in explanations of local cultural change and eastern contact as a type of boat, long identified as 'Mesopotamian', found in Gerzean paintings and in rock carvings. In his study of the rock art of the Armant region, where he located numerous representations of boats from the Nile deep into the Red Sea Hills towards the Sea itself, Winkler used comparisons with boat paintings on Gerzean pottery for dating purposes and with them adopted the older view that the 'type of boat with tall vertical prow and stern is, among other evidence, proof of a Mesopotamian influence in Egypt' (Winkler 1938:26). Even on his own terms Winkler's hypothesis is weak. the distinctions within his classification of rock drawn boats are not as clearcut as he argued, nor is their distribution as restricted as his proposition would require. He himself later located his 'Mesopotamian' type of boat on the west bank of the Nile and it is now known 130 kilometers south of the First Cataract (Engelmayer 1965), significantly modifying the pre-eminence of the Wadi Hammamat in the distribution of this motif. Nor yet have such representations been found anywhere near to the Red Sea itself. In view of the fact that the contestants with the high-hulled boats on the Gebel el-Arak knife handle (for so long the key artefact in the eastern invasion hypothesis) all wear Egyptian costume, it must be seriously doubted whether the ships with rising prows and sterns have anything to do with Mesopotamia, where there is no evidence of the character of sea-going craft in the fourth millennium BC. It looks as if the apparent similarity of boats in the arts of Egypt and Mesopotamia at this time is no more than a similarity between simple river and lake boats made independently from comparable materials (Landström 1970). Direct sea contact between lower Mesopotamia, be it from Sumer or Elam, and Egypt at this time round Arabia and up the Red Sea may not be categorically ruled out (Johnstone 1980:171ff; van Loon 1977:3); but in the absence of any positive archaeological evidence in its favour, and no analogy in Dynastic times, its probability must be rated so low as to

rule it out of consideration here in favour of other routes for
which the positive evidence is at present so much stronger even if
not, in the nature of such things, conclusive.

Any attempt to sketch the pattern of evidence for cultural
transfers from Mesopotamia to Egypt in the second half of the
fourth millennium BC cannot be considered complete without
some attempt to come to grips with two of the most elusive elements. They have both long held a place in studies of this phenomenon, not least in Frankfort's. The least contentious, and most
tractable, in archaeological terms, is the question of the origin of
monumental mudbrick architecture in Egypt. In a special paper
devoted to this topic in 1941 Frankfort attributed it to Mesopotamia, arguing that there was no evidence for extensive use of mudbrick in Egypt before the Dynastic period; that there is nothing in
predynastic architecture which would lead into the mudbrick
architecture of the First Dynasty; and that mudbrick building in
Mesopotamia had gradually evolved to the point of complexity
first found in Egypt before they are known to have been in contact. There has been little fresh archaeological evidence from
Egypt to challenge the first two points, despite revived fieldwork
and a growing attention to settlements archaeology in predynastic
studies (Hoffman 1980:155ff). But new interpretations of old data
indicate that some kind of case might be made out for local development. In his excavations at Naqada, Petrie cleared a predynastic mudbrick complex of rectangular buildings within a perimeter
wall, though details were never published (Baumgartel 1947/60,
II, 133–4; Kemp 1977:197–8). In the revived excavations at
Hierakonpolis in 1969 it was made clear that the use of niched
mudbrick façades had not been confined to funerary structures
in early dynastic Egypt, for part of a large non-funerary building
so decorated was then uncovered (Weeks 1971–2:29ff). This supports the view that the *serekh* (the stylized niched façade in royal
names) was copied from the walls of the royal residence. In cemetery T at Naqada were grouped some brick-lined predynastic
tombs that may be the burial places of predynastic rulers, ancestral to the large brick tombs of Dynasty I at Abydos (Kemp
1973). It is, of course, possible that these predynastic examples all
post-date the earliest contact between Egypt and Mesopotamia
and would therefore not challenge Frankfort's basic case. If
so, the argument for foreign transfer in this instance has been
strengthened by the discovery of the town of Habuba Kabira in
Syria, considerably nearer to Egypt than anything like it known
before, with mudbrick architecture identical to that known at sites
like Uruk in south Mesopotamia.

Frankfort was prepared in 1951 to discount the enduring
impact of every known aspect of Mesopotamian cultural stimulus
in predynastic Egypt save one, the invention of writing: a problem
which has long divided the experts (contrast Wilson 1951:38, and
Helck 1971). Unequipped as I am to discuss the matter myself, I
will merely set out what appears to be the present consensus.
Writing is not archaeologically attested in Egypt until the outset
of the First Dynasty, when inscriptions, generally short, appear in
a wide variety of contexts: on grave stelae, on sealings, on plaques
of wood and ivory, on vessels of baked clay and stone. Carved
slate palettes and ceremonial stone maceheads of some size show
scenes in which the ruler is represented by a falcon, or other royal
beast, and the provinces (*nomes*) by their emblems. If a local prehistory is sought for these devices it has to be traced through pot-
marks and ships' standards on Gerzean pottery (Hoffman 1980:
290ff). It is only at the outset of the First Dynasty that major political figures are certainly identified by their names, written on the
rebus principle: cat-fish + chisel = *Narmer*. The apparent sud-
denness of the appearance of a writing system at this time, rather
than the isolated symbols or emblems previously documented, has
been the main argument for a foreign catalyst. Only Sumer is
known to have had a certainly older system; the 'Proto-Elamite
system' of southwest Iran (Khuzistan) seems at present to be
slightly younger than that of Sumer (Le Brun and Vallat 1978)
and 'with the exception of numerals, proto-Elamite signs were not
genetically connected with proto-Sumerian signs' (Vaiman 1972:
133). What similarities there are between the writing systems of
Sumer and Egypt are matters of internal characteristics not of
appearance. As Hawkins has defined them recently, they are both
'mixed logographic-syllabographic scripts, both using class
determinatives formed from common logograms as aids to reading' (1979:146). The form of the scripts and their syllabaries,
which ultimately reflect the structures of the two different primary
languages involved, Sumerian and Egyptian, diverge markedly.
Both the Egyptian sign-list and its syllabary are of native origin.
Whatever the nature of the foreign stimulus, it was so radically
transmuted into the local idiom as to leave no categorical indication of its presence.

The character of the contact

Any explanation of the impact of the cultural transfers indicated by this data will be affected by conclusions about the direction of the contact, or more precisely by the identification of the
intermediaries through whose hands it passed. I have already indicated why any direct contact, which would have to have been by
sea round Arabia, is now considered unlikely. It is most economi-
cal to argue at present that in prehistoric, as in historic, times
Sumer and Elam were in contact with Egypt, if at all, through
Syrian intermediaries. There is no force in traditional arguments
for substantial military incursions or migrations into the Nile Valley from the east, nor yet any convincing indication either of
Mesopotamian or Elamite craftsmen or emissaries active in Gerzean Egypt. Two lines of communication are then possible, either
by land down the coast and then across northern Sinai, or by sea
from a port on the Lebanese or Syrian coast, to the Egyptian
Delta; trade which, again on historical analogy, would have been
in the hands of Levantine not Mesopotamian sailors and carriers.
A land route direct across northern Arabia, before domestication
of the camel, would seem not to have been possible, though more
widespread use of the domesticated ass as a beast of burden
played a vital part in the expansion of long-distance trade in the
Near East in the fourth millennium BC wherever water was
readily available. The absence of lapis lazuli, and of Mesopotamian type seals and pottery, between Syria and Egypt at this time
might be seen either as evidence for a sea-route or, on Beale's
'bypass phenomenon' (1973:144), as indicative of direct contact

between one or more Egyptian controllers and Mesopotamian traders or their representatives at settlements like Habuba Kabira in Syria.

Whatever the line of contact, and both might have been used, it is clear that Egypt's links with Mesopotamia may only be explained as one aspect of an exchange network already well established when, early in the Gerzean period, distinctive Mesopotamian artefacts and lapis lazuli first reached the Nile Valley. As Marfoe (p. 26) has taken the pattern of Egyptian interaction with the Levant as the subject of his contribution to this volume, I will confine myself to certain specific points relevant to the fourth millennium BC, which is not his main concern, and to Egypt. Marfoe defines two phases in prehistoric trade between the two regions, only the first of which really concerns us here, for by the later Gerzean periods, when there are marked changes in the scale and intensity of contact between Egypt and Palestine, fresh cultural transfers from Elam or Mesopotamia are no longer evident, though lapis lazuli continued to arrive until the break after the reign of Djer already mentioned (p. 39). Although we have no way at present of gauging, even crudely, the level of exchange activity in the first phase, Marfoe is probably right to regard it as low. But there is still much uncertainty over the source of the primary materials evidenced in the archaeological record. It has been widely assumed that the presence of such woods as Cedar, Cypress (or Juniper) and Pine, as well as resins, in early predynastic contexts indicate contact by land or sea with the Lebanon or Syria (Brunton and Caton-Thompson 1928:62–3; 'foreign timbers' in Lucas 1962:429ff). Yet it is quite possible that they reached Egypt from North African or more local sources (Nibbi 1981:1ff; especially the paper by Quézel quoted there). Then again silver, first evident in the Amratian period (SD 30–8), has been attributed both to Anatolian and to local sources (Prag 1978). Recent analyses have indicated that Lucas may well have been right years ago when he argued that the earliest Egyptian silver was a locally occurring natural alloy of silver and gold containing enough silver to be white in colour (Stos-Gale and Gale, 1981a, 1981b). The possibility of some early contacts with Anatolia, however, remain; a fresh analysis of the lead model hawk from grave 721 at Naqada (SD 44–64) revealed that: 'the high silver content. . . and its lead isotope composition prove that the lead did not originate within Egypt' (Stos-Gale and Gale 1981b:115).

From sources in Sinai much closer to Egypt, as early as the Badarian period, came copper and turquoise, moved overland in pack-ass caravans by the tribesmen of the source region, who penetrated deep into Lower Egypt up the Wadi el-Tih. At the western end lies the archaeological site of Maadi, positioned at the apex of the Delta, like some of Egypt's later capitals. Here Palestinian pottery is much commoner than on any other predynastic site in Egypt and here are true underground houses, as in Chalcolithic Palestine, which are otherwise unknown at this time in Egypt. Ample provision for storage and traces of a metal industry emphasized the role of this site as a nodal point on which external supply and local redistribution networks focussed (Hoffman 1980:200ff). Whether by land or sea, all this long-distance contact with Western Asia would have passed through Lower

Egypt, which recent research has shown was settled roughly as early as the Nile Valley and does not deserve the neglect it has received until recently in studies of predynastic Egypt. Research there is hampered by natural conditions and the area has suffered by comparison with the better known parts of the Valley in Upper Egypt, as it also has from speculative historical reconstructions which may misleadingly project backwards the pervasive dualism of Dynastic Egyptian ideology. The earliest representation of what was later to be known as the Red Crown of Lower Egypt is on a sherd from an Amratian grave at Naqada in Upper Egypt (Petrie and Quibell 1896:44, pl.III.75) and on the Palermo Stone the earliest line of rulers, before the First Dynasty, contains seven surviving names and figures wearing this Crown (Edwards 1971:1; Jenkins 1980; pl. 22).

Before exploring the social and political importance of the Mesopotamian contact within Egyptian predynastic communities, some attempts must be made to put a balance into this commercial exchange network. In terms of archaeological visibility the commercial intercourse between the two areas seems only to have run in one direction, from east to west. Here, our only guide at present is historical analogy. In the fourteenth century BC, when there is the first clear documentary evidence of direct diplomatic contact and gift exchanges between Babylonian kings and Egyptian pharaohs, Babylonia generally sent horses and chariots, silver and lapis lazuli, bronze (tin) and oil; Egypt most often gold, but occasionally fine furniture and textiles (Brinkman 1972). If such a pattern were to be postulated earlier, the horses, chariots and the bronze would be ruled out as later innovations; but the basic pattern of lapis lazuli, silver and oil in exchange for gold might very well have applied before 3000 BC. Naqada, which was in all probability the centre of a Gerzean state in Upper Egypt, bore the ancient name *Nubt*, probably deriving from the ancient Egyptian for 'gold' on the account of the proximity of gold mines in the eastern desert accessible from the Wadi Hammamat. It might be 'that the town obtained its name because possession of gold, working it and trading in it, were its outstanding characteristics, just as in historic times Egypt was the land of gold' (Baumgartel 1970: 480). Scientific attempts to 'fingerprint' Sumerian gold are being undertaken, but have not so far identified significant trace elements (Meeks and Tite 1980).

The pattern of Egypto-Mesopotamian contact in the second half of the fourth millennium BC is then characterized by a traffic of low intensity in luxury items probably passing through Syria. It embraced small-scale acquisition of lapis lazuli from a very distant source imported for local manufacture; small objects like seals, which mark property (but whether at this stage for individuals, corporations or kin-groups is debatable), and denote authority; and a flow of foreign information that may have stimulated the local development of monumental mudbrick architecture and a writing system over a period of one or two centuries. All three were taken up by an elite in Gerzean communities either for personal ornaments/currency, or for restricted classes of ceremonial and votive objects. There is virtually no indication – so long as the significance of the isolated 'Mesopotamian' pots remains obscure – for the mixture of subsistence and luxury goods involved in Egyptian exchange with the adjacent parts of the Levant.

Explaining the interaction

(a) In Egyptian society

The fundamental question to which this argument leads has been stated over the years in a variety of ways, each closely reflecting the explanatory models for cultural change current at the time of writing, but each seeking to define the extent of alien influence in the emergence of the Pharaonic state in Egypt towards the end of the fourth millennium BC. Today it might perhaps be phrased in the following terms: did the establishment of a long-distance exchange with Mesopotamia alter significantly the productive activities of local Gerzean communities in Egypt and, consequently, help transform them, in a manner Kohl, for instance (1975, 1978), has recently seen as crucial in the evolution of complex ranked societies in the ancient Near East, or did it merely offer information from a more developed society to be copied or emulated by an elite in communities already partly stratified from other causes at the time of initial contact?

With archaeological data that allows no precision in establishing the relevant order of the major critical factors invoked in current explanatory models of early state formation (Webb 1975, for a good summary) – population pressures, warfare and long-distance trade – a definition of the extent of development towards a complex society within Egypt at any particular time before the First Dynasty is extremely hazardous. Nor is the problem simplified by a sharp difference between some of the leading scholars in this debate as to what signifies most in describing the evolution of the state at this time, whether it be increased social ranking and centralization of authority, to be traced in archaeologically recognizable wealth differentials (Adams 1966) or an increased number of tiers in the hierarchy through which information was channelled (Johnson 1975; Wright and Johnson 1975; cf. Weiss 1977), archaeologically pursued through survey and location analysis. As Butzer has pointed out application of central place theory to the Nile Valley is inappropriate: 'In the Egyptian case it is probable that terrain-related site location, access to riverine transport and irrigation basins, and the role or status of prominent cult centres played a primary role in settlement patterning' (1976:72). His research has thrown into prominence the local units into which Egypt was divided from earliest recorded history, and almost certainly much earlier: the *nomes* or provinces, whose 'standards', as shown in historic times from the earliest monuments of Dynasty I onwards, may already be represented by the 'ship standards' painted on Gerzean pottery (Newberry 1913). As Butzer points out, in challenging Wittfogel's (1957) despotism hypothesis for Egypt, any political ramifications of irrigation there were localized and restricted to the small geographical areas represented by the *nomes*: 'One might argue that hydraulic agriculture provided the indispensable economic resource base for the complex, state-centred society that had emerged in the form of the Old Kingdom, yet high economic productivity is essential to any complex society. More distinctive may be the socio-economic anchoring of the Egyptian *nomes* into the explicit ecological framework of the riverine oasis. These primeval *nomes* appear to have provided the necessary political infrastructure for the military ventures that over several generations of strife led to the unification of Egypt' (Butzer, 1976:110–11).

As has often been indicated the crucial point in respect of the Nile Valley's relationship to external trade-networks is the absence of a number of points of access. Two areas only are vital to control of the main external systems of trade: the delta in the north, which is relevant here, and Nubia in the south, which is of great importance, but not for the question under consideration here. Because the Valley is only open at a very restricted number of points to supply lines, once political control has been established over them, it is relatively easy to maintain a monopoly over external trade contact. It is currently assumed that the driving force in this process came from Upper Egypt, where two exceptional concentrations of population, at Naqada and at Hierakonpolis, in turn assumed control of a nascent state, during Gerzean times, which then pushed into Lower Egypt (Kaiser 1964; Kemp 1977). Certainly it is this southern region, with its monopoly of the crucial archaeological information, that appears to have ultimately controlled the systems both for internal and external exchange in the Valley, for onto it focussed communications north and south by river, east and west by ass caravan, at the critical time.

Even before the Gerzean period external trade was bringing to Egypt exotic, prestigious materials which would have conferred power and status on those controlling their distribution within the local exchange networks. They were significantly older. By the Badarian period, at least, metals and pigments, shells and stones, were widely traded between the Valley and the peripheral regions, both as raw materials and as finished goods, whilst marked differences in wealth are indicated by the quality and quantity of exotic or prestige goods buried with some of the dead and the precocious appearance of tomb robbers (Brunton and Caton-Thompson 1928:38ff). If the process is to be taken back a stage further, to the source of the wealth that allowed for the growth of internal exchange systems in the Badarian period, Carneiro's (1970) 'circumscription hypothesis' of state-formation may be appropriate. Competition for the more agriculturally productive areas, between and within *nomes*, postulated by this model, or more specifically for the stored surpluses from the best farming land (for it was they which gave their controllers the economic muscle to manipulate exchanges) would have generated more and more complex tribal organization in which the power of individual chiefs was steadily increased. In a word, it was the initial struggle for the means to exchange as much as the power it then gave to control internal distribution systems, independent of tribal restraints, that served to rank early societies in the Nile Valley. Any substantial foreign, long-distance trade would have been keyed into this existing network in which, in the absence of a market economy, certain dominant rulers (or chiefs) may have been controllers by the end of the Amratian period (Naqada I) (Hoffman 1980:343ff).

Their acquisition of luxury items in Naqada II, which is what the Mesopotamian connection brought them, would have had little or no economic significance, but it would have been of great value to them in maintaining and extending the existing socio-political hierarchy within their own communities, whilst increasing the chances of extending their clientage to groups whose rulers had no such access to desirable goods. As from the outset of the Pharaonic period in Egypt, in marked contrast to the city-state pattern of Sumer, economic administration was controlled by the Pharaoh through the state bureaucracy, it was clearly an ancient indigenous pattern of authority. Formerly independent local rulers had finally become the dependants of a single dynasty (Dynasty O), so dominant that its members probably already controlled expeditions to exploit the mineral wealth of the peripheral deserts and trading contacts into Syro-Palestine, by the century or so before the formally listed Dynasty I inaugurated by (Narmer.)

It is only in mortuary archaeology that this trend may be erratically detected in Gerzean times. In at least two cemeteries, at Naqada (T) and at Hierakonpolis (Case and Payne 1962:15) there are groups of tombs of unusual size and wealth, physically separated from the main cemetery, that many scholars now believe to be ancestral to those of the First Dynasty at Abydos. 'Tombs not only played a critical role in the political transition from Predynastic chiefdoms to a centralized state ruled by a divine king, but they also constitute our principal information for the nature of this change in Egypt' (Hoffmann 1980:267–8). These early 'royal' tombs are dated Naqada IIc–III. If I am correct in dating the first impact of a Mesopotamian connection to the early Gerzean period (Naqada IIa–b), then it does appear to have preceded the most obvious archaeological evidence yet available in Egypt for marked social ranking and the artistic representation, on the walls of the 'Painted Tomb' at Hierakonpolis, of what has been described as 'a commentary indicating how in rapid stages the chieftainship of tribal savagery grew into the kingship of a civilized state' (Case and Payne 1962:15–16). But, at this point, we must turn back to Frankfort (1951:49ff), who so clearly distinguished the differences in these pristine states, graphically showing that there may be no simplistic conclusion that the emergent Pharaonic state emulated a Mesopotamian or Elamite state-system, since they are radically different. Even with the scattered archaeological evidence to hand it is apparent that a broad spectrum of stimuli from Western Asia, including the more developed region of southern Mesopotamia, were available, reaching Egypt with varied impact, and that some elements in this spectrum were selected for emulation within certain sections of Gerzean society in response to factors, not all conscious, operating within their own culture.

It is hard for us to reconstruct the Egyptian milieu which selected certain motifs and rejected others, for even in Mesopotamia we have no real idea what they signified. To Egyptians they were presumably regarded, at the simplest level, as symbols of the power and authority of the distant peoples who controlled access to such desirable minerals as lapis lazuli, perhaps also, for a brief period in the 'Uruk IVa' horizon, to all goods of Syro-Anatolian origin reaching Egypt. It might then be a case of actively selective emulation, as defined by Irene Winter in her recent study of the better documented relationship of Assyria and northwest Iran in

the ninth century BC, based on earlier studies of comparable phenomena by such scholars as Caldwell, Flannery and Renfrew (Winter 1977:377ff). But, this concept implies, indeed requires, that the cultural transfers were sufficiently formidable in the minds of the aspiring local Gerzean rulers for them to regard such foreign symbols as potent enough to merit adoption. It is here that the selection of motifs has a particular importance, for it was not icons of triumph in war or in the hunt that were adopted, for Amratian and Gerzean imagery had its own formulation of these power exercises over man and nature. Remarkably, even the most famous, the Mesopotamian master-of-animals on the Gebel el-Arak knife-handle, that might seem an exception to this generalization, shows the hero dominated by, not dominating, the flanking lions in a manner peculiarly Elamite (or Iranian). If it represented power or authority, it was very equivocal in its significance. No Egyptian Pharaoh was ever to be seen so dominated by man or beast. No such ambiguity (at least to the modern eye) surrounds the supernatural monsters and other animal motifs chosen. They indicate a selection inspired not by military dominance, which on my general interpretation would have been beyond the Egyptian experience of Mesopotamia and Elam, but by a much more elusive impulse, motivated by religious scruple rather than military competition or emulation.

It is hardly possible to extend the analysis, for only one of the knife-handles on which these motifs are particularly concentrated has been found in an archaeological context. This late grave (Naqada III) at Abu Zaidan (no. 32) was not exceptionally rich in conventional terms (Kantor 1944, Fig. 12, with important revisions in Needler 1980). Metal was absent from the grave as excavated and apart from simple pottery it held three fine flint knives, a single carved ivory handle (reconstructed, after seiving, from fragments), a serpentine cosmetic jar, a schist cosmetic palette and a stone bracelet. The sex of the occupant is not recorded. Miss Needler (1980) has argued that the carved ivory knifes, of which only six are yet recorded (Asselberghs 1961: pls. 31–41), are 'iconographically and stylistically... more closely related to the commemorative palettes and other monuments of the Unification Period (Naqada III) than to the Hierakonpolis Painted Tomb of the Middle Gerzean period'. They are a distinctively local Egyptian type of artefact; but whether they denote status, say a princely ranking, or special social function, perhaps in cult rituals, may not yet be assessed. But, whatever the conclusion, one thing remains as clear now as it did to Frankfort thirty years ago. Local Egyptian ideology was already so developed and pervasive that even these isolated motifs appear only briefly and are then absorbed to the point of oblivion in Egypt's own highly distinctive imagery. A comparable transformation is equally evident with the cylinder seal; it was centuries before it was finally ousted by local stamp types, but by Dynasty I it was already carved and used in a manner without parallel in Sumer or its periphery (Frankfort 1939:292ff).

(b) Betwixt Sumer and Egypt

Marfoe's admirable contribution to this volume (chapter 3) with which I largely agree, removes the need for me to pursue this issue very far. In view of its current popularity I should perhaps emphasize my agreement with Marfoe that Wallerstein's (1974) distinction between core, semi-peripheral and peripheral areas of economic development, and his argument that it is interaction among these disparate levels that stimulates growth, does not seem particularly fruitful in application to this case. But, since I have adopted a particular interpretation of the means by which Mesopotamian contact was made with Egypt through Syria in an 'Uruk IVa' horizon, it should perhaps be justified more definitely. Particularly when its brevity may have been crucial in determining the impact of the connection within Egypt.

The excavation of a south Mesopotamian community, or colony, implanted into northern Syria on the Euphrates at Habuba Kabira is one of the more remarkable archaeological discoveries of the past fifteen years. So far as it is possible to judge, it represents a deliberate Lower Mesopotamian penetration up the Euphrates (and its tributaries, if sites like Brak are also to be brought into this perspective) during the earlier Protoliterate period (Strommenger 1980a) to secure direct control of vital raw materials and luxuries from the Syro-Anatolian region and to regulate exchange of goods from the east and south-east passing this way. Herodotus (I:194) has told us how such riverine trade accommodated itself to the nature of the river: 'Every boat carries a live donkey – the larger ones several – and when they reach Babylon and the cargoes have been offered for sale, the boats are broken up, and the frames and straw sold and the hides loaded on the donkey's backs for the return journey overland to Armenia'. This penetration does not seem to have outlasted the Uruk IV period by very long in its original form; relatively soon it had to make way for local control, which may well have been stimulated to develop by this very intrusion.

How such colonies were administered – in other words what social and political patterns were momentarily transferred to Syria with them – is a matter still of surmise, as is the impact of writing on the local evolution of literacy. If Habuba Kabira's parent city was indeed Uruk, as is commonly assumed, though it is only one of a number of possibilities, it would also usually be assumed that the 'colonial' settlement was administered as if it were the public household of the temple rather than of the crown, which is commonly taken to be a later development in Sumer. It would equally be taken for granted that any mercantile enterprise at this early date was under the direction of the temple household, not of the Crown, or private individuals. But such substantial revisions of our understanding of political and social structures in third millennium Sumer (Gelb 1979, 1980), and of the role of the merchant in Mesopotamia at this time (cf. Hawkins 1979), have emerged in the last decade, that caution is now called for in any assumptions about the Uruk IV–III horizon. Not least when work in progress on the archives of this time from Uruk itself promises significant clarification on many such fundamental questions (Green 1980). Cities like Kish, Nippur, Ur and Uruk were each the focus of varied patterns of urban growth and may well have had distinctive socio-political establishments from an early date. Whatever the case, in marked contrast to the earliest Pharaonic situation in Egypt, there are traces from Uruk IV down

through the third millennium BC, at cities as distinct as Kish and Uruk, of popular assemblies with some influential role in city government. Again this highlights, as Frankfort so often emphasized, the contrasting traditions of the two pristine states.

It is unlikely that anyone today would wish to explain the emergence of Egyptian Early Dynastic society, in the second half of the fourth millennium BC, through invasion or migration from a 'higher civilization' to the east in Lower Mesopotamia. The view that a fresh and vital, if undefined, 'influence' from that quarter may explain certain things in the 'Unification Period' (Naqada III) has not lost support quite so completely, though the latest major treatment is not in favour of it as a significant factor (Hoffmann 1980). It has been argued here that, although there certainly was contact, it was earlier and indirect. Lower Mesopotamia briefly, in the early and middle Gerzean period (Naqada IIa–c), fed into an existing exchange and interaction network between the Levant and Egypt some cultural baggages – in Braudel's sense – whose arrivals are archaeologically visible in Upper Egypt, if not yet always in Lower Egypt, some which are not. They were active in Egypt, not so much in 'triggering off' or accelerating social differentials or politico-economic centralization, as in generating new conceptions that sharpened the self-awareness and distinction of already well-established tribal rulers and the favoured elites through whom their power was exercised. They were not active in the same way in Palestine, since a similarly susceptible political establishment had not yet emerged there; their role in Syria is more obscure, since less archaeological data is at present available.

In Egypt what may have been transferred and accepted is only part of the problem; no less interesting is the question of what may have been transferred and not accepted. On the positive side it is a matter of assessing the impact of certain Mesopotamian ideas (of record and communication: seals and writing), of Mesopotamian techniques (monumental mudbrick architecture) and of Mesopotamian images or visual formulae, whose precise original meanings may have been as obscure to the Predynastic Egyptians as they are to the modern commentator, but which clearly filled some gap in their own imagery at the time of initial transmission. The Lower Mesopotamian (Elamite) repertory from which I have argued these motifs came, was much greater, alert-

Fig. 4.2. *Egyptian prehistoric chronology*

(Petrie 1939)	(Kaiser 1957)	
Badarian (SD 20–9)		
Amratian (SD 30–7)	Naqada I (SD 30–8)	c. 3800/3700 – 3600/3500 BC
Gerzean (SD 39–60)	Naqada II (SD 38–63)	Predynastic c. 3600/3500 – 3200/3100 BC
Semainean (SD 61–78)	Naqada III (SD 63–80)	Protodynastic (Dynasties O and I) c. 3200/3100 – 3000/2900 BC

Fig. 4.3. *Comparative diagram of archaeological chronologies*

	Egypt	Palestine	Syria	Lower Mesopotamia (Sumer)	S. W. Iran (Elam)
c. 3200/3100 BC	(Djer) Dynasty I (Narmer/Hor-Aha)	Early Bronze II Early Bronze Ib (Arad IV)		Early Dynastic I (Uruk III)	Susa 16
	Dynasty 'O' (Naqada III)	Early Bronze Ia		Uruk III (Jamdat Nasr)	(Stratigraphical Break)
c. 3500 BC	Naqada II (Gerzean Period)	Intermediate Phase	Habuba Kabira (South)/Jebel Aruda	Uruk IVa b c	Susa 17 Susa 18
c. 3800 BC	Naqada I (Amratian Period) Badarian Period	Chalcolithic Period		'Ubaid Period	

Note: both the overall synchronisms and the absolute chronologies are only approximations.

ing us to the exercise of choice in Egypt by the arbiters of religious imagery in the mid-Gerzean period. This takes us into questions as much beyond the scope of the present essay as beyond the evidence from Egypt at present available for their investigation.

Chronological Note

Since this chapter is in a thematic volume covering a broad spectrum of material, there may be readers to whom Egyptian prehistoric terminology and chronology is unfamiliar. Fig. 4.2 and comments are intended for their guidance.

As the pioneering work on the later prehistoric period in Egypt was based almost exclusively on the evidence of cemeteries, no stratigraphic sequences were readily available. At the very end of the nineteenth century Petrie was thus forced to evolve a relative chronology based not on stratigraphy, but on a comparative study of the pottery he had found in a number of cemeteries, notably those at Naqada, Abadiya and Hu. He studied the association of various types of pottery in grave-groups statistically and deduced fifty-one consecutive stages of development numbered 30–80, leaving 1–29 for subsequent discovery of later material. These stages he called 'Sequence Dates' (SD). This is merely a convention which assumes neither a correspondence to absolute dates not that the steps are of equal length. Petrie's system is increasingly subject to critical analysis and revision, but it still remains fundamental. Kaiser's revisions are the main published ones; he, like some other scholars, has adopted the name of the largest cemetery Petrie excavated, 'Naqada', to denote the main phases rather than Petrie's terminology based on other site names. Absolute chronology is still very uncertain, as comprehensive series of Carbon-14 determinations are not yet available for the periods in question.

Fig. 4.3 presents the comparative chronology used here.

Acknowledgements

My interest in this subject has been sustained and stimulated over many years by discussions with the late Dr Elise Baumgartel and my colleague Mrs Joan Crowfoot Payne, who has most kindly checked various specific points in predynastic chronology for me; I am also grateful to Mrs Ruth Amiran and to Dr Pirhiya Beck for their advice. They do not necessarily agree with the opinions stated here.

Note
1 That is, for the purposes of this paper, ancient Sumer and Elam.

Bibliographic Note
Publications on relevant topics that have appeared since this paper was written are listed below.

1. *Artefacts and foreign relations*
Davies, W. 1981   'The foreign relations of Predynastic Egypt: Palestine in the Predynastic period' *The SSEA Journal* (Toronto) XI(1), 21ff.
Needler, W. 1984   *Predynastic and Archaic Egypt in the Brooklyn Museum* (The Brooklyn Museum, New York)
Prag, K. 1986   'Byblos and Egypt in the fourth millennium B.C.' *Levant* XVIII, 59ff
2. *Chronology*
Shaw, I. M. E. 1984   'The Egyptian Archaic Period: a reappraisal of the C-14 dates' (1) *Göttinger Miszellen* 78, 79ff
3. *Early writing systems*
Arnett, W. S. 1982   *The Predynastic Origin of Egyptian Hieroglyphs* (Washington; University Press of America)
Jasim, S. A. and Oates, J. 1986   'Early tokens and tablets in Mesopotamia' *World Archaeology* 17, 348ff
Ray, J. D. 1986   'The emergence of writing in Egypt' *World Archaeology* 17, 307ff

4. *Faience*
Continuing research has done nothing so far to reject the view that, on current chronologies, the first production of faience was in Western Asia, before the earliest appearance of green-glazed faience beads in graves of the Amratian Period in Egypt (Naqada I). It should then perhaps also be included on p. 39 here as an example of stimulus innovation from Western Asia:

Kaczmarczyk, A. and Hedges, R. E. M. 1983   *Ancient Egyptian Faience: an analytical survey of Egyptian Faience from Predynastic to Roman Times* (Aris and Phillips)
Moorey, P. R. S. 1985   *Materials and Manufacture in Ancient Mesopotamia: The Evidence of Archaeology and Art: Metals and Metalwork, Glazed Materials and Glass* (BAR International Series No.237; Oxford), especially pp. 136–7

Part three

Regional interaction and crisis

Chapter 5

**Commercial networks in the
Ancient Near East**

Mogens Trolle Larsen

Introduction

This chapter seeks to reconstruct and describe a commercial system which flourished during the first couple of centuries of the second millennium BC, and which linked such distant areas as Afghanistan, the vast plains and deserts of the Iranian highland, the Mesopotamian alluvium, the Syrian plain and the Anatolian plateau. The sheer enormity of such a geographical area gives rise to a number of very serious problems, of course, and it forces me to make use of a good deal of imaginative guesswork and more or less informed reconstruction. My preoccupation will be the available textual documentation, which means that my analysis will have a quite narrow focus, primarily on Mesopotamia and Anatolia, the only places from where texts come in this period. My attempt to include the other regions as a kind of periphery therefore relies on an understanding of the texts from the 'center'. These terms are accordingly used at the outset in a neutral sense, defined on the basis of documentation alone. Whether it will be meaningful to introduce elements of an economic or political character in the definition will have to be dealt with in the light of the results of this analysis.

It is obviously essential, therefore, to discuss the nature and value of this documentation and I shall attempt to provide a brief overview of the textual corpus available for this task and a preliminary evaluation of the biases built into it.

Documentation

There are serious limitations to an analysis which relies

entirely or predominantly on textual sources from the period in question. Few sites have produced texts which are directly relevant here, and even fewer have been properly excavated; the distribution in terms of temporal and geographical space is very uneven; many texts have no known provenience, i.e., not even the site where they were excavated can be established with certainty, and the exact archaeological context for most of the remaining texts is unclear.

The texts allow us to catch glimpses of a system, and we may confidently assume that they are basically non-representative in terms of the overall structure. It is therefore no surprise that this evidence has given rise to a variety of different opinions and interpretations. These relate to fundamental questions such as the importance and volume of foreign trade, and the relationship between the private and the public sector in commerce (Adams 1974; Yoffee 1981). Even problems of a simpler nature often lead to disagreements, such as the location of towns and even countries mentioned, some of them as sources for basic commodities traded. To top it all, there is some uncertainty about even the correct translation and interpretation of key terms which denote the most essential trading goods, for instance one of the metals which play a vital role in the commercial system: some scholars maintain that it was lead, others that it was arsenical

copper, and most appear to support the view that it was tin (Muhly 1973, 1976).

These are parameters which define the limitations of any analysis, so we have to proceed with some caution, realising that the evidence is likely to be vague, non-representative and even occasionally misleading.

Fig. 5.1 summarises the main textual sources and indicates some of the most serious problems. The uneven distribution in time and space is obvious, and this is coupled with the vast difference in the depth of documentation from the various sites: compare the rich archives from Kanesh, containing more than 10,000 texts and covering a quite short period, with the downright scanty evidence from most of the other sites, often no more than 10 or 15 documents. It is rare to have strictly contemporary evidence which could allow us to link even two sites; moreover, when this promising situation occurs, the texts are likely to stem from different types of context so that they refer to distinct aspects of the commercial systems and illuminate the concerns of unrelated socio-economic institutions. Our reconstructions have to rely on a confusing mixture of evidence: private letters and contracts from one site must be related to information from royal inscriptions, administrative archives from a palace or a temple, the odd diplomatic letter – even a passage in a literary or lexical text.

Fig. 5.1. *Summary of main textual sources*

Time[1]	Place	Type of document	Contacts	Imports	Exports
2025–2000	Ur	admin.	Magan	copper, stone	textiles, wool, oil, barley
1930–1865	Ur	admin.	Dilmun	copper, ivory, pearls, spices	wool, silver, wheat, sesame
1920–1840	Kanesh	private	Assur	tin, textiles	silver, gold,
			East Anatolia	copper, wool	tin, textiles
1810–1790	Ur	private	Dilmun	copper	silver
1810–1765	Kanesh	private	Assur	textiles, tin?	silver
1790–1780	Larsa	private	Eshunna	silver?	?
			Susa	tin?	?
			Sippar	tin	silver, gold
			Zagros	slaves	?
1785–1760	Mari	dipl. and admin.	Susa/Assur?	tin	?
			Syria	wine, wood	tin
			Babylonia	?	wine, wood
			Anatolia	horses?	?
			Cyprus	copper	tin
1785–1600	Sippar	private	Eshnunna	tin	paint
			Zagros	slaves	oil, aromatics
			Syria	wood, wine, oil, aromatics	tin
			Assur	tin?	silver?

So our difficulties stem in part from the questions of interpretation when we have texts, and in part from the black holes
when a period is undocumented and the white areas on the map
where no texts from any period are available.

The organisation of the trade

The period covered by this chapter was a long one and on
the political plane it saw several rather drastic changes. It begins
with the last third-millennium empire, Ur III, a highly centralised,
bureaucratic structure which marked the last period when Sumerian traditions were still predominant; after 2000 BC followed a
period of decentralisation with several political centers growing
up in the region which had been under direct control from Ur.
The Akkadian language and Akkadian traditions in the political
and socio-economic field became more and more important. In
the phase called 'Isin-Larsa' down to *c.* 1800 BC we are confronted with a very complex political situation, a fluid and constantly
changing system of alliances and rapid shifts in the fortunes of the
various cities and small territorial states (Edzard 1957).

One of the small states which developed out of the ruins of
the Ur III system was the city-state of Assur, located on the Tigris
in northern Mesopotamia. This little settlement became the center
for a far-flung system of international trade which is illuminated
by the archives from Kanesh, and for that reason it plays an
important role in this context (Garelli 1963, Larsen 1976). It
flourished as an independent state during the nineteenth century
BC, but became part of a larger territorial unit around 1800 when
a shortlived kingdom was established in the north, encompassing
the region of the Jezira, the middle Euphrates with Mari, the
Tigris region including Assur and even areas east of the Tigris,
reaching into the Zagros valleys. When this collapsed after one
generation Hammurapi of Babylon built up his kingdom which
managed to unify the entire southern alluvium under one centralised government. This state existed – albeit in a somewhat
shrunken shape – down to around 1600, when a strange Hittite
raid from Anatolia toppled the last king of the line and paved the
way for the new Kassite rulers.

Apart from the Ur III phase and certain shortlived political
initiatives the entire period under scrutiny is characterised by a
multitude of small political units, city-states or not very large territorial states. This is obviously of relevance for our understanding of the commerical patterns of the period, and it marks a sharp
contrast with the ensuing Late Bronze Age (see Liverani's article
in this volume, chapter 7), which was characterised by large states
and empires which met directly at fairly well-established borders.

If we concentrate on the socio-economic system of the central Mesopotamian region we see a transformation of the Ur III
pattern, in which a centralised bureaucracy is the dominant feature, towards a system in which private accumulation appears to
become steadily more and more important. The texts from Ur
illuminate this process well, as described in the studies by Oppenheim (1954), Leemans (1960) and Butz (1979). The first group of
documents in Fig. 5.1, administrative texts from the late Ur III
phase, are extremely terse and reveal little; they are concerned
with the relations between temples and state officials on the one
hand and travelling traders on the other, and it seems that the
investments referred to stem from government funds. We cannot
know whether the traders were really a kind of official carrying
out specialised functions for the temples etc., or whether they had
other, privately financed activities as well. Also the second group
of texts show some relationship between travelling traders and
temples, since they are concerned with 'tithes' paid to the Ningal-
temple, representing goods that stem from trips to Dilmun; these
texts may show a system of temple investment in the trade at Dilmun, but again we cannot say precisely what role these investments played in the overall system. Finally, the texts from around
1800 appear to relate to either purely or at least predominantly
privately financed commercial ventures. The letters exchanged
between traders and the few investments contracts indicate that
we are dealing with an example of the classic pattern of venture
trading, so well described for the early trade on the Mediterranean. In fact, as pointed out by Oppenheim, the investment
contract resembles the classic *societas maris*, which regulates the
relationship between the investor and the travelling trader. It is a
system which is characteristic of trade over water, where each
transaction stands as an independent venture, in contrast to the
systems in which long-term partnership contracts are set up to
regulate the relations between a resident investor and his factors
abroad.

A crude distinction between a market economy and an
'embedded', status-oriented system has little relevance for the
Mesopotamian evidence from any period[2]. We are faced with a
system which allows for a fluctuating relationship between a central authority and a private sector; in certain periods we seem to
have a very strong central control which can reduce for instance
traders to a status as officials. The so-called 'balanced accounts'
from Umma, probably the main commercial center in the Ur III
state, appear to provide us with evidence for such a situation: they
are annual audits reckoned in silver equivalencies of commodities
and money which has flowed through the hands of traders, and
they reflect a system of control which may well indicate that the
traders had only quite limited access to private investments
(Snell 1982).

Even in the later phases of the Middle Bronze Age it is clear
that the palace exercised some degree of control over the commercial system and specifically over the association of traders known
as the 'harbour'. The traders of the various towns were organised
in a *karum*, a term which denotes both the physical reality of a
special merchant quarter and the community of traders in the
town. This was led by a royally appointed man through whom the
contacts with the central authorities were regulated. The traders'
association has certain obligations towards the palace of course,
being charged with the selling of products which came from taxes
or from the production in the palace sector, and the procurements
of commodities which were needed from abroad (Kraus 1958,
1984, Larsen 1976, Charpin 1982, Stol 1982).

It seems clear that investments based on accumulations in
the private sector came to play a more and more important role in
the life of such traders, but the administrative and bureaucratic
system exhibits a remarkable degree of stability and continuity.

As said, we are dealing with fluctuations and not with drastic revolutionary changes.

The clearest case is illustrated by the extensive Old Assyrian archives from Kanesh in Anatolia. The texts all stem from private merchant houses located in what was called the Kanesh 'harbour'; this community was established by traders who had their home base in the town Assur, several hundred kilometers away on the Tigris, and it was predominantly inhabited by men who represented private firms who had their main seat in Assur itself.

The trade was financed on the basis of private investments, with only occasional references to what may be temple funds. Partnership contracts here were long-term agreements which set up structures which may be described as a simple form of a company (Larsen 1977). The family firm was clearly the organising element in the trade; 'our paternal house' was always located in Assur of course, and it was presided over by the patriarch of the family. This was where purchases of tin and textiles were carried out for the money arriving from Anatolia, and where the caravans back to Kanesh and the other Assyrian settlements in Anatolia and northern Syria were arranged and equipped. The family would have a trusted man in Kanesh, usually a son of the boss, who handled all the different affairs of the firm at that end, receiving caravans from Assur, selling the goods either for cash in the market or by way of commission contracts with traders who travelled around from town to town in Anatolia, paying taxes to the local authorities, handling debts, lawsuits etc. And around him, both in Kanesh itself and scattered in other towns he would have a staff of junior members of the family (Larsen 1982).

There was a king of Assur and he had important functions of a ritual nature apart from being the leader in some manner of the city-assembly which appears to have constituted the true political and judicial power in the system (Larsen 1972, 1976).

Similar social and commercial systems presumably existed in other areas and phases of the Middle Bronze, but the evidence from for instance southern Mesopotamia is, as pointed out, less clear. We can see that trade was the occupation of several members of the same families, even over two or three generations (as described for instance by Leemans in his study of the Old Babylonian merchant 1950); and the scanty evidence from Ur refers to the late trade over the Gulf to Dilmun and contains letters exchanged between persons who regarded themselves as members of a special group of 'Dilmun-travellers'. It seems reasonable to conclude from the evidence which we do have that it was here – as elsewhere – the family which organised the different relations of partnership, representation and agency.

Goods and production areas

Obviously, Fig. 5.1 does not inform us about all traded commodities or all areas that played a direct role in the commercial system. We cannot even be sure that the sites which are actually represented were of the first importance in the system. However, a seemingly logical pattern does emerge from the information available, one that can be taken as the basis for further analysis.

This system can be presented in simplified form:

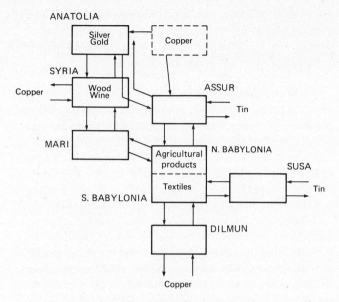

Fig. 5.2. Commodities: schematic model.

The commodities which reappear in many parts of the system are metals, textiles and certain agricultural luxury products such as fine oil, spices and aromatics. Basic agricultural products such as wool and even more clearly grain play a limited role in the documented pattern. The common distinction between luxury goods and utility goods, so important for the original Wallerstein argument according to which trade in precious goods was 'non-systemic', must be discussed in the concluding remarks, but there is no obvious reason to introduce it at this point of the analysis (Wallerstein 1974).

Tin

The system as delimited in my schematic model (see Fig. 5.2) represents simply the regions from which we have direct textual evidence. Most of the goods exchanged within this system in fact originated there, one of the significant exceptions being the metal tin. This comes into the system at two points: at Assur in the north, and at Susa in the south; it is obvious that it must come from further east, across the Iranian plateau, for the two towns mentioned are located strategically in relation to two of the most important crossings of the difficult Zargos mountain chain. Assur and Susa then represent the pipes through which tin was channeled into the Middle Eastern system at this time, taking the north Mesopotamian route to northern Syria and Anatolia from Assur, and the southern route to the main cities on the alluvium from Susa.

The origin of tin appears to be established with the finds from Afghanistan where surface occurrences of ample supplies have been reported recently (Cleuziou and Berthoud 1982). How the ore reached Mesopotamia, the organisation of the extremely long haul across very rugged terrain with donkey caravans as the most likely system, and how much was transported – all this remains unknown. Statistics are obviously not available for this period, but the Old Assyrian documents, which illuminate only the imports to Kanesh from Assur, provide direct documentation of some 13.5 tons over 40–50 year period (Veenhof 1972) – a figure which can safely be raised to at least 80 tons as a conservative estimate of the total trade. We must accordingly reckon with a yearly inflow of very substantial quantities of tin into the system delineated by my chart, running into several tons.

While it is apparent that such a trade must have been based on rather elaborate socio-economic systems in both Iran and Afghanistan – of which I know nothing – it seems likely that these links in the larger systems will remain undocumented by texts. Writing was apparently not used in these regions at this time, an interesting reflection of the diversity of the individual elements in the pattern of trade.

Copper

Copper too came into the Near Eastern core area from outside: from Oman, ancient Magan, which had provided copper for southern Mesopotamia during the third millennium; from eastern Anatolia in the region around the ancient city of Durhumit which must be sought in the Pontic area[3]; and slightly later from Cyprus which delivered copper to Syria.

Copper must obviously have been traded in truly vast quantities. A document from Ur refers to single consignments of more than 18 tons coming by ship from Oman, indicating the scale of this trade (Leemans 1960:50); in the Assyrian trade on Anatolia we find a reference to a single shipment of 15 tons, and the fifteen largest shipments mentioned there (out of hundreds of such references) in all amounted to nearly 35 tons (Garelli 1963 and Larsen 1976:92).

Such large quantities were of course difficult to transport over land, so in the case of truly long-distance trade in copper we find that it relied on waterborne transportation, the best examples being Oman and the Persian Gulf in the south and Cyprus and the Mediterranean (plus the Euphrates river) in the north. This also explains why several sources for copper were apparently used concurrently, serving different parts of the system: Oman delivering copper to the alluvium in the south, the Pontic region supplying Anatolia and northern Mesopotamia, and slightly later Cyprus providing copper for the Levant and Syria.

Precious metals

The sources for silver and gold are more difficult to establish. These metals functioned as money within the system and are therefore present in all the various links. The one source known to me is central Anatolia from where very significant quantities were sent back to Assur in payment for the tin and the textiles received, and it also seems probable that the cities on the alluvium received at least a large part of their silver via Assur. The import over a 40–50 year period from Anatolia to Assur can be estimated to at least 10 tons of silver on the basis of the figures available. Gold may also have come to southern Mesopotamia from the Indus area (Leemans 1971).

Textiles

The southern Mesopotamian region appears to have been the main producer of the textiles present in the trade. It is interest-ing to note that since all textiles at this time are made of wool, there must obviously have been production centers in all parts of the Near East. Imports to any region must therefore have been introduced in competition with local products; it seems self-evident that they cannot have competed on price in view of the ubiquitous technology and the cost of transportation. Looking again at the Old Assyrian trade on Anatolia for statistical data we can observe that the presently available texts give detailed information concerning 14,500 pieces of cloth imported to Kanesh from Assur, again over a 40–50 year period; a conservative estimate of the total trade in this period must be some 100,000 textiles. It is reasonable to assume that a large part (probably most) of these textiles had been produced in southern Mesopotamia, shipped to Assur where they were sold on the market, shipped further on to Kanesh in central Anatolia, and finally sold somewhere on the plateau (Veenhof 1972: part two).

The basis for such a trade must have been a production of specific high-quality textiles which had a great prestige value in areas such as Anatolia. It should be emphasised that it is impossible to point to very significant differences in levels of technology within the area delimited by my chart, so it was not a question of ancient Mesopotamia trading with 'barbarian' Anatolia (cf. Schneider 1977:24).

We have very elaborate documentation for textile production in the period of the Ur III empire, down to around 2000 BC (cf. Waetzoldt 1972). In this highly bureaucratised and centralised state the various productive sectors of the economy had been regulated and concentrated in certain centers on the alluvium, and textile production was characteristic of the capital city of Ur and the provincial town of Lagash. Ration lists inform us that some 12,000 female weavers of semi-free status worked in Ur, and that more than 15,000 persons were directly engaged in weaving and preparing textiles in Lagash. Waetzoldt estimates that the annual production in Ur alone was some 24,000 pieces. These fell into many different categories and qualities, and the Sumerian bureaucrats reckoned that one of the simple types demanded 27 workdays to complete, whereas the most luxurious type took a weaver no less than 1,200 days to finish! This probably included the time it took to prepare the wool, but the fulling of the cloth took an extra 90 days. The textiles produced measured no more than three or four meters in length, so we can see that these were incredibly elaborate products[4].

Whereas it seems unlikely that the following, more chaotic period continued this well-organised system of production on the same scale, it is clear that palace-organised establishments with hundreds of weavers continued to produce large amounts of high-quality textiles during the entire period in question here in the main cities on the alluvium. A single document from Mari in the eighteenth century BC mentions more than 850 names of men, women and children, perhaps captured in a recent raid, who are organised in the palace weaveries (Dossin 1964a and b, cf. Rouault 1977).

Wool

Wool too was exported in significant quantities, but bulk

shipments were presumably only feasible with water-borne transportation as in the case of copper; exports from Ur to Dilmun and Magan are attested. According to Waetzoldt only the poorer qualities of wool are known to have been exported.

Grain

The Gulf is also the only place where shipments of grain are mentioned in quantities of any significance, although ships carrying grain and wine move down the Euphrates from Syria to Mari and probably beyond[5]. The suggestion that grain was a major export article to such areas as the Iranian plateau (cf. Kohl 1978, 1979) seems to me to lack any safe foundation; land transport of goods with a high bulk–value ratio can never have been a significant element in the commercial pattern (see also Leemans 1960:115).

Syrian products

Fig. 5.2 points to the existence of a significant production center in Syria, from where wood, wine and various aromatics were exported. The Amanus range with its cedars occupies a central place in much Mesopotamian writing, both as a semi-mythical place in literature and as a goal for military expeditions looking for plunder. The importance of links with the Syrian region has been underscored by the finding of the Ebla archive which is of course some hundreds of years earlier than the period I am dealing with, but which demonstrates the existence of a strong political power in the region and close commercial ties with Mesopotamia channeled through Mari on the middle Euphrates[6] So the situation in our texts has a long history behind it.

The structure of the system

Any attempt to analyse the overall system must of necessity begin with the evidence from Kanesh which describes the Old Assyrian commerce. In fact, this corpus is so varied and now also so relatively well understood that it has relevance for historical reconstructions which reach far beyond the Ancient Near East.

The Old Assyrian trade was quite simple: tin and textiles were sent from Assur to Kanesh to be sold, i.e. exchanged for silver; this was sent back to Assur to be invested in new consignments of tin and textiles (see Fig. 5.3).

Assur was a center for transit trade. The tin exported from there to Anatolia and to other parts of the Greater Mesopotamian region came to the market in Assur from the east, ultimately from Afghanistan, but presumably carried into Assur by men who only controlled the last leg from somewhere in the Zagros region. We do not know who carried the tin to Assur, but it does seem reasonably clear that it was not brought by men of Assur itself. When merchants in the city write to their colleagues in far-off Anatolia they never appear to contemplate going anywhere in order to buy tin; they sit in Assur waiting for it to arrive. Either it was brought by Assyrians who specialised in the furnishing of the market in Assur, and who had little or no direct relation with the men who controlled the trade with Anatolia; or the tin was brought there by men from other towns – and the evidence concerning textiles strongly supports this latter view.

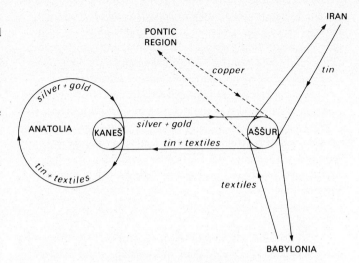

Fig. 5.3. Old Assyrian trade: schematic model.

One of the categories of textiles sold on the Anatolian market was known as 'Akkadian', i.e. originating in southern Mesopotamia. There are references to the import of such cloth to Assur, and all texts which we have agree that Akkadian textiles were brought by Akkadians , i.e., traders from the Babylonian towns (Veenhof 1972:98–103). It is surely likely that some Assyrians went to the south, and the contacts between these groups of merchants must have been intense (Walker 1980, Leemans 1960: 98–102). But as things stand now we must maintain that the traders of Assur left it to others to supply the market there with the essential commodities which were meant for export to Anatolia. In contrast, the Assyrians were certainly present in Anatolia in considerable numbers.

It is difficult to say how large a population Assur had in any period, and it is certainly extra complicated for this early phase which is so poorly represented in the archaeological record; however, it seems unlikely that it can have had more than 15,000 inhabitants in all within the walls of this really quite small township, and it is a fair guess that 1,500–2,000 men were directly engaged in the trade on Anatolia (Veenhof 1977). So if some 10 per cent of the total population pursued these activities, is it in fact reasonable to assume that the community could have been actively engaged in large-scale trade with other areas as well?

The Old Assyrian trade was therefore concentrated on the north Syrian and Anatolian market, and it was consequently dependent on a constant flow of supplies of both tin and textiles to Assur itself. It is possible that this situation is reflected in a royal inscription which comes from Assur and stems from the period just before the documentation from Kanesh starts, i.e. a time when the trade was being expanded into Syria and Anatolia. This text refers to a liberalisation of taxation for traders from the south, presumably an abolition of taxes and other hindrances to a free flow of trade (Larsen 1976). Such a step would be a logical consequence of a growing Assyrian commercial involvement in the west.

The texts from Ur referred to earlier bear witness to a similarly restricted commercial operation: a very heavy involvement in one specific commercial circuit, bringing large quantities of copper from Oman and Bahrain into southern Mesopotamia; there is no evidence referring to other commercial links, for instance with cities and countries further north on the alluvium. As already mentioned, the merchants who were engaged in this commerce referred to themselves as 'Dilmun-travellers' (Oppenheim 1954, Leemans 1960:39), thus indicating the highly specialised nature of their activities. We have no way of deciding for certain whether this is a skewed picture due to the limited documentation, but in fact it seems not unlikely that these two bodies of evidence show us a fundamental feature of the commercial system of the period. The limited resources in manpower alone argue for a specialisation which then resulted in a system of circuits which interacted with each other in various ways.

Another such circuit may be described for a triangle linking Susa, Eshnunna and Larsa. The handful of texts dealt with by Leemans (1960: chapter 3; cf. also Leemans 1968 and Veenhof 1972:143, note 247) refer to shipments from Eshnunna to persons in Larsa, and in at least some of the cases the trip went via Susa. Some of the contracts refer to small amounts of silver which are to be brought to Larsa, probably as extras on top of a commercial consignment. Even though the texts which we have therefore do not deal with the basic commercial operation, but only with the special arrangement designed to give the transporters some gain as well, it does appear that the object of the operation is the purchase of tin at Susa; if the deadline set is not met the transporter has to pay what is described as the 'profit' accrued to the amount he is bringing – clearly showing the commercial nature of the entire procedure.

We seem to gain a small glimpse here of a commercial circuit which connected these three cities, and it appears that merchants at home in the town of Larsa in the south were in control of this particular branch.

Conclusion

So, in this period of small political units we find a commercial system which consisted of a series of interlocking circuits, feeding each other and overlapping at certain nodal points. There were, as already noticed, several possible points of entry and exit into the central area, and there are potentially competing routes crossing the entire region, for instance along the two main rivers. There was some movement of people beyond the strict frontiers of such circuits, of course; we hear of envoys from Dilmun at Mari for instance, perhaps traders on their way even further along the Euphrates route towards Syria.

The system described here was obviously vulnerable to limited breakdowns, but it would also appear that it had a high degree of flexibility. The small political units which combined to make up this patchwork of connections were liable to be hit by a variety of destabilising factors, and with the destruction of a strategically placed city a real gap could develop in the chain. On the other hand, such gaps could be closed by other small states, or detours could be found around a political vacuum in most instances.

During the third millennium we have examples of the same

elements, notably from the palace archives found at Ebla in Syria which refer to the production of and trade in very substantial amounts of textiles, but it seems impossible at the moment to reconstruct a similarly grandiose regional system. Furthermore, we also have indications of a quite different system of satisfying demands, namely wars or raids which in most instances were directed towards precisely those areas which produced such essential commodities as wood and metals. Such campaigns have in fact been explained as designed to establish key points in a protective system set up to guard caravan roads, but the existence of isolated forts such as the Old Akkadian one at Tell Brak cannot explain all such campaigns.

The period following upon the one described here presents a different system again, dominated by large territorial units; as pointed out by Zaccagnini (chapter 6), nearly all of the extant evidence for trade is phrased in the terminology of diplomatic exchanges of gifts.

These geo-political differences obviously had a profound impact on the transformation of socio-economic and commercial patterns and procedures, but there is a danger in stressing this point too strongly, for the material available is simply not sufficiently clear or representative. It seems very probable indeed that the different elements in the commercial system which have been outlined here formed a complex mix which was present in the region at all times, although the emphasis on one or the other single element changed.

The central area of the Near East, from the Zagros to the Mediterranean, and from the Gulf to the Taurus and sometimes beyond to the Black Sea, appears to have formed a natural unit; few goods had to be introduced from outside, and there was a developed network of routes and exchanges within the region. Egypt is conspicuously absent from the evidence from this period, but that is undoubtedly partly to be explained by the lack of evidence from the Syro-Palestinian region. The trade on Anatolia opens up the possibility that some of the tin brought there from Assur found its way to the Aegean area, but nothing can be said for certain about it. And the extent to which Cyprus as a producer of copper became drawn into the Near Eastern system cannot be adequately described at the moment.

If we are to operate with the concepts 'center' and 'periphery' we must begin with the fact that the Near Eastern core area contained several centers. During the period in question they did not compete politically, except for some isolated instances, although there were of course constant conflicts within each of these regions: southern Mesopotamia shows a long series of wars among the city-states, so does Anatolia and Syria. But there is little evidence for inter-regional conflict. Instead, the intense contacts manifested themselves in the form of commercial links which surely in many instances were regulated by way of written treaties of some kind.

Within this conglomerate 'center' or core area we find elements of a regional specialisation, in production as well as in commerce. Again, Assur is the clearest available example, and it is evident that the very existence of the city was connected with trade. It has been pointed out by Oates (1968) that its hinterland has insufficient agricultural resources to support a major settlement, and the site itself is strategically located in reference to several routes. During the Old Assyrian period there was certainly some textile production in Assur, but its *raison d'être* was clearly its function as a transit center: a market for important categories of commodities and a commercial center from which the penetration of the Syrian and Anatolian markets was directed.

The expertise built up here in the field of commerce formed one of the basic elements in the trade towards the west. The construction of elaborate systems of accounting, of investment and partnership structures, and of an administrative system of great elegance and efficiency led to a commercial organisation which in its complex details is paralleled only millennia later by the traders of the Mediterranean cities. The famous 'commercial revolution of the thirteenth century' in Western Europe, which was characterised by a major shift in business organisation away from the travelling, itinerant trader towards the sedentary businessman seated behind his desk – is paralleled in many details by the material from Kanesh (Roover 1965, 1966).

I am convinced that similar commercial circuits existed side by side with the Old Assyrian one, interacting with it, and maybe having an organisational structure which was equally elaborate. One indication of our ignorance is the fact that several major Old Assyrian commercial establishments or 'harbours' were located in northern Syria, and we know practically nothing about their activities. It seems safe to guess that they were somehow linked to commercial circuits in Syria and Palestine.

Looking at the southern Mesopotamian region with its many large urban centers we find a much greater emphasis on production and consumption in our documentation. But it is also clear that we are faced with a very open system with numerous external contacts reaching across the Gulf to Dilmun (Bahrain), Magan (Oman), and ultimately Meluhha (Indus); via the Khuzistan plain and Susa in the south and via other more northerly passes and roads through the Zagros onto the Iranian plateau – and ultimately all the way to Afghanistan; along the Tigris to Assur and the north Mesopotamian Jezira plain towards Anatolia – ultimately to the Black Sea and perhaps the Aegean; and along the Euphrates via Mari and Emar to Syria, Palestine – and ultimately Cyprus.

We are in other words dealing with a highly interactive world in which it is possible to follow commodities flowing from one end to the other. However, it seems that while goods could move over this entire system, the same was only to a limited extent true of the traders. Rather, the central Mesopotamian region exhibits a pattern of transit centers which were located in the periphery of the production area: Assur, Sippar at the gateway to the Euphrates route, Mari further upstream, Eshnunna at the opening of the major route through the Zagros via Hamadan, Der on the road to Elam and Susa itself; in the Gulf we have Dilmun. These places regulated much of the contact between the Mesopotamian plain and the surrounding world, feeding the cities on the alluvium with needed imports.

It may perhaps not be too adventurous therefore to suggest a pattern with three important production centers: the alluvial

plain of southern Mesopotamia, Syria, and Anatolia; and with a number of commercially specialised interstitial societies – with Assur as the best known example.

If this is an adequate description of the Near Eastern core area, what are we to do with the 'periphery'? Should we simply assume that the borders which have been outlined here are a function of the textual documentation, determined by the spread of literacy and perhaps the chance of discovery? Would this mean that we should posit the existence of a continuing series of sociopolitical structures similar to the ones found in the 'core area', so that there is no real center–periphery contrast, but rather an everexpanding horizon of centers in constant interaction with each other?

To my mind such a uniform landscape is as improbable as the idea of a Mesopotamian center 'generating' peripheral, dependent societies in Iran or Afghanistan by the creation of specialised economies which became dependent on the import of foodstuffs from the Mesopotamian granary (Kohl 1978, 1979).

If we look briefly at two of the areas which were drawn into the commercial system described here, the Zagros and Anatolia, we shall see how difficult it is to reach simple solutions which can be claimed to have a general relevance.

The Zagros seems best understood as a peripheral region, at one and the same time a barrier and a funnel, both blocking off the Iranian plateau and areas beyond from the Mesopotamian plain and providing linking lines of contact through a few passes. The ebb and flow of state formation, settlement patterns and population density in the Zagros valleys is surely to be seen to a very large extent as a function of the contacts that are channeled through the mountains. It cannot simply be understood or adequately described in terms of events or developments in the Zagros itself; it is in a decisive way connected with the relations between lowlands and highlands, west and east. Developments both in the north of the Zagros in the valleys around the ancient Shusharra (Eidem 1983, Laesse 1959) and in the south around Elam and the other states in that region (Stolper 1982) have been linked in a clear way with Mesopotamian events and pressures. The Shemshara material seems to show a phase of centralisation and precarious state formation, which should perhaps be linked with the tin trade. Our lack of precise knowledge of the Iranian side during the second millennium prevents us from even speculating about similar pressures from the east. We have to remind ourselves constantly that there just is no way in which we can at the moment offer a satisfactory description of the mechanics of and background for the traffic in tin which went all the way from Afghanistan to Mesopotamia. Nor do we have any clear evidence concerning the precise nature and scope of the involvement of Indus-culture groups in this and other commercial links with the west (Lamberg-Karlovsky 1972).

The Old Assyrian commercial penetration of Anatolia represents obviously a vitally important phase in the history of the region, even though it is impossible to say anything certain about the precise effects of this activity. The burning down of the 'harbour' at Kanesh at one point may even be directly linked to the struggles which eventually led to the creation of a large territorial state under Hittite leadership. The Anatolian political system reflected in the Old Assyrian documents was one of small kingdoms, often in conflict with each other but also having some degree of collaboration in their dealings with the foreign traders. In what ways did the Assyrian presence, the introduction of writing, of new systems of social and political organisation, and of intense economic activity – which surely must have touched some Anatolians deeply – in what ways did this contribute to the political process which resulted in the creation of the Old Hittite empire? I have no answer to this question. What was the effect on the Anatolian societies in terms of stratification, elite and status markings, ideological or perhaps religious concepts?

In fact, were it not for the strange fact that the Old Assyrian traders at Kanesh in central Anatolia left their archives in the ruins of the burnt-down houses in their 'harbour', we would probably be completely ignorant of the elaborate commercial system which was developed there. The trade was of very large proportions, as we can see from the texts, but it left practically no archaeologically traceable remains. The houses in which the Assyrians lived were of local type, as was the pottery found in them; and the main elements in their imports, tin and textiles, are not available. This is understandable for the textiles, but it is surely rather strange that not even metallurgical analyses have given clear signs of an increase in the use of tin bronzes in the region at this time (Eaton and McKerrell 1976, McKerrell 1977). Maybe analyses of more material, with a stricter and more limited temporal and geographical horizon would give us more information, but postulating the Old Assyrian commercial system on that basis would surely be deemed somewhat risky.

The trade in textiles is of special relevance for an understanding of the connections between the Assyrians and the Anatolian states. That the textile trade was of supreme importance will hardly come as a surprise for anyone who is at home in medieval or early modern European economic history. The Italian and the Flemish cities built their wealth on trade in cloth, and the Levant Company – to take a more recent example – exported English broadcloth to Aleppo and exchanged it there for silk. Cipolla (1976:59) notes that 'as late as the end of the sixteenth century, cloth accounted for about 80 per cent of the total exports of England while textile materials, groceries, timber, and wine were the four main categories on the import side'. [7] Statistics are of course not available for Mesopotamia, but these figures would surely be close to the actual situation there some 3,500 years earlier.

Jane Schneider (1977) has pointed out – in a critique of Wallerstein's thesis – that the trade in precious goods, the exchange of precious metals or stones for finished products, first of all textiles, has been a characteristic feature of expanding empires and core areas since Antiquity. The evidence adduced here certainly supports such a view and shows the importance of textile production for the urbanised, densely populated states.

The Old Assyrian evidence throws light on some of the important features of such an exchange, and of special relevance is an incident reported in a letter: we are told that some enterprising Assyrians had begun trading within Anatolia in locally pro-

duced woolen cloth which could serve as an imitation of the most common Assyrian import; an Anatolian production of one of the basic import commodities was obviously feasible, and it demands little imagination to understand that it would constitute a real threat to Assyrian interests since it must have been considerably cheaper. However, this traffic was apparently stopped abruptly by the bosses and the city assembly in Assur who issued strong warnings and fined very heavily the traders who were proven to have taken part in the scheme (Veenhof 1972:126–8).

This leads back to the problem briefly raised earlier: how was it possible to send woolen cloth all the way from southern Mesopotamia to central Anatolia, in fact to the Black Sea coast, when such textiles could in principle be produced anywhere in the region? The incident referred to indicates clearly that part of the answer lies in the commercial expertise developed by certain groups such as the traders from Assur, who had built up an elaborate network of contacts which covered northern Syria and Anatolia. Quite obviously, they were not only able to control the truly long-distance trade linking Assur with Kanesh, but they also had a firm grip on the commercial contacts linking the various small states, to such an extent that they could protect their own wares from unwanted local competition. Or did this encourage local initiative to exploit trade in the Anatolian fabrics which the Assyrian traders had to leave alone?

However, this can only be part of an explanation. It is essential to keep in mind that most of the trade served what we would call luxury needs or demands, and this again is due in part to the demand structure in the social systems and in part to the technological constraints on transportation. Thus, import goods in these systems were clearly meant to satisfy the demands of an elite, demands for luxury items which marked rank and status. Think of the many kilos of lapis lazuli found in princely graves at Ur and other places in Mesopotamia, stone which had been transported all the way from the mountains of Afghanistan (Herrmann 1968). The Mesopotamian textiles, no doubt elaborate and extremely beautiful, must have played a similar role not only in Anatolia, but in all regions to which they were imported.

The commercial pattern in the Middle Bronze Age exhibits a combination of utilitarian goods and luxury products, and I am not arguing for the priority of one of these groups. Nor do I propose to enter a discussion of the proper definition of these categories. Rather, the evidence discussed indicates the futility of a sharp distinction in terms of systemic importance.

The commercial system delineated here was obviously constituted by a multitude of diverse and quite different single units. In huge regions like Iran and Afghanistan, which appear to have been closely involved in the commercial exchange, writing was not used, a fact which must have had repercussions for the way in which the transport and exchange could be arranged. And the Anatolian scene shows us the meeting of intensely different social, cultural and political traditions. While the society of Assur with its commercial establishments abroad appears to reflect in its institutions and balance of power the importance of the private families who dominated the commercial and economic life, the Anatolian kingdoms appear to be highly centralised, palace-oriented societies with scores of royal officials keeping control over the economy. The differences appear to concern even such features as family structure and the position of women, but in spite of this we find all kinds of interaction across the various boundaries, even numerous marriages between Assyrian men and local Anatolian women.

Assur is equally different in a number of respects from the typical southern Mesopotamian society – although, as pointed out, we must assume that there were other city-states which can be compared to Assur. The large palace-run production facilities of the south have no parallel in Assur, where the royal palace is not mentioned ever as an economically important institution (Larsen 1972, 1976).

It seems reasonable to explain this special Old Assyrian society in the light of the functions it fulfilled in the wider commercial system. The trade run by family firms must have had the same or at least similar effects to those which can be observed in for instance the Italian cities which built their wealth on foreign trade, and the emergence of a kind of merchant aristocracy is reflected in the creation of political and juridical institutions through which the power and aspirations of the families could be channeled.

The wider systemic patterns which could encompass the periphery are certainly beyond my reach. It seems important to begin with a better understanding of the interplay within the core area of the Near East between constraints of an ecological and geographical nature and the specificities of political, social and cultural traditions.

Notes

1. The primary source for the information contained in Fig. 5.1 is still Leemans 1960 with additions in 1968; see also Klengel 1979 for a general overview with much discussion of detail, Crawford 1973 for a discussion of some questions of Mesopotamian exports, Veenhof 1972 and Larsen 1976 for the Old Assyrian trade, and Malamat 1971 and Finet 1977 for more specific details.
2. See Adams 1974, Gledhill and Larsen 1982, and Yoffee 1981 for some statements on this question; cf. also several articles in Lipinski 1979.
3. I prefer this interpretation to the idea expressed previously, that the copper came from Ergani Maden in southeastern Turkey (Larsen 1976:91).
4. Such textiles are described as being 'royal'; this designation is also used about textiles sent to Anatolia, cf. Veenhof 1972:192–3, with reference to 'Akkadian textiles of extremely fine quality, royal clothing'.
5. See Burke 1964 for details of the transit trade and taxes levied at Mari on ships from Syria bound for Mesopotamian towns; cf. Klengel 1979; for wine see Finet 1977.
6. Pettinato 1979 gives references to documents from Ebla which involve thousands of textiles in single transactions. A complete volume of administrative texts dealing with textiles has been published by Biga and Milano 1984.
7. A few figures will indicate the scale of the textile trade: around 1550 England exported from London annually *c.* 133,000 'short cloths' (Cipolla 1976:259); Florence produced 70–80,000 pieces of cloth per year before the Black Death (Lopez, Miskimin and Udovitch 1970:112); and Venice had an export of some 25,000 pieces annually in the sixteenth century (Lane 1973:309).

Chapter 6

Aspects of ceremonial exchange in the Near East during the late second millennium BC

Carlo Zaccagnini

1. Introduction

The topic of ceremonial exchange in the Near East of the second millennium BC has been one of my main interests in the past ten years: the main results of my investigations were published as two essays on gift exchange, in the late Bronze Age[1] (Zaccagnini 1973) and in the Old Babylonian period (Zaccagnini 1983a). The treatment of the issue of gift-giving, in its manifold aspects (modes of exchange, economic and political functions, ideological implications, etc.) inevitably led me to take into account a series of related matters, such as the general framework of the circulation of goods (Zaccagnini 1976), the organizational aspects of trade (Zaccagnini 1977), the salient features of transfers of movable property (Zaccagnini 1979a and Maidman 1980), and the patterns of spatial mobility of qualified manpower (Zaccagnini 1983b).

One of the main concerns was to elaborate and make use of an adequate heuristic model that could provide useful tools for appropriate socio-economic enquiries and allow us to overcome the well-known tenuity of historical investigations devoted to ancient Near Eastern economies. It seemed to me that an obligatory starting point for any research on gift (also in relation with trade) in the ancient Near East ought to be the epoch-making *Essai sur le don* of M. Mauss, and that the subsequent theoretical elaborations of K. Polanyi and his successors (the so-called substantivists in the field of economic anthropology and sociology) could be considered as useful methodological guidelines for the interpretation of Western Asiatic sources. The long discussions that took place with M. Liverani[2] and other younger scholars of the University of Rome concentrated upon the feasibility of resorting to methodologies traditionally alien to our specific field of research, which was characterized by a massive presence of philological know-how and by a very poor standard of historical tooling. It was thus no surprise that the reactions to our methodological concern, and to the issues deriving from it, were muted within the Assyriological world and the most interesting and stimulating confrontations took place with scholars of different scientific formation and interests (e.g. anthropologists, historians and philologists of classical antiquity, etc.).

The aim of the present chapter is not to summarize the main results of these past researches, but to add further materials towards a discussion that ought to include the themes of trade and of 'fiscality' as segments of one and the same discourse. In other words, it should be clear that the practice of gift exchange in the Late Bronze Age does not exhaust the entire range of the circulation of goods *within* the various socio-economic organizations and *between* them. Leaving aside the fiscal systems that operated inside each state formation, as well as between 'great' kingdoms and tributary states, exchanges among foreign countries in the form of trade did take place and we have clear evidence for it, both as concerns of 'private' merchants and 'royal' traders that operated on behalf of the palace organizations.[3]

In section 3 I will discuss the topic of the ideological

superimpositions on – or better, interpretations of – the acts of exchange: these, as such, were neutral (i.e. non-connoted) 'performances', which could, however, be described and presented in terms of 'gift' and/or 'tribute' and/or acts of trade. This is not to deny the existence of a network of commercial relationships, carried out by merchants (*tamkāru*), according to well-established operative procedures, deeply rooted in Near Eastern economic traditions; i.e. the existence of trade as a *fact* and not simply as an ideological viewpoint. In short, it can be said that Amarna and Ramesside trade between courts were most often carried out *in the form of* exchanges of gifts (Liverani 1972a:297–9). In this respect, see the significant oscillations in the terminology of the sources, that often alternate/couple the terms *mār Šipri* 'ambassador, envoy' with *tamkāru* 'merchant' (Zaccagnini 1973: 127). With respect to trade activities run by private merchants outside the sphere of the palace, I surmise that resorting to gift procedures must have been fairly sporadic. On the other hand, a quantitative evaluation of the sphere of gifts vs. that of trade is impossible, also because no conclusive evidence is available for the latter, in terms of either quality or quantity of transacted goods.

2. Use value vs. exchange value of gift-items

In the course of the past few years, some Italian colleagues with whom I had the opportunity of discussing the topic of ceremonial exchanges in ancient societies raised the question whether one should leave the substantivist model or modify it in the light of the marxian formulations concerning commodities and money,[4] in particular with reference to the concepts of use value and exchange value. At the present time, it is my belief that, in spite of certain limitations, the substantivist model can still be profitably employed for analysing the phenomenon of gift exchange, bearing in mind that the model requires some adaptations (especially with respect to the theoretical elaboration of the commercial pattern of transaction, i.e. trade and market exchange). This does not imply an incompatibility of the above model with some marxian concepts concerning values and modes of evaluation of goods: while it would be extremely difficult to attempt a comprehensive interpretation of the phenomenon of gift exchange in the light of the marxian formulations, it seems nevertheless that some significant aspects of this practice can be better investigated and appreciated by employing certain marxian methodological guidelines.

The appurtenance of goods to two (or more) levels of appreciation and circulation is a well-known fact in 'primitive'/ 'simple' societies; the same phenomenon has also been singled out in Western Asiatic economies, although the operative implications in the various patterns of exchange are not so drastic as those that have been observed in various African and Pacific societies. In other words, the ancient Near Eastern circuits of exchange are not so rigidly patterned as to exclude the feasibility of 'conversions' (i.e. the exchange of luxury prestige goods with subsistence commodities): on the contrary, goods belonging to different levels participated in the same circuits of exchange in a fairly loose way (Zaccagnini 1973:170–9; Liverani 1979a:26–7).

The determination of the value of a gift-item proceeds from its use value but goes far beyond it, since it results from a combination of its exchange value (in strict commercial terms), viz. its rate of exchange with other standard commodities – silver in the first place – that were used for the determination of 'prices' with non-economic, i.e. symbolic, traditional, 'moral' connotations attached to the gift-item (Liverani 1979a:25–6 and Zaccagnini 1973:178). Indeed ancient oriental sources offer scarce evidence for the operation of non-commercial elements in the evaluation of goods. On the contrary, the stress is systematically laid on the exchange value of the gifts, in a more or less explicit way, sometimes from the donor's and quite frequently from the receiver's side (Liverani 1979a:27–30; Zaccagnini 1973:78–9, 117–23). In this connection, I may perhaps recall a couple of instances in which one can feel a somewhat different attitude towards the evaluation of the commodities that are sent or requested as gifts. For example, the request of a daughter of Zimri-lim to her mother: 'Send me something that may please me, and I will rejoice [over it]. Please, be not negligent toward me!'[5] – in this case, the stress is laid upon the family ties that link the two women. See also a passage of a broken letter sent by the king of Hatti to an unknown king (perhaps the king of Arzawa), where a complex matter of exchanges is dealt with: 'Concerning the gift of the king of Aḫḫiyawa, about which you wrote to me, I do not know how the situation is and whether his messenger has brought anything or not. Now then: I have taken a rhyton of silver and a rhyton of pure gold from the gift of the king of Egypt and I have sent them to you'.[6] As was pointed out by Liverani (1979a:25), this passage provides evidence for a dual circulation of prestige goods in opposite directions, closely resembling some well-known Melanesian mechanisms of transfers of gift-items. Aside from the dynamic aspects of these exchanges, it seems important to stress the extra-economic elements of appreciation of the exchange commodities, i.e. the possible 'story' of these vessels, that came as a gift from abroad and after a while were sent to another party, in a sort of chain of ceremonial transfers. The rhytons (*bibrû*) were appreciated not only because they were valuable articles, presumably of high artistic quality, but also because they had a role as standard gift-items, which circulated from one court to another.[7]

As I mentioned before, examples of this kind are sporadic in the Late Bronze Age documents. As a rule, the stress is laid on the exchange value of the goods: the way this factor is brought to attention varies according to the style and the dynamics of the partnership, the rank of the parties, etc. The topic of the commercial evaluation of gift-items has been dealt with at length and it seems unnecessary to go through the matter once again. Rather, I would like to pinpoint another aspect connected with the evaluation of gifts, viz. the constant tendency, expressed by the party who is waiting or asking for a gift, to minimize its exchange value and to underscore its use value. This mental attitude/rhetorical device is constant throughout the second millennium: in the following sections I will quote some examples.

As for the first point, I will not touch on the topic of the complaints over having received less or other than what was expected: for this, there is abundant evidence in the Middle

Bronze and Late Bronze Age sources. I shall instead focus upon another styleme, which can be roughly summarized as follows: 'What I am asking from you is nothing/is not much for you: you have got plenty of it, you are rich, [etc.]'. A couple of OB passages can be quoted here: 'In your eyes, let it [i.e. the request item] not seem too expensive';[8] 'The wish [for] which I wrote to my father is not even worth one *qa* of barley, but I will rejoice as if my father had given me one mina of silver'.[9] Good examples are provided by the Amarna letters: see, e.g., the recurrent expression about the great quantity of gold in Egypt ('abundant like dust') that are used in support for the request of that metal[10] and notice the interesting elaboration of this topos in El Amarna EA 16: 14–16: 'Gold in your country is [abundant like] dust: one [just] gathers it up. Why does it stick to your eyes? [i.e., why are you not giving it?]' (Zaccagnini 1973:66 and n. 22).

With respect to the second point, there is a wide range of variants in underlining the functional requisites of the awaited gift; in this case, the basic motive that generates the various expressions is this: 'The gift is not requested because of its exchange value [i.e. with a view to an accumulation of wealth or a reutilization in a commercial circuit], but primarily because it is needed.' The functional link between a gift-item and its utilization was presented in a more or less plausible way: in fact the stress which is laid upon the value of use of the goods reveals an important aspect of the ideology of gift-giving and represents a significant rhetorical device that was currently employed in the requests (Zaccagnini 1973:61–9; 1983a:§8.2).

The OB letters offer very good evidence for expressions concerning primary needs that *must* be satisfied: the personal state of distress suffered by people who claim to be starving, thirsty, to have no clothes and to be cold, etc., is often greatly emphasized, with vivid and at times grotesque effects (Zaccagnini 1983a, §8.2.1). I will simply quote one passage, the literary character of which is immediately apparent: 'With respect to [the fact] that among my brothers I am [the only one who is] not provided with food, my partners got hold of 2 *qa* of flour and 2 *qa* of drink, and you have [also] given them meat [and] fish for nourishment. What have you given me?. . . [Through not] eating and drinking I have become weak: moreover, I have no clothes to wear. I had asked for a garment from you, but you had no mercy on me. I shed my tears and my weeping upon you. Since I have none in whom I can trust, I am dead forever. I am mistreated. . . For 25 days [I do not know any more] how a garment is made. . . I am hungry and I am cold'.[11] Clearly enough, these requests only apply to subsistence goods, whose value of use was easily appreciated: the nature and the formal aspect of these demands is an elaborate begging for alms.

In other instances, in which the requested item was of more 'personal' character or more precious (e.g. gold), the stress on the value of use was less generic. Instead of mere need, we meet specific functional justifications, that are put forth in various degrees of plausibility, in a more or less skilful way. Typical is the case of gold, which was requested by the Asiatic rulers from the XVIII Dynasty pharaohs: in many a case the party who is asking for gold tries to justify his requests by stating that the precious metal

is needed for achieving a specific work, which of course implies that gold was not wanted exclusively because of its preciousness, but because of its value of use (Zaccagnini 1973:69). Gold (immediately after women) was the most appreciated item in non-commercial transactions: the statement that it was needed for casting an object or for making a work – interestingly enough, it was very seldom specified what sort of work had to be achieved – obviously aimed at giving the impression that a simple storage of wealth was not pursued.

The case of gold is indeed typical and illustrates at best the distortion in moving from exchange value to use value, which was employed in gift-transactions by parties who were well aware of the negative aspects attached to asking (Zaccagnini 1983a: §8.1). Maybe the clearest example of this shift is provided by a famous passage of a letter to Amenophis III from the king of Babylon, who is asking for an Egyptian princess to be sent to him as a wife: 'Since you, my brother, not permitting your daughter to marry, wrote to me saying: "From ancient times a daughter of the king of Egypt has not been given to anyone", [I say]: Why do you speak thus? You are a king and you can do as it pleases you. If you give, who shall say anything?. . . There are grown-up daughters and beautiful women. Send me a beautiful woman, as if she were your daughter: who is to say: "This woman in not the daughter of the king!"?'[12] Women belonged to the highest level of exchangeable goods in ceremonial circuits (Liverani 1979a:31–3): the 'exchange value of an Egyptian princess was extremely high indeed, also because, to all appearance, it was extremely difficult, if not impossible, to get one of them as wife' (Zaccagnini 1973, 17). The sharp refusal of Amenophis originates from a disparity of opinion between him and the Asiatic kings in their respective evaluations of Egyptian princesses (and women in general) as possible gift-items.[13] The arguments of Kadašman–Enlil are differently shaped: he would desire an Egyptian princess (i.e. a highly appreciated commodity), but would be satisfied also with an Egyptian beauty – whatever her status – that could in any case meet with the requirements normally expected in Asia from an Egyptian princess.[14] In other words, what is here called for, is not a commodity of a given exchange value, but a commodity (or a substitute for it) *which is needed tout court.*

A somewhat different case is that of specialized palace personnel, who were sent from one court to another, during the Amarna and especially the Ramesside period: in most cases these movements concern physicians and conjurers who were sent from Egypt and Babylon to Hatti. The dynamics and the forms according to which these displacements were effected closely resemble those of gift exchange: from the viewpoint of their evaluation, foreign specialists were of course appreciated because of their professional capabilities (use value) but also because they were considered a precious (and exotic) item, in a way similar to the foreign princesses who were sent in marriage. In other words, the exchange value of this highly specialized personnel was taken into the deepest consideration. The functional basis for the requests for specialists was at times expressly stated: for example, Ḫattušili III asking for a sculptor from Babylonia states: 'I wish to make some statues to put them in my family house'.[15] The same

Ḫattušili asked Ramses to dispatch him a physician, in order to prepare medicaments for his sister, so as to let her bear a baby (Edel 1976). See also an Amarna letter from the king of Cyprus, where the request for a conjurer[16] is preceded by the announcement that a plague was raging in the island, killing everybody and that one of the king's sons had died.[17]

The stress laid on the *need* to receive a specialized professional is often coupled with the assurance that he will not be detained abroad: at times very intricate arguments on this subject take place among the Great Kings of the Ramesside period (Zaccagnini 1983b: §4.7). Both parties aim at making one point clear: the specialist is not a precious commodity that was transferred to become part of the wealth of a foreign court (like silver, gold, women, etc.), but was a (valuable) item which was requested out of necessity: when the necessity was over, the specialist should be sent back home. However, as in the case of gifts, there is clear evidence that the exchange value of these people – all of them were officials of the Late Bronze Age palace organizations – was an important factor in the dynamics of these ceremonial interactions. A couple of examples can be quoted here: in EA 19, the king of Ugarit requests the Pharaoh, his overlord, to send him two black servants and a physician: in spite of the fact that Niqmadu claims (a) that there are no physicians at his court (which seems extremely improbable), and (b) that he has been ill and is on the way to recovery (i.e. stress is laid on the functional need for a doctor), there seems to be little doubt that the request for a physician stands on the same level as that for two dark-skinned Nubian servants, i.e. foreign people to be shown at court as interesting rarities. Ḫattušili's request for an Egyptian physician to heal his sister is also illuminating: Ramses' reply – that the woman is 50 to 60 years old and no physician can possibly help her to bear a child – aims at demonstrating that the alleged *need* for a doctor has no basis: thus Ḫattušili's demand is politely but firmly rejected.

3. Ideologies of exchange

The identification of the ideological structures that operate in the representation of the acts of exchange gives us the opportunity to attempt an historical evaluation of the international relations during the Late Bronze Age, which may go past the 'evenemential' aspects *reflected* in the sources. Of course, this is not to say that facts are irrelevant, but simply that facts were patterned according to definite rhetorical procedures, stemming from definite ideological settings, and depending on the genre of the texts (e.g. letters and treaties vs. 'historical' narrations in the form of celebrative royal inscriptions). I will concentrate now on the ideological factor.

The theoretical model that interprets the acts of exchange in terms of interaction among partners of equal rank is emblematically expressed through the ideal of brotherhood and consequent mutual love: this takes place when the parties are in communication with one another (e.g. in letters and treaties). On the other hand, when one party speaks for the benefit of another audience (e.g. when the addressee of the message is not the counter-party, but the receiver of inner political propaganda),

foreign interactions are interpreted in total contrast with enemy countries, hostile monarchs, who are fought against, brought to submission, obliged to pay tribute, etc. (See Liverani 1979c, 1973b; and Zaccagnini 1973:133–4).

I totally share the views expressed by Liverani (1979c), who has convincingly demonstrated (a) the ambiguity of the acts of exchange that are recorded in ancient Near Eastern documents – that these acts are in any case very difficult, if not impossible, for us to grasp, in their factual historicity; (b) the operation of different ideologies, with specific narrative codes, in recording the same acts of exchange. The latter, whatever the genre of the texts (commercial accounts and letters, diplomatic letters, celebrative inscriptions, iconic representations, etc.) are practically lost to us: our unique basis of information and object of inquiry consists in the records of these acts: consequently, our main task is to decode the message of the texts and to grasp the ideological apparatus underlying them.[18]

The interaction between monarchs of the Late Bronze Age are thus differently shaped, according to the ideological model that has been adopted for the interpretation of the acts of exchange. Once again, I would like to stress the contemporary operationality of the 'reciprocative' and 'redistributive' modes of transaction: to them must be added the 'commercial' model.[19] Liverani has ingeniously illustrated three examples of intermingling and interference of the various levels of presentation of the same event (or of similar events): the Amarna correspondence vs. Egyptian celebrative inscriptions (i.e. reciprocity vs. redistribution) (see also Zaccagnini 1973:133–4), the story of Wenamun (i.e. commercial bargaining reported in a narrative that is strongly ideologically connoted, mainly in a redistributive sense), the report (texts and reliefs) of Hatšepsut's expedition to Punt (i.e. iconic representation of a trade venture, coupled with epigraphic records consistently Egyptocentric, in their ideological apparatus) (Liverani 1979c:19–26).

In this connection, I would like to call attention again to the sources pertaining to the Amarna exchanges: not only the contemporary use of the reciprocative and the redistributive models, but also the operationality of the commercial mode of transaction is clearly attested. The first point need not be discussed again; as for the latter point, I have already treated the interrelations between the ceremonial and the mercantile levels of interaction (Zaccagnini 1973:117–124). Some distinctive features of the 'lower' level of exchanges, that patently emerge in contexts of formalized ceremonial exchange, have been pointed out; e.g. explicit evaluation of gift-items, including the use of silver and the mention of 'prices', iteration of requests, scarcity of politeness formulae, non-inclusion of the dynamics of the exchanges in the framework of ceremonial reciprocity (brotherhood, love, generosity, etc.), and so on.

In addition to this, it should be noticed that another important piece of documentary evidence for the commercial level of interaction is provided by the Amarna corpus, namely the inventories of goods that are sent as *gift-items* from or to Egypt: EA 13 (presents from Babylonia), EA 14 (presents to Babylonia), EA 22 and 25 (presents from Mitanni). No doubt the reasons why these inventories were compiled were of a practical order: the giver sent them along with the goods recorded therein, so that the receiver might check the integrity of the shipment upon the arrival of the caravan; in the second place, records of important dispatches of gifts, as in the case of bridal gifts and dowries in international marriages, were compiled and kept in the palace archives for the sake of book-keeping, should these goods become the object of litigation or restitution (e.g. dowries, in case of divorce); on a more general level, one could invoke the presence of these records in the archives of the receiver of the gifts to remind him of *past* shipments, in the course of *present* negotiations.[20]

Notice, however, that the items listed in these inventories are accurately described and precious materials like gold and silver are carefully reckoned in minas, shekels and fractions of shekels. It has been pointed out (Zaccagnini 1973:81) that the way these gifts are described aims at providing the receiver with all necessary elements for a commercial evaluation of them, without resorting to the use of silver, i.e. the most common means of evaluation of goods at that time. In spite of this, there is hardly any doubt that the 'message' conveyed to the receiver by means of these texts is the following one: 'What I am sending you as dotal gifts (or the like) consists of A, B, C..., which is worth x, y, z, ...' The commercial character of the substance and form of EA 13, 14, 22 and 25 is thus patent. The significance of this datum can be fully appreciated in consideration of the fact that these same conveyances are *contemporarily* qualified '(forced) contributions' (*inw*) that are due to Egypt[21] in Egyptian celebrative royal inscriptions, and 'gifts' (*šulmānu*) in international correspondence (letters).

The easiest way to combine the presence of these inventories of gifts with the data provided by royal inscriptions and letters – all referring to the same event – would be to consider the 'event' – i.e. the transfer of a certain amount of commodities from one court to another – as neutrally, i.e. factually *reported*, in the lists, and differently *interpreted* in the other texts, according to the peculiarities of their respective ideological framework. In other words:

factual level		transfer of commodities	inventories
ideological interpretation	redistributive key:	'(forced) contributions' (*inw*)	royal inscriptions
	reciprocative key:	'(greeting-) gifts' (*šulmānu*)	letters

This interpretation could find reasonable support in some passages of the Amarna letters, where lists of gifts are hinted at, in order to focus the partner's attention onto the *fact* of certain dispatches of goods, to which the lists themselves would bear unquestionable witness.[22]

However, I believe that such an interpretation is not wholly satisfactory, inasmuch as it fails to take into account the *connotative aspects* (= the ideology) of the inventory lists[23] and takes for granted that the data recorded therein represents the neutral (i.e. non-connotated) *event*. On the contrary, *the very fact that these lists were compiled* (and were compiled in the way we have seen)

makes it clear that the commercial pattern of interaction was fully operative together with the reciprocative and the redistributive ones. The three of them stand on the same level and apply to the same 'performance' (a dowry, a *terḫatu*). The historical referent thus becomes ambiguous for us, since it functions as mere support for different representations of a given set of data; for us, all of these representations have the same degree of credibility and there is no reason whatsoever to privilege one vs. the others, in an impossible quest for historical objectivity.

4. Rhetorics of the reciprocative code

Once it is ascertained that the same historical episode (in our case, act(s) of exchange) was compatible with different ideological interpretations and consequently was differently presented, according to the audience to whom the episode would be related, it becomes perfectly clear that we should not be too much troubled about the reconstruction of an alleged historical truth free of the distortions operated by the records (e.g. 'gift' or 'tribute' or unqualified conveyance; exchanges between 'brothers' or deliverances from vanquished to victorious parties or neutral acts of trade; etc.). Rather, it is essential to concentrate our attention on the sources (the well-known *plaisir du texte*: R. Barthes) (Zaccagnini 1981:262), in order to attain a satisfactory level of understanding of their narrative codes and a sound comprehension of the ideology underlying the texts themselves.[24]

In this connection, it may be useful to offer some summarizing and concluding remarks on the ideology and the rhetorics of the reciprocative model. A first point necessarily concerns adoption on a vast scale of this transactional mode in international contacts during the second half of the second millennium BC. There is no other period in three thousand years of ancient Near Eastern history in which the ideology of 'brotherhood' among parties – who recognize each other as subjects of equal rank and interact on the same factual and formal level – is so coherently and consistently employed. As I have tried to show in my essay on gift exchange in the OB period, every aspect of the dynamics and the formalities of ceremonial exchanges during the Late Bronze Age easily finds significant antecedents in the Middle Bronze Age sources. Yet, totally new and absolutely typical of the Amarna and Ramesside periods is the adoption of the reciprocative model as the pattern *par excellence* of the diplomatic interactions between Near Eastern political entities. Of course, along with the scheme of 'brotherhood', other schemes are employed in unbalanced relationships: 'lord' vs. 'servant'; 'father' vs. 'son' (Zaccagnini 1973:125–34, 149–70), but this simply confirms the compactness of the former scheme, to which the others are functionally related.

It is not immediately apparent why the pharaoh, the king of Mitanni, the king of Hatti, etc. should mutually call themselves 'brothers', who 'love' one another, send each other 'gifts', send each other *letters*, etc. It was not like this before, it would not be like this during the first millennium BC, in spite of the fact that military, political and 'commercial' interactions did and would take place between foreign states. On a first approximation, it may be suggested that the XV–XIII centuries BC were an epoch of unique confrontation and balance of great powers, some of them emerging, others in decline, but with no outstanding hegemonic formation. The dynamics of the military and political events that took place is too well-known to be recalled here; rather, it might be noticed that a series of confrontations, mainly in individual lines of interaction, took place; the presence of various inter-links among the main lines of communication brought about a solid network of far-reaching connections, which covered the entire Near Eastern area and the Levant. Hence the adoption of the model of 'brotherhood', which implies and demands good relations among parties, on a parity level.

On a further approximation, it would seem that an important aspect of the interactive model adopted in the Late Bronze Age is that of 'family' groups that correspond with one another, i.e. the various courts are viewed as (great) households that stand on the same socio-economic level and are in reciprocal contact for their mutual benefit. The addresses of the letters exchanged between the monarchs (i.e. the chiefs of the palace administrations) of this period perfectly summarize the components of these households: the king (= addressee of the letter), his house(s), country, wives, sons, chief officials, soldiers, horses and chariots: to all of them the greetings of the sender are dispatched. The sender, in his turn, informs the addressee of the well-being of his household. Thus a whole state formation is metaphorically represented as a family (micro-) structure and interactions between state formations are shaped and formalized according to the pattern of inter-family relations. There is one step forward in this process of 'privatization' of 'public' affairs, i.e. the various monarchs, in a way, act as members of *one* big family, that comprised all Great Kings who mutually recognized one another in their political status. The metaphor of the family is comprehensive and offers a global solution to the matter of international relations. Parity of rank, from the point of view of kinships ties, necessarily means 'brotherhood' (Zaccagnini 1973:108–17): thus the pharaoh, the king of Hatti, the king of Babylon, etc. are 'brothers' in every respect, as long as there is interaction among them.[25] Should no interaction take place, the concept of brotherhood is decidedly rejected: the best example is provided by a letter of Ḫattušili III to Shalmaneser I: the relevant passage runs as follows: 'You became Great King. But why do you still speak about brotherhood and about going [together] to the mount Amana? What is this brotherhood? Why should I write to you about brotherhood. Whoever writes to another about brotherhood: are they not friends those who write to each other about brotherhood? But why should I write to you about brotherhood? You and I, were we borne by one mother?!'[26] In this case, notwithstanding Ḫattušili's formal acknowledgement of the status of Great King achieved by Shalmaneser, the metaphor of brotherhood is not taken into consideration, because the idea of establishing a substantial partnership is not accepted: hence the uselessness of speaking about brotherhood: 'Since [my father] and my grandfather did not write to the king of Assur [about brotherhood], you too do not write to me [about brotherhood] and status of Great King! [I do not] want it!'[27] These passages hardly require any comment; I would rather like to point out an element of particular interest; in connection

with the use vs. non-use of the concept of brotherhood. It has been suggested[28] that KBo XVIII 24 is the first tablet of the letter KUB XXIII 102, two passages of which have now been quoted: the incipit of KBo XVIII 24 is: 'Thus says the Sun, Great [King]: to Shalmaneser [Great King, king] of Assur, *my brother*, say: . . .' I need not stress the significance of the discrepancy between the qualification 'my brother' in the opening formula of the letter – yet notice the absence of any greeting to the king of Assur – and the detailed argumentations against the feasibility of speaking about brotherhood between the two of them.[29] Thus the word in line 2 of KBo XVIII 24, to all appearance, is a most interesting lapsus, favoured by the standardized character of these addresses, a lapsus that shows up in the light of the subsequent words of the letter.

What is the *substance* of this incessantly invoked brotherhood? Late Bronze Age sources are clear: brotherhood means love, friendship, a favourable attitude towards the other party, and so on (Zaccagnini 1973:111–17, 1983a: §4.1.2.). Without this, the status of 'brothers' is reduced to a mere formality, which can at most mean that two kings are of equal rank, and is not at all productive of a true partnership. The metaphor of 'love' that binds two 'brothers' is consequential in its manifestations: satisfaction or dissatisfaction about the dynamics of the relationships are consistently expressed in terms of 'joy', 'pleasure' vs. 'sorrow', 'grief' (Zaccagnini 1973:114–16). The best examples of this passionate relationship are provided by the Mitannian letters of the Amarna archive: Tušratta's epistolary style is unique in its constant resorting to a phraseology that is typical of the family sphere and in which ample space is reserved to the rhetoric of sentiments. But the same attitude is current throughout the epistolographic material of the Late Bronze Age.

The *issues* of being 'brothers' that 'love each other' consists in keeping in mutual touch, in exchanging letters and presents. Later on I will come back to the topic of the necessity of being in touch; I will now briefly deal with the matter of sending gifts. Some passages of the Amarna letters explicitly state the necessary link between a good relationship and the sending of gifts: the most incisive formulation is to be found in a letter sent from Babylonia: '[Between] kings there is brotherhood, friendship, alliance and [good] relations [if] there is abundance of precious stones, abundance of silver, abundance of [gold]'.[30] In another letter sent from Babylonia, a similar statement is inserted in a very interesting argumentation: 'As they say, in my brother's land there is everything and my brother needs nothing: in my land too there is everything and I need nothing. However, we received from the hands of the kings (our predecessors) a good relationship from a long time ago and we send greeting gifts (lit.: greetings) to one another. May this relationship endure between us':[31] in other words, there is no 'economic' need for sending each other goods,[32] because Egypt and Babylonia were (or boasted to be) totally self-sufficient; in spite of this, a long-standing relationship had been established, and this could only mean that gifts were exchanged. Compare another letter from Babylonia: 'Since my fathers and your fathers established friendly relations with one another, they sent nice presents to one another and did not refuse to one another any requests for good things'.[33] A very close association between the establishments of good brotherly(/sisterly) relations and (regular) dispatches of gifts is also attested in some Ramesside letters subsequent to the peace-treaty between Hatti and Egypt: Ramses' wife Naptera to Ḫattušili's wife Puduḫepa (KBo I 29 + KBo IX 43), Ramses' son Šuḫatapšap to Ḫattušili (KUB III 70) and Ramses' mother Tuya to Ḫattušili (KUB XXXIV 2; cf.Tuya's fragmentary letter to Puduḫepa: 426/w) expresses in a very similar way the same concern about being close and loving friends and sending each other gifts (Zaccagnini 1973:40–3; Edel 1974).

The *ultimate meaning* of these relations consists in keeping in constant touch, in being recognized as partners of equal rank and socio-political status, who send, accept and reciprocate gifts: kings who participate in the ceremonial circuits of exchanges are members by full right of the Late Bronze Age court society, and vice versa. The *conditio sine qua non* in order to play an official – not necessarily a factual – role in this highly formalized scene is to accept the rules of the game: those who do not intend to act or are prevented from acting as 'brothers', 'lovers', etc. are automatically cut off. Of course this does not mean that they are formally out of the scene where a well-known play takes place. The Amarna letters from the king of Cyprus to the pharaoh – taken as a whole – illustrate at best a clumsy yet highly original attempt to conciliate the factual *and*[34] commercial with the ceremonial levels of interaction. The poor standard of their formal features helps a lot in singling out many basic components of the 'upper' level, which – in this case – is only partially integrated in the 'lower' one.

The above quoted passage EA 7:33–9 provides a good example of the attitude towards keeping up mutual contacts for the sake of the contacts themselves and not because there is any material need from both sides. Obviously the historical relevance of statements like those in EA 7 is purely ideological and is totally unrelated to their degree of factual likelihood. I have already commented on the semantic range of the world *šulmānu* 'greeting gifts', which is tightly associated with *sulmu* 'greetings' in the Akkadian terminology of the Late Bronze Age (Zaccagnini 1973: 202–3. cf. Kestemont 1976:164); the interchange in the use of the two terms is at times noteworthy: people who wish to 'listen' (*šemû*) to the *šulmānu* of the other party[35] and people who 'send' (*šapāru*) the *šulmu* to each other.[36] The urge to be in constant touch (i.e. to send greetings, to exchange gifts) has good OB parallels (Zaccagnini 1983: §4.2.2.) and can be considered the epitome of the reciprocative ideology applied to the ceremonial sphere of exchanges. The structural reasons of such an urge are traceable under the formal cover of diplomatic politeness: one of the main differences in the dynamics of the commercial vs. ceremonial pattern of exchange is the contextuality versus scalarity themes in counter-performances. This means that, in the latter case, each move is at the same time the reply to a former counter-move and the presupposition/stimulus for a subsequent counter-move: clearly enough, the game must have no interruptions – hence the frequent pleas for a regular and constant flow of envoys carrying messages (and gifts). The frequent mentions of past relations between (fore)fathers of the present partners, or between one party and the father of the other one, always aim at ensuring a similar continuity now and forever – the examples provided by the Amarna corpus are extremely abundant (Zaccagnini 1973: 139–47).

The ideological and operative implications of the reciprocative model are not limited to the sphere of the various individual relationships, but stretch over the general network of international connections. It is totally inherent to the topic of the gift that the partnerships be limited to contacts between two parties, with no interferences from third ones. Utopian as this may sound, there is hardly any doubt that it was felt intolerable that A exchanged gifts with B and at the same time with C, who, in his turn, was not (or claimed not to be) in friendly relations with A. Thus the king of Babylon to the pharaoh 'Now [as for] the Assyrians, my subjects, I did not send them to you: why did they come to your country on their own? If you want to be my friend, let them make no business. Send them back empty-handed!' Notice the derogative qualification of the exchanges between Egypt and Assyria, that are qualified as 'purchases, business (*šīmāti*)'; in Burnaburiaš' opinion it is not conceivable that Egypt and Assyria – the latter defined as 'vassal, subject' of Babylonia – might exchange gifts, since the pharaoh already exchanges gifts with Babylonia: the two lines of exchanges are incompatible.[37] Similarly Ḫattušili III to Kadašman-Enlil II: 'The question of the messenger [of the king of Egypt . . . The king of] Egypt [received] your [gifts and you] have received [his gifts]. Now, [you are grown up: if you] send [a messenger to the king of Egypt], should I prevent you [from doing this]?'[38] In the correspondence between Cyprus and Egypt, the style of which is an almost unique mixture of the ceremonial and commercial codes, the very same concept is differently formulated: 'Do not compare me with the king of Hatti or the king of Babylon: as for me, whatever gift my brother has sent [to me], I have returned to you twice as much.'[39] I need not point out the significant interference of the two levels of interaction: the king of Cyprus speaks of 'gifts' (*šulmānu*) and at the same time underlines the economic advantages of exchanging with him rather than with other Asiatic kings. Whatever the style, the theoretical principle that should inspire these international relations is the same in the three passages that have been quoted above.

Summing up, it can be said that the outstanding character of the phenomenon of gift-giving consists in its 'personal' aspect (Zaccagnini 1973, 189–193): the theoretical framework in which ceremonial exchanges are inserted is thoroughly consistent with the idea of pertinence and exclusiveness of the gift. As for the former point, there is no need to stress that gifts differ from merchandise in that they are not neutral items of exchange but, as a rule, are directly related to the person to whom they are given. The latter point is more delicate. If we recall the Maussian definition of the gift as a 'total social phenomenon', we may perhaps understand why the involvement of the actors who participate in the game is so deep: the rhetoric of ceremonial exchanges forms a rigid and coherent structure, in which the moral and social connotations attached to the acts of exchange are – at least in principle – predominant over the economic aspects. I have already pointed out that one and the same historical event (in our case, one or a series of acts of exchange) could undergo various interpretations. In the light of this, it is interesting to underline significant differences which are implied in the exchanges. The redistributive representations (i.e. 'tributes') are based on the principle that a plurality of givers pay their (forced) homages to a higher authority: it is essential that tributes be abundant and, above all, of various provenances. Thus the accounts of single conveyances from one country to another are often coupled by summarized and cumulative representations of many tributes, all standing on the same level.

In principle, the commercial pattern of exchange is neutral with respect to the number of participants who perform acts of trade: the only limit is of course that of the maximization of the economic profit, which might lead one party to try and exclude or reduce the activity of others (competition in trade is not a novelty). This is not the place to deal with the themes of long-distance trade (e.g. segmentations of long chains of exchanges) or of the technical modalities through which partnerships were organized with a view to business profits. Suffice it to recall that the *low* level of ideological connotation of commercial acts of exchange include a basic indifference towards the number and the personality of the subjects that participate in it.

On the contrary, the sociology of ceremonial gift exchange, with its far-reaching moral and 'public' implications, is much more complex: the quintessence of the attitude displayed by the Asiatic kings – there is no comparable evidence for the kings of Egypt – is that it is not admissible to exchange gifts with an actual or potential enemy/rival of one's own partner. To exchange gifts means to be on friendly terms with someone, to be his 'brother', to 'love' him: thus it is not possible to be 'brother', 'lover', etc. with A and with the enemy, the competitor, or whatever of A. To this effect, the metaphor of the Late Bronze Age gift practice is extremely consequential, with respect to thorough personal engagement of the participants in this sort of rite.[40] The Amarna and Ramesside sources offer consistent evidence for the pattern of restricted exchanges (A→B, B→A), with which we have been dealing so far. With respect to the pattern of extended exchanges, a possible hint of a wider circulation of gift-items, which follow certain itineraries in opposite directions, is possibly provided by a letter from Ḫattušili III to the king of Arzawa (?), already commented upon.[41] The scheme $A \underset{\rightleftarrows C}{\overset{\nearrow B}{}}$, with B and C in a situation of mutual incompatibility, would be considered unacceptable either by B or C. On the other hand, it is not admissible that a 'gift' might be confused with a 'tribute': the complaints of the king of Babylon made because the pharaoh displayed the Babylonian chariots (that had been sent as a 'gift') together with the chariots of the Egyptian vassals (that had been collected as Syro-Palestinian 'tributes') – upon the occasion of a ceremonial parade in Egypt – demonstrate the deep difference between the two codes of representation and their respective ideologies.[42]

In conclusion, if the interpretation of the acts of exchange took place according to the code of ceremonial gift-giving, the actors of the Late Bronze Age international scene played their roles[43] in a very clearly defined way; but the same thing happened whether the chosen code was the redistributive or the commercial one: I have commented on some cases of superimposition of two or three codes with reference to the same event. These occurrences demonstrate that the seeming incompatibility of the various registers of interpretation is not a *factual* one, inasmuch as it only concerns the *ideological* sphere of evaluation of the event itself. Modern historians of the ancient Near East have often been misled in their reconstructions by the uneven presence of documents related to the three levels and by the enduring dream of attaining the historical *truth* embedded and possibly disguised in the sources.

Notes

1 This chapter is part of the research program 'Models of production and exchange in the ancient Near Eastern civilizations', directed by me at the University of Bologna and financed by the Italian Ministry of Education. Professor M. T. Larsen has read the manuscript and offered valuable criticism and suggestions, for which I owe him my sincere thanks.

2 Shortly before the publication of my 1973 book, M. Liverani wrote his pioneering essay on the Amarna trade (Liverani 1972a), which has now been translated into English in Liverani 1979a: 21–33.

3 To quote only the example of Ugarit, see the *tamkāru ša mandatti* discussed by Liverani (1962: 83–5, and 1979b); for a different view see Heltzer 1978, especially 121–31. The activities of these merchants who acted as palace officials were the object of international agreements with the king of Hatti (cf. Liverani 1962: 82–3) and with the king of Karkemish (ibid. 112–15). On the other hand, people like the well-known Sinaranu were active in trade independently of the palace organisation (ibid. 85–6; Heltzer 1978: 132–5).

4 Especially *Capital*, Book 1, first section.

5 *Archives Royales de Mari* 43: 27–9.

6 *Keilschrifttexte aus Boghazköi* II: 11 rev. 11'–14'; cf. Zaccagnini 1973: 73.

7 See the interesting fragment of a letter from Hatti to Cyprus, *Keilschrifttexte aus Boghazköi* I 26, recently commented on by Knapp 1980, in which the king(?) of Alashiya is requested to send to Hatti precious commodities, including rhytons.

8 *Textes cuneiformes de Louvre* XVII 68: 10–11.

9 *Albabylonische Briefe* II 151: 20–5.

10 EA 16: 14; 19: 61; 20: 52, 55; 24: III 92–4; 26: 41–2; 27: 50, 106; 29: 146, 164.

11 *Altbabylonische Briefe* V 160: 5–8, rev. 2'–10', 14'–15', 17'.

12 EA 4: 4–13; cf. Zaccagnini 1973: 17; Liverani 1979a: 31; Pintore 1978: 57.

13 Franco Pintore maintained a thoroughly different view in his book; my arguments were presented in 1979b, but Franco's sad departure prevented us from going on with the debate which had only started.

14 I do not totally share the opinion expressed by Liverani 1979a: 31, n. 58.

15 See *Keilschrifttexte aus Boghazköi* I 10 and *Keilschrifturkunden aus Boghazköi* III 72 rev. 58–60; cf. also Canby 1976.

16 EA 35: 26

17 Ibid. 13–14, 37–9. The use of pestilence as a rhetorical device for carrying out a complex bargaining with the pharaoh has been pointed out by Liverani 1979a: 23–4 with n. 12, and by me in 1973, 74.

18 Cf. Zaccagnini 1983a: §7.1. For similar methodological concerns applied to another group of ancient Near Eastern documents – neo-Assyrian royal inscriptions – see my remarks in 1981: 259–262.

19 For a definition of the three modes, with respect to the use of the key-words 'gift', 'tribute' and 'commercial (commodity)', see Liverani 1979c: 11.

20 See e.g. EA 24 III 35–43, translated in Zaccagnini 1973: 29, n. 78, where Tušratta reminds Amenophis III of the dowries sent from Mitanni on the occasion of the marriages of his aunt with Thutmosis IV and of his sister Giluḫepa with the same Amenophis III.

21 The term *inw* has recently been discussed by Liverani (1979c: 13–14). He convincingly demonstrates that *inw* denotes 'contribution', but that it always bears strong political connotations, Egypto-centric in nature; these 'conveyances' are considered to be due to Egypt as a consequence of a state of inferiority of the giver, whether due to a military defeat or in homage to the fame of the pharaoh.

22 The best example is EA 24 III 35–43, mentioned above in note 20.

23 Cf. the observations by Liverani (1979c: 17–19) concerning the 'deformation' of the acts of exchange referred to in the administrative texts.

24 Clearly, two textual genres in particular have been subjected to analyses of this nature: royal inscriptions with a historical content, and letters. With respect to the first category see in general Liverani 1973b; for more specific studies see e.g. Liverani 1972b, 1973a, 1977, 1979d, Fales 1979, 1982, Zaccagnini 1981, 1982. For the 'historical' narrations of the Old Testament see Liverani 1974a, and on a more general (and radical) level 1979e and 1980. With respect to letters seen in addition to the works already mentioned the important contributions of Liverani centered on the Amarna corpus: 1971a (now translated into English in 1979a: 3–13), 1974b, 1983. For the neo-Assyrian period see e.g. Fales 1974.

25 For the antecedents of the terms 'brother', 'brotherhood' see Zaccagnini 1973: 116, and 1983a, § 4.1.1. A significant hyperbole of this concept can be found in a text from Ugarit: 'See, my brothers, I and you are brothers: sons of one man we are brothers ... We are one man.' PRU IV, 133 (RS 17.116): 21'–23', 28'; cf. 1973: 110 with n. 72 for similar occurrences.

26 *Keilschrifturkunden aus Boghazköi* XXIII 102 obv. I 5–16: cf. Zaccagnini 1973, 110–11 and 44 with n. 128 for bibliographical references.

27 Ibid., lines 17–20.

28 By H. Otten, *Archiv für Orientforschung* 22(1968–9): 112–13.

29 Notice that in lines 5–20 the term 'brotherhood' (ŠEŠ-*UT-TA*/ ŠEŠ-tar) occurs 8 times!

30 EA 11: rev. 22–3.

31 EA 7: 33–9.

32 Cf. Liverani's treatment of the topic of 'irrational' exchanges in the Amarna period in 1979a, especially 22–6, where he deals with the extreme case of exchange of identical products. For a comparable situation see *Keilschrifttexte aus Boghazköi* I 14 rev. 6'–10': 'It is *customary* that, when kings seize kingship, the (other) kings of the same rank send them nice presents: a royal dress and pure oil for the anointment.' Cf. Zaccagnini 1973: 33 with n. 86.

33 EA 9: 7–16.

34 I have already shown that mere acts of exchange are not necessarily and automatically acts of trade, liable to ideological *interpretations* in terms of reciprocity and/or redistribution.

35 E.g. EA 37: 8–10, 14–16: 17: 53–4; 19: 73–4; cf. Zaccagnini 1973: 202–3 with n. 65.

36 *šulma šapāru* obviously means 'to write/send greetings', but its semantic extension at times includes the meaning 'to send gifts', or at least alludes to it. The best example is provided by a passage of EA 7, where the king of Babylon after complaining to Amenophis IV for not having received his 'greetings' (lines 21, 23, 30: the verb is *šapāru*) states that both Egypt and Babylonia had everything and were in need of nothing; yet they accepted the old and welcome habit of 'sending greetings (*šulmu*)' to each other. There is hardly any doubt that what is really alluded to with *šulma šapāru* (38) is 'to send gifts'; cf. Zaccagnini 1973: 203.

37 EA 9: 31–5. M. T. Larsen suggests a complementary explanation for Burnaburiyaš' statement, viz. that in addition to the practice of gift exchanges there existed another level of interaction among foreign courts, namely exchanges conducted in a purely commercial way; hence the urgent appeal: 'They should not even be allowed to make purchases!' This interpretation is very convincing; cf. Zaccagnini 1973: 124 with n. 160. References to Assyrian 'merchants' operating abroad are in the treaty between Tudḫaliya IV and Šaušgamuwa of Amurru (Kühne and Otten 1971: 14–17; IV 14–18), and in the 'Poem of Tukulti-Ninurta' (Ebeling 1938: 18; II 4–9; cf. Zaccagnini 1973: 124 with n. 159.)

38 *Keilschrifttexte aus Boghazköi* I 10 and *Keilschrifturkunden aus Boghazköi* III 72 obv. 72–5.

39 EA 35: 49–53; cf. Vincentelli 1971.

40 The same incompatibility in situations where two Great Kings and one small king interact is perfectly illustrated in two passages from the Šuppiluliuma-Šunaššura treaty (Weidner 1923: 104; III 50–5, 60–3), for which see Zaccagnini 1973: 190–1. Kestemont (1976: 164) has objected that the term *šulmānu*, in this context, does not refer to a gift but has a precise juridical meaning and denotes a 'proposal (of agreement)'.

41 *Keilschrifttexte aus Boghazköi* II 11 rev. 11–17; cf. Zaccagnini 1970: 15, and Liverani 1979a: 25, n. 24. According to Liverani lines 11–12 reflect a promise of the king of Hatti to send to Arzawa(?) a gift received from the king of Aḫḫiyawa.

42 EA 1: 89–92, discussed by Liverani 1979c, 15–16.

43 In his book F. Pintore (1978) has singled out and analysed in detail the 'masks' of the 'suitor' and that of the 'giver' in international marriages.

Chapter 7

**The collapse of the Near Eastern regional
system at the end of the Bronze Age:
the case of Syria**

Mario Liverani

I could not pretend to synthesize in a few pages the subject indicated by the title of this chapter, especially if 'synthesis' is considered the act of systematically presenting the basic elements and results of the entire analytical process. In this sense, the present chapter is not at all a synthesis, it is rather a preliminary note, a list of problems whose solution is actually impossible in most cases. I had planned to write the whole chapter in the form of interrogative sentences: this approach would be entirely justified by the present state of our knowledge, but much too burdensome in style. I have therefore left out most of the question marks, but it is only too evident how many of my proposals are still tentative, how many are in need of further work, and how much may be open to drastic revision.

The Late Bronze Age system

The character of inter-regional contact in every period is conditioned by types of political management, socio-economic structure, technological equipment, and so on. Since all of these factors underwent notable changes from the Late Bronze Age to the Iron Age I period, it is reasonable to look for the consequences of (or connections between) these changes and the change in trade relationships (and in inter-regional relationships in general) at the end of the second millennium BC. Establishing relationships between single historical events and the course of foreign trade (as has sometimes been proposed) is very difficult, and, in my opinion, too dependent upon the vagaries of the evidence.[1] On the

other hand, basic connections between the socio-political structure and trade patterns of a given period are beyond doubt. The possibility of grasping something of this relationship in the period of the final collapse of Bronze Age civilization is especially opportune because this was one of the most dynamic periods in all of ancient history.

The political system of the Late Bronze Age in the Near East and in the eastern Mediterranean was characterized by large regional units (the result of a development of many centuries, impossible to sketch here), each endowed with a higher authority of regional extent, and a system of lower-level, local authorities with cantonal or city-specific jurisdiction. In the political language of the period the higher level is that of the 'great kings', and the lower level is that of the 'small kings', the latter subject to the former who are alone recognized as independent powers.[2] In the Syro-Palestinian area in particular two features are to be underscored: (a) The Syro-Palestinian *cultural* unit was not coterminous with the two *political* units into which it was divided, the centers of which were outside the region (in Egypt for the south, Mitanni and later Hatti for the north). In the case of other regions, the cultural unit was better associated with the political unit; (b) In the Syro-Palestinian region the double level of political rule (great kings vs. small kings) was particularly evident because of the fragmentation of territory into a number of small, autonomous kingdoms, each with local dynasties. In other regions the lower level, represented in Syro-Palestine by the small kings, can be represented otherwise, due to more advanced processes of unification which eventually led to the local level of government being purely administrative in character.

With respect to inter-regional relations, the political system just outlined is characterized by two important ideological features, which give a peculiar character to the entire period. The first feature was the parity of rank. This was of course a fiction, a convention which does not reflect the actual economic, demographic, or military power of the partners to a transaction. At any rate, the partners in an inter-regional relationship, when of the same level (i.e. a great king with another great king, a small king with another small king) considered each other as equal in rank, as 'brothers' in their metaphorical terminology. The high frequency of paritetical treaties in the fifteenth to thirteenth centuries BC shows that the concept of equal rank was formalized into a set of established conventions. The second feature is the juridical-administrative responsibility of each king in the territories under his authority. In cases of theft, murder, accident, etc., a formal procedure was employed – complete with denunciation, inquiry, indemnity – which gave satisfaction to the victims, even if the culprits were not identified. (See most recently Klengel 1980.) Responsibilities and procedures in such cases were specified according to the convention of rank. One great king would ask for satisfaction from another great king under whose general authority the territory where the incident had occurred was situated. The great king responsible for giving satisfaction to his colleague of equal rank would, in turn, entrust the task of investigation to the small king of the city where the incident occurred. The small king would, in turn, consider responsible the inhabitants of the village nearest to the place where the incident occurred.

With this background in mind, and admitting a great deal of simplification, the mechanics of inter-regional contact in the Near East during the Late Bronze age can be outlined as follows:

(1) *Setting*: at the higher political level ('palace' level). Merchants, messengers, prospectors, etc. belonged to the Palace; 'private' activities were (ideologically and factually) less important. Every great king could contact other kings of equal rank; he could also contact his own, dependent small kings (and could do this from a favourable position!); contacts between a great king and little kings not under him were considered incorrect. The main stream of inter-regional relationships had, accordingly, to follow the specific vertical (levels of rank) and horizontal (regional/local units) pattern outlined above.

(2) *Typology*: mainly exchange of gifts (Zaccagnini 1973); also exchange of specialists (artisans, physicians, exorcists, artists, etc.) (Zaccagnini 1983b; Edel 1976), women (inter-dynastic marriages) (Pintore 1978), and messages (oral and written) which were properly the instruments for other exchanges but could acquire a value of their own. Of course this is a 'mental typology'. As I have tried to show elsewhere in texts from the Late Bronze Age, the same act of exchange could be considered both as a gift-exchange (when addressing a partner) and as a tributary contribution (when addressing the inner public) (Liverani 1979a). We

could say that gift exchange was the 'code' of inter-regional exchange in this period.

(3) *Ideology*: the basic ideas were reciprocity and brotherhood, both expressed with obsessive insistence in the letters accompanying the exchanges. Other ideological values,[3] generosity and disinterest (even in the specific form of an augmented restitution), the contrast between self-sufficiency and exchange, the personalization of the gift, were less distinctive. The ideological complex was quite coherent.

(4) *Extent*: due to the strict formalization of political relationships and juridical responsibilities, and to the palatial setting of the exchanges, it is obvious that trade was blocked by one's neighbors. Every great king was in contact with adjacent great kings, and if he wished to proceed beyond he was obliged to pass through them. This meant that he could not proceed. Single objects and single persons could, of course, travel over longer distances, but only as a result of different passages (cf. Liverani 1979a: 25, n.24). Means existed for easily blocking messengers and merchants which included the right to detain them, the imposition of customs and preference deductions, and the withdrawal of juridical guarantees and military protection (most famously Kühne and Otten 1971: 14–17 (Rs IV 14–18)). Structurally, the only relationship possible was that with the adjacent regional unit, with no possibility of avoiding it or passing beyond.

Sea trade

The system of sea trade in the Late Bronze Age was strictly dependent upon the general conditions just described. Various fleets were active in the eastern Mediterranean (also in the Red Sea, considered here for comparative purposes). In the Late Bronze Age there was certainly no 'thalassocracy', but a conditioned coexistence. There was an Egyptian fleet, fleets from the

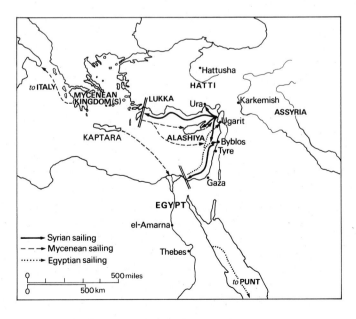

Fig. 7.1. Syrian sailing in the Late Bronze Age.

coastal Syro-Palestinian towns (the Ugaritic one is the best known), a fleet from Alasia-Cyprus, one from Ura in Cilicia, and a Mycenaean fleet (or fleets from various Mycenaean political units).

Although the evidence is scanty and uncertain, it seems that Syrian sailing was rather cautious, confined to hugging the coasts, probably for technical reasons. Direct contacts between Cyprus and Egypt, and between the Aegean and Egypt, on the contrary, are attested (see McCaslin 1980: 102–7). Moreover, as already noted, contacts were limited to adjacent regions, with only limited possibilities for venturing beyond. Therefore Syrian ships (also Cypriote and Aegean ships) could not go beyond the eastern Delta, which acted as a barrier against contact with inner Egypt or the Red Sea. On another front, the Mycenaean region blocked (or at least drastically hindered) direct contacts between Asia and Egypt, and the central Mediterranean and Europe respectively. Syrian sailing was thus restricted by both political and technical barriers. Ugaritic ships reached southward to all of the harbors of the Syro-Palestinian coast as far as the eastern Delta; to the west they reached Alasia–Cyprus and Ura in Cilicia (the sea-gate of Hatti), only occasionally arriving in Lycia or Crete (Kaptara), due to the hindrance of Mycenaean hegemony (Casson 1966; Linder 1981). In sum, Syrian sailing in the Late Bronze Age was structurally blockaded and bound to the coast with little hope of alternative outlets.

Traded goods

Leaving aside Syrian exports in timber, olive oil and purple-dyed wool textiles, it is important to note the fact that trade in metals seems to have been characterized by a concentration of production in conveniently controlled areas and by intensive inter-regional trade. This is especially true of copper, which during the whole of the Bronze Age arrived in the Near East from two principal mineral-rich regions: Alasia–Cyprus in the west, and Magan-'Oman in the east (Muhly 1973: 192–9 and 220–32). By drastically over-simplifying, we can say that a large part of the copper circulating in the Late Bronze period in Syria–Palestine, Egypt, the Aegean, and Anatolia (not forgetting the Ergani mines) was Cypriote copper (See especially Vincentelli 1976: 20–2; and cf. Stech Wheeler, Muhly and Maddin 1979: 139–52). Something similar could be said of the Egyptian monopoly of gold (with lesser technical value, but higher symbolic value) (see Edzard 1960: 38–55; Helck 1962: 399–402); and possibly of Iranian tin (but the problem of tin is much more complex (see Muhly 1973: 288–335; cf. Leemans 1968: 201–10; Dossin 1970: 97–106; Malamat 1971: 31–8; Muhly 1976: 97–104). Such a high degree of source specificity for raw materials of a metallic nature is comparable to several non-metallic examples, such as Afghan lapis-lazuli, or incense and myrrh from Punt, or the Syrian products already mentioned above.

The Amarna letters exchanged between the Pharaoh and the king of Alasia are illustrative of the procedures by which raw materials were acquired between developed states (Knudtzon 1915, no. 33–40). For the procedures for gaining access to raw materials in under-developed (non-urban) countries, the Hatshepsut expedition to Punt is likewise illuminating (Naville 1898: LXIX–LXXVI; Stevenson Smith 1962: 59–60, and fig. p. 61. Text: Sethe 1961 (1927) 315–54 translated in *Ancient Records of*

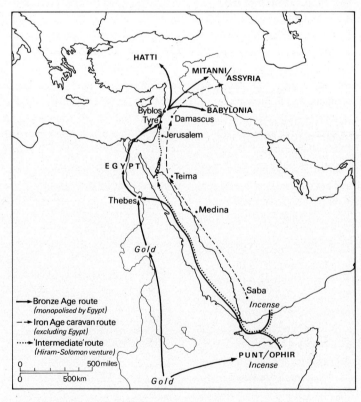

Fig. 7.2. Gold-incense routes from Late Bronze to Iron Age.

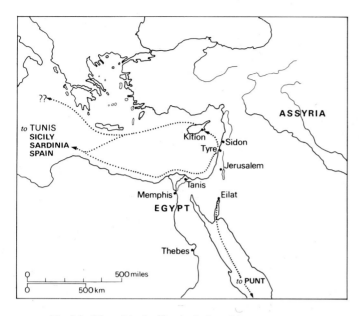

Fig. 7.3. 'Phoenician' sailing in the Iron I Age.

Egypt (ARE) II 1252–95). If we were to try to 'imagine' trade contacts between the Near East and Europe in the Late Bronze Age, this text provides the more reasonable model. I just want to emphasize how much this system of monopolistic production and intensive inter-regional trade was bound to the political system characterized by regional units, with contacts carried on at the highest political level (palace), and limited by necessity to adjacent units.

The collapse

The collapse of Near Eastern civilization at the end of the Bronze Age is a problem even wider than the subject of the present volume. Only a few points will be recalled here, with particular reference to inter-regional contacts, and limited to the Syrian case. While it is true that the crisis is rather extended and takes place at roughly the same time over a large area, it is all too evident that the specific features of the collapse in each region constitute a case of their own, dependent upon the specific socio-political, economic, demographic, and technological features of that area. In general, I belong to that group of scholars who consider (both on a theoretical level, and in the case of the Late Bronze Age crisis) internal factors of socio-economic dynamics to be pre-eminent, and the external (migratory) factors to be rather limited from a quantitative point of view. They represent the result more than the cause of the crisis, coming as part of a response with a sort of 'multiplier' effect.

Limiting myself to the Syro-Palestinian area, I have repeatedly tried to point out the direction in which the socio-economic crisis developed (Liverani 1975 and 1979f). The Syrian system of the Late Bronze Age was based on a convergence of interests held by the king and the class of high functionaries (*mary-annu*, scribes and administrative personnel, merchants, etc.), and dependent upon a particularly crude exploitation of the village

communities. The periodic measures of debt cancellation and release of enslaved debtors, so typical of the Middle Bronze Age, are no longer to be found (Liverani 1971b). The growing number of runaways, seeking an escape from their economic plight, are hindered by treaties of reciprocal extradition (Liverani 1965). The traditional systems of adjustment within the family or the village sphere are eroded by the growing consideration of land and work as merchandise. In regard to material culture, this situation seems to be reflected in a certain degradation of basic, domestic culture, in contrast to an accentuated concentration of luxury goods and conspicuous consumption in the royal palaces.[4] In regard to territorial exploitation, this situation is reflected in some depopulation of rural areas, and in a marked concentration of settlement in coastal or valley areas better provided with land and water (cf. the classical article by Alt 1959 (1925); more recently Aharoni 1967: 160–3 and *passim*. These general sketches have been confirmed by archaeological surveying in various areas). The coincidence of a mass of runaways, and the desertion of non-irrigated lands, produces a growth in nomadic (or semi-nomadic) groups which in some regions supplied the political and ideological pole of attraction for the rural villages who no longer felt any solidarity with the royal palace (see the important article by Mendenhall 1962). In addition to the separation of peasants from the capital city, and their joining nomadic tribes, a second weakening factor for the palace is the disengagement of the military aristocracy (*mary-annu* and others), and in general the higher specialists who were tightly linked (by their function) to the development of the urban-palace complex. At the apex of the crisis (when a shock of external origin is certain for the Syrian coast), the royal palace could not rely upon the (mainly economic) support of the villages, too crudely exploited in the past, or that of the aristocracy (mainly military). Moreover, the particular concentration in the Palace of all the elements of organization, transformation, exchange, etc. – a concentration which seems to reach its maximum in the Late Bronze Age – has the effect of transforming the physical collapse of the Palace into a general disaster for the entire kingdom.

In this general framework, some elements are more directly linked with the features of inter-regional relationships than others. The status of the merchant in the Late Bronze Age was that of a Palace dependent (Zaccagnini 1977); but during the thirteenth century his relations to the Palace underwent some changes in the context of the disengagement of higher specialists already mentioned (see Liverani 1979b for Ugarit; Reineke 1979 for Egypt). Other categories aimed at transforming their service into a sinecure: typical of this is the case of the *maryannu* with the development of a threefold process of hereditary acquisition of rank, substitution of service by a yearly payment, and total exemption from service (Liverani 1974c: 350 and 1979f: 1344-5). At the moment of the collapse, such categories of personnel would not be able to furnish their military service for the protection of the Palace, not to survive without the Palace and consequently they were eliminated (there is no more mention of the *maryannu* after the final Bronze Age crisis). Merchants, on the contrary, aimed at accentuating the private aspects of their work, adding personal activities (exchange, financial services) to their institutional activity for the Palace, obtaining from the king customs exemptions and freedom from service, until they acquired a significant level of autonomy and wealth (the case of Sinaranu of Ugarit is typical). At the moment of the collapse, the merchants were in a position to survive without the Palace organization, and to continue their personal activities in a different framework.[5]

Another element of the crisis which influenced trade was an end to political and juridical guarantees covering inter-regional traffic. There was no longer any 'great king' negotiating with his colleagues in adjacent regions; further, the 'small kings' either ceased to exist or else no longer were able to control by coercive police or judiciary intervention, countries which had become hostile, and in which the tribes acquired more and more territory and authority. Brigandage on land and piracy at sea seem to have played a role in the collapse; and obviously the lack of security on the roads and the lack of support points (such as the Palaces) accelerated the breakdown of inter-regional trade, especially the regular high-level trade in the form of gift-exchange and specialists-exchange between Palaces of equal rank. The same was probably true of metal production, particularly copper production. It is reasonable to suggest that the temporary disappearance of the Palace organization in producing and re-distributing activities had left distant trade partners unprovided for, thus compelling them to look for other sources for such essential materials.

Summing up, the collapse of royal palaces (which in the Late Bronze Age were the basic and almost exclusive agents in long-distance trade) produced a complete crisis in inter-regional contacts requiring their re-casting in another form. This is both because the very protagonists of trade disappeared (kings, scribes and ambassadors, palace merchants, palace specialists, etc.), and because the political and juridical organization of trade was destroyed (juridical guarantees, alliance treaties, military protection, financial indemnifications, free pass and credit letters, etc.). Even the linguistic channel (letters in the Akkadian language and in cuneiform script) which, in the Late Bronze Age, was employed in inter-palatine contacts in Mesopotamia, Anatolia, Syria–Palestine, Egypt, and Cyprus, came to an end when scribes and scribal schools (which were part of the palace administration) were eliminated by the final collapse of the palaces. It is possible that the systems of silver equivalence upon which trade was based also underwent substantial alteration in the twelfth century.

Factors in the process of restructuring the regional economy

During the same period in which destabilizing factors led directly to the final crisis, other factors were active which proved decisive in the process of renewed structuring following the crisis. Sometimes the very same factor was effective both in breaking down the old order and in re-shaping the new; in other cases, on the contrary, we see an inversion of the main trends of the times, or a reaction against destabilizing factors.

Some factors were related to the territorial distribution of settlements, an element of obvious importance for establishing transport routes, and therefore important for the very existence of trade (at least land trade). The territorial pattern of Syria–Palestine in the Late Bronze Age was based on the virtual restriction of settlements to irrigated land (coasts, valleys), with a progressive de-population (already begun in the Middle Bronze Age) of the inner plateaus where the large urban centers of the Early and Middle Bronze Age had been. In the Late Bronze Age, capital cities and the agricultural territory dependent upon them constituted something like a discontinuous series of islands embedded in large tracts of pastureland (now devoid of agriculture) and wooded high-lands (not yet submitted to tillage) (see Rowton 1967: 261–77 for wood distribution and Rowton 1965 for socio-economic effects). This territorial pattern corresponded well with the concentration of communications in the Palace, the system of juridical guarantees and treaties, and the 'outer' and hostile character attributed to the nomadic element. Toward the end of the period (and beginning probably in the south) we witness an inversion of the trend, a trend which continued to develop in the Iron I period. The large palace-towns of the Bronze Age were mostly destroyed, and the urban settlements of the Iron Age were smaller, more diffuse, and more numerous than in the Late Bronze period. In the inner plateaus (depopulated or under-populated for centuries) the sedentary population grew rapidly, probably due to a trend towards sedentarization among nomads. The previously wooded hills were subject to colonization (Aharoni 1947 and 1967: 217–21). Lastly, we witness a centrifugal expansion of the nomadic element, thanks to the dromedary, towards the large deserts, the long caravan routes, and the far-away oases, previously irrelevant in historical terms. This inversion of the Late Bronze Age pattern towards an expansion of settlement was based (as is well known) on the availability of certain technological elements either new, improved, or else more widely employed than in earlier times. The lack of adequate data and sound studies on most of these technological elements is still a serious obstacle to a reasonable reconstruction of the period.

The use of the domesticated dromedary had no direct bearing on trade with Europe and the Mediterranean, but it was a factor of primary importance in permitting the expansion of settlement and caravan routes towards the inner plateaus which characterized the Iron Age (cf. most recently Briant 1982: *passim*). As for sailing techniques, I personally am not aware of precise innovative elements introduced about 1200 BC which could be said to characterize Iron Age I shipping in contrast to Late Bronze Age navigation. However, I am strongly inclined to postulate some such innovation, since we get the impression of a sudden widening of the sea routes and of a technical and operative freedom which distinguishes sailing of, so to speak, an 'Homeric' type, from the cautious coast-hugging of the Late Bronze Age. This widening of sea travel is quite similar to (and contemporary with) the opening of caravan routes from Transjordan to South Arabia and the substitution of the dromedary for the ass.

Also influencing settlement patterns, as well as travel patterns, was the availability of more efficacious systems for holding water. Generally speaking, there are two problems: (1) to dig pits deeper than before, so as to reach lower water tables; and (2) to obtain better water-proof plaster for cisterns than previously available. On both counts, the archaeological evidence ought to be adequate enough to present a sound, general sketch, but such an outline is still wanting, and the proposal is nothing more than a reasonable hypothesis.[6] From the texts we obtain only a few insights into these problems; interesting data but too scattered to prove useful for the construction of any quantitative sketch. But note, for example, the three stelae of Seti I from Redesiyeh (text: Kitchen 1973: 65–70; translation in *ARE* III 169–95), dealing with the problem of excavating pits in order to equip the road to the gold mines; and see also the Kubban stela of Ramses II, where his luck in reaching the water table at 20 cubits is contrasted with the unsuccessful digging of Seti I down to a depth of 200 cubits (text: Kitchen 1973, II/7: 353–60; translation in *ARE* III, 285–93). Moreover, the expansion of agriculture into hilly regions and arid lands required technical procedures in soil preparation (clearing woods, hill terracing, construction of transversal barrages in wadis, etc.) which also seem to undergo a substantial development towards the end of the second millennium.[7] These developments are, however, less important for inter-regional contacts.

Lastly, iron: although the progressive and partial character of the substitution of iron for bronze in work tools requires maximum caution, nonetheless this element must be taken into account (see Waldbaum 1978; Wertime and Muhly 1980; Stech Wheeler, Muhly, Maxwell Hyslop and Maddin 1981: 245–68). Iron ploughs are an obvious advantage in bringing new areas under cultivation, as are iron tools for wood clearing (mostly achieved through fire) and for excavating pits or cisterns. But even at a stage before that of the practical employment of iron tools, there was another way in which the new iron metallurgy was effective in influencing patterns of inter-regional contact. It has not been stressed enough that the new impulse towards iron-working, probably contemporary with a crisis in copper supply, must have been accompanied by renewed activity in metal prospection, indications of which are to be found both in the archaeological data (the most obvious case being the development of mining at Timna (see Rothenberg 1972a: 63–111)) and in texts (see e.g. some texts of Ramses III: Erichsen 1933; translation in *ARE* IV, 408 (cf. also *ARE* IV, 29–34)). This renewed activity of metal prospectors contributed in a significant way to the re-shaping of the map of metal supply from the Late Bronze Age to the Iron I period. I presume that two elements were important: the first element is a technical one, i.e. the fact that iron ores are more widespread (even if in less substantial concentrations) than copper ones. The second element is a commercial one, i.e. the crisis (at least momentary) of the copper supply at the palace level. The two elements could have contributed to the same result, and it is not important to know which element preceded the other. Just to give a hypothetical example: Ramesside metal prospectors in the Araba, looking for copper mines to substitute for the Cypriote copper obtained now with increasing difficulty, may have detected iron ores as well; or, conversely, in looking for iron they may also have found copper mines.

In any case, the pattern of metal supply seems to undergo two basic changes – two changes apparently contradictory but in fact complementary. First, in Iron I we notice direct access to distant metal-producing areas which were previously inaccessible (except through many passages) due to the system of regional

units centred on royal palaces. (On this widening of trade, see the next paragraph). On the other hand, there seems to be a more far-flung and careful exploitation of the inner territory (i.e. in our case: Syria–Palestine). For the large monopolies of metal production of the Late Bronze Age, connected by efficient palace trade, the Iron I period substitutes metal production on a local scale. The same holds true for metal working: the rather sophisticated palace installations necessary for bronze working are substituted by the iron worker's much more accessible and movable equipment.

A marginal note on the factors of restructuring: Ramesside Egypt seems to have played an interesting role, more so if we consider that some elements (the dromedary, iron) remained foreign to Egypt for many centuries. Metal prospection, the digging of pits, the revival of Red Sea sailing, and new relations with the nomads of the Sinaitic-Transjordanian areas are all themes characteristic of Ramesside inscriptions. Perhaps it is not only a question of better documentation (in comparison with other kingdoms of the same period), but also a question of a state administration particularly attentive in looking for new solutions to technical and commercial problems. It would probably be rewarding to study in detail the endeavor of Ramesside Egypt to re-define its presence in Asia, a presence which had been planned in a completely different way at the beginning of the eighteenth dynasty. For gift-exchange with Asiatic great kings and relations with the Cypriote copper monopoly, Egypt tried to substitute direct exploitation of Sinaitic metal resources. For the tributary pattern, best represented by the yearly collection tour among the Syro-Palestinian vassal kinglets, Egypt tried to substitute trade (Wenamun's text is illustrative of some aspects of this change: see Hans Goedicke, *The Report of Wenamun*, Baltimore–London, 1975)). For a diffused type of political control, Egypt tried perhaps to substitute the presence of Philistine mercenaries in key positions, and so on. This attempt to maintain some sort of control in the Syro-Palestinian area notwithstanding the political and technological changes, resulted in failure, probably because Egypt remained foreign (for historical and for structural reasons) to the most meaningful innovations of the times, from the re-shaping of settlement patterns to the new role of the tribe, from iron metallurgy to the use of the dromedary. But this is another problem, and the failure does not diminish the interest of the attempt.

The restructuring of inter-regional contacts

By considering the problem in a rather abstract way, the effect of disintegration and restructuring the pattern of relations typical of the Late Bronze Age should produce a new pattern typical of the Iron I period. This abstract procedure, with all its risks, is made partly necessary by the scarcity of written documentation in the period immediately following the final crisis of the Late Bronze Age; a scarcity which is not fortuitous and will not be supplemented in the future, and one which is itself an effect of the crisis (eclipse of scribal schools and palace administrations). The general reliability of this sketch is partly confirmed by documentation from subsequent periods; but it is necessary to repeat that in ascribing most of the changes to the apex of the crisis (twelfth century) we adopt a rather simplified and arbitrary point of view. The change may have had an inner chronology much more complicated than it is now possible to detect. In any case, without trying to establish too detailed a reconstruction, and by restricting ourselves to the basic elements of change (the elements of 'longue durée'), we can outline a pattern which should be considered a likely and reasonable one, rather than a real and proven one.

Considering again the same elements used above for the Late Bronze Age pattern, we obtain the following sketch:

(1) *Setting*: no longer exclusively palace-centered. Some palaces still exist, and the archaeologically attested palace destructions are spread through time with no period absolutely devoid of palaces. There is no period of the Judges in the Biblical sense (Liverani 1980). Residual palaces carry on some trade (this point can be ascertained by a look at their furniture and household goods), but they have a different organization and less responsibility. They are flanked and challenged by other political bodies as well. Palaces are no longer the exclusive agents of trade. On the caravan routes of the Syrian and Transjordanian hinterland the main trade agents are now the nomadic tribes – and it must be recalled by contrast that the semi-nomadic tribes of the Bronze Age were engaged in trade only occasionally, functioning more as an obstacle to the circulation of goods and men than as an agent thereof. To what extent this pattern also holds true for the Mediterranean sea-trade, i.e. to what extent groups of pirate-sailors not tied to a specific land were active in trade ventures, is not clear, but the problem does exist (see the narrative of Wenamun). Moreover, alongside the palace and the tribe we must consider the trading activities of 'private' agents (i.e. urban, but non-palace agents). This is the final result of that trend towards autonomy in the merchants' status that we have already outlined for the thirteenth century. For the Iron I period the documentation is very scanty indeed (see again Wenamun), but this element accords well with the process which leads from Late Bronze conditions to the emergence of some sort of 'trade aristocracy' in the Phoenician towns. Finally, in outlining a situation no longer exclusively centered on palaces, we should also note the end of that forced trade which in the Late Bronze Age was built up through payment of tribute by the little kings of Syria and Palestine to the great kings of Egypt and Hatti.

(2) *Typology*: there is a shift from the conventional pattern of gift-exchange to a more properly commercial pattern. The key factor is again the change in the status of the merchant. In the Late Bronze Age the merchant was a palace official whose task was to supply goods not available locally. He was allotted an amount of silver (or other goods) by the palace administration, with which he had to settle accounts at fixed times. This type of merchant was active for his own profit only as a sideline (Liverani 1979b: 495–503). In the Iron Age the merchant is active mainly for his own sake, and the very supply of raw materials becomes an activity which is carried out for profit, stimulated not by royal

order but by advantage. The difference is in part a material one, but in part also one of mental pattern. The narrative of Wenamun again contains hints for understanding how the very same procedures already employed in the Late Bronze Age were now re-cast with a new underscoring of the commercial elements instead of the political and ideological elements (Liverani 1979a: 20–3).

An analysis of the trade terminology also reveals interesting trends. In the Bronze Age the pair *môtār/maḥsōr* finds its place in the (yearly) balanced accounts settled by palace administration and merchants, with the meaning 'surplus'/'deficit'.[8] In the first millennium the meaning is 'profit'/'loss' (Prov. 21:5) in the frame of a financial approach to trade activity. The entire terminology of trade underwent semantic changes which can be studied in this connection: this has already been done for the root *kly* (Late Bronze 'to consume'/Iron age 'to spend') (Milano 1978) and could be done for *mḥr* (from 'equivalence' to 'price'), for *mkr* (from 'to exchange' to 'to sell'), and for the new words *rkl* and *sḥr* (itinerant selling) which did not exist in the Bronze Age (see Speiser 1961: 23–8).

(3) *Ideology*: in the context of gift-exchange, the most relevant concepts were those of generosity and disinterest (namely in the ideal of giving back more than received). Now it is reasonable that, in line with what has just been said, profit came to be highly valued. Further, the exclusive valuing of imports, and silence on exports (so typical of the royal point of view, centered on the problem of power) in the Bronze Age, is at least mitigated in the first millennium when production for export and exchange are considered in a positive light (consider Ezekiel's 'prophecy' on Tyre).[9]

(4) *Extent*: the break-up of regional empires (and also the availability of new technologies) was effective in widening the extent of contacts. 'Private' merchants were no longer obliged to pass through royal palaces, and could probably operate in a more far-flung and yet more intensive way. They were no longer only interested in obtaining raw materials, but also in selling artifacts, and most probably came into closer contact with common people. They were no longer limited to adjacent regions by formalized political relationships, but could move over greater distances. The possibility for cultural influence spreading through trade relationships increased both in intensity and geographical extent.

Sea trade

The pattern of sea trade was re-shaped accordingly. With reference to the Syro-Palestinian (now to be called 'Phoenician') sailing trade, and with exclusive attention to the problem of extent, the situation seems to be as follows:

(a) We possess written records of great interest on sailing ventures in the Red Sea (tenth century), i.e. the joint expedition of Tyre and Jerusalem, starting from Eilat and arriving in Ofir (Yemen and East Africa) in search of gold and exotic merchandise (I

Kings 9: 26–8; 10:11; 10:22; II Chron. 8:17–18). These ventures
are pertinent here by way of analogy; an analogy not yet sufficiently underscored. It is necessary to consider these ventures
in the context of the shifting of the gold route from the Late Bronze
Age to the Iron Age, subsequent to the change in political and
technological circumstances. In the Late Bronze Age, as often
mentioned in written sources, gold arrived in Asia, via Egypt,
which monopolized its position as intermediary.[10] Gold came to
Egypt either directly from mines in Upper Egypt and Nubia,
or from East Africa (Punt), via the Red Sea and the Wadi Hammamat (Vercoutter 1959: 120–53). Incense and myrrh followed
the same route. In the Iron Age, the breakdown of the Egyptian
monopoly, the development of settlements in Transjordan and
the Hijaz, and the use of dromedaries on caravan routes originating in Southern Arabia, all meant that gold and incense could
reach Syria and Transjordan directly from Yemen, avoiding the
Egyptian passage and making exclusive use of the land route. The
attempt by Hiram and Solomon is somewhat unusual: they
tried to avoid Egypt, and to reach the source (Ofir) directly, but
make use mainly of the Red Sea route (a sea route apparently not
employed by Egyptians since Ramses III). In any case, this venture shows that in the tenth century Phoenician sailors were able
(in technology and organization) to travel directly to any distant
goal, without the support of regular intermediate points, and
to draw directly from the producing countries and thus obtain
increased profits.

(b) In the Mediterranean, I would propose that the situation was
somewhat similar, although we lack records of comparable detail
and reliability. The collapse of the Mycenaean world freed Syrian
(now Phoenician) sailing from its western barrier, just as the
Egyptian collapse freed its Southern border. We can suppose that
the availability of improved sailing techniques[11] permitted longer
and bolder routes to be followed without the need for intermediate support stations. The new needs of metal supply (partial
crisis of Cypriote copper? Interruption in the arrival of Iranian
tin? Search for iron?) made the exploration of far western metal
sources (Sardinia, southern Spain, etc.) advantageous. It is well
known that the traditional dating for the foundation of Cadiz and
other Phoenician colonies in the far West have been discarded as
being too high (about 1100 BC) in comparison with the archaeological remains from these regions and the intermediate harbors
(in Sicily, Tunisia, etc.). However, the dates are not too far from
that of the Hiram–Solomon venture to Ofir. Although it is
obvious that such dates are to be discarded as foundation dates
for 'colonies' (a phenomenon quite alien in the twelfth to tenth
centuries!), they are reasonable as chronological bases for the first

trading activities which may have left no substantial archaeological traces and which required no intermediate landing places to
have been pre-arranged. In the Mediterranean, as in the Red Sea,
the Phoenician sailors, 'free' from the technical and political
barriers of the Late Bronze Age, were able to travel directly to
their far-away goals, and thus gain direct access to gold (Ofir) and
silver/tin (Sardinia, Spain).

Acknowledgement
My best thanks are due to Dr Dan Potts for a thorough revision of
my English.

Notes
1 Cf. e.g. the criticism in *Oriens Antiqvus* 8 (1969, pp. 342–343 to the 'political' explanation that Merrillees 1968 gives for the end of Cypriote pottery imports into Egypt.
2 Tadmor 1979: 3, labels the situation as 'The Club of the Great Powers'.
3 I have to refer to my monograph (still unpublished) 'Prestigio e interesse. Ideologia e prassi dei rapporti politici nel Vicino Oriente durante i secoli XV–XIII,' where the different ideological values are treated in detail.
4 The trend is quite evident, but we still lack any socio-economically oriented analysis of the archaeological evidence.
5 The opposed trends and results in the development of *maryannu* and merchants' status are briefly described in Liverani 1978, Reports: 191–8.
6 The hypothesis has been suggested by Albright 1931: 132, and resumed by Aharoni 1967: 219, and emphasised by Frankenstein 1979 and Gottwald 1979: 655–60, but an analytical treatment is still lacking.
7 The problem should be studied on the basis of textual data (e.g. Jos. 17: 14–18 on wood clearing) and archaeological data (especially the hill terraces, see for the moment de Geus 1975: 65–74, and Gottwald 1979). The general trend (innovative develop-ment at the beginning of the Iron Age, after a stasis in the Late Bronze Age) seems to be clear and generally accepted, but – once again – the analytical studies are still lacking: cf. for the moment Stager 1975.
8 See my remarks on the terminus technicus *mḥsrn* in Liverani 1979b: 503; the administrative procedure goes back to the IIIrd millennium (see now Powell 1977: 23–9).
9 Ezekiel 27: 9–25, where trade is seen as an itinerant activity (*rkl, shr*), and export items are produced especially (*mᶜśh*) in order to obtain imports. By the way, the term '*zbwn* for 'merchandise' points to the 'silent trade' procedure described by Herodotus IV. 196 (which differs from van Dijk 1968: 75–6; Lipinski 1985).
10 See Edzard 1960 and Helck 1962. F. Pintore (1983) contains inter-esting hints on the displacement of the trade route between Egypt/ Arabia and Palestine.
11 The pivotal question (not to be answered for the moment, in my opinion) deals with the acquisition of 'Mycenaean' sailing tech-niques and sea routes by the 'Phoenicians'.

Chapter 8

Center and periphery in Bronze Age Scandinavia

Kristian Kristiansen

Introduction

It remains an astonishing fact that thousands of impressive stone built barrows (cairns) are scattered along the coasts of the Gulf of Bothnia, hundreds of miles north of the central settlement areas and production areas of the Scandinavian Bronze Age (Fig. 8.1). We find a similar phenomenon along the Norwegian coast (Fig. 8.2).[1] In an environment dominated by Stone Age technology, with only a few imported bronzes, these north Scandinavian parallels in stone to the south Scandinavian barrows in grass and turf (Fig. 8.3) have puzzled archaeologists for many decades. They are part of an old debate in Scandinavian archaeology concerning the cultural and economic interrelationship of central and marginal areas during the Scandinavian Bronze Age.

The classic problem was whether to regard the evidence of a few Bronze Age objects and numerous monumental coastal cairns as evidence of a Bronze Age Culture or should they rather be seen as detached fragments that were incorporated into a completely different cultural and economic context, based on a Stone Age subsistence (a recent summary of the discussion is found in Bakka 1976). In reality we are dealing with a much more highly differentiated pattern which has been obscured by opposing two *complementary* concepts – that of culture and that of economy. Moreover, the rapid increase of new empirical evidence in recent years on both settlement and ecology in northern Scandinavia has rendered this old dichotomy obsolete. It seems, then, that devel-

opments in both theory and data make it worthwhile to attempt a reinterpretation of the relationship between central and marginal areas during the Bronze Age in Scandinavia. It should be stressed, however, that the following is to be regarded as a preliminary outline with no attempt to cover but a selection of the evidence.

Topographical framework

The research area comprises Scandinavia and the coastal areas around the Baltic Sea, including the lowland areas of the present northern Germany and northern Poland (Figs. 8.4 and 8.5). From northern Norway to northern Germany (the Elbe-knee) this represents a distance of approximately 2,200 kms as the crow flies. The same distance from the Elbe to the south extends into the central Sahara. Most of central and northern Scandinavia is dominated by old bedrock, the Hercynian folds stretching from northern Scandinavia to southern Norway, appearing again in northern England, Scotland and Ireland. Denmark, southern Sweden and northern Germany are dominated by fertile brown soils, moulded during the last glacial. In combination with the long coastline and the potential for fishing this makes it one of the most fertile agricultural areas in the temperate zone. Less fertile areas are mainly found in southwestern Jutland/northwestern Germany and in central Sweden lying outside the last glacial. However, stretches of fertile agricultural land are also found in central Sweden, around Stockholm, and in several areas along the Norwegian coast, especially the Oslo area, the area around

Fig. 8.1. Coastal cairn from Western Norrland in Sweden (photograph Evert Baudau, University of Umeo, Dept. of Archaeology)

Stavanger and further to the north the Bergen and Trondheim areas.

With respect to natural vegetation, central and northern Scandinavia is dominated by the fennoscandian coniferous forests (pine, spruce and beech), and in the mountains alpine vegetation ('fjeldmark'), while southern Scandinavia is dominated by deciduous forests, in Sweden mixed with some coniferous forest. The areas of deciduous forest generally correspond with brown soil areas.

Climatically the division extends east–west. The coastal areas of western Denmark and Norway being dominated by Atlantic climate, whereas the rest of Scandinavia is dominated by Continental climate. In combination with the Gulf stream along the Norwegian coast, this implies a rather mild winter climate allowing agriculture to be practiced very far to the north.

Economic setting

Let us first consider the economic and ecological setting. In recent years paleobotanical research has clarified that farming penetrated northern Scandinavia during the Neolithic along coastal strips of land suitable for mixed farming and fishing (articles in Sjøvold 1983). In the northern Bothnian Sea, farming, mainly restricted to cattle husbandry, was practiced in the later Neolithic in some places (Broadbent 1982: 18; Baudou 1982). The evidence is quite scanty, but becomes more reliable from the Late Bronze Age which marks an expansion period (Engelmark 1976, Huttunen and Tolonen 1972). By the transition to the Iron Age this farming pattern had disappeared in the north, due to climatic deterioration. Further to the south, in southern Finland, the introduction of farming displays a rather similar sequence, although in some areas an expansion stage can be established already during the Early Bronze Age (period II/III), whilst the farming practice does not disappear at the transition to the Iron Age (Tolonen 1981 and 1982; Vuorela 1981 and 1982; discussion in Edgren 1984, Zvelebil and Rowley-Conwa 1985). In northern Norway cattle husbandry defines the Early Neolithic, whereas agriculture did not appear until the Later Neolithic. Permanent pastures were established during the Bronze Age, especially during the Late Bronze Age (Vorren 1979, Vorren and Nilssen 1982). Similar sequences may also be found further to the south (Mikkelsen and Høeg 1979). Due to better climatic conditions (the Gulf Stream), the impact of farming was much stronger than in the Bothnian Sea area.

Fig. 8.2. Coastal cairn from Bohuslän, Western Sweden. (Photo: Marianne Djurfeldt, Goteborgs arkeologiska Museum).

What we find then is a pattern of farming practice that followed the south Scandinavian cycles. Deviations appear especially in terms of the intensity of farming (the impact on the landscape was much less significant, settlement was less dense), agriculture did not play any significant role until later, and in periods of climatic deterioration farming retreated further south (Gräslund 1981, Fig. 2). Expansion stages, transforming the landscape into permanent pastures, took place in southern Scandinavia already during the Middle and Later Neolithic (in some areas from the Battle Axe Culture, in others from the Dagger Period (Berglund 1969, Andersen *et al.* 1984, Digerfeldt and Welinder 1985, Aaby 1985, Odgaard 1985)). In central and northern Scandinavia this expansion did not take place until the Bronze Age, in some areas from the Early Bronze Age (e.g. Gotland; Carlsson 1982), in other areas from the Late Bronze AGe or Early Iron Age (Engelmark 1982, Fig. 2; Welinder 1974 and 1982). The paleobotanical data of recent years thus confirm the implications of previous archaeological distribution maps as a reflecion of farming (for Norway discussed by Sverre Johansen 1979 and 1982; northern Sweden in the series *Early Norrland* and Baudou 1982; Finland in Siiriäinen 1982).

The distribution of bronzes clusters distinctively on what is

still today regarded as the central agricultural areas. Outside these areas, in the mountainous tracts and along rivers, we only find a few scattered bronzes, but numerous finds of stone and flint tools (Johansen 1981 and 1983, map 1 and 4). They belong to the same tradition as the central farming areas, indicating a common cultural tradition. The marginal settlements performed specialized seasonal hunting and fishing combined with some farming when possible (Hofseth 1980; Mikkelsen 1980; Odner 1969). The same is true of many coastal settlements along the Norwegian coast (Skjølsvold 1978; Magnus and Myhre 1976: 155 ff). Further it has been suggested that large scale seal hunting in the Gulf of Bothnia was an essential economic background to the expansion of Bronze Age culture and society (Siiriäinen 1980).

In the interior of northern Scandinavia autonomous fishers, hunters, gatherers still persisted, but were in regular contact with the farming and fishing population along the coast. The nature of this interaction is still a matter of debate (Selinge 1979: 96 ff and chapter 6). The northern hunter-fishers belonged to the Russian Arctic Bronze Age tradition, in opposition to the coastal farmers (Bakka 1976: pl. 16), and also distinguished themselves in stone technology (Baudou 1977) (Fig. 8.6).

On this basis then, it can be stated that there exists no

Fig. 8.3 Barrows from Northwestern Zealand in Denmark (photograph: The Ancient Munument Directorate)

major dichotomy between southern, central and northern Scandinavia in terms of subsistence. Variations existed in terms of adaptation to regional and local variation in topography and climate. Fishing and some hunting was obviously part of the economy to the north, and a regular exchange between hunters and farmers took place in most of central and northern Scandinavia. However, both to the north and the south the Middle and Later Neolithic 'laid the groundwork for the introduction of bronze and provided the social environment in which it would gain symbolic value' (Broadbent 1983: 20). And we might add the introduction of the ritual system and the symbolism of monumental burials.

Thus, we can now turn to a discussion of the significance of the evidence of cairns, rock carvings and bronzes as to the nature of the Bronze Age in northern Scandinavia. We are here basically dealing with ritual evidence and although many of the bronzes are tools used in subsistence, their deposition is often ritual. To understand their context some basic aspects of the meaning of ritual must be outlined.

Ritual, power and prestige

Ritual provides a powerful framework for the establishment and legitimation of rank and political power of an elite (for a discussion see Bloch 1977: 329 f.; Goldmann 1970, chapter 23). By institutionalizing certain practices and beliefs (songs, dances, myths etc.), cyclical repetition takes the world out of history and

out of time. What has become ritualized cannot be questioned; 'belief' does not exist in primitive social organization. But, perhaps more importantly, ritual tends to be exclusive – it can only be performed by those that are, in some way or another, qualified. The nature of these qualifications represents the crucial point. In tribal social organization they are often linked to social prerogatives – such as direct descent from mythical ancestors, or kinship relations with powerful 'chiefs' and gods from outside. When access to outside exchange networks and mythical power is unified, a powerful combination of ritual, social and economic dominance is established (e.g. Helms 1979, chapter 4 and 6).

'Exchange is the code through which status information is communicated' states Goldmann (1970: 496). This is true in two senses: firstly a monopoly of exchange rests on a monopoly of ritual/mythical information and social and ritual practices. Secondly, such information is always linked to the employment of specific social and ritual symbols. An axe is not just an axe, and a sword is not just a sword. The employment of the long sword in the Early Bronze Age was linked to the spread of a warrior ideology among tribal elites from the Mycenaean/Euradian area. The war chariot and the stool also belonged to this complex (Kristiansen in press). In the same way the employment of monumental burials not only demanded knowledge of its ritual, but more significantly it demanded as well acceptance of the principle of demonstrating and distinguishing an elite in burials.

Material evidence is thus closely linked to a system of ritual

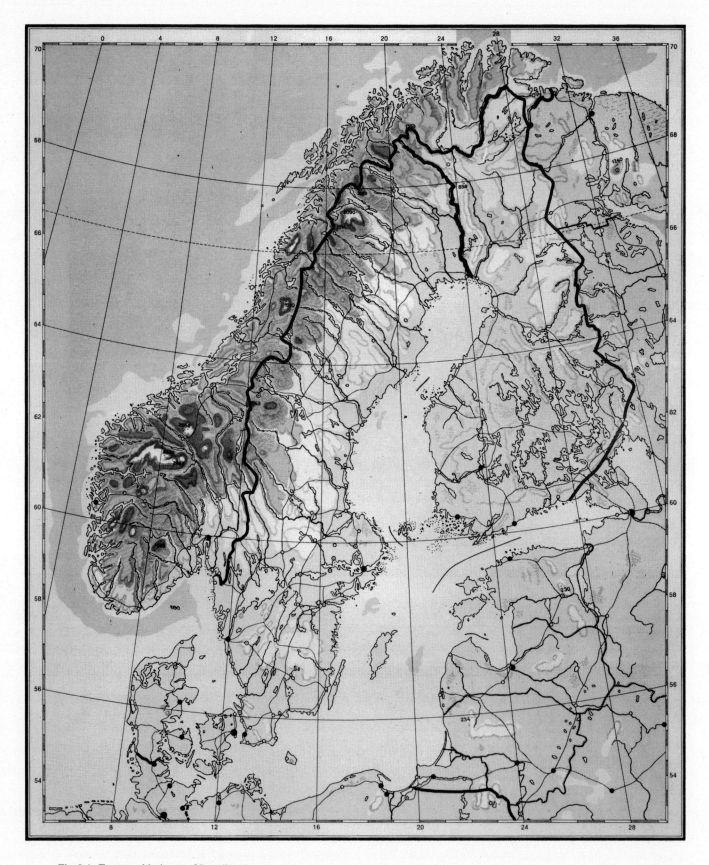

Fig. 8.4. Topographical map of Scandinavia

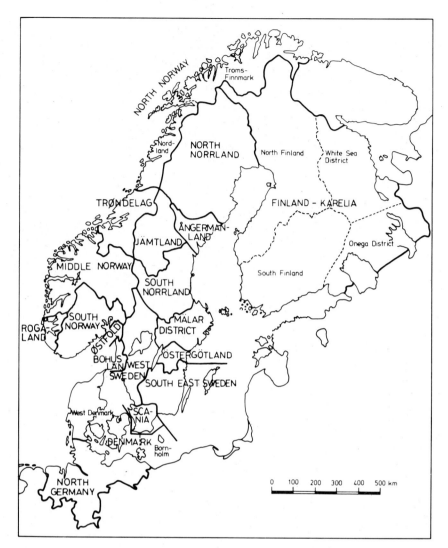

Fig. 8.5. Geographical regions in Scandinavia (after Malmer, Fig. 1)

and social practices. Some items, such as small axes could perhaps more easily be adopted independently of such social and ritual practices due to their utilitarian functions. Barrows/cairns, however, are part of a complex ritual, just as are specialist ritual equipment like lurs and gold cups. In an intermediate position we find swords and ornaments, whose adoption is related to knowledge of their use and social value (Kristiansen 1982 and 1984c; Levy 1982). It is the specific combination of these elements that defines various degrees of social and ritual complexity, both locally and regionally.

I thus propose that social organization during the Bronze Age was based on a close relationship between prestige goods exchange and the ideology of (foreign) tribal elites. This was sustained by a complex ritual system to which alone the elite had access. The whole of Scandinavia was embraced by this process, but to varying degrees. Only in southern and part of central Scandinavia do we find all diagnostic material features of the fully developed system of tribal elite ideologies. This includes, besides monumental barrows, the regular employment of prestige goods, such as complex ornaments and weapons in burials and other

ritual depositions (Fig. 8.7), complex ritual gear (e.g. lurs, ritual axes, horsegear) (Fig. 8.8) and rock carvings with ritual scenes, demonstrating the employment of prestige goods and ritual gear (Fig. 8.6). In some of these areas such objects were only deposited occasionally, in contrast to Denmark/Skåne, where bronze was more abundant. A less developed social hierarchy, but still dominated by the ideology of (foreign) tribal elites, is found in marginal areas in central and northern Scandinavia. It is characterized by cairns, simpler rock carvings and a few bronzes.[2] In these areas simpler tools, such as the Late Bronze Age stone axes, often replaced bronze axes in ritual (Marstrander 1983). The spread of a prestige goods ideology that in a few generations became dominant throughout Scandinavia took place during the Early Bronze Age (period I) and was firmly established from period II in northern Scandinavia following the dating of the cairns (Broadbent 1983, Fig. 2) and the rock carvings (Malmer 1981), beginning around 1500 BC.

Having discussed the economic and ideological setting, I shall finally try to outline the operation of the system in terms of

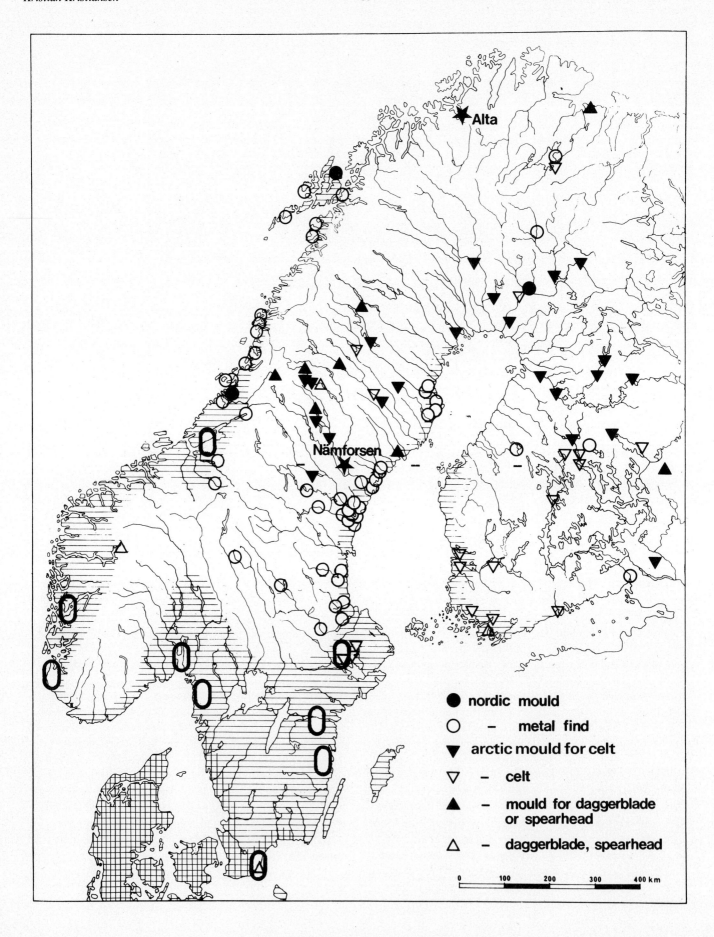

nordic mould

– metal find

arctic mould for celt

– celt

– mould for daggerblade
or spearhead

– daggerblade, spearhead

0   100   200   300   400 km

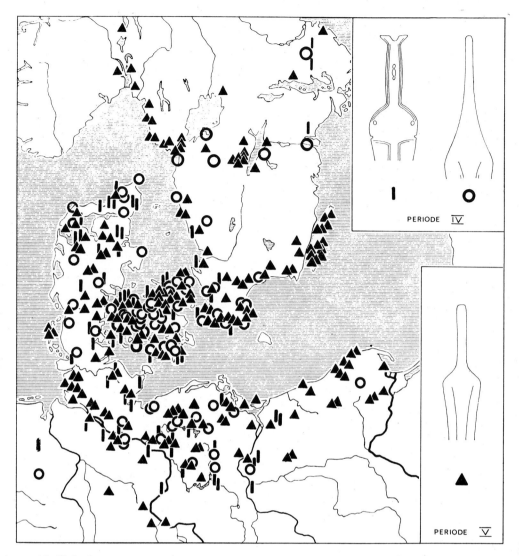

Fig. 8.7. Areas with chiefly elites during the Late Bronze Age, based on the deposition of swords (after Struve 1979, pl. 46 with additions).

the social organization of production and exchange between centers and peripheries.

Center and periphery

In what way is it possible to talk about centers and peripheries in a tribal context such as Bronze Age Scandinavia? To answer this we have to define their relationship. A basic criterion is their position within a larger regional system and their degree of organization, complexity and accumulation. Thus southern Scandinavia was directly dependent for its social reproduction on its participation in the larger European network of bronze exchange. It follows that northern Scandinavia should be defined as a periphery from the point of view of its relationship to southern Scandinavia. It may thus be defined otherwise in relation to a circum-

polar system (Moberg 1970, Malmer 1975) that is not considered here, but which may have acted as a periphery to Eurasian Bronze Age societies. Scandinavia may thus exemplify a more universal relationship between tribal centers and peripheries in temperate regions.

However, it is necessary to define more precisely in what way and to what extent the various central and marginal areas were dependent on each other. Ekholm and Friedman (1985) have recently suggested a distinction between centers and peripheries defined by *dependent* and *independent* peripheries. Although they are discussing the relationship between highly developed state-like centers or empires and their peripheries, the distinction may also be applied when discussing center and peripheries within a tribal framework. *Dependent structures* 'are those that depend on the

◀   Fig. 8.6. Generalized map of Nordic Bronze Age Culture with cairns (vertically hatched)/barrows (cross hatched) and the distribution of respectively Nordic and Arctic moulds and bronzes in Northern Scandinavia. Major regions of rock carvings defining centers of ritual superiority are encircled with a heavy line (modified after Bakka 1976, pl. 16; Hyenstrand 1984, maps 18–19; *Norsk Historisk Atlas* 1980, maps 11–13; Oldeberg 1974–6, 92–93, and Bandou 1960).

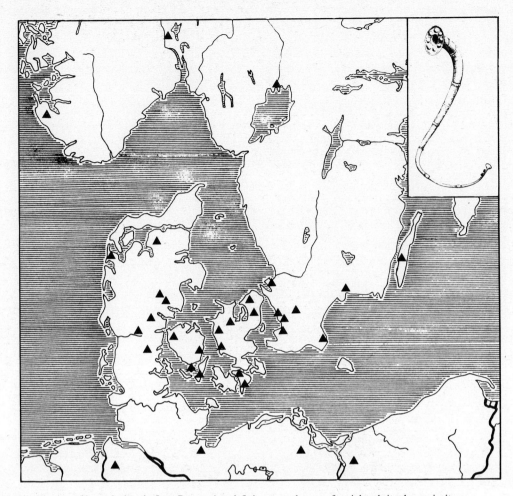

Fig. 8.8. The distribution of lures during the Late Bronze Age defining central areas of social and ritual superiority

larger system for their reproduction but are neither centers dominating their own peripheries nor peripheries dependent on a center' (Ekholm and Friedman 1985: 114). It would seem that this definition matches the situation in southern and central Scandinavia with respect to their position in relation to Europe as well as in relation to northern Scandinavia. *Independent structures*: 'These are structures whose operation is characterized by internal cycles of reproduction that are not connected to global cycles. However, such structures are clearly not independent with respect to their conditions of reproduction which depend on their location in the larger system' (Ekholm and Friedman 1985: 114).

If we define internal cycles as an independent subsistence base, e.g. fishing and hunting, then this definition may be applied to the hunter–fishers of northern Scandinavia who were probably also dependent to a certain degree upon exchange with coastal fishers and primitive farmers. Defined more broadly, we may also include the whole northern region in its relation to central Scandinavia.

The above defines certain guidelines for classification and interpretation. However, the situation is even more complex when we also consider the local relationship between e.g. coastal farmers and inland hunters. I thus propose two types of center/periphery

relationships for Bronze Age Scandinavia:

(1) One based on organizational complexity and dependency on a *regional* scale. Here I propose a distinction between southern, central and northern Scandinavia, reflecting a declining degree of complexity and dependency. The center/periphery relationship is an indirect one based on the dynamics of regional cycles of production and alliances. The nature of these relations will be discussed later.

(2) One based on direct center/periphery relationship on a *local* scale, where a central area exploits its hinterland by ideological, political and/or economic means. Such centers or dominant chiefdoms did probably exist in southern Scandinavia both in the Early (Kivik/Skallerup) and Late Bronze Age (Lusehøj, Seddin). In northern fenno-Scandinavia the relationship between coast and inland is different from that of central Scandinavia as the two groups do not conform to the same culture and sibsistence. Thus the relationship was rather an indirect one of reciprocal exchange and ideological dominance.

In order to add some flesh and blood to these propositions we shall take a new look at the evidence in an attempt to delineate a processual and explanatory framework for the operation and structure of center/periphery relationships throughout the Bronze Age. If we first consider regional dynamics, a broad correlation can be observed between agricultural expansion, the ritual deposition of metalwork and the position of rock carvings. During the Early Bronze Age the region around Ostergotland represents a rich and important center of both rock carvings and metalwork, especially during period I (rock carvings and settlement: Norden 1925, Burenhult 1973: 100 ff; metalwork: Oldeberg 1974–6, Jacob–Friesen 1967, maps 1–2; landscape and settlement: Carlsson 1982). From periods II–III southwest Norway is a central region, from where expansion took place (metalwork and settlement: Møllerop 1962, Myhre 1980: 66–106; rock carvings Fett and Fett 1941; landscape and settlement: Simonsen 1975). These two Scandinavian regions were influenced respectively from eastern and western Denmark.

During the Late Bronze Age a new expansion in metalwork takes place. In Sweden the Mälar region is now the central region (metalwork: Baudou 1960; settlement and rock carvings: Kjellén and Hyenstrand 1977; landscape and settlement: Welinder 1974) and in Norway it is the Oslo fjord region and Bohuslän in Sweden (metalwork: Johansen 1981; rock carvings: Marstrander 1963 and Nordbladh 1980; landscape and settlement: Hafsten 1958, Furingsten 1984). Influences are now channelled from eastern Denmark and northern Germany. There is a correlation in all these regions between the flourishing of metalwork, farming and rock carvings. There is less abundance of metalwork outside the central regions, more local imitations and less complexity in ritual and rock carvings.

Throughout the Bronze Age there existed direct alliances between these Scandinavian centers and Denmark/Scania as reflected in metalwork. Chiefly alliances could take place over hundereds of kilometers, especially over the open sea, along coasts and by passing many local settlements. Thus, the maintenance of regional centers depended upon a complex interplay between agricultural expansion (surplus production) and participation in alliance networks with southern Scandinavia that gave access to exotic ritual information and prestige goods (Kristiansen 1978 and 1981, Welinder 1977).[3]

The maintenance of this interregional network, however, also depended upon the local organization of center/periphery relations. Regional centers were more successful than other areas in Scandinavia in dominating local alliance networks and directing the surplus to be employed in creating alliances with southern Scandinavia. Several recent studies have indicated such a local organization of C/P relations. Thus, in terms of ritual complexity of rock carvings Gro Mandt has been able to demonstrate a local C/P structure in western Norway (Mandt 1972) and the same is true in other areas (Kjellén and Hyenstrand 1977: 27 f and 31 ff; Nordbladh 1980: 44). In southeastern Norway, Øystein Johansen has suggested a similar structure based on metalwork (1981), and the same is true of Denmark (recent works by Jensen 1981 and Thrane 1982). Also in Mälar region not alone the Kung Bjørn barrow (Almgren 1905) but recent settlement studies as well may be seen to point in the same direction (Jaanusson 1981; articles in Hyenstrand 1984a). Moreover, in Finland Unto Salo had made

suggestions of a local small-scale hierarchy, as evidenced in 'The size and location of cairns' (Salo 1983; also Seger 1983).

Such local structures tended to favour coastal farming populations with access to both alliance networks and a richer productive potential. Thus I propose that C/P relations were an essential structural feature of Bronze Age society. They formed a hierarchy from local to regional and interregional C/P structures and tended to direct surplus towards local and regional centers of strong chiefdoms in a system of unbalanced exchange. However, between regional centers of chiefdoms more direct links of trade and alliances could often be established. And strong chiefs from regional centers might send out expeditions to establish new alliances or even found new settlements in more distant areas. If successful, they might lead to overall changes in alliances and regional centers (Kristiansen 1978 and 1981).

It can also be suggested that trade and exchange at a larger scale took place at ritually defined regional meeting places. Perhaps this might be suggested for southern Scandinavia by the systematic grouping of hundreds of cooking pits in some of the very large settlements or settlement agglomerations in central Scandinavia (Thrane 1974) and by some of the major concentrations of cairns of firecracked stones (Hyenstrand 1978) and perhaps also by some of the central places with hundreds of rock-carvings, such as the much disputed Nämforsen in northern Scandinavia. A few isolated hoards with south Scandinavian bronzes in the marginal areas of Fenno-Scandinavia may testify to such long-distance trading expeditions from central Scandinavia settlements.

Thus C/P relations were an inherent feature of the operation of Bronze Age Society at both local and regional levels. The ability to direct surplus towards both local and regional centers was due to their superior ritual position, as reflected in more elaborate metalwork of ritual gear and/or scenaries in rock carvings. Local and regional peripheries were integrated into this ideological framework of ritual superiority, making possible their economic exploitation in a system of unbalanced exchange, whether as part of marriage alliances, gift-exchange or trade. Such a structural hierarchy of shifting regional and local C/P relations also provides a framework for explaining stylistic variations in pottery and metalwork.

The impetus to extend a basically south Scandinavian ideology even to the most remote areas, however, was social and economic. The peripheral areas in Scandinavia must have had material advantages that made it possible and worthwhile to maintain alliances with the more southerly regions. Alliances and exchanges are dependent upon the capacity to produce a surplus to give feasts. Here southern Scandinavia had a strong potential being one of the most productive regions in temperate Europe in terms of natural conditions of fertile soils and good fishing waters. Some of these products, such as dried fish or perhaps sheep and cattle, might have been part of the exchange with central Europe. But the extraordinary wealth and richness of the south Scandinavian Bronze Age calls for something extra. Besides amber, this was most probably exclusive furs from northern Scandinavia and maybe other products such as seal oil/skins (Fig. 8.9), although the evidence is scarce.[4]

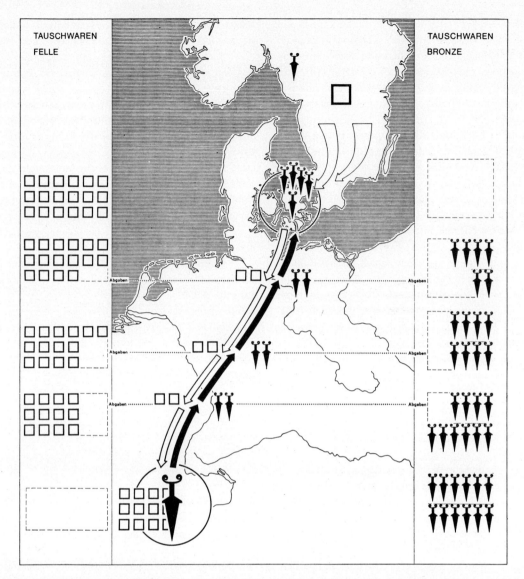

Fig. 8.9. Generalized map showing the changing rate of exchange between furs (to the left) and metal objects (to the right) from Scandinavia to Central Europe. Southern Scandinavia is considered to control exchange relations between Northern/Central Scandinavia and Europe (after Struve 1979, pl. 72)

The diffusion of Scandinavian ritual and ideology north-ward should thus be seen as a combined result of regular contact between local settlement units, in combination with more organized trading expeditions extending over long distances. Only in this way could the ideology of south Scandinavia have been accepted and integrated by all local settlements along the coastal areas. And its basis was a pre-existing Late Neolithic network; thus we do not have to think in terms of population movements on any larger scale. However, southern Scandinavia also received ritual influence from the north. As suggested by Mats Malmer, the south Scandinavian rock carvings were an indirect result of an ideological integration between northern and southern Scandina-via. In several localities a temporal overlap is demonstrated, e.g. reflected in reciprocal stylistic influences (Fett and Fett 1941: 137; Hagen 1969; in opposition Bakka 1973), perhaps most clearly at Nämforsen and Alta (Helskog 1985).[5]

This whole process represented the integration of the entire Scandinavian region into an international network of C/P rela-tions that linked the Aegean/Mediterranean region, Central Europe and Scandinavia to a common if transformed ideological framework. In this way it was able to transcend barriers of dif-ferent subsistence strategies and differences in the level of social organization. Instead such differences could be manipulated by ritual and ideological means.

With the decline of international exchange networks of prestige goods at the transition to the Iron Age, the whole system of center/periphery relations collapsed. The various regions devel-oped autonomous cultural and economic traditions. When we are again confronted with center/periphery relations in the Iron Age their foundation is not ritual superiority but commercial and mili-tary dominance.

Dedication

This article is dedicated to professor Evert Baudou in Umeaå as a tribute to his wide ranging contributions to Scandinavian Bronze Age research and to north Swedish archaeology, and to Professor Paul Simonsen in Tromsø for his contributions to the archaeology of Northern Norway.

Notes

1 It should be noted that cairns were also built during the Iron Age. Some of the largest along the Norwegian coast have turned out to belong to the late Roman/Germanic Iron Age, which was also an expansion phase in Norway (For cairns in general see Magnus and Myhre 1976, Meinander 1954, Baudou 1977 and Hyenstrand 1984b: 54 ff), and discussion in Bertilssom 1981.

2 This is not the place to enter a detailed discussion and definition of regional variations in terms of social and ritual complexity. Firstly, they fluctuate throughout the Bronze Age (Kristiansen 1978 and 1981) and secondly it represents a major research project that is already being carried out by a number of persons (Thomas Larsson, Hans Lundmark, Marie Louise Stig Sørensen) supplemented by several local studies (in Hyenstrand 1984a). Hyenstrand (1979 and 1984b) has provided some important general guidelines, just as the many earlier typological classifications of metalwork, such as Baudou (1960), provide a valuable empirical background. Larsson (1984) and Lundmark (1984) have provided an interesting methodological framework for analyzing regional variation in organizational complexity, and has presented some interesting preliminary results.

3 The abundance of rock carvings of ships – often whole fleets – in the central region gives ritual testimony to the importance of successful trading expeditions by sea and along the long coastlines of Norway and Sweden (Malmer 1981: 11 ff).

4 Neither archaeological nor literary evidence from the Mediterranean and the Near East indicate the employment of exotic furs during the Bronze Age. On the contrary furs were rather taken to characterize more barbarian countries. Hides, however, were widely employed and were imported, e.g. from Nubia to the Aegean. Hides were also subject to tribute and taxation.

Also in the well-preserved burials from the Early Bronze Age of Denmark (period 2, 1500–1200 BC) textiles are obviously a symbol of status, not furs. Cow-hides were employed as shrouds, indicating the symbolic value of cattle. The caps in the male burials, on the other hand, imitate fur being covered with a thick pile by oversewing (Broholm and Hald 1940). Just as amber is never found in south Scandinavian burials after the beginning of the Bronze Age, due to its high exchange value, the same could be true of furs. I want to thank Torben Holm-Rasmussen and John Lundd of the Antiquities Department of the National Museum in Copenhagen for having researched the ancient literature and reference works on the use of furs and hides.

5 The rich rock carvings from Alta in Artic Norway have underlined the cultural interrelation between the Arctic, central and southern Scandinavia as reflected in ship design. Also this remote area, with rich hunting/fishing settlements, was influenced by the major social and ideological changes in the Bronze Age. Thus from 1700 BC to 500 BC boats are much more numerous than during the Neolithic, and they are no longer depicted in hunting and fishing scenes but are found alone in association with travelling, gods, spirits or people – reflecting the importance attached to the organization of travelling and trading expeditions, and to the control over boats, fishing and trade (Helskog 1985).

Part four

**Imperial expansion and its hinterland:
zonal contrasts**

Chapter 9

**Imperial expansion under
the Roman Republic**

Daphne Nash

Our people, by defending its allies, has become master of the whole
world   (Cicero *de Rep.* 3.23.35)

The aim of this chapter is to examine the dynamics of expansion
of the Roman empire during the second and first centuries BC.[1]
The formation of the Republic's empire was a complex process,
expressive of the political development of Roman society during a
period of rapid change in Rome's place within the Mediterranean
world. The traditional aims of the narrowly constituted and
exclusivist military oligarchy which had laid the foundations of
the empire during the third century proved incompatible with the
demands of administering permanent overseas possessions.
During this last phase of its hegemony, the Senatorial oligarchy
experienced increasing difficulty in maintaining its traditional
structure when confronted with the many and varied consequences of the territorial and economic expansion set in train by its
very success in pursuing its fundamental military aims.

   The following discussion will be concerned primarily with
one period of Roman imperial expansion in order to examine the
relations between Rome and its neighbours in a particular historical context. This period opens at the end of the third century BC
with the defeat of Carthage and the beginning of rapid growth in
Rome's overseas empire. It closes in the early years of the first
century AD with the secure establishment of Augustus' administration, which brought about lasting changes both within the
organisation of the Roman state and in its management of the
empire.

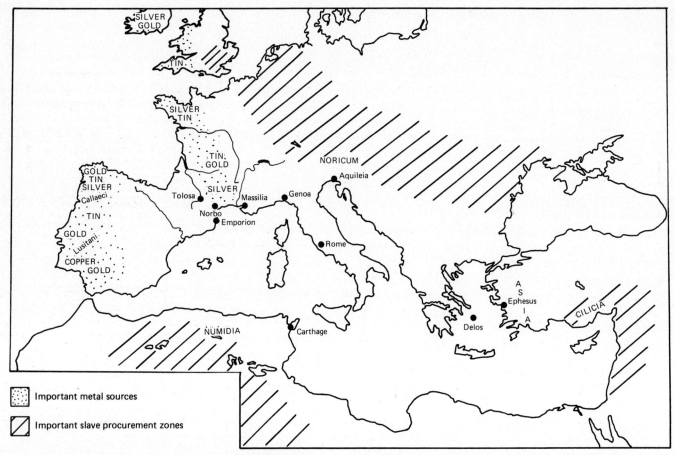

Fig. 9.1. Extra-provincial resources during the Late Republic.

Rome's meteoric development during the late Republic would have been impossible without labour and revenues from outside Italy, and indeed from outside the directly administered empire altogether.[2] The principal beneficiaries of these resources were the two leading sections of the Roman ruling-class: the office-holding Senatorial oligarchy with their monopoly in military leadership; and the wealthiest propertied families outside the Senate. This upper echelon of the so-called Equestrian Order included as its wealthiest members the *publicani* who formed companies to manage state contracts in the provinces (Badian 1972).

This division of the Roman ruling-class was in origin no more than a *de facto* distinction between very wealthy Romans who had held Senatorial office, and those who had not.

During the second century, however, an increasingly sharp separation of functions began to emerge between these two groupings. This development was directly related to problems arising from the management of a growing empire without any bureaucracy under Senatorial control other than *ad hoc* committees of Senatorial legates formed from time to time for such purposes as drawing up the charter of a new province or distributing public land. The split which arose within the Roman ruling-class served an important function for the Senatorial oligarchy, for it enabled the Senate to divest itself of many of the costs and risks

attendant upon the long-term management of the empire, particularly in the economic sphere.

This was, therefore, a distinctive period of Roman political history – the late Republic – during which the internal struggles of the Roman oligarchy gave rise to exceptionally rapid and extensive territorial expansion outside Italy, and also to violent conflict within the political heartland itself. Just as imperial expansion forced splits and sub-groupings within the ruling-class of Rome, so on the territorial plane, a clearly stratified regional system took shape. By annexing provincial territory, the frontier that separated directly administered Roman territories from the outside world moved forward repeatedly, bringing progressively more remote societies into contact with the Mediterranean world for the first time, and this had important consequences for resident societies on both sides of the imperial frontier.

In relating to its hinterland, four distinct zones concentric upon Rome may be identified, and their characteristics will be outlined in what follows. The first zone was a heartland consisting of Rome itself and Italy. The second consisted of the directly administered provinces, which together with Italy constituted the Roman empire. The third zone was composed either of allies and official friends of the Senate, or of enemies when its members were in conflict with Rome. This zone, close to the empire, was an important source of perishable goods and foodstuffs for the city-based economy of the empire, and the demand for subsistence had a marked effect upon the development of communities in the third zone of the periphery. The fourth zone was a remote periphery which can be seen to have been recognisably involved in the economic maintenance of the Roman empire, but which lay outside the immediate political concerns of Rome and about which most Romans claimed little knowledge or interest. This zone primarily supplied durable goods such as minerals, manufactured exotica, and slaves (fig. 9.1). During the Republic, the frontiers which divided these zones from one another moved gradually outward from the Mediterranean, with consequences which will be reviewed below.

Rome in the late Republic

Late Republican Rome was not to be surpassed by another European city either in size or in the scale of its consumption for nearly another millennium. As the administrative centre of a growing empire, the city was also the principal arena of civilian competition within the Roman ruling-class, enacted in the voting assemblies, Senate and law courts. The city was the single most important object of both official and private ruling-class expenditure, drawing to itself labour, foodstuffs and materials from every direction, and promoting the development of a wide range of manufacturing and export industries both at Rome and more widely in Italy. In the late Republic the Roman ruling-class still owned their most important estates in Italy, and lavish sums were spent upon the maintenance and embellishment of Italian towns and cities in addition to the extravagant expenditure upon Rome.

The expansion of the Roman economy after the Second Punic War (218–202 BC) therefore gave rise to an urgent and increasing need for food for the city population, for building and strategic materials to support civic and military enterprises, for luxury goods and skilled slaves for ruling-class display, and for barbarian slaves for use in most aspects of production. The mid-second century, from the 160s to the 140s, was an important milestone in this development. In 167 the inhabitants of Italy were permanently exempted from paying tribute, symptomatic of the changes in the Roman economy. For the first time dependable revenues from overseas provinces made it possible to confer this important privilege upon Rome's domestic hinterland. The 150s saw a marked upturn in the activity of the labour-intensive Italian, and especially Campanian, wine export industry (Tchernia 1983, Peacock 1984), which contributed at this time to a very greatly increased general demand in Rome and Italy for slaves of all kinds. The conquests of the first half of the second century, especially in the eastern Mediterranean, fostered the development of a Roman ruling-class appetite for expensive luxury goods from Greece and the east, heightened rather than sated by the plunder from Greece and Carthage in 146 BC. The rising wealth of the same ruling-class gave rise in the 140s to widespread investment in monumental construction work both in the city and in Italy.

At the same time, the city became a major centre of population. During the early second century BC many wealthy Romans had acquired large Italian estates on conquered territory, sometimes by illicitly appropriating unallocated public land and

sometimes by dispossessing less successful smallholders, many of whose difficulties were a consequence of unprecedentedly long absences abroad on military service. Since these large estates were commonly run with slave labour (Plutarch *Ti.Gracch.* 8), the dispossessed began to drift into the city, and this process gave rise to Senatorial concern on many counts, not least of which was a relentless decline in the numbers of Romans eligible for military service at a time when military service was still contingent upon a minimum property qualification, and military needs were fast increasing (Brunt 1971).[3]

From the mid-140s onwards, various attempts were made to alleviate this predicament, by land reforms, the settlement of new citizen colonies, and the provision of a subsidised grain dole in the city. Persistent resistance to such measures by traditional oligarchs within the Senate, and particularly to those measures which entailed relinquishment of misappropriated public land, led to the beginning of a century of civil bloodshed in 133 BC, and created a large and vigorous constituency of support for those politicians willing to mobilise it in the voting assemblies or, eventually, in arms, against the intransigence of the 'optimate' oligarchy (Velleius Paterculus *Roman History* 2.3.3, Cicero *de Rep.* 1.19.31). The epithet 'popularis' was coined in this epoch to describe those Senators who depended upon the support of the city population, the dispossessed, indebted, and veteran soldiers (Cicero *pro Sestio* 45ff), and it was on the basis of this conflict within the Senate that the ultimate internal struggles of the Roman Republic were thrashed out. During the second half of the first century BC the most successful of the great *populares*, Julius Caesar and his heir Octavian (later Augustus), succeeded in carrying out the necessary reforms, but only at the cost of Caesar's assassination by an 'optimate' faction, and a final and unprecedentedly violent episode of civil war which among other things destroyed the last recognisable remnants of the Republican oligarchy.

Oligarchic aims and the growth of empire

The governing body of the late Republic was the Senate, composed of some 600 publicly elected magistrates and ex-magistrates, under the leadership of two consuls. Relative to the total size of the Roman ruling-class this was a very small and disproportionately wealthy and powerful elite. The Senate was the senior legislative body of the Roman state, and it alone could negotiate with foreign states and communities. Only the Senate could declare war or a state of emergency, and only Senators could hold military commands. At the same time, normal tenure of all elected magistracies was for a single year and there were restrictions upon re-election, so that there was a high turnover of personnel in elective office, and most Senators could expect to hold several major posts in the course of their careers.

The political struggles of the late Republic and its consequences for the outside world were a legacy of the emergence of Rome to mastery in the Mediterranean during the third century BC under the leadership of a small elite group within the Senate consisting of members of some half-a-dozen exceptionally influential families. This traditional oligarchy had had a long and illustrious history, and some of its fundamental aims and imperatives, although now increasingly inappropriate, nontheless continued to play a key role in the development of the political economy because of the immense prestige of their exponents. In this respect, their military aims were especially important.

From the earliest times, the Roman state had been almost continually at war with one or another of its neighbours. Roman property-owning citizens all had an obligation to undergo periods of military service as young men, and the senior elective magistracies all carried military responsibilities. The military component of every Senator's career, initially under the authority of a more senior commander but ultimately in independent command of a legionary army in a province, was of especial importance for the formation of the Roman empire. During the late Republic legitimate military activity was confined to areas outside Italy, obliging even those Senators disinclined to travel to become involved in warfare and in the administration of a province. Every Senator therefore gained experience of both civilian and military responsibilities, since spells of office in Rome alternated with military appointments abroad. Internally, too, the military dimension of struggles and rivalries within the late Republican oligarchy was perhaps their single most distinctive feature, and governed the course and outcome of the civil wars.

A central collective oligarchic aim may be described most simply as an attempt to enjoy as many as possible of the benefits of winning an empire while delegating to others as many as possible of the associated costs. This aim had many and varied manifestations, some of whose consequences will be explored in what follows. Thus, in the military arena, so central to oligarchic aspirations, non-Roman allies bore an unduly large share of the burden of winning the empire while being excluded until 70 BC from any share in its government (Velleius Paterculus *Roman History* 2.15). Similarly, in political life, it was very difficult for a 'new man', in whose family there might even have been several generations of junior Senators but not yet a praetor or consul, to gain election to those senior and militarily important posts, and thus found a new noble line. By the same token, the large, wealthy and influential Italian ruling-class was excluded altogether from the Senate until 70 BC, and thereafter it was technically illegal for Senators to possess a ship or to invest heavily in commercial enterprises. While in practice this ordinance was widely disregarded by wealthy Senators, it did serve to maintain the exclusion from the Senate of the greater part of the wealthiest stratum of the Roman ruling-class as a whole, whose capital was heavily and openly invested in commerce. This meant that they could hold neither magisterial office nor military commands. In this way, too, in the economic sphere, a substantial proportion of the costs and risks associated with sustaining the empire and the privileges of its ruling elite were borne throughout this period by non-Senatorial groups within the citizen body and by foreign communities outside the empire altogether.

At an individual level, the principal aims of any Senator's political career were the tenure of magisterial office in Rome, from which a provincial command might arise, and the accumulation of a private fortune with which to promote his political career, support a lavish standard of domestic display, attract a large following of supporters, and invest in Italian land and property and in personal loans and related ventures.[4] While abroad and in a military command, most Senators' actions were likely to be governed by an overriding concern with their future in the city and in Italy. Thus, for instance, Julius Caesar's Gallic conquests of 58–51 BC were undertaken with a view to strengthening his political position relative to his military rival Pompey and his erstwhile patron Crassus, and his commentaries on the Gallic wars seem likely to have been written in 51 to publicise his achievements in a city with a strong anti-Caesarian faction at a time when he hoped to stand *in absentia* for a second consulship at the elections of 50 (Holmes 1911: 202f).

An ambitious commander might seek the coveted reward of a triumph for his military successes on his return home. There was no greater public honour. A triumphing general processed through the city like a deity, displaying his plunder, the proceeds of which – a vital source of state revenue – were deposited in the treasury, and led a train of prominent captives, many of whom were put to death afterwards. The triumphal celebrations and public distributions from booty were immensely popular in the city. It was, however, a traditional qualification for the exceptional distinction of a triumph that a general have added territory to the possessions of the Roman people, and this, together with the more or less annual turnover of provincial governors, each with similar aims and needs, added relentlessly to the momentum of expansion of the empire during this period. The very existence of permanent overseas provinces, seen from this perspective, was a monument to the personal achievements of the most ambitious and successful late Republican Senators.

For individual Senators, the financial rewards of successful military activity were as important as, if less openly vaunted than, its political rewards. Although there were in practice a variety of routes to senior office, several successful spells in the provinces on the staff of a general, and finally as an independent governor, was probably the most reliable means of achieving a good political career and a private fortune besides. The early stages of every Senator's career were particularly expensive relative to his income, encouraging young Senators to seek posts on the staff of promising generals.[5] Viewed from this perspective, provincial and foreign territory represented a vast reservoir of potential private revenues to be tapped by Roman military activity.

Thus, throughout their careers, the costs of electoral and magisterial expenditure in Rome were routinely recovered during provincial appointments, and senior commands were naturally most remunerative. Even noble families might fall into serious debt if the record of high office were not maintained in successive generations. This was for instance the case with the Julii Caesares in Caesar's youth, and his debts when he was due to go to Spain as propraetor in 61, in part a legacy of his lavish expenditure as aedile in Rome in 65, were so great that he was almost prevented from leaving the city. Plutarch (*Caesar* 11) says that it was only the fact that his wealthy patron M. Crassus paid off his most pressing debts and stood surety for a further vast sum of 830 talents (*c*.21,464 kg) of silver that enabled him to go. His ensuing

ferocious and seemingly ill-justified assaults on the Callaeci and
Lusitani made it possible to pay off all his debts on his return and
to finance the next stage in his career as well. He later made many
millions in Gaul as proconsul, allegedly flooding the Roman market with so much gold that the price of bullion fell by one third
(Suetonius *DJ* 54).

Some of the political consequences of this relationship
between Rome and its overseas territories may be observed in the
clash between individual generals and the Senate which began
very shortly after the acquisition of the first major overseas
provinces. As early as 187 L. Scipio Asiaticus was tried in the
Senate on a charge of having accepted a substantial bribe from
king Antiochus to secure advantageous terms after his surrender
to Rome. During his trial Scipio is said to have torn up his
account books in disgust that he should have been held to account
for a 'mere' four million *asses* when he had put two hundred
million into the treasury (Livy 38.55). Struggles such as this
within the Senate were now almost inevitable because a general in
action overseas had of necessity to make many *ad hoc* arrangements which he hoped would subsequently be ratified in Rome.
There was no other way in which a provincial war could be run,
since even the most efficiently organised long-distance communication was slow and very vulnerable to interference.

There was, therefore, also ample scope for profiteering and
corruption. Conflicts arising from this source were to dominate
much of the political life of the late Republic.

Attempts were made to minimise these conflicts, for
instance by restricting the tenure of provincial commands to a
single year, making rapid advancement to senior magistracies difficult, and making repeated tenure of consulships and proconsular
commands more difficult still.[6] In practice, however, all these
provisions were breached in times of political stress or military
emergency, particularly during the first century BC. Naturally, it
was the most prominent and experienced Senators who secured
repeated consulships, dictatorships, or prolonged provincial commands. C. Marius held seven consulships at the end of the second
century, primarily to meet the Cimbric emergency. Pompey held a
protracted command against Sertorius in Spain from 77–71, and
another in the East in 66–62. Julius Caesar commanded in Gaul
from 58–51, and shortly before his death had been voted Dictator
for life. Augustus forged his unique solution to the crisis of the
late Republic on the basis of an unbroken series of consulships
from 31 to 27 BC.

The oligarchy had good reason to fear the results of personal economic gain from military commands because of the use
to which a private fortune could be put in times of political stress.
The emergence of the military protagonists in the struggles of the
late Republic was facilitated by the inherent military aims of the
Republican oligarchy. It also drew upon another traditional
aspect of Roman public life.

From the earliest times, a Senator's prestige and political
influence had been dependent not simply upon his military
achievements but upon the number and standing of his personal
adherents or 'clients' at home and abroad (e.g. Q. Cicero *Com-
ment.Pet.* 1.9). In times of stress during the late Republic this
archaic system of patronage could be mobilised by members of
either Senatorial faction to raise gangs in the city or private
armies from the countryside.[7] Thus, in 83, the young Pompey
raised three legions in support of Sulla from his father's veterans
and dependants in Picenum, long before he had reached the minimum age to stand for Senatorial office. Pompey attached himself
to the traditional oligarchy, but this method of pursuing political
aims was especially characteristic of 'popularis' leaders. In the
mid-first century Caesar's patron M. Crassus, one of the wealthiest Romans of his day, is alleged to have said that no-one
deserved to call himself wealthy unless he could raise a legion
from his own income (Pliny *NH* 33.47), and several of the
protagonists in the disturbances of the first century BC did precisely that. The opening words of Augustus' own account of his
achievements openly boast of this entry upon public affairs after
Caesar's assassination in 44 BC: 'At the age of nineteen, on my
own responsibility and at my own expense, I raised an army with
which I set the Republic free from its oppressive domination by a
faction' (*RG* 1.1).

During the first century BC veteran soldiers became an
especially important class of adherents for these leaders, and
influential generals vied to provide well for the retirement of
soldiers they had commanded, if necessary on lands confiscated
from proscribed opponents, and would appeal for their military
help as necessary during civil conflicts. The emergence of what
were in effect private armies was a characteristic development
within the Senatorial oligarchy of the last century of the Republic,
and the need for land on which to settle veteran soldiers was an
important influence upon the Senate's attitude to its territories.

By the end of the third century BC, the military preoccupa-
tions of the Senate had begun to cause grave economic difficulties
for the State. The treasury had proved unable to meet the costs of
warfare in the final war with Carthage (Lewis and Reinhold 1966:
223ff), and this problem grew in proportions during the Mediterranean wars of the early second century. The Senate's habitual
sources of revenue, heavily dependent as they were upon military
activity, did not suffice to meet the costs of long-term military
commitments on this unprecedented scale. During the Second
Punic War the Senate had borrowed heavily from other citizens,
and found it difficult afterwards to repay its debts. Thereafter,
wealthy equestrians began to use their capital to play an essential
economic role in the exploitation of the empire, forming companies to purchase state contracts for taxes, military supplies and city
provisions, on the understanding that they would fill these contracts at a profit to themselves (Badian 1972). The treasury could
not have met its commitments, and especially those related to
perennial military activity abroad, without this support, so
the arrangement was to the mutual benefit of both ruling-class
fractions.

It was in this area that some of the most characteristic
features of the political economy of the late Republic became
manifest: the contradictory nature of the two main sources of
Roman state revenue, and the formal separation and partially
conflicting aims of the ruling-class groups most closely associated
with their respective procurement. Two main classes of state

revenues in Republican Rome can usefully be distinguished: those directly derived from military activity at the expense of alien populations, and those which were exacted through channels of civil administration and were levied upon citizens as well as upon aliens. During this epoch, procurement of the former was the exclusive prerogative of the Senate. The latter were mainly managed by non-Senatorial groups of behalf of the Senate. Both sources of state revenue had always existed, but military revenues seem to have been the mainstay of the Roman economy until at least the mid-second century BC.[8] Since the heaviest single item of state expenditure was traditionally the army, it might be possible to describe the primitive Roman state as a self-sustaining military economy, with an adequate agrarian subsistence base, and surplus revenues acquired primarily from the windfalls of warfare. The idealised late Republican image of the simple life of the 'early Romans', epitomised by the Dictator Camillus called up from his plough in 387/6 BC to save the city from the Gauls, reflects, albeit in exaggerated terms, something of the character of the primitive Roman state, so much in contrast with the new economic conditions to which the state was having to adjust during the late Republic (see e.g. Pliny *NH* 33.11.148).

Military revenues

Military revenues were the immediate economic proceeds of warfare: plunder itself, cash from the sale of captives and plunder, ransom obtained in exchange for war prisoners not sold as slaves, and war indemnities exacted from a defeated community such as Carthage. These revenues were gained at the cost to the state of fielding an army and losing citizen soldiers' lives. The Senatorial treasury always had shallow reserves, and any shortfalls in military revenues were made up by levying a tribute on citizens to meet the costs of warfare. This unpopular practice was discontinued in Italy in 167 BC, but was an important prototype category of administered revenue levied on a regular basis in the provinces after the Second Punic War.

During the course of the second century the balance of state expenditure began to change, and with it, the strain upon the treasury became insupportable. Heavy sums were now being spent upon the maintenance of the city and its population, until by the 140s when Polybius was writing, civic expenditure had begun in aggregate to rival military expenditure as a recurrent tax upon state resources (Polybius 6.17). At the same time, for a variety of reasons, military costs also began to rise very steeply. State expenditure was now for the first time in Roman history permanently raised well above a level which could be met by the unpredictable if occasionally spectacular proceeds of warfare.

For the current argument, changes in military expenditure were of especial importance because they had far-reaching implications for the formation of the empire. Not only were more armies being fielded than ever before, but the composition of the army changed twice, first at the end of the second century and then again in 70 BC, each time permanently raising the cost to the state treasury (cf. note (8) below).

During the second century, the Senate still employed the unique and highly successful military system that had achieved Roman mastery in the western Mediterranean. No major ancient state at this time could defend its interests, much less pursue imperial expansion, with an army drawn exclusively from its own citizen body. During the fourth and third centuries BC all the larger Mediterranean states other than Rome habitually supplemented their citizen forces with foreign mercenary soldiers, at high financial cost and at serious political risk, as the mercenary rebellion at Carthage in 240 demonstrated very clearly. Rome, by contrast, succeeded in paying relatively little for the armies that won her supremacy in Italy, and during the third and second centuries laid the foundations of an extensive Mediterranean empire.

Rome did not employ mercenaries. In Roman armies at that time landowning Roman citizens formed the core of the infantry legions, and a nucleus of cavalry. They paid for their own arms and equipment, but by the second century were receiving both subsistence and a salary from the state while on campaign. They also received a share of any spoils of war. To make up the full military complement, the Roman Senate also compulsorily recruited at least an equal number of infantry and three times as many cavalry from the autonomous allied communities of Italy (Polybius 6.26). Although allied troops were provided with subsistence and a share of the spoils, and fought under Roman military leadership and discipline, their salaries were paid not by Rome but by their own communities. The advantages of this arrangement for Rome were obvious.

This arrangement worked well while warfare was confined to Italy itself, enabling soldiers to return home annually, and allies, heavily drawn from the warrior communities of Central Italy, welcomed the chance of winning rich spoils from Roman wars. It was breaking down by the end of the second century under the stress of radically altered political and economic conditions. These changes affected both the citizen and allied sections of the army. Where citizens were concerned, the pool of potential Roman recruits had begun to contract alarmingly. The continual warfare of the early second century caused heavy loss of life, and long spells of military service abroad often left absent soldiers without a livelihood on their return, because their estates had fallen into disrepair in their absence, their families were in debt, or they found that they had been forcibly dispossessed by unscrupulous neighbours. Without land, they were no longer eligible for military service, and without employment in the countryside they had little alternative but to drift into the cities.

Attempts between the 140s and 120s to implement land reforms to restore this class of free smallholders, and thus both to alleviate much social distress and replenish the reservoir of army recruits, met with obstinate resistance within the traditional Roman oligarchy, some of whose estates and possessions were threatened.[9] A succession of demoralising wars in Spain throughout the second century, followed by a series of catastrophic defeats by Gallic and German war bands in the last decade of the century precipitated radical military reforms at Rome.

C. Marius, an ambitious 'new man', held a first consulship in 107, and his successes in 107–105 against Jugurtha in Numidia inspired the hope that he might be able to save Italy from the Cimbri and Teutones whose raids and repeated destruction of

Roman consular armies during the previous decade had caused panic in the city and the expectation of another Gallic sack. Marius was elected, exceptionally, to a second consulship in 104, and instituted lasting military reforms. With the disciplined army he trained during 104–103 while waiting for the Cimbri and Teutones to return to southern Gaul from Spain, he defeated the Teutones and Ambrones in 102 at Aquae Sextiae and in 101 helped his colleague Catulus to annihilate the Cimbri near Vercellae.

Marius' army reforms included extending eligibility for military service to the poorest but also the largest class of Roman citizens, who, having no land to tend, were prepared to serve for long periods as professional soldiers. This reform entailed certain costs to the treasury, however, since landless soldiers were utterly dependent upon the State for their livelihood, and came to expect a grant of land as a reward for long service. This cumulative demand soon began to cause grave difficulties in Italy, unresolved until the time of Augustus.

The financial cost of recruiting landless citizens was soon greatly compounded by the enrolment of the Italian allies as Roman citizens in the census of 70 BC, after the bitter conflict of the Social War described below. This meant that in future wars the Roman treasury was obliged to pay Italian troops for their services, and though the continued recruitment of allies from Transpadane Gaul mitigated the consequences of this change, it nonetheless brought about an enormous increase in military expenditure to the Senatorial treasury.[10] Against this background the violence which attended the political unification of Italy, described below, can occasion little surprise. It was a process intrinsic to the expansion of the Republican empire but in conflict with narrowly defined oligarchic interests.

Provincial administration

The Roman state had always had some administered revenues in the form of rent on public land and mines, taxes on certain sales and the manumission of slaves, transport and harbour dues, and war tribute, but they had traditionally taken second place in importance to military revenues. This reliance upon military sources of revenue might be satisfactory for a small state with few imperial responsibilities and low internal costs, but was not an adequate basis for the economy of a large empire. It was now vitally important for the state to secure dependable and perennial revenues through administrative channels, relying upon warfare as a source of essential but unpredictable supplements to this income. From the early second century BC, the overseas provinces began to meet this need. The most important categories of provincial revenue were tribute, levied on land and population, rent on mines and transport and harbour dues levied at ports and markets. These revenues were above all a tax upon the agrarian produce of the provinces, and upon commercial activity everywhere in the Roman empire.[11]

The early history of the immensely rich province of Roman Asia is paradigmatic in this respect (Magie 1950): a province left to the Roman people by royal legacy rather than conquered by force of arms, it was accepted in 133 BC amid conflict in the Senate about the appropriate uses to which its enormous tax revenues could be put. A strong claim was made to use the money to finance land reforms and the settlement of citizen colonies abroad, to alleviate the social problems alluded to above. In common with most other eastern provinces, Asia had had a long history of tax production for a succession of overlords and empires, and under Roman rule it proved to be an important testing-ground for methods of exploiting such a possession (Lewis and Reinhold 1966: 343).

An important distinction now emerged between two uses of the Latin term 'provincia', related to the division within the Roman ruling-class alluded to above, and the separate economic functions of each of its two major fractions. Administered revenues were not directly collected by the Senatorial governor of a province and his staff, although it was the governor's responsibility to see to it that they were collected. Instead, their collection fell to equestrian contractors and their agents, and to local nobilities whose cooperation with the Roman administration frequently earned them the hatred of their own populations but the gratitude of Rome, acknowledged very often by individual grants of citizenship.

The first, and most primitive, meaning of 'provincia' was the sphere of official responsibility and legitimate military activity allotted to a Roman general with *imperium*, and it was under this meaning that the Provinces in the other sense were conquered. In the first sense of the word, provinces were the oldest source of new land and military revenues for the Roman state, and owing to the persistence of military imperatives within the Roman ruling-class, 'provincia' continued to hold this meaning throughout the late Republic. Provinces in this sense were of course the special preserve of the Senatorial oligarchy, and the ambiguity in the meaning of the term left scope for any Senatorial governor to extend the territorial limits of an established Province if he could demonstrate to the satisfaction of the Senate that in so doing he was acting in defence of the interests of the Roman people by conquering its enemies. Although in principle a province in the military sense had definable limits – and parts of Julius Caesar's army mutinied in 58 BC, seemingly because their officers, mindful of optimate attitudes in Rome, objected to Caesar overstepping the obvious interpretation of his command – it was within the brief of a general in the field to give a liberal interpretation to the 'interests of the Roman people', in the hope that his actions would subsequently be ratified by a grateful Senate. In this way, much fresh territory was continually added to the empire.

A Province in the second sense was captured or ceded external territory directly administered by the Roman Senate and without a foreign policy of its own. It was a territorial entity with explicitly defined frontiers, governed in accord with the edict of each incoming governor, which covered the regulation of taxes, the relationship between different classes of community in the province, and judicial arrangements. In general, pre-existing systems of revenue collection and local jurisdiction were altered as little as possible when a province was annexed, providing that they were compatible with the requirements of the Roman administration (e.g. Sicily: Lewis and Reinhold 1966: 346ff). A Province in this sense was therefore a permanent sphere of Roman administration, yielding regular revenues in the form of tribute, rent on property and mines, and a range of taxes and duties on goods and services. Contracts for tax revenues and for the procurement of supplies were let at Rome by the Censors at quinquennial auctions. Thus, equestrian companies were able to establish relatively long-term commitments in the Provinces, seeking to meet their obligations to the state at a profit to themselves.

Provinces were therefore areas within which Roman property quickly spread. Confiscated provincial territory might be taken as state property and made subject to rent accruing to the treasury, or it might be sold or allotted to private owners. As a consequence, Roman investment outside Italy was always heaviest in the formally administered Provinces, as surviving roads and monuments demonstrate. In the 70s BC Cicero described the Province of Transalpine Gaul, in the vicinity of Narbo Martius, as 'so crowded with Roman citizens, that scarcely a commercial transaction took place without a Roman being involved' (Cicero *Pro Fonteio* 5.11,13). There was a grain of truth in this exaggeration; Narbo Martius was the first and most important Roman colony in Gaul, founded in 118 BC (Levick 1971), and an important commercial centre (Cicero *Pro Fonteio* 5.13).

The late Republic was therefore a period during which Rome and Italy constituted themselves as consumers of revenues from elsewhere. As providers of the widest range of revenues, the provinces enabled the centre of the empire in Rome and Italy to undergo great economic expansion on the basis of conspicuous consumption and luxury commodity production (cf. Garnsey 1983).

The emergence of the Equestrian Order

The formation of the Equestrian Order as a distinct grouping within the Roman ruling-class relates very closely to the Senate's failure to create any permanent internal bureaucracy to administer provincial revenues. Senatorial governors could not and did not manage the long-term finances of the provinces they governed. Instead, they relied upon equestrian companies with many years' experience of working in a specific Province. The *publicani* seem to have had little difficulty in persuading a succession of annual governors to cooperate with them in their exactions, for instance by providing them with a cavalry escort with which to harass reluctant communities (Cicero *ad Att* 5.21; cf. note 4). In this way, equestrian wishes began to have a marked influence upon the development of the empire, particularly in the tax-rich eastern provinces.

In some respects both Senators and equestrians had convergent interests in the Provinces. There were very great fortunes to be made there by both sections of the Roman ruling-class, and this brought the wealthiest members of the equestrian order – the *publicani* and their associates – into close association with the Senatorial oligarchy. Cooperation or collusion between them enabled Senatorial capital to be invested both legitimately and illicitly (Cicero *in Verr.* 2.69ff) in equestrian business, while the military management of the provinces, essential for the security of equestrian business, was itself a source of equestrian revenues when for instance the sale of war captives took place (Cicero *ad Att* 5.20.5 etc.). But conflicts of interest also arose.

A conscientious governor, like Gabinius in Syria in 55 BC (Broughton 1952: 218) or Cicero in Cilicia in 51–50 BC, might seek to curtail equestrian activities in favour of the provincial communities, whose gratitude was of especial importance to a 'new man' in Roman politics. But this risked antagonising the local *publicani*, and even Cicero did not carry out all his generous plans. Similarly, equestrian companies might find they had bid too high for tax concessions, and would then find themselves embattled with the Senate when they sought to have their bids remitted, as occurred over the Asian taxes in 61–59 BC.

In Rome itself, conflicts between Senatorial and equestrian interests were enacted in the courts (Gruen 1968). Since the Second Punic War, Senatorial courts had proved ineffective in curbing abuses by their peers, and the first equestrian extortion court was instituted by C. Gracchus in 122 BC. Here, Senatorial governors returning from provincial commands could be held to account for maladministration. Conviction by this court could deliver a severe check to the progress of a Senator's career. The equestrian extortion court was originally created by 'popularis' legislation to protect the interests of provincials, the Roman people and the oligarchy alike from the potentially disastrous consequences of unbridled Senatorial rapacity in the provinces. It also represented the first formally constituted equestrian political institution.

By creating a non-Senatorial court to sit in judgement upon Senators, this enactment put the old *de-facto* division between Senators and equestrians on a new footing (Cicero *de Leg* 3.9.20; Varro in *Non. Marcell.* p.728L). The now more sharply defined division between them was a cardinal feature of the political economy of the late Republic, theorised on behalf of the optimate oligarchy in speeches and letters by M. Cicero. The creation of the first equestrian court thus unexpectedly marked an important turning-point in the relationship between the two major groupings within the Roman ruling-class, and the vicissitudes of these courts and battles over the composition of their juries was to play a key role in the political struggles of the late Republic.

The internal affairs of the city of Rome in this period were consequently dominated by increasingly dangerous rivalries not simply among the wealthiest and most powerful members of the Senatorial nobility described above, but between the Senate and the upper echelons of the Equestrian Order. At the heart of these struggles was the management of Rome's growing empire, for it was in the provinces that office-holding magistrates and ex-magistrates and equestrian contractors for state revenues and supplies were most closely associated with one another. We may now turn to the effects that these struggles had upon the formation of the territorial empire.

The formation of an Italian heartland

Until the mid-third century when the conflict with Carthage had begun in earnest, Roman expansion had essentially been within Italy, at the expense of its Italian, Etruscan and Greek neighbours (fig. 9.2). The piecemeal character of this process over a period of three centuries meant that during the second century the constituent communities of Italy had a range of different ties

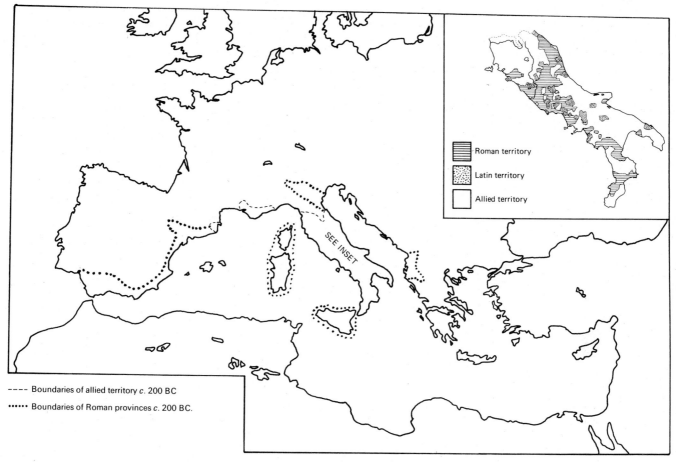

Fig. 9.2. The Roman world *c.* 200 BC.

with Rome (Sherwin-White 1973). These were to provide models for the relations subsequently established with overseas dependencies. Confiscated or conquered territory in a belt across central and northern Italy was defined as Roman public land. This was most closely associated with the city, and constituted the innermost core of the early empire. Here there were numerous enclaves and colonies of Roman citizens presiding over an essentially provincial population. Land which had not been sold freehold to Roman citizens was either farmed or grazed for a rent to the treasury, and during the second century stretches of such land were also at times illicitly appropriated by wealthy Romans and treated as though they were their legitimate private possessions, with consequences outlined above.

Outside Roman territory, the oldest Roman dependency, Latium, had a peculiarly close relationship with the city. Until 150 BC, Latins permanently resident in Rome were in fact entitled to Roman citizenship, although thereafter automatic access to the citizenship was confined to wealthy Latins who had held magistracies in their own communities and thus had performed especially valued services for the Roman Senate. Instead, Latins temporarily resident in Rome were given limited voting rights in Roman elections, and in 122 BC were accorded the much coveted right of appeal against the actions of Roman officials.

Although nominally autonomous until 89 BC, when they received full Roman citizenship with the rest of Italy, the Latins were in fact subject to Roman foreign policy and military discipline. The Roman army depended heavily upon the Latins, and Roman conquered territory was garrisoned not only by citizen colonies, but by communities with Latin rights. These were populated by Latins, and by poor Romans who thereby surrendered full citizen rights. Latin colonies in Italy and Cisalpine Gaul were especially important as military recruiting grounds, and together with Roman colonies performed essential functions in the establishment of Roman culture and discipline in conquered territories. Rome's relationship with the Latins, as it developed between 150 and 89 BC, was the model for the Latin rights subsequently accorded to many provincial communities outside Italy as a privileged status short of full citizen rights.

Elsewhere in Italy during the second century BC the Greek and native Italian communities were autonomous allies of Rome. Their inhabitants had no systematic access to Roman citizenship, and were bound to Rome by individual treaties. There were two categories of alliance. The first was an equal alliance which recognised the mutual autonomy of both partners, obliged the ally to help Rome in defensive wars and entitled it to request similar help from Rome. The second was an unequal alliance, which obliged the ally to provide military aid for any Rome war, and in general to respect Roman authority. Latins and dependent allies furnished well over half the manpower of all Roman armies until 70 BC, and consequently played an essential part in the conquest of the empire.

Equal alliances were, however, frequently converted into unequal ones, since even an equal alliance imposed constraints and burdens upon the ally which might lead to rebellion. This was commonly punished by reinstatement of the alliance on less favourable terms. This model of alliance, together with the tendency towards degradation of the privileges of allies, was in due course extended to overseas allied communities, and by the late second century BC a majority of Roman allies everywhere were subject to an unequal and firmly subordinate relationship with Rome.

This relationship with the allies was very much to Rome's advantage. Where the Italians were concerned, treaties of alliance obliged them to give military assistance at their own expense but under Roman leadership, as described above, while excluding their nobilities from access to the Senate or to senior military commands in Roman wars, thus preserving the hegemony of the Roman oligarchy. The allies therefore bore a very large share of the labour of winning the empire, but had no direct part in its government. This exclusion became increasingly frustrating and anomalous with the growing closeness of the association between Romans and Italians in the economic exploitation of the overseas provinces after the Second Punic War.

Italian agriculture and commerce in fact made as essential a contribution to the growing Roman economy as did Italian soldiers. From the beginning of the second century, the Italian allies of Rome invested heavily in independent commercial activity in the provinces, with special emphasis upon the sale of Italian wine and the procurement of slaves for Italian and Roman markets (e.g. Cicero *Pro Fonteio passim*; Tchernia 1983). Transport and harbour dues levied both in the provinces and in Italy raised large Roman revenues from this vigorous trade. Since the allies bore all the costs and risks attached to this commerce, the Roman government derived economic benefit even in this non-military sphere from maintaining the alien status of the allies.

Faced with the intransigent refusal by the Senate to admit them to Roman citizenship, and thus potentially to a share in the government of the empire, the Italian allies finally rose in a concerted rebellion in 91 BC, with the aim of either securing the citizenship or of destroying Rome altogether and setting up an alternative Italian state. They were led by generals from the Central Italian warrior states whose military contribution had been heaviest. The Roman Senate was victorious, but at excessive cost, and the oligarchy withdrew from its now untenable position. At the close of this so-called Social War of 91–89 BC the Italian allies, together with the Latins and some of the inhabitants of Cisalpine Gaul, were enfranchised at Rome, though it was not until 70 BC that they were actually included in the census and thus able to receive the practical benefits of their newly acquired citizenship.

The resolution of the Social War therefore meant that the whole of Italy south of the Po became for the first time a homogeneous block of Roman territory, and this innermost core of the Roman empire now became ever more closely identified with the political and economic concerns of the city. This initial consolidation and enlargement of the Roman heartland was followed in due course by further expansion into the North Italian Plain (fig. 9.3), and was accompanied at each step by a complementary spread of Latin rights into adjacent provincial areas, primarily in the north-western quadrant of the empire. This development served an essential military function, since provincial Latin communities could still be called upon to supply soldiers on the traditional self-financing basis.[12]

Rome's earliest province north of the Apennines had been Cisalpine Gaul, divided into two zones either side of the Po. The conquest of the area, begun in the late third century, was complete by 100 BC, and it then became an abundant source of cheap foodstuffs, wool and other raw materials for the city of Rome (Polybius 2.15), as well as a prolific recruiting ground for soldiers. Cisalpine Gaul was the first area outside Italy to be incorporated into the Italian heartland. Thus, the southern, Cispadane, area seems to have received citizenship after the Social War in 89 BC together with the rest of Italy, while Transpadane Gaul was accorded Latin rights. In 49 BC Caesar gave full citizen rights to the Transpadanes and Latin rights to the leading communities of the old Republican provinces of Transalpine Gaul and Spain. Augustus finally extended the Italian heartland to its geographical limits at the Alps by abolishing the old province of Cisalpine Gaul and incorporating it into the administrative area of Italy. New colonies were now routinely placed overseas to cater for the needs of veteran soldiers and to provide a reservoir of recruits. This expansion of the Roman heartland was made possible by the growing capacity of the overseas provinces to sustain the privileges of such a large imperial centre.

Economic development in the provinces

The pattern of relationships between Rome and the inhabitants of the Italian peninsula before 91 BC was in many ways replicated outside it as Italy ceased to provide Rome with some of its customary services and revenues. Foreign communities, whatever their status, were openly regarded as being the most legitimate of all targets for Roman economic and military exploitation, and the Senate generally displayed little practical concern for the wellbeing of their inhabitants. In so far as they constituted foreign territory, the provinces too were acknowledged as essentially and legitimately exploited areas. Here, however, the fact that they were also Roman possessions and responsibilities, in which different sections of the Roman ruling-class had important vested interests, meant that their needs and grievances could not lightly be ignored by the Senate.

Roman economic activity took a variety of forms in the provinces. On behalf of the government, food and materials might be directly requisitioned as a component of tribute, or compulsorily purchased at a fixed price below market value (e.g. Cicero *in Verr.* 3.70.163). Where taxes were collected in cash, market trade proliferated to generate the necessary silver coinage. Everywhere, free commerce developed to provision provincial towns and Italian markets, and this was the most important link between provincial territory and the outside world, promoting the formation of trading networks that reached far into alien territory (Haselgrove, this volume). Allied communities embedded in provincial territory played an especially important role in articulating these dendritic networks, as described below. This activity seems generally to have encouraged the development of appropriate manufacturing and extractive industries, and the surplus production of leather, wool, grain, pottery, and metals not only in the provinces themselves but in alien communities close to their frontiers. Thus although intensive Roman exploitation might eventually prove damaging to the agrarian sector of a provincial economy (Duncan-Jones 1980), in the shorter term it gave rise to increased prosperity at least among provincial elites, reflected in the growth of urban centres everywhere.

Trade across provincial borders with foreign communities was handled by a multiplicity of Italian and provincial traders acting on their own behalf or on behalf of larger companies. Long before their enfranchisement by Rome, the activity of Italian traders based in the provinces had earned them a reputation for rapacity not only in the provinces but in the territory of external allied or friendly communities. Diodorus (5.25.3) commented on their greedy purchase of Gallic slaves at what he regarded as the astonishingly low price of an amphora of wine per slave, and Cicero (*Pro Fonteio* 9.20) drew attention to equestrian resentment at having to pay state tax on such traffic as it passed through provincial territory. Revenues from this source were handsome: six silver denarii per amphora on its way out of Transalpine Gaul and presumably a further import duty on the returning slaves.[13] Strabo (4.6.7, 4.6.12) likewise described incidents during the second and first centuries BC in Noricum and the Alps where Italians, lured by the prospect of exploiting local gold deposits, so antagonised the native chiefs that the Senate had officially to curtail their activites in the interest of maintaining peaceful relations with the important Celtic kings in the territory of whose dependants the deposits lay.

Suitably placed provincial centres such as Narbo and Tolosa in Gaul, or Aquileia on the Adriatic (Alföldy 1974) acted as bases for large-scale commercial activity beyond the frontiers. By the same token, the close economic ties between the provinces and cooperative alien communities situated close to the frontier encouraged the development of marketing systems in the close vicinity of the empire and the formation of towns in places where none had previously existed.

Where western Europe is concerned, the dense distribution of Campanian wine amphorae and ceramic dinner services in the frontier zone and beyond during the second and early first centuries BC is evidence for the lively trading relations established with autonomous Gallic communities, yielding ample taxes on traffic across the frontiers (Nash 1978a: 112–113; Peacock 1984; Tchernia 1983; Galliou 1984). During this period ties of official friendship were formed with native kings and states behind the imperial frontier, facilitating trade with them in commodities and especially in slaves, and forming an almost unbroken belt of alien communities and states in close and dependent relationship with Rome. At the same time, these foreign friends relieved the empire of certain strategic and military concerns. They therefore performed essential, if indirect, functions for the Roman state. These arrangements worked well in the interests of the Senate in the short term, and at the same time boosted the fortunes of the external communities which cooperated with Rome, making ties of friendship with the Senate a privilege much sought after by barbarian princes (Caesar *BG* 1. 35.2; 1.44.5; Augustus *RG* 31–3).

Rome's relations with communities outside the empire

The establishment of permanently administered overseas provinces defined the geographical frontier with the outside world, separating Roman territory both from autonomous allies and official friends, and from external enemies of the Roman Senate.

Certain essential commodities, especially scarce metals and most slaves, had of necessity to be obtained from areas far from the heartland of the empire, and sometimes from immense distances, since for geographical or social reasons they were not sufficiently available within provincial territory to meet the needs of the growing empire (fig. 9.1). Whereas the Senate was eager to possess silver and gold mines, rent on which accrued to the treasury, the procurement of the slaves that were needed in tens of thousands for agricultural and industrial service within the empire was a different matter. Within provincial territory, the only legitimate source of slaves was capture in warfare, a preserve of the Senatorial governor and his army. The non-Senatorial traders who provisioned Roman and provincial markets were obliged to obtain slaves either by purchase from victorious generals in the field, or in trade with communities external to the empire. Until 88 BC the Aegean port of Delos was the single most important source of such slaves, marketed there by Mediterranean pirates. These remained the chief eastern source of slaves until Pompey's elimination of organised Mediterranean piracy in 67 BC thrust this trade outwards to the frontiers of the empire. From this time onwards, Central Europe and Gaul became the leading sources (Crawford 1977). Commercial trade for slaves undoubtedly fostered the first-century expansion of 'European' warrior communities such as the Belgae and Germans, whose perennial warfare generated a rich harvest of captives. It also boosted the fortunes of middlemen communities in immediate contact with the empire, such as the Aedui. This dynamism probably underlies some of the social and historical developments described by Haselgrove in this volume.

It was clearly an advantage for the Senate to be able to rely on external communities to organise the procurement of exogenous commodities and slaves, and while the relationship remained advantageous to the Senate, foreign friends and allies were treated with a measure of respect. Under this arrangement, much of the profit from management of peripheral supply networks was taken by alien nobilities and therefore kept outside the empire, and this generally led in the short term to a period of marked political and economic growth on the part of Rome's external associates.

Overseas allies

Few Roman provincial areas under the late Republic were

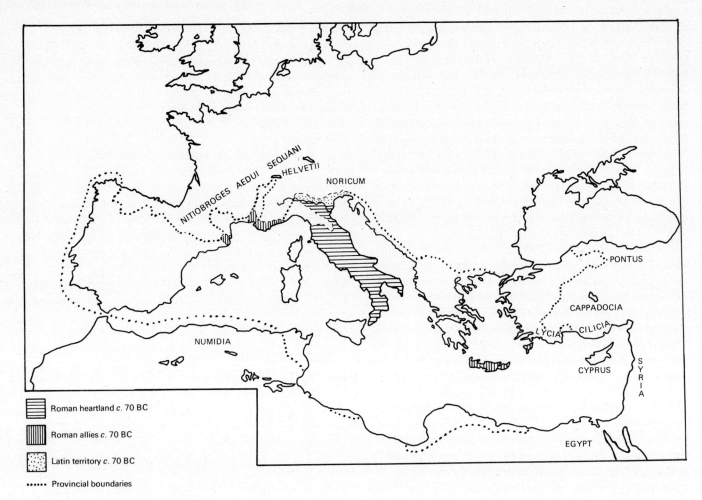

Fig. 9.3. The Roman world *c.* 70 BC.

homogeneous blocks of directly administered subject territory. Most were punctuated by areas of allied territory as well as by Latin or citizen colonies, as had been the case in second-century Italy. Overseas allies were in the closest of all geographical and economic proximity to the empire, frequently embedded deeply in surrounding provincial territory. In general, Rome received a range of vital economic and strategic benefits in return for recognising the ally's formal autonomy and immunity from direct interference. In the overseas provinces, as in Italy, treaties of alliance might range from terms of relative equality as in the case of Massilia, to severe subordination as in the case of Carthage.

Rome's overseas allies paid a high price for their titular freedom, recalling what had been expected of the Italians before their final rebellion. Rome tended to abolish territorially strong allies, and those that remained were generally important commercial centres able also to provide policing services and military or naval assistance when required. Massilia, for instance, supervised the vital overland route between Italy and the Rhône delta, linking Rome with its western provinces, provided naval support in Roman wars, and helped to police the pirate-infested Ligurian coastline. It was also an important port of long-distance trade, linking Italy and the Mediterranean with the Rhodanian corridor and northern Gaul.[14]

In the economic sphere, all but a few especially privileged allies were subjected to harbour dues and transportation taxes when dealing with the Roman provinces. In view of their commercially based economies, this was an important tax upon their prosperity. In the west, allies such as this, which always possessed important ports of long-distance trade, included Massilia and her chain of coastal dependencies, Emporion, Carthage until her destruction in 146 BC, and the Ligurian port of Genoa. These cities and markets played a vital part in the economic development of adjacent provincial areas, forming as they did nodal points on long-range commercial networks.

Official friends

The distinction between a Roman ally and an official friend of the Senate or *amicus* is not always easy to recognise. Perhaps the main difference between them was one of emphasis, since under peaceful conditions *amici* seem to have made less of a direct military contribution to the Roman state, supplying fewer auxiliary soldiers except under emergency conditions, such as Caesar's Gallic wars. Official friends' ability to manage commercial networks, often procuring durable materials or slaves from a very great distance, seems to have been their most important contribution to the empire, together with their ability to supply it with food and perishable goods, and to act as a buffer state between the empire and its remoter periphery.

Perhaps because of this indirect relationship with their foreign friends, the Senate seems not to have acknowledged any obligation to defend them unless it was very obviously in their own interests to do so. In attempting to define the character of official friendship with Rome, Appian (*Celt.* 13) suggests that it was always more a prestigious than a practical arrangement for the friend. The Aedui, for instance, Rome's longest-standing and most valued Gallic friends (Caesar *BG* 1.43.7), pleaded with the Senate in vain in 62 BC for help against their German enemies (Caesar *BG* 1.44.9), and when Caesar did respond to their renewed appeal in 58 it seems largely to have been motivated by his own ambitions, since it gave him the excuse he needed to take his military campaigns deep into free Gaul. It is not in fact clear that at that moment Roman interests were under any real threat, as he wished to claim in justification for his decision to attack one *amicus*, the German Ariovistus, on the behalf of other, Gallic friends (*BG* 1.31.16, 1.33). The kings of Noricum, by contrast, whose function as a buffer state on the north-eastern frontier of Italy was very highly valued at Rome, won a concession in 170 BC to purchase horses in Italy, together with lavish diplomatic gifts, as an apology from the Senate for unwarranted interference by a Senator who had overreached his command (Livy 43.5).

For an *amicus*, therefore, the main attractions of the relationship with Rome were the prestige it conferred, and trading concessions with the empire. These could be, and often were, used to extend the client community's influence within its own region and thus to strengthen the basis of its ties with Rome. In this way, the Kings of Noricum were able to gain hegemony over neighbouring communities in the Alps during the second century, and in the late second century BC the Aedui were able to detach themselves from their apparent third-century subordination to the leading chiefdoms of the upper Rhineland to become an influential Celtic state in their own right. Tacitus (*Agricola* 14), thinking of the growth of the southern British kingdoms during the early first century AD, commented that the Romans were in the habit of using kings to enslave others on their behalf. The Republican Senate and Augustus alike encouraged the growth of official friends' influence and power so long as it enhanced the efficiency of the services provided for the empire. Thus, for instance, a succession of conspicuously strong autonomous Gallic societies formed near the frontiers of the western provinces as they expanded, first in Cisalpine Gaul in the third century BC, then in the Alps in the second century, at the head of the Rhône valley in the early first, and finally in Germany and southern Britain during the second half of the first century BC and the first century AD (cf. Haselgrove, this volume). Contact with the Roman empire might therefore have a marked influence upon the economic and political development of official friends of the Senate, encouraging the formation of politically centralised states where they had not previously existed.

Enemies
The Roman empire's dependence upon its neighbours gave rise not only to the broadly peaceable and contractually regulated relationships with allies and official friends outlined above, but also to hostile and predatory relations with communities defined as enemies. While some measure of responsibility was acknowledged for allies and even for friends, reflected in an undertaking not to interfere gratuitously in their internal affairs, enemies were regarded as legitimate military targets for whose welfare no concern need be evinced.

This outlook served a practical purpose. No guilt or responsibility need attach to the plunder or destruction of enemy communities, the enslavement of enemy populations, or the seizure of enemy territory, because all enemies were by definition regarded as having provoked their just treatment by Rome. Thus, before the Senate or a Roman general could open hostilities it was necessary for recognised grounds for retaliation to be established and ritually acknowledged. Junior Senators had ample opportunity to learn the appropriate techniques for legitimizing warfare during their service on the staffs of senior commanders. Julius Caesar's career in Spain, Gaul and ultimately in the civil war illustrates their effectiveness.

So pervasive was this Roman outlook upon the external world that all extra-provincial territories were liable to be regarded generically as enemies unless specifically designated as friendly. This was especially so in the less socially developed areas of temperate Europe and Africa where perennial native brigandage and periodic raids on provincial territory lent validity to the habitual Roman view, and where when border warfare was not currently in progress it could very easily be provoked in order to justify a Roman attack.

This automatic attitude can be seen in the written works of contemporary Roman authors. Thus, in describing the essentially peaceable wine trade between the province of Transalpine Gaul and the Celts of south-western Gaul or the Aquitanians, Cicero (*Pro Fonteio* 9.19) spoke of wine on its way 'to the enemy'. Likewise, at the end of his life, reviewing his enlargement and consolidation of the empire, Augustus could proudly boast that 'those external peoples whom I could safely pardon, I preferred to preserve rather than to exterminate' (*RG* 3.2 cf. Vergil *Aen.* 6.847–53).

This Roman outlook upon the outside world may be regarded from the standpoint of the current discussion as an intrinsic aspect of the Senate's habitual practice of making others bear the less acceptable costs of its own expansionary tendencies. At this period, the Roman state was constantly seeking fresh territory, an imperative lent especial urgency with the expansion of the citizen body in 70 and the impact of the needs of veteran soldiers thereafter. Individual Senators also all required opportunities for military achievement. It was therefore absolutely necessary that there exist an arena for military aggression for the welfare of whose inhabitants the Senate need take no responsibility. The Republican oligarchy could contain its internal stresses to only a limited extent, as the almost continuous civil disturbances between the 130s and 31 BC reveal. The long-term use of provinces as an arena for the resolution of its conflicts posed grave difficulties because of the Senate's ultimate responsibility for their welfare, as the painful history of the province of Asia, particularly, demonstrates. Thus, the Roman state actually needed extra provincial enemies about whom it need have little or no concern, and in attacking and plundering whom it could actually claim righteous justification (cf. quotation at head of this chapter).

With enemy communities profitable trading relations might nonetheless also be undertaken, but this was probably always a matter for private enterprise, unprotected by official agreements or treaties. Under these conditions, the enemy had no redress against extortionate dealings, but those trading ultimately on Rome's behalf had equally to bear very considerable risks with no official protection other perhaps than a reasonable conviction that any damage to themselves might be eagerly seized upon by the governor of an adjacent province as an excuse for opening hostilities on the enemy. This justification was used under Caesar's governorship of Transalpine Gaul to conduct campaigns in the Alps (*BG* 3.1.2).

Although external territory was sometimes ceded to Rome by peaceable means, particularly in the eastern Mediterranean, in the West, Roman territorial expansion under the Republic was almost invariably the outcome of military conquest at the expense of enemies. As a result, enemy territory outside the provincial frontiers came in effect to be regarded almost as a reserve of potential Roman possessions, exploited indirectly in the short term, but perpetually threatened with conquest in the longer term, as reflected in the spasmodic outward movement of the provincial frontier in Spain and Gaul during the second and first centuries BC.

Thus, there was an inherent tendency for the Roman Republican empire to expand. Its expansion was not, however, allowed to proceed indiscriminately, and not every returning governor's arrangements were ratified by the Senate. One reason for this was the Senate's apparent concern to avoid annexation of overseas territories that might prove to be excessively costly to administer relative to any revenues they might reasonably be expected to yield. This consideration was particularly relevant to barbarian communities with poorly developed administrative structures which meant that taxes would be difficult to collect. After the initial wars against such a community, which yielded military revenues, the recurrent costs of actually administering and policing a reluctant and even recalcitrant subject might be far less attractive than the revenue to be derived from the same community through transport tax on trade with it augmented by periodic protection moneys from its government if it were left free.

This was the case with Britain at the end of this period. Strabo (4.5.3, 2.5.8) said that some of the British kings had procured the diplomatic friendship of Augustus, and thereafter submitted so willingly to customs duties on traffic between Britain and Gaul that there was no need to annex and garrison the island. One legion at least and some cavalry would have been needed to carry off the tribute, while the expense and danger to the army would have offset the tribute money. In addition, transport taxes would have had to be lowered if Britain had been annexed.

At this time, therefore, Britain held few attractions for the Roman government. It is doubtful whether Caesar's raids in 55–54 BC, which staked a notional Roman claim to annex the island, yielded any appreciable revenues. The situation was rather different in AD 43 when the conquest of what had by then become a strong and wealthy provincial nobility seemed a more attractive proposition. Similar considerations probably led the Romans to postpone the annexation of Transalpine Gaul north of the Isère (Stevens 1980) after the wars of 125–121, whereas by the mid-first century BC the Aedui, Averni and their neighbours had become capable of forming the core of a stable provincial administration.

Thus while the main imperative of Roman expansion originated within the Roman political economy, the relationships into which the Republic entered with external societies themselves exercised a positive influence upon the process of expansion of the empire, by continually generating conditions which could prompt or justify annexation of external territory, usually on grounds of defence of the interests of the Roman state. The characteristic lurching expansion of the Roman empire during the late Republic was a product of the very contradictory influences and imperatives which governed relations with the outside world.

This interaction can be traced very clearly in the history of Rome's relations with the Gauls and Germans, who were both geographically and historically Rome's closest European neighbours. Warfare had always been a prominent feature of Rome's contact with the Gauls, and few Roman governors of the Transalpine province failed to add some permanent territory to it, within the limits described above (e.g. Cicero *Pro Fonteio* 5.12). Major wars, especially in 123–121, 103–100 and 58–51 led to massive additions to Roman territory. Julius Caesar's conquests were at the expense of both friends and enemies of the Roman state, including many societies previously unheard of at Rome. Belligerent warrior societies, such as the first century Allobroges (Dio Cassius 37.47, Caesar *BG* 1.6.2), did not always make attractive or profitable provincials, but sustained economic growth in external border areas such as central and eastern Gaul between 121 and 58 BC, or Britain between 50 BC and AD 43 might render them attractive and cooperative subjects later on. The western provinces eventually formed the most stable and enduring possessions of the Roman empire, reflected in the first century AD Jewish historian Josephus' amazement at the complacency of the Gauls who 'submitted to being the milch cow of Rome' under minimal military supervision (*BJ* 2.16.4 [371–3]). In the first century BC the Republican Gallic province produced the first non-Italian Senators, and in AD 48 the emperor Claudius admitted the first northern Gauls into the Senate. Later still, in the early second century AD, it was the oldest overseas western province, Spain, which furnished the first non-Roman emperor in the person of Trajan.

The outer periphery

Beyond the outermost horizon of acknowledged allies, friends and known enemies of the Republic, lay societies which had no direct contact with the Roman empire, and about whom the Romans seem to have denied much knowledge or interest. Writing in the 140s BC, Polybius (3.37.11) described the inhabitants of Atlantic Gaul as nameless societies about which nothing would be known until someone was intrepid enough to investigate them, despite the fact that these communities had been well known for several centuries to Carthage and some of the western Greeks. Polybius dismissed as an unsubstantiated sailors' yarn the detailed account of the coastal regions of northern Europe given by the Massiliote Pytheas, who explored them in the late fourth century, thus exemplifying one of his Roman captors' habitual attitudes to the alien world (Strabo 2.4.1, cf. 1.4.3). In similar vein, writing under Tiberius in the early first century AD, the geographer Strabo described the nomads of the northern steppes and Africa as of no use at all to Rome, merely requiring to be watched (Strabo 6.4.2, cf. 5.2.7).

The contribution that was in fact made to the Roman economy by nomads and other barbarians far distant from the frontiers of the empire and beyond even the curiosity of the Roman ruling-class was clearly not appreciated by Strabo or his contemporaries, but should not for that reason now be underestimated. Although little involved in the supply of perishable goods and foodstuffs to the empire, many highly prized exotica, and some vital raw materials, came from these distant realms, including tin, amber, ivory and silk, the producers of which might on occasions be as ignorant of the Roman empire as the Romans were of them. Tacitus for instance (*Germania* 45) recounts the amazement of the inhabitants of Jutland, who collected amber from the beaches, that there were actually people who valued such a commonplace material. The outer Gallic periphery, despite Roman ignorance, was the Republic's principal source of tin, and the Gallic north and Germany became one of the most important sources of barbarian slaves in the first century BC, traded south for the expendable trappings of Mediterranean civilization. This zone therefore constituted the outermost periphery of the regional system centred upon Roman Italy at this time.

The list of commodities which ancient writers record as obtained in exchange with barbarians nearly always included slaves as a matter of course. Thus, for instance, in a different but comparable social environment, Strabo described the trading post of Tanais, originally established by the Greeks on the estuary of the river Don on the northern shores of the Black Sea to deal with Asiatic and European nomads (Strabo 11.2.3). In his own time in the early first century AD, the nomads brought slaves, hides, and 'such things as nomads possess' to Tanais and were given in exchange clothing, wine and other manufactured items. In the 50s BC Caesar said that the ferocious German Suebi, who had little contact with the Mediterranean world, traded with foreign merchants, not so much in order to purchase anything in particular, as to dispose of their spoils of war (*BG* 4.2.1). In the context, it is difficult to envisage that this plunder consisted in anything other than human captives.

The perennial inter-tribal warfare among the warrior communities of the Steppes, Central Europe and most of the North-West meant that whenever there was a market for slaves in the Mediterranean, northern Europe and Asia represented a vast

reservoir of potential slaves (cf. Piggott 1965: 229 ff). The same was true of Spain and Africa, and it would be possible to trace developmental processes in the history of the kingdom of Numidia very similar to what may be observed in the major kingdoms of the Gallic periphery. Most of the Mediterranean goods which were given in exchange for slaves were perishable, and wine seems to have occupied a particularly important place in the slave trade with the Gauls. The Celts everywhere were notoriously eager to import wine, whose consumption at princely feasts generated a continuous demand for more. By the same token, barbarian slaves in the Roman economy could only be replaced quickly and in large numbers by purchase, and this gave rise to a continuous cycle of reciprocal demand by both parties to the exchange of wine for slaves. The dynamism of this trade rooted as it was in elite consumption on both sides of the relationship, was fundamentally complementary and self-perpetuating.

In Gaul, Narbo Martius certainly had a slave market, and so did Aquileia at the head of the Adriatic, at which Strabo says the Illyrians acquired olive oil and wine in wooden casks, giving the Aquileians slaves, cattle and hides in return (5.1.8). Since much wine must everywhere have been transported overland in skins and casks, the surviving evidence for the distribution of Republican wine in the form of Italian amphora sherds is probably no more than a dim reflection of the real extent of trade in Mediterranean wine outside the Roman empire at this time.

The close of the Roman Republican epoch

The Roman Republican epoch terminated around the end of the first century BC (fig. 9.4). Internally, the Republican military oligarchy failed to preserve its traditional structure under the stress of possessing an empire. It had proved impossible to restrain the accumulation of wealth and political prestige by the most ambitious and successful of its members, or to rule an empire without an integrated military and bureaucratic structure. From the mid-second century to the end of the civil wars in 31 BC, Roman politics were dominated by the careers and rivalries of a few very powerful and wealthy Senators, variously allied with sub-groupings of the Senate and with different sections of the equestrian order. Their struggles culminated in the career of Octavian, who defeated all his rivals to achieve sole mastery of the state in 31 BC. Under pressure of powerful groups outside the Senate, it had also proved impossible to maintain the narrow exclusiveness of the circle of traditional Roman Senatorial families, and by the death of Augustus few scions of the ancient noble families remained in the Senate, while Roman citizenship and domestic territory had spread uniformly to the Alps.

During the late Republic, this northwards movement of the territorial boundaries of Italy had greatly enlarged the political constituency of the Roman heartland and led to the beginning of a dilution of the old Senatorial oligarchy, as the right to gain entry to the Senate was extended within Rome's immediate periphery. This process gathered pace during the civil wars of the mid-first century BC, when Caesar was taunted with admitting Gauls to the Senate (Suetonins *DJ* 80) and membership of the Senate as a whole swelled to excessive proportions.

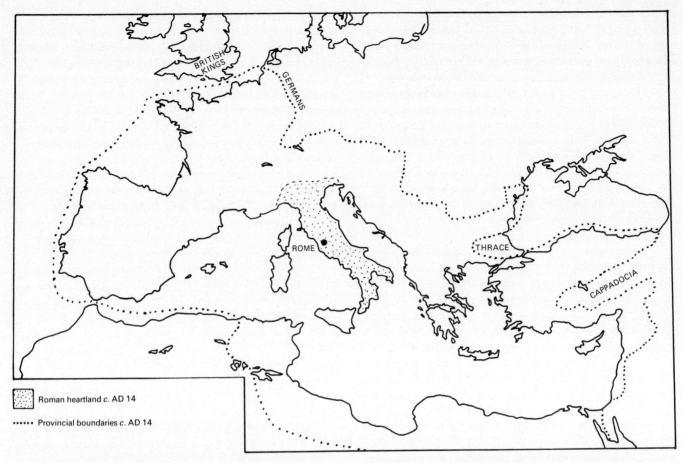

Fig. 9.4. The Roman world *c*. AD 14.

The late Republic ended with the resolution of the civil wars in the firm subordination of the Senatorial oligarchy to the authority of Augustus. He gradually reduced the Senate in size, and deprived it of its traditional military responsibilities. All senior commands were reserved for himself and his immediate circle, opportunities for triumphs were confined to selected generals from his own household, and he disbanded all but 28 of the 60 legions in the field in 31. (Scullard 1963: 216; Brunt and Moore 1967: 41; Brunt 1971b: 498 ff). While this posed serious problems in the short term because of the veterans' insistent demand for land, in the longer term it signalled the creation of a small but highly disciplined imperial army.

Augustus divided the provinces into two groups: those where there was always military action, primarily on the frontiers, which he had kept as his own responsibility; and the rest, with their capacity to produce tax revenues in abundance, which he allowed the Senate to administer. Provincial governorships routinely became of longer duration, approximating more closely to professional appointments, and men of equestrian standing or even imperial freedmen were accorded a part in provincial administration. Thus, a greater degree of integration between Senatorial and equestrian functions was achieved than had been possible under the Republican dispensation. In effect, these changes reconstituted the Senate as Rome's first imperial bureaucracy. Deprived of its central place in Roman political life, of its

government of foreign policy, membership of the Senate and tenure of the elective magistracies declined in prestige with astonishing speed during the late first century BC, until eligible Romans had first century BC, until eligible Romans had positively to be encouraged to stand for office.

Externally, the empire now also began to reach its tenable limits. In the West, Augustus consolidated provincial territory by finally completing the annexation of Spain and the Alps between 26 and 16 BC, and this brought to an end a long series of relatively unrewarding wars that had begun in both areas early in the second century BC. Further east Noricum was peacefully ceded to the empire in *c*.15 BC. In the century which followed Caesar's conquest of Gaul, British and German communities close to the new Roman frontier underwent what by now had become familiar processes of internal development (Thompson 1965), eliciting the usual Roman response, though now with more equivocal results. German expansion in the first century AD provoked Augustus and his successors into further largely unsuccessful attempts to extend the Rhine frontier northwards, and here the Roman empire had almost reached its definitive limits by the end of the first century BC. Augustus' loss of three legions under P.Quinctilius Varus in the Teutoburger Forest in AD 9 constituted the first serious setback to attempted Roman expansion in Western Europe.

Southern Britain was taken by Claudius in AD 43 following

the dissolution of the strongest of the two paramount kingdoms of Britain, that of Cunobelinus in Essex and Hertfordshire, and in the early second century AD the furthest extension of the British frontier finally penetrated Scotland. In those areas of the British Isles that remained outside the empire, primarily Ireland and most of Scotland, contact with the empire continued to involve the supply of slaves and eventually, in the fourth century AD, mercenary soldiers. These relationships fostered the expansion of warrior economies of classic Celtic type in Ireland and Scotland.

Thus, during the first century AD the pace of Roman territorial expansion began to decline, and at the end of his life Augustus enjoined his successors to defend rather than to extend the Empire (Scullard 1963: 268). A fresh epoch then opened in the relationship between the Roman imperial centre and its European periphery during which the Irish, Scots and Germans replaced the Continental Celts as the closest, most vital, and also the most threatening, neighbours of the north-western provinces of the empire.

Notes

1 I would like to thank Dr T. G. Ashplant, Miss B. M. Levick and Dr M. J. Rowlands for their helpful comments upon earlier drafts of this paper. The views expressed here are, of course, my own responsibilities.

2 For more detailed discussion of the history and economy of this period, with fuller documentary citations, see e.g. Brunt 1971b, Crawford 1978, Duncan-Jones 1974, Frank 1938–41, Greenidge and Clay 1960. Hopkins 1978, Lewis and Reinhold 1966 and Sherwin-White 1973. Broughton (1952) is an invaluable guide to the ancient source material. Classical authors cited may be consulted in the *Loeb Classical Library* editions.

3 The number of slaves employed in Italian and Roman agriculture at this time can only be guessed at, but was very large. 90,000 slaves, mainly of European origin, joined Spartacus' revolt in 73–71, and the Sicilian slave revolts of 135–132 and 104–100 reveal the considerable extent of agricultural slavery there too.

4 Thus e.g. M. Brutus had made extortionate loans to the town of Salamis in Cyprus, and Pompey had made such heavy loans to king Ariobarzanes of Cappadocia, one of Rome's client princes, that during the 50s he was barely able to recover the interest on his loans. The governor of Cilicia, at least, seems to have had some responsibility for seeing that these Senatorial loans were repaid (Cicero *ad Att.* 6.1.3 etc.).

5 The office of aedile, though not essential for a Senatorial career, was the first elective office to confer full senatorial dignity on its holder, and because of its popularity with the city population, was much aspired to by ambitious junior Senators. Aediles had responsibilities within the city which included the maintenance of roads and aqueducts, distribution of the corn dole, and the provision of public games. Although aediles received a state grant, they were expected also to spend freely from their own pockets. In 58 BC, the curule aediles M. Aemilius Scaurus and P. Plautius Hypsaeus staged exceptionally magnificent games with funds acquired while

junior officers on Pompey's staff during his eastern command in the sixties (Broughton 1952: 195).

6 The Dictator Sulla's legislation in 81 BC was a milestone in this process (see Broughton 1952: 74ff). He imposed a clear structure on Senatorial careers, and his provincial legislation (the *lex Cornelia*) remained in force until revised by Julius Caesar.

7 Thus, for instance, consular and tribunican legislation was passed in 64 BC to try to limit the attendants upon candidates for elections, and to make formal associations (*collegia*) illegal (Broughton 1952: 161).

8 Michael Crawford (1973) has demonstrated that the output of the Roman Republican silver coinage can be correlated fairly closely with the number of legions in the field during most of this period. A striking correlation also exists until the 160s between the annual output of silver coinage and revenue from Roman triumphs and ovations as recorded in the *Fasti* and by the historian Livy. It is only after this date that the seemingly simple relationship that had prevailed until then between military revenues, coinage output and military pay breaks down. A combination of high revenues from provincial taxes, and increasing civic expenditure is probably responsible for this change.

9 Cicero (*de Officiis* 1.24.124–5; 2.21.73–24.85; see Lewis and Reinhold 1966: 254ff) gave eloquent voice to this point of view. 'And how is it fair that a man who has never had any property should take possession of lands that have been occupied for many years or even generations, and that he who had them before should lose possession of them?' . . . 'And what is the meaning of an abolition of debts, except that you buy a farm with my money?'

10 There is a sharp and sustained increase in the output of silver coinage at this time (Crawford 1973), perhaps largely attributable to this change in military expenditure. It is interesting in this connection to note that there was an abrupt drop in the output of silver coinage at Rome in the 20s BC, when the civil wars had ended and Augustus disbanded more than half the soldiers under arms.

11 The experimental abolition of Italian harbour dues in 60 BC was abandoned under Caesar's dictatorship as unprofitable.

12 Some at least of the native silver coinages struck within the Republican provinces of Cisalpine and Transalpine Gaul may be accounted for by this practice (cf. Nash 1978b).

13 *Pro Fonteio* 9.19. By way of comparison, the annual wage for a legionary soldier at the time was 120 denarii per year, raised by Caesar to 225.

14 As an 'equal' ally, Massilia was entitled to ask Roman help in her own defensive wars. Her appeal for help against the Oxybii and Deciates in 154 BC led Rome into its first Transalpine war, but the territory then reclaimed was correctly handed over to Massilia to safeguard. Erosion of Massilia's independence began in the late 120s when, again responding to an appeal from Massilia this time against depredations by the Salluvii, Allobroges and their allies (Stevens 1980), Roman conquests in Massilia's hinterland established provincial territory in the Rhône valley and thus for the first time separated Massilia from the immediate contact with free Gaul which had become as important a source of revenue as it had been under very different historical conditions during the fifth century BC (Nash 1985). On Massilia's relationship with Rome see Ebel 1976 and Goudineau 1983.

Chapter 10

**Culture process on the periphery:
Belgic Gaul and Rome during
the late Republic and early Empire**

Colin Haselgrove

> Evolution is not stable in space. It is usually characterised by a
> spatial shift in centres, very often one that is, more specifically, a shift
> from centre to periphery.
>
> (Friedman and Rowlands 1977: 269)

There can be few areas or periods which exemplify better
those processes which are the substance of the generalisation at
the head of this chapter than the northwest provinces of the
Roman Empire, most particularly Belgic Gaul.[1] Conquered in
the 50s BC by Julius Caesar, one of the dominant personalities of
that expansive phenomenon that was the late Roman Republic,
Belgic Gaul was to develop into a wealthy province, which in turn
became in its own right a centre, at first *de facto* under the
Gallic emperors, and finally *de iure* with the partition of the
Empire under Diocletian. Indeed, under Constantine the Great in
the early fourth century AD, one of the major cities of Belgic
Gaul, Augusta Treverorum (modern Trier) has some claim to the
title of the capital of the Western Empire.

It was a transformation, the magnitude of which can hardly
be over-emphasised, a shift in centres which should probably be
counted amongst the major factors in laying the foundations for
the birth of European capitalism. In the course of only three centuries, the initiative, economic as well as political, may be seen to
have passed from Italy and the Western Mediterranean to temperate Western Europe, never to be completely regained by
the former zone. Though short lived in itself, the 'Gallic empire'
that was born by AD 260 established a pattern which persisted

through the Industrial Revolution and into the twentieth century;
a fact which the emergence and disappearance of a series of
centres represented by the succession of unwieldy empires –
Merovingian, Carolingian, Angevin – interspersed with such
strong political and economic entities as Anglo-Saxon England or
Medieval France, have served only to obscure. When viewed as
an evolutionary phenomenon on a world scale, the persistence of
a zone or Western 'centre of gravity' is as impressive as its success
is remarkable in achieving world dominance under capitalism,
only some fifteen hundred years after its birth. In this respect, it is
indeed an irony that capitalism's most famous critic, Karl Marx,
should, of all places, have been born in Trier.

In the context of a volume devoted to the study of regional
systems, the aim of this chapter then is to examine the initial
stages of an example, which if the argument advanced above is
accepted, may have been of no small relevance to the development
of our own society. This initial phase constitutes the process by
which an area right at the heart of temperate Western Europe,
Belgic Gaul, was transformed into the periphery of a wider system. Yet it will be argued that its relations with Britain and also
Germany were as important as its relations with Rome, and this
development has its origins before the formal incorporation of the
area as a province of the Empire. It is not, however, the purpose
of this chapter to embark on a detailed discussion of the conditions and forces which subsequently led to the elevation of this
formerly peripheral area to the status of a centre in its own right

within the western Roman Empire; the most important being the massive military concentration along the Rhine engendered by the presence of the frontier with Free Germany. These have attracted a massive literature, albeit passively, in the context of the history of the Empire as a whole from the time of Gibbon onwards (e.g., Gibbon 1896; Mommsen 1909; Rostovtzeff 1957).

By contrast, although useful general summaries exist (Brogan 1974; Drinkwater 1983), relatively less attention has been paid to conditions in Belgic Gaul in the earliest post-conquest period,[2] and in particular, to the processes experienced by the indigenous social formations in the crucial quarter century which intervenes between Caesar's exerting Roman mastery on Gaul and Augustus achieving it. Yet the state of Gaulish society and culture as it emerged from the phase of restructuring which followed the advent of Roman rule was a crucial constituent of all further developments. Culture generates its own dynamic, while affording the basic matrix upon which other forces external as well as internal operate; it is at once an active and a passive ingredient in change, whatever the scale of the social or political unit involved, and whatever the dictates of the wider system to which it is exposed. Our understanding of the changes which Belgic Gaul was to undergo as a province of the Roman Empire entails as much an appreciation of the likely nature of the indigenous society and its component structure, as a knowledge of the part which specific historical circumstances and the wider economic and political context were to play in shaping that society and its culture. To these questions, the present chapter is addressed.

Principles of social reproduction

The analysis of phenomena bridging the transition from prehistory to better documented societies has always posed problems. It is evident that our starting point must be the archaeological record and that only processes which find clear expression in material culture and physical remains can be investigated adequately (cf. Haselgrove 1979), but as yet there are few signs of consensus over the methodology to be employed, or of a solution to the inferential problems inherent in the movement from material culture to meaning, or from physical form to process. Of necessity analogies and generalisations must be invoked, both in the interpretation of specific contexts, and in the assimilation of regional sequences to broader patterns of human development, though in the end, our interpretations will only be as good as the assumptions upon which they rest.

The approach followed in this paper is explicitly materialist, and will employ generalisations with their foundation in the French structural-Marxist tradition (cf. Godelier 1980) and in the formulations of Wallerstein (1974), as subsequently elaborated in various works (e.g., Ekholm and Friedman 1980; Friedman and Rowlands 1977). At its core is an insistence on the study of social reproduction defined with respect to the wider regional systems within which individual formations interact, rather than a concern with social institutions *per se*. The level of model-building is inevitably relatively abstract, but has already been helpful to our understanding of social dynamics at various periods of later European prehistory (cf. Nash 1975; Rowlands 1980). This is

particularly true of the close of the first millennium BC, when judicious interplay between the material remains of indigenous societies, and the outsider's viewpoint in the surviving classical texts – biased and lacking the requisite temporal and geographical specificity though the latter frequently are – considerably strengthens the analysis, affording valuable insights into the interaction between Mediterranean and European societies and, on occasions, closer definition of local social formations and an opportunity to evaluate our generalisations in a reasonably controlled context.[3]

The model focuses on competition for ranking and mechanisms for the accumulation of wealth available to local groups linked by kinship and alliances played out within a wider sphere of regional exchange. Two distinct structures can be envisaged; a 'developed' form which is, in effect, a transformation under certain conditions of a 'basic' form. The expansionist tendencies of such 'transitional' systems have been fully documented by Rowlands (1980). In very general terms, local groups derive their social identity from participation in corporate groups at increasing levels of inclusion. The social unit of most immediate relevance is the clan, to which individuals owed their loyalty and social-status, and at the highest level, territorial groups composed of a number of clans, the anthropologist's tribe. The principles for common action in these larger corporate groupings are, however, likely to be weak and restricted to such matters as shared ritual, ancestry or territorial ties, and it is at the level of the constituent domestic-groups that competition for rank is played out. This occurs in a wider arena of differential success in the formation of alliances through gift exchange and marriage, through which wealth is accumulated and external labour recruited; the more extensive its alliance network, the more successful the group. Similarly, since productivity is determined by group size, larger groups will dominate smaller ones through their superior capacity to accumulate the labour and wealth necessary to meet their exchange obligations. In essence, a multiplier effect operates in expanding the reproductive success of local descent groups.

Assuming the conduct of alliance formation to be in the hands of the heads of domestic-groups who are in a position to divert surplus wealth to their personal advantage, inter-group competition can also serve to reinforce internal ranking and to sustain the head's control over the reproduction of the group. It is possible to see how from this 'basic' form, intensification of these processes and manipulation of such opportunities can lead to the development of more absolute forms of ranking, as a consequence of increasing polarisation between 'wealthy' and 'impoverished' groups; the latter gradually losing their capacity to participate in status-building activities and ultimately losing their separate identity and thus being reduced to becoming dependents or clients of the wealthier groups. With this reduction of the poorer groups to client status, we have, in effect, the emergence of an elite stratum, cross-cutting the old clan boundaries, and defined instead by external alliances, relations to land and absolute differences of wealth. In these 'developed' forms, competition for rank continues within the elite stratum, now based directly on the ability to accumulate wealth and to use it to gain higher status in the wider tribal structure. As Rowlands (1980) and others have stressed, transformation to 'developed' forms and the emergence of an elite is rarely a self-contained process, but rather contingent on the tribal system's position in a wider system of social production, more often than not reflecting its incorporation into an expansive trading network offering the accumulation of new forms of wealth and imposing new kinds of demands on its productive structures.

In the context of late Celtic societies, it would seem that the 'developed' form of the system, which predicts the existence of some degree of absolute ranking between the elite and their dependents (defined in terms of overt wealth distinctions), provides the more appropriate model, although various references to the German tribes (Tacitus *Germania* 26; Caesar *BG*, VI, 22) are suggestive of different systems for the control of social reproduction and would caution against the whole-sale application of this model in the German-speaking areas and those parts of Belgic Gaul with Trans-Rhenine settlement. However, the classical sources leave us in little doubt of the existence of an elite in Celtic society, among whom competition for rank was intense and alterations in status frequent. Wealth and social standing were inseparable; the individuals who could expend most in status competition, on gifts, feasts, and their dependents, were by definition the most powerful (e.g., Athenaeus IV 36–7, 40 quoting or paraphrasing Poseidonios' lost *History XXIII*). Both Polybius ((*History* II, 17) and Caesar (*BG* VI, 15) underline the importance of competitive success in enabling individuals to maintain or enhance their standing and attract dependents and adherents; the power of the aristocratic elite was reckoned in terms of the number of their clients and these would remain with them only so long as they maintained their support through success in warfare and in displays of hospitality. Similarly, a number of references show that wealth in precious metal ornaments, weaponry, cattle and later coinage and its circulation within the clientage system was fundamental to the overall process of social reproduction, and as such was in the control of the elite (e.g., Polybius II, 17; Diodorus Siculus V, 27).

It is important to stress that in this system, dominance is dependent on the control of circulation and exchange, rather than on production *per se*, although the former cannot be completely separated from the productive surpluses needed to support such transactions and hence the resources in land, livestock and minerals required to generate them. This is immediately apparent when we consider the interplay of different forms of circulation and sets of productive relations (Fig. 10.1). As Nash (1975, 1978c) has argued, there were at least three separate circuits of accumulation, involving discrete systems of circulation based on the separation of internal and external exchanges with warfare simply being a non-reciprocal form of the latter.

Vertical exchanges between superordinates and subordinates have already been dealt with to some extent. A number of the sources (e.g., Caesar *BG*, VI 13) imply the existence of what might be termed 'unfree dependents' or near slaves among Gaulish societies of the first century BC, with whom the elite will have had rather different relations than they had with their 'clients' or free dependents. In return for the loan of the means of production

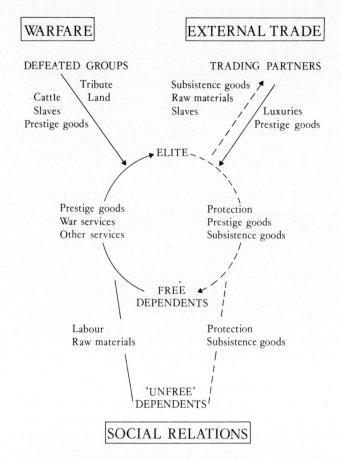

Fig. 10.1 Principal mechanisms open to the elite for the accumulation of wealth.

and a certain degree of protection afforded to them by the elite, the 'unfree' dependants will have had to render labour services of various kinds; the significant difference between them and the clients, and the determinant of free status of the latter, was that only they could own land and valuables. In return for the protection of their patron, the loan of extra land and the distribution of valuables and spoil, the clients were expected to render a variety of services and rents in livestock or other valuables. In theory, it was open to clients and free dependents not only to compete with one another to improve their own status, but to aspire to achieving elite rank in their own right. In practice, however, this would normally be precluded by the elite's control over the circulation of valuables and their ownership of almost all the productive land,[4] reinforced it is to be presumed by ideological sanctions and by their access to ritual knowledge. The categories of wealth appropriate to the sphere of internal circulation are thus essentially those which could be locally produced, such as livestock, weapons, and latterly, one assumes, coinage, and with the majority of the population including free dependants having to borrow their means of subsistence in return for rents or services, the continued reproduction of an absolute distinction between the elite and their dependents could be regarded as assured.

The overwhelming preoccupation of Celtic societies with warfare in the eyes of the classical world, is in fact intimately bound up with the system of social reproduction (e.g., Strabo *Geographica* IV 4.2). Success in warfare effectively offered any group, and above all individual members of the elite, the possibilities of an unbalanced exchange with their competitors; stock and valuables could be obtained as booty, and with conquest, new land and slaves. These could be used both directly and indirectly in the regulation of the clientage system, as the goods acquired could be used to attract extra clients, and slaves and land could be worked to produce a larger surplus; individuals could also be of value as hostages for the tribute payments of the defeated, and as pawns in the wider arena of alliances and marriages.

The third mechanism for the accumulation of wealth which was open to elites resided in the sphere of peaceful external relations, including alliances and gifts exchanges as we have already seen, and organised trade networks. Through furnishing resources and manufactured goods only available beyond the boundaries of local societies, these seem to have been a key feature of the initial process of elite separation and of subsequent competition within that stratum. The development of mutually exclusive spheres of circulation involving categories of wealth items appropriate to the different sets of relations between an elite and their dependents, and between elites, noted above, presumably has its origins in the former process, just as continued hierarchy will effectively have depended on the separation being maintained.[5] Thus, although theoretically there is nothing to preclude any of the craft products and other goods made available by the development of new long-distance trade networks being redistributed internally, in practice their penetration of these societies is likely to have been highly selective, with the circulation of each category of import being restricted to individuals of the appropriate rank.

The importance of organised trade networks initiated by expansive state societies as a mechanism for wealth accumulation in this kind of competitive society lies in the capacity they have to bring about the dislocation of traditional reproductive cycles, and a significant increase in their degree of political centralisation (cf. Haselgrove 1982). Their role in this is essentially two-fold: through unleashing in enormous quantities a whole series of commodities not previously available to the local communities, they allow the development of absolute differences of wealth between individuals and a degree of elaboration of the social hierarchy of a different order from previously, and secondly, by imposing different kinds of demands on the productive structures of the local system. At the very least, the need to mobilize larger and larger quantities of exportable resources in order to capture prestige imports entails significant intensification of production, and in the case of resources not available within the domain, we must also envisage the formation of additional alliances and exchanges networks to effect their procurement from yet further afield (Haselgrove 1982).

As a stimulus to the transformation of indigenous productive structures, the action of these imports is effectively indirect, with, for reasons which were elaborated above, the most valuable items being assimilated as prestige goods in the sphere of elite circulation and consumption, although other categories may well have been redistributed further down the hierarchy in the general process of competition for rank. However, the intensification of production beyond subsistence is primarily mediated by other mechanisms; the manipulation of clientage relations; increased manufacture of wealth items appropriate to internal circulation or the redesignation of other prestige goods previously restricted to elite activities to that sphere; and increased tribute. In an archaeological context, it should be possible to detect such differentiation in the structuring of mortuary deposits and settlement evidence.

Historically, the context for the establishment of an organised trade network by an expansive core state often seems to be the early stages of a developmental cycle similar to that outlined recently by Ekholm and Friedman (1980). Initially, this is characterised by the formation of a periphery of more centralised polities in the areas directly exploited by the Centre, although in time these develop their own peripheries supplying commodities unavailable within the primary domain (cf. Rowlands 1980); inevitably, the degree of elaboration achieved by individual polities depends significantly on pre-existing local social conditions as well as the degree of commercial interest to which they were subject. In this phase, therefore, there is a stimulation of local commercial and industrial economies under the umbrella of a massive importation of real wealth to the Centre, accompanied in relative terms by a significant polarisation of wealth among the peripheral communities.

Sooner or later, this phase gives way to the establishment of empire proper, through outright conquest and the gradual absorption of nominally allied peoples, bringing with it an increase in economic activity (Ekholm and Friedman 1980). As the accumulation of wealth at the Centre far outstrips real production, there is rapid inflation and increasing costs. This, combined with increasing opportunities in the provinces brought about by the conditions of conquest, incorporation and over-exploitation, leads to an outflow of merchants, and producers, and as a result, a rapid decentralisation of accumulation in the empire as a whole. As the total accumulation is greater than the proportion which is still drawn into the centre, this phase gives way to one of crisis and competition between the core and the emergent centres of the periphery, with the eventual collapse of its hegemony.

Applied to the process of Roman economic and political expansion which led to the formation of the province of Belgic Gaul in the first century BC, this model enables us to outline the following stages in its development; first, the emergence of a periphery of strongly centralised polities around the boundaries of the Roman *Provincia* in the south of Gaul, an area which must have had a degree of contact with the Mediterranean world over a long period, and where, in the absence of conditions which would allow the emergence of hegemonies based on a monopoly over external exchange, we may envisage the existence of a highly competitive but relatively acephalous society (cf. Rowlands 1980) until the new opportunities afforded by the opening of the region to an enormous volume of trade by Roman entrepreneurs from the second century BC onwards. The second phase of development amounts to the incorporation of areas at a greater distance from the Mediterranean, including Belgic Gaul, into an outer periphery as the polities of the inner periphery sought to expand their productive base. This was followed shortly by the Roman conquest of *Gallia Comata*, both the highly centralised *civitates* of Central Gaul and the corona of less developed polities to the north and west; this period lasted for several years as resistance to incorporation was gradually overcome and the indigenous communities adjusted to Roman administration and taxation. The fourth and final phase, saw the transformation of Belgic Gaul in a remarkably short time into an extremely wealthy region as a result of the commercial and productive opportunities opened up by the Conquest and the presence of the army along its frontier in the Rhineland. We may now proceed to examine each of these phases in greater detail, although the final stage will be subjected to scrutiny only to the extent that developments also had their impetus in local conditions.

Formation of a periphery I: Roman trade and Central Gaul

Apart from the material record, our primary source of evidence for Gaulish society and its political divisions by the middle of the first century BC is Julius Caesar's *Commentariorum de Bello Gallico* (*BG*). In its time, this text has been accused of a miscellaneous array of shortcomings, ranging from plagiarism on a grand scale (Tierney 1960) to biases, misrepresentation and selectivity engendered by the propagandist purpose for which it was compiled (Stevens 1951). As a result, for long scholars have tended to dismiss the indications of political and social variations in time and space at which both categories of evidence hint. Instead, Caesar has been divested of any value as an original source and the various groups he identifies as separate *civitates*, translated and interpreted simply as 'tribes', the constituents of an indefinite and undifferentiated tribal society, a conceptualisation which is not only plainly misleading, but devoid of any anthropological insight.[6]

However, in recent years, a number of studies have appeared in which the value of Caesar's text as an independent source has been reinstated (Nash 1976), and the complexity and level of the social organisation, which he describes for at least parts of Gaul reconsidered. Champion (1980), for instance, has emphasised the long and careful preparations undertaken by the Helvetii over a period of two years after they had taken the decision to migrate, involving the collection of sufficient transport and food for everyone involved in the movement. Others such as Crumley (1974) and Nash (1975, 1978c) go further and argue that by the period of the Gallic War, the communities of Central Gaul around the periphery of the Roman *Provincia* (as the south of France was then called), including most notably the groups known as the Arverni, the Bituriges and the Aedui, display evidence of a degree of socio-economic differentiation and political centralisation little different from those characteristics shown by a whole range of societies grouped together by anthropologists, and other comparative scholars, as examples of the so-called 'early state' (cf. Claessen and Skalnik 1978).

For both Crumley and Nash then, we can perceive in the *civitates* of Central Gaul, a series of small states, each with at least one central place or *oppidum*, the fortified administrative centres of each territory, housing a permanent non-agricultural popula-

tion, and a locus of specialised productive activities and for both local and long-distance exchange. Some *civitates* appear to have possessed specialised trading centres in addition to their central places; Strabo (*Geographica* IV, 2.1) refers to the Aedui with their *polis* at Cabyllinon, the modern Châlons-sur-Saône, presumably from its location an entrepôt (Fig. 10.2), and their *arx* at *Bibracte*, also referred to by Caesar (*BG* I, 23) as their largest and richest centre, a conclusion which is reinforced by the evidence excavated from its site at Mont Beuvray (Déchelette 1914).

As Fig. 10.3 shows, Crumley and Nash differ markedly in their reading of Caesar's text in terms of the hierarchical organisation of these 'states' or *civitates*, and in their interpretation of the principles of stratification at work, and the processes behind the pattern of increased differentiation which they perceive in the categories and institutional terms employed by Caesar to communicate the characteristics of these groups to his audience at Rome. However, they do not disagree on the two particulars of most relevance to this chapter; that the textual evidence, backed up by the physical remains of the archaeological record, is indicative of a socio-political organisation and degree of economic specialisation completely different in nature and scale from that which preceded it, and secondly, that the actual formation period of the states was short, and intimately linked to the beginnings of the expansion of Roman political and economic interests beyond the north coast of the Mediterranean.

It is reasonably certain from various references in Caesar's narrative (e.g., *BG* I, 2–3) that at the time of Roman military intervention, the central Gaulish state was in its infancy; numerous attempts to overthrow the new order were still being mounted, and it is unsurprising that the Roman offers of alliance and federation were welcomed by the councils of a number of these *civitates*, such as the Aedui, whose position they would now ensure.[7]

Various factors must have been important in the process through which this series of states developed, among them population pressure and increased warfare consequent on the ending of opportunities for mercenary service in the Mediterranean world after the third century BC (cf. Nash 1975). However, in terms of the principles of social reproduction proposed here, it is the opportunities opened to the elite by a dramatic increase in foreign trade, and the resultant dislocation of the traditional structures of social reproduction, to which we must accord paramount importance. In this particular situation, the foreign trade was the product of Roman interests in the areas of Europe north of the Alps, a process which was dramatically intensified with the establishment of their *Provincia* in the south of France.[8] This trade finds archaeological expression in the massive export to Gaul of wine amphorae (Peacock 1971), associated bronze services, and fine tablewares in the black-glazed Campanian pottery (Nash 1975).[9] In return for these, the Romans were clearly interested in a variety of commodities (Haselgrove 1982; cf, Strabo *Geographica* IV, 5.2), including a range of raw materials and even agricultural products. However, it seems probable that above all else at this period, the Romans were interested in obtaining slaves to work in Italian agriculture, a need which seems to have reached its peak in the

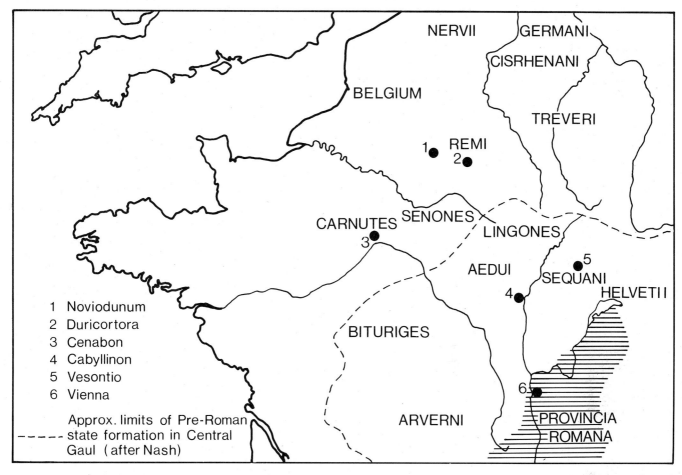

Fig. 10.2 Location of major population groups in central and northeast Gaul.

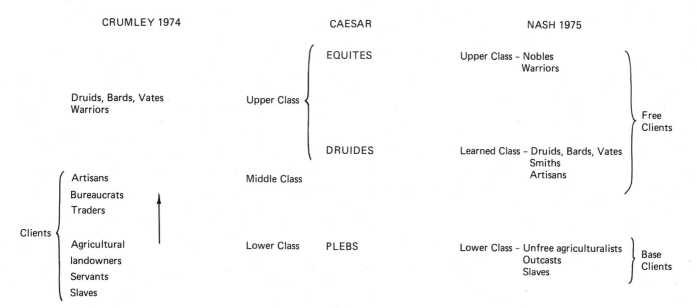

Fig. 10.3 Alternative interpretations of late Gaulish society based on the account given by Julius Caesar.

later second century BC, and an exchange which seems to have operated very much in their favour, as in Diodorus Siculus' comment on Italian merchants and their love of lucre:

> They transport the wine by boat on the navigable rivers, and by wagon through the plains and receive in return for it an incredibly large price; for one jar of wine they receive in return a slave, a servant in exchange for the drink. (V, 27, translation Tierney 1960)

This demand for slaves must have generated an increase in warfare almost inseparable from that consequent on the overall demise in stability of this period, but this mode of acquisition of slaves is one that must have had serious consequences in the traditional processes of social circulation and reproduction.[10] The export of the captives must have imposed a constant demographical burden, while the loss as slaves of previously free dependants, until then kept as hostages and recoverable as ransom, rendered their lands available for appropriation by the elite.

The increase in warfare and external trade made possible an unprecedented cycle of wealth accumulation for successful groups in conjunction with their demographic and territorial expansion. In many cases, some of these may originally have been among the lower ranking groups of the elite, which suddenly found themselves in a geographical situation that left them far better placed to gain access to the new sources of wealth offered by external trade and thus to elevate their status within the tribal hierarchy in contrast to previously higher-ranked groups which suddenly found themselves possessed of advantages that no longer counted. With time, however, of necessity a limited number of successful groups emerged as powerful and wealthy, able to control territories of far greater scale than would have been possible under the earlier conditions of competition.

It is at this point in the overall process of wealth accumulation and growth of coercive power that Nash (1975) would place the institution of the state. The constitution of the state represents, in effect, both a mundane solution to the complexity of the new scale of polities in maximising the efficiency with which tribute could be mobilised and surplus extracted from the subject territory, and a permanent alliance in the self-interest of the successful groups holding power to ensure the reproduction of their position, both by preventing the emergence of challenges from other groups gaining access to new forms of wealth,[11] and in precluding their own subjugation by a group even more powerful than themselves.

With the inception of state organisation, the primary concern of the ruling elite will have been the legitimation of their own position and power; at first through the manipulation of ideological constructs and the institution of strict rules to confirm the *status quo*, and in the longer term through the development of formal legislation, always backed up in the last resort by the ultimate sanction of the threat of institutionalised resort to coercive force. In the event, however, the evolution of these states was suddenly arrested by Caesar's military intervention in 58 BC. As a result of the degree of centralisation and territorial consolidation which they had already achieved, these Central Gaulish polities

seem to have been adopted with only minor adjustments as the basic administrative units of the subsequent provincial organisation, apparently retaining many of their pre-Conquest boundaries (Nash 1978c); the whole process of their incorporation into the Roman Empire being remarkably smooth and swift (cf. Drinkwater 1983). In Belgic Gaul, this does not seem to have been the case, for reasons which must now be examined.

Formation of a periphery II: Belgic Gaul and beyond

Armed then with a body of generalisations pertaining to the structuring principles at work in the reproduction of the late Iron Age societies in Gaul, and some insight into the particularities of the early state as it seems to have developed in the zone bordering Roman *Provincia*, a consideration of specific developments in Belgic Gaul becomes possible. As a reflection of the disruption occasioned by the special circumstances of the Gallic War and Caesar's conquest of the region, and for the purposes of the analysis, we may conceptualise the process in terms of two phases, to all intents equivalent to the first and second halves of the first century BC respectively, at which point a major restructuring of the settlement pattern, involving the foundation of the 'public towns' as the focus of the new Roman *civitates* (Brogan 1974) took place.

Although our knowledge of the pre-Roman settlement pattern in north-east France has been transformed in recent years by the programmes of aerial reconnaissance initiated by Agache (1978) and others, it has yet to be complemented by the systematic excavation of many late Iron Age settlements, particularly rural sites, and as a result, our understanding of the situation there in the first half of the first century BC still depends heavily on the testimony offered by Caesar. This is unfortunate, as more than for some other areas, there must be a suspicion that in his account of Belgic Gaul, Caesar elaborated a number of the political and ethnic distinctions to serve political ends at Rome in order to overcome the criticisms and doubts about his motives made by his opponents (cf, Stevens 1951); a suspicion which extends to his account of Britain and Germany.

Be that as it may, there is sufficient in his narrative to imply a considerable degree of cultural and social heterogeneity in the region compared with the zone to the south. Thus, although in his introduction to the Commentaries he treats the Belgae as a separate people with their own distinctive language, customs and laws (*BG* I, 1), one of the most important points to emerge from modern critiques (e.g., Hawkes 1968) is that it was only a part of the population which lived between the Rhine and the Seine which gave itself this name. The territory occupied by these groups, referred to by Caesar as *Belgium*, seems to have coincided roughly with the modern regions of Picardy and Upper Normandy and its inhabitants do seem to have had a capacity for common action at least in the face of the Roman invasion (*BG* II, 4), even, it has been suggested, to the extent of adopting uniform currency measures (Scheers 1977). *Belgium* had ethnic links and close ties to south-eastern England (*BG* V, 12) and one individual is recorded as controlling land on both sides of the Channel (*Ibid*, II, 4). Outside this territory, however, we find several other important population groups who are differentiated on a variety of grounds. Caesar's allies, the Remi (*BG* II, 3 etc); the *Nervii* and the Celtic- speaking *Treveri* who both on the evidence of Tacitus (*Germania*, 28) laid claim to Germanic ancestry; and the variety of smaller groups referred to collectively as the *Germani Cisrhenani*. They seem to have been the product of full Germanic settlement across the lower Rhine, as part of the process of expansion of Germanic speaking groups which, if only with much qualification, we can perceive at work in the later first millennium BC (Fig. 10.2). Cross-cutting these are other distinctions introduced by Caesar, even if he himself does not always seem to have noticed their significance (Hachmann 1976). In connection with *Belgium* and the *Remi*, he speaks of heavily fortified settlements called *oppida*, apparently similar to those encountered elsewhere in Gaul, whereas the *Nervii* and other coastal groups such as the *Morini* and *Menapii* did not, when in danger, take refuge in fortified towns, but in swamps, fens or forests (*BG* II, 28; III 28–9 etc.). It is unlikely to be an accident that Caesar regarded the *Morini* and one of the groups within the *Germani Cisrhenani*, the *Eburones*, as *barbari*, or the *Nervii*, who would not allow the importation of wine or other luxuries (*BG* II, 15), as a *gens* and as *homines feri* (*BG* V, 34; VI, 36). All these have implications for differences in the social structures of the groups between the Seine and the Rhine, even if Caesar himself had no clear notion of the real ethnological background (Hachmann 1976), or of the structuring principles which articulated the reproduction of the different kinds of social formations he encountered.

If groups in that part of Belgic Gaul qualified as *Belgium* may have had close links with Britain, it is equally clear that the Germanic origins (of whatever order and reality) of the major part if not all of its population attested by the *Remi* (*BG* II, 4), could point to the existence of similar ties with trans-Rhenine population. Indeed, Caesar (*BG* V, 55) complains of intrigues with, and promises of money to, this group by those hostile to him, although elsewhere he was to claim that the two 'peoples' were constantly at war (*BG* I, 1).

Taken at face value, these attributes of decentralised behaviour and a dispersed settlement pattern which necessitated something of a piecemeal conquest, would suggest that political conditions in Belgic Gaul were in no way comparable to those in the zone of state formation to the south. However, it may be that to do so would be to impose a distinction which is altogether too rigid, elevating comments which properly applied only to the coastal and marshland communities in the extreme north, to a more general characterisation of the area between the Rhine and the Seine. Certainly, whether or not Caesar intended it, such a picture is at variance with the other evidence of these communities which we possess. Particularly along the southern fringes of Belgic Gaul in the Aisne Valley and the Mosel region, there are massive fortified sites (Wheeler and Richardson 1957) such as Condé-sur-Suippe, Pommiers, the Titelberg, and Villeneuve-St-Germain,[12] which are little different to those such as Bibracte further to the south and should betoken a similar degree of centralisation in these areas. It is possible that Caesar's *Belgium* will, of course, yield evidence of similar nucleated settlements; indeed his usage of the principal settlements of the area such as

Samarobriva (Amiens) for winter quarters renders this more than likely.

One is drawn to the conclusion that behind the pattern of variation implicit in Caesar's account of Belgic Gaul, we can actually discern a more consistent trend, one of increasingly political centralisation the closer we move towards the zone of state formation in Central Gaul. It is only in the extreme north and east, in the coastal areas inhabited by the Nervii, the Germani Cisrhenani and other population groups, and across the Rhine, that we encounter a dispersed settlement pattern and other attributes of genuinely acephalous communities. Further south, however, the degree of political centralisation and socio-economic differentiation seems to have been rather understated, and in the area immediately bordering Central Gaul, we can perceive a belt of *civitates* which seem to share a number of significant characteristics with those of their southern neighbours who had already achieved full statehood.

At first glance, it might be thought that as in Central Gaul the explanation of this pattern and the impetus to political centralisation in Belgic Gaul lay in an evolving relationship between its populations and the Mediterranean world. Evidence of pre-Caesarian contact is afforded by finds in burials such as Hannogne or Château Porcien (Flouest and Stead 1977) and by an ever increasing number of finds of Republican amphorae (Fig. 10.4) in the north east, although a significant number of these, as well as all the findspots in south east England, presumably postdate the conquest. One site, the Titelberg, has also produced Campanian pottery (Rowlett *et al.* 1982).

The significance of this material, however, is difficult to assess. Caesar observes that being farthest removed from the Roman Province, Belgic Gaul was least often visited by merchants with luxuries for sale (*BG* I, 1), although the geographical specificity of his remarks is not beyond question. There is certainly nothing to compare with the massive quantities of amphorae from sites to the south, such as *Bibracte*, or Cabyllinon where 24,000 amphorae were dredged from the River Saône.[13] The bulk of the contact, therefore, is likely to have been indirect and somehow mediated by the halo of newly established states around the boundaries of *Provincia*. Even with the notoriously pro-Roman Remi, the manner in which they placed themselves at Caesar's service in 57 BC does little to suggest that previous relations were direct, although their favourable disposition to Rome, even if motivated by their circumstances (Hachmann 1976), may have been of longer standing.

The evidence we have is, in fact, much more susceptible to interpretation in terms of the model of peripheral expansion which has been noted above and elsewhere (cf. Rowlands 1980). To meet increased demands from their Mediterranean trading partners, the states and polities of Central Gaul will have had to expand their own productive base. It seems likely that this will have been achieved at least partly by expanding their own exchange relations with more remote populations to the north, which will have had the additional advantage of gaining access to extra specialised products, such as furs, not available to them locally. Hence, a dendritic growth of alliance and exchange

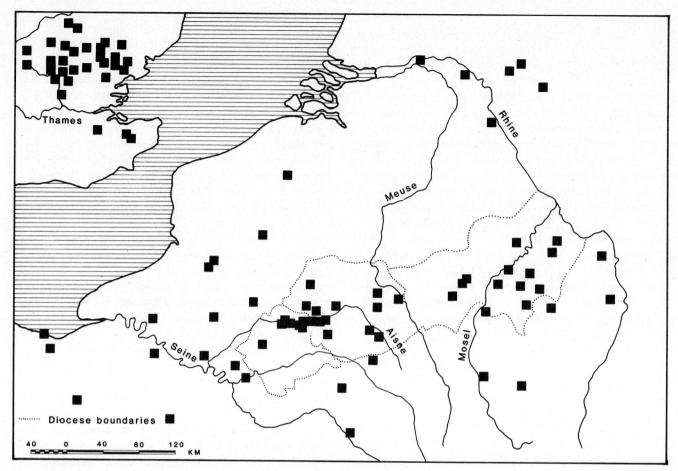

Fig. 10.4 Findspots of late Republican amphorae in southeast England and northeast Gaul.

networks would serve to expand the region of procurement and to re-orientate an ever increasing flow of commodities to the centres in the south (Rowlands 1980). Where slaves were a commodity of particular importance for exchange, as seems to have been the case for the Roman world, peripheral expansion is more likely to take the form of raiding and more generalised warfare before more stable alliance relations are established. Hence, the by-now relatively stable states of Central Gaul are likely to have promoted the growth on their own periphery of more unstable polities to the north as a means of ensuring the exportable surplus needed to satisfy the demands of their Mediterranean trading partners, setting in motion a dynamic whereby this periphery expanded outwards, as former relations of warfare were consolidated by conquest or transformed into more peaceful alliance and exchange networks between increasingly powerful and centralised polities.

The evidence is certainly consistent with the view that it was just such a process of peripheral expansion accompanying the commercial expansion of the Mediterranean core which was disrupted by Roman military intervention in the affairs of *Gallia Comata*. Increasing unrest and warfare is surely reflected in the Late La Tène foundation or re-occupation of the many strongly defended sites in north central France and the Rhineland (Collis 1975; Wheeler and Richardson 1957) and equally, whatever the difficulties of precise dating, it is clear that this trend predates the

Roman invasion. It is not unlikely that the kind of 'crisis' model of the sudden nucleation of a hitherto dispersed population into large fortified settlements proposed by Collis (1982) is relevant here, and is certainly testable – in some cases, even the names of the sites, e.g., Caesar's *Noviodunum* of the Suessonnes (*BG* II, 12), are indicative of a relatively abrupt and dramatic transformation. In more general terms, the countless references to be found in *De Bello Gallico* to the instability of conditions prevailing in Belgic Gaul are consonant with a state of warfare in which the capture of slaves was an important preoccupation. It could be that from a British point of view, one of the most important passages: 'maritima pars ad eis qui praedae ac belli inferendi causa ex Belgio transierant . . . et bello inlato ibi permanserant atque agros colere coeperient' (*BG* V, 12) reflects genuine misunderstanding and misrepresentation on Caesar's part of the processes at work, i.e., an instance of peripheral expansion taking the form of raiding before more stable alliance relations could be established.

There is much to suggest that fewer but more powerful groups were emerging which controlled large territories by taking advantage of more stable alliance relations with the zone of state formation to the south from which wine and Italian drinking vessels were obtained in return for slaves and other commodities. This is particularly likely in the case of the populations inhabiting the southern fringes of Belgic Gaul, in the Seine Basin and Mosel valley, where geographical location put them in an excellent position to manipulate and monopolise dendritic networks stretching into the vast hinterland of Britain, the Low Countries and Germany. Caesar, for example, refers to the Bellovaci as the largest and most influential of the Belgic tribes, and to the dependants of another powerful group, the Treveri, while the existence of alliance structures of the kind envisaged seems confirmed by his comment that the Bellovaci had always lived under the 'friendly protection' of the Aedui, until their leading men induced them to sever the connection and take up arms against Rome (*BG* II, 14; IV, 6).[14]

It is not clear whether or not such groups had reached a degree of centralisation sufficient for the leading groups to have constituted themselves as a state along lines parallel to those suggested for the *civitates* of Central Gaul (Nash 1975). Significantly, nowhere in Belgic Gaul is there any sign of the development of a bi- or trimetallic system of coinage similar to those in the zone to the south (Allen and Nash 1980), and, on balance, it seems unlikely that by the time of the war against Rome even the groups on the southernmost fringes of the region had reached a level of economic development comparable to Central Gaul. What is certain, however, is that Caesar's conquest, when it came, was to have a decisive influence on the subsequent development of Belgic Gaul, altering political conditions and the whole basis of social reproduction, dramatically and irreversibly.

The incorporation of a periphery: the Roman Conquest

The likely effects of the Gallic war on Belgic Gaul have been examined elsewhere (Haselgrove 1984) and will only be summarised here. The most immediate consequences are likely to have been those arising from the cost of actually waging war. Payments of various kinds would have had to be made to clients, for the recruitment of mercenaries, as bribes and as inducements to form alliances. Indeed, Caesar specifically complains of the Treveri in connection with the latter (*BG* V, 55). Moreover, if precious metal coinage (though subject to the same general rules of use as other forms of wealth) had by this stage in the evolution of Gaulish societies replaced many of the traditional forms as a means of payment (cf. Nash 1981), then a massive increase in the minting of coinage will have been necessary to finance the war. Analysis of the dies suggests that the striking of coinage during the war was of an order of magnitude of some ten to twenty times greater than previously (Haselgrove 1984), perhaps even higher if as seems likely, earlier production was episodic over much longer periods. This increase in minting can hardly have been achieved without the coining of metal recovered through melting down many of the other forms of valuables, e.g., torcs, previously confined to the sphere of elite circulation and gift exchange. Very considerable strain was in fact experienced in mobilising the necessary quantities of precious metal. In the course of the war both the weight and standard of gold coinage fell dramatically (Scheers 1977); gold experienced a debasement from a purity of over 60 per cent to 45 per cent or even less. Indeed, the war clearly went far to establish the principle of coinage as a token, the authority or prestige of its issuer now being accepted as guaranteeing

coin as a means of payment at a certain rate, in contrast to the older system with its emphasis on precise weights and on the direct convertibility of different forms of wealth in precious metal (Spratling 1976), a development which was to be of considerable importance in the post-war period.

Although beyond the limits of precise quantification, it is clear that financing the war and the cost of the defeat experienced by the Belgic groups will have had a dramatic effect on the amount of wealth left in the region. At least four mechanisms for its loss from circulation can be identified; the loss of coins and valuables in hoards that were never recovered, to which may be added large quantities leaving the region to purchase mercenary support and as personal wealth taken by defeated members of the elite, such as the chiefs of the Bellovaci who fled in 57 BC (*BG* II, 14). Both of these will have had the converse effect of increasing the amount of wealth in circulation in the recipient areas. Finally, the Belgic groups will have lost a great deal of their wealth in booty to the Roman army and in the exaction of tribute imposed after each defeat. Again exact figures are difficult,[15] but it is known that Caesar brought so much gold back with him from Gaul that the price of the metal in Rome fell sharply, much of it stripped from the temples where the spoils of war were generally dedicated (*BG* I, 1; Suetonius *Div. Iulius* 54.2). It is probable that much of the wealth in precious metal will have been taken out of circulation permanently in the very first year of the war, with whatever reserves there were being dissipated in the string of unsuccessful revolts that follows. Even Rome's allies such as the Remi are unlikely to have been completely exempt from tribute, although the relative amount of wealth left in circulation must have been greater than in many of the other *civitates*.[16] It is no accident that the only coinages in gold, albeit extremely debased, with a possible claim to post-Conquest striking are found in the territory of the Remi and the Treveri (Haselgrove 1984). Finally, when Caesar was forced by increasing political pressures in Italy to leave Gaul in 50 BC, he levied a tribute of forty million sestertii on *Gallia Comata*, which though far from extortionate, was set at a less favourable rate than has sometimes been claimed (Drinkwater 1983).

A further significant consequence of the war was certainly demographic, including the loss of warriors, and individuals taken as captives and sold into slavery, or hostages who were not redeemed; this must have resulted in a significant drain of people away from the region. The *Nervii* are reputed, for instance, to have lost 99 per cent of their men capable of bearing arms in a total force of sixty thousand[17] (*BG* II, 28). In rare instances, as with the Atuatuci, Caesar seems to have sold whole populations into slavery, the total number of persons included in the sale being reported as fifty-three thousand (*BG* II, 33; III, 16). The motive was evidently to make an example of them for rebelling against treaties with him. It may be presumed that as with gold, the demand for slaves in Italy is likely to have fallen temporarily whilst the loss of productive capacity is likely to have had far more harmful consequences for the region.

In fact, Caesar's treatment of his defeated enemies was by and large consistent, and governed both by the short-term military consideration that relative leniency would lessen the likelihood of groups rebelling while his armies were under pressure, and the longer-term consideration of leaving intact a framework which would provide the basis for the administration and exploitation of a future Roman province, a process which would require not only the cooperation of an elite, but the labour power of the remainder of the population. For similar reasons, certain powerful groups such as the *Aedui* and the *Arverni* were treated with leniency even after their rebellions, while in the other cases, individual members of the elite who had remained loyal were substi'-tuted for those who had rebelled as in the case of Cingetorix of the *Treveri* (*BG* VI, 8). In general, Caesar's policy seems to have been one of buttressing the position of the local elites, to whom a number of valuable concessions were given. Hirtius actually records how in 51 BC, wintering in Belgic Gaul, Caesar bestowed rich gifts on the elite, and refrained from imposing any fresh burdens to promote their continuing loyalty to him (*BG* VIII, 49). Either then, or more probably later, individuals were also granted Roman citizenship (Drinkwater 1983), in effect linking their self-interests to those of the Julio-Claudian house by making them its clients. It may be assumed that these alliances and treaties with the most powerful elites were concluded in terms comparable to the privileges which emerged in the legislation of Augustus which created the Gallic provinces, probably at the time the first census was instituted in 27 BC (Drinkwater 1983); the *Remi* presumably became an allied 'state' (*civitas foederata*), while the Treveri were certainly a free 'state' (*civitas libera*). In addition, groups which had been loyal were rewarded by being vested with dependent groups or clients, which increased their territory and population;[18] thus both the *Carnutes* and the *Suessiones* appear to have been placed under the control of the *Remi* (*BG* VI, 4: VIII, 6). One may

speculate that the territorial structure of the late-Roman archdioceses such as Reims (Fig. 10.5) and Trier has its origins in the arrangements made at this period.[19]

Caesar's policy then was the creation of a framework which would provide the administrative basis for the future province, through identifying the interests of influential elite groups, who will have continued to believe themselves to be free allies, with those of Rome. The measure of its success is first, and foremost, that after what was by any standard a brutal war of conquest, and a departure which if planned, was also precipitate, *Gallia Comata* was to give the Roman world remarkably few problems over the next quarter of a century (at a time when it was firmly preoccupied elsewhere) until the new emperor Augustus was able to turn his attention to the reorganisation of the province in 27 BC.[20] Much, however, of the trouble that there was occurred in Belgic Gaul, and as early as 46 BC, D. Junius Brutus Albinus, Caesar's successor as governor of the Province, had to suppress another revolt of the Bellovaci (Livy *Epitome* 114). In 39 BC, Agrippa campaigned in the northeast, and this was followed by C. Carrinas' campaign against the *Morini* and their Belgic and Germanic allies in 30 BC, while in 29 BC, Nonius Gallus defeated the *Treveri*, who had also invoked their Germanic alliances. Four years later, a campaign of retribution was launched against Germans who had slaughtered visiting Roman traders by M. Vinicius (Drinkwater 1983), and between 19 and 17 BC, Agrippa returned to Gaul for a second term as Governor, again having to deal with problems in the northeast which had German backing.

Thus, while there were uprisings in other parts of *Gallia Comata* during this period, notably in the southwest, and Belgic Gaul as a frontier zone occupied a relatively vulnerable position, the occurrence of so much unrest in this region,[21] and not, for instance, among the states of Central Gaul, is a question which calls for some discussion. The answer, I would suggest, lies in the difficulties experienced by elites in maintaining their position relative to their dependent populations in the wake of the Gallic wars, in comparison to the more developed and centralised polities in the zone of pre-Caesarian state formation.

There can be little doubt of the complexity of the problems involved in maintaining the existing social order in the immediate post-conquest period, notwithstanding the Roman backing enjoyed by the elite, and possibly the presence of garrisons among those of the Belgic populations reduced to tributary status (*civitates stipendariae*). Most serious of these is likely to have been the loss of almost all of the traditional wealth forms, in a society whose reproduction and expansion had previously been geared to the circulation of treasure items among members of the elite and other valuables, such as coinage and cattle, between the elite and their subordinates – with the deprivations that parts of the landscapes are likely to have been subjected to, even the expansion of herds of livestock may well have proved a problem. Of the traditional avenues to elite accumulation of wealth, which might have allowed replacement of some of the lost bullion, warfare and predation on their neighbours was now closed to them as an option by the *Pax Romana*.

Moreover, a patron's power and prestige had traditionally

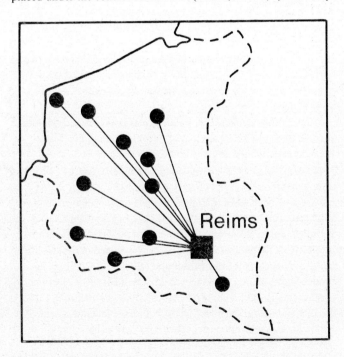

Fig. 10.5 The metropolitan see of Reims at the end of the fourth century AD.

been reckoned in terms of the number of his clients, and in the size of his armed retinue, yet the keeping of the latter would pose an obvious threat to Roman supremacy.

One of the more critical foci of discontent, to which Roman misunderstanding of the essentially reciprocal nature of Gaulish patron–client relations probably contributed, is likely to have lain in the relationship between the ruling groups and previously independent elites who had been bound to them as clients. Their discontent at this and the requirement to furnish tribute which was then forwarded to Rome as tax, can only have been accentuated by any problems the dominant groups experienced in fulfilling their obligations as patrons by distributing valuables and other elite trappings to their clients. At another level, a consequence of Caesar's consolidation of these clients and their own dependents into continuous territories and a hierarchy dominated by his allies, may have been to deny them the possibility of concluding alliances with their equals outside the region, previously such an important element in the system of social reproduction. The abolition of these horizontal relations, or at least their restriction to members of the ruling echelon, can only have contributed further to the difficulties experienced by the local elites in maintaining their own positions.

It is to be presumed that the Romans will themselves have understood something of the pressures to which the leading groups were now exposed, and will have done their best to alleviate them as long as this did not involve a clash with their own interests. It is clear from the evidence of a number of sites that the ruling elites were allowed not only to maintain, but even to embellish the defences of their principal settlements (cf. Collis 1975), even when these had proved impregnable to Roman arms as in the case of *Gergovia* (*BG* VII, 36–53), as a symbol of their continued authority. It is possible that the ruling groups of the allied and free states were, in fact, allowed to maintain an armed retinue, and weapons were certainly interred in the burials of the elite down to the end of the first century BC, e.g., at Goeblingen – Nospelt (Thill 1967) in the territory of the *Treveri*. What is certain is that, in the Caesarian tradition, the Gallic elite were able to raise and command their own forces to serve as auxiliaries with the Roman army for some time after the conquest, and as late as AD 21, Tacitus refers to 'a cavalry regiment – raised among the Treveri but serving with us in Roman fashion' (*Annales* III, 40).

In the short term, this policy will have had obvious advantages: it took the younger members of the elite and their clients out of circulation in their own *civitas*, and if they survived, they would return to their home territories 'Romanised' in their attitudes, and more important, in the identification of their self-interests with those of Rome.[22] In the long term, the mechanism generated contradictions which could be related to the unrest in Belgic Gaul during the later first century BC since younger members of the elite were offered an opportunity through the traditional mechanism of success in warfare to accumulate wealth on a scale denied to the ruling elite at home and would then return to the *civitas* to find themselves excluded from the political process.

It has always been clear from the pattern of post-Conquest hoards that the Romans not only allowed the continued circula-

tion of indigenous coinage in the province (cf, Scheers 1977), but actually tolerated the continued minting of coin, with the availability of metal the only determinant of its composition. It has recently been suggested that this coinage was used to pay the auxiliary contingents serving with the Roman army,[23] which would certainly be consistent with its presence at the forts in the Rhineland. Whether or not this constituted its primary purpose, it is clear that striking even a largely token inscribed coinage in bronze and potin will have had considerable symbolic importance in constantly reiterating the authority of its issuers, the ruling group, and above all, their continuing ability to make payments to dependents and a means whereby direct intervention in local exchange could be sustained, thus affording them mechanisms for continuing to mobilise other commodities and resources for export.

While redefinition of the valuables acceptable in the discharge of social obligations was clearly one of the options open to the elites of Belgic Gaul,[24] its success will clearly have been dependent on continued group consensus. This raises the wider issue of whether this would have been ideologically manipulated by the elite to legitimate their continued hegemony, which also has direct consequences for our interpretation of the material remains, as the precise symbolism employed will depend on the structures of signification invoked by a particular group. As Giddens (1979) has argued, this almost invariably involves, as one aspect, 'the naturalisation of the present' through the reification of existing social relations as fixed and immutable, effective as in nature. By inhibiting recognition of historical processes of change, the interests of the dominant group in the preservation of the *status quo* are sustained. Other, complementary, ideological forms may also be suggested; the interests of the hegemonic group could be projected as being in the interest of the Community as a whole. Alternatively, an ideology of denial may have operated, where through inversion, the existence of hierarchy and its contradictions may be denied.

The power of religious ideology in the Celtic world is implicit in the apparent security of the vast amounts of wealth dedicated and deposited on sacred sites;[25] notwithstanding the desperate need for precious metal to finance the cost of the war against Rome, the treasures of the sanctuaries remained inviolate for Caesar to plunder them (Suetonius, *Div Iulius* 54.2). Caesar comments that it was common practice after a victory for the spoil to be dedicated on consecrated ground, and that it was almost unknown for anyone to dare, in defiance of 'religious law', to conceal their booty at home, or to remove anything placed on the piles, with the sanction of death by torture for anyone who broke the rule (*BG* VI, 16). While the practice cannot be taken too literally in view of the importance of warfare as an avenue to the accumulation of wealth open to the elite, it is clear that we have an instance of religious ideology being invoked to maintain the position of the elite by denying their clients the possiblity of entering into competition with them. The subtlety of the political and ideological process is also apparent in his further comment that the 'magistrates' suppress what they deem it advisable to keep secret and only publish what they deem it expedient for the people to know (*BG* VI, 20). Continued investment in sanctuaries will

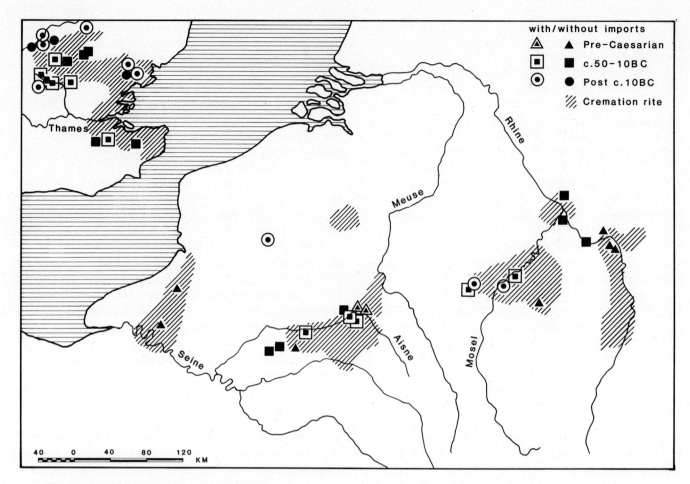

Fig. 10.6 'Wealthy' burials in southeast England and northeast Gaul.

have been an important strategy open to the post-conquest elites attempting to maintain their status, and it may be suggested that the origin of the great rural sanctuaries of Roman Gaul (Agache 1978) is to be seen in this process; the dearth of valuables for dedication promoting as an alternative form of display, investment in institutional facilities and buildings. It should be more than coincidence that the structural sequence at sanctuary sites such as Trier Altbachtal had its beginnings in the later first century BC. An early assimilation of Celtic and Roman religious ideology will also have had its part in this process of legitimation.

Also relevant is the marked differentiation in mortuary rite which develops in restricted areas of northeast Gaul at this period against a background of cremation burial, particularly along the Aisne and the Mosel (Fig. 10.6). Similar features extend to the Welwyn group of the Thames estuary. When the traits characteristic of the complex are set out, the high degree of correlation between the artefact categories present in each region is apparent, mirrored by distinctions in grave form (Fig. 10.7). A most interesting feature of the burials is the juxtaposition of Roman imports such as wine amphorae and associated bronze and silver vessel services, with what must be interpreted as traditional symbols of authority and status, such as buckets, wagons and horse-gear, weaponry and shields, and in one case apparently a bear-skin robe cremated with its wearer at Heimbach-Weis (Collis 1977), paral-

leled by the Welwyn Garden City burial in southeast England. The tradition clearly had pre-Caesarian beginnings, but the majority of the burials are undoubtedly of post-Conquest date.[26] It is likely that the relatively small number of cremations reported (cf, Haselgrove 1982) is indicative of a minority rite, and that the majority of the population disposed of their dead by alternative mechanisms. There are several features of these 'wealthy' burials which suggest ideological manipulation of the disposal of the dead and would be consistent with an identification of sectional and community interests in the legitimation of the 'new order' of the post-Conquest period.

The very consumption of large quantities of what we assume to have been valuables is an obvious inversion of the reality claimed for the period, and as such must be symptomatic of 'the naturalisation of the present through the reification of the immutability of existing social relations' (cf. Giddens 1979). Moreover, the rites and symbolism adopted must be seen as projecting the desirability of the alliance with Rome and the benefits of acculturation on the part of a class who owed their position to this relationship. At burial sites such as Goeblingen – Nospelt (Thill 1967) the message is reiterated in everything from large-scale wine consumption to the cremation rite; the power and continued success of the ruling groups was indissolubly linked to the Roman alliance.

ATTRIBUTE	GROUP Thames	Mosel	Arras	Aisne	Seine
Flat grave crem.	X	X	?	X	X
Rect. enclosures	X	X		X	
'Vault'	X		X	?	
Tumuli	X	?		(?)	X
Amphoræ	X	X	X	X	
Imported æ,æ vessels	X	X	?	X	?
'Imported' pots	X	X	X		
Local æ (bound) vessels	X	X	X	?	X
Wrought iron items	X	(?)	X	?	
Wagon/Harness	(x)	(x)		X	X
Weapons	(x)	X		X	X
Brooches, beads	X	X	X	X	X

Fig. 10.7 Attributes of the principal late Iron Age Burial Groups in southeast England and northeast Gaul.

Though the nature of archaeological evidence precludes certainty, it may well be that burial was now one of the few occasions on which such consumption would have occurred; the fact that it did occur in the process of disposal of the dead must in any case be significant. Shennan has recently suggested that this may relate in some way to the problem of succession to power in societies where the rules of succession are not clear and leave open the possibility of competition (Shennan 1982), the rich burials received by some individuals being as much an indication of the alliances and resources which could be mobilized by the leaders of the next generation, as a reflection of the dead person's position. Given the problems confronting the Belgic elites in the later first century BC, this suggestion has much to commend it.

A further idea which may well be relevant to the elaboration of this burial rite is the observation of Goldstein (1981) that formal bounded areas for the exclusive disposal of a group's dead are likely in periods when there is an imbalance between society and its critical resources, such as land. In effect, the group's rights to control or use crucial but restricted resources are attained and legitimised by lineal descent from the dead, and its rights constantly reaffirmed through the existence of an exclusive disposal area. Of the few resources still available to the post-Conquest elite to maintain their position, the ownership of land and thus the capacity to generate a surplus, is the most obvious, and consolida-

tion of their control over its disposal will have been crucial to them, particularly in those areas which were experiencing a temporary shortage of cultivable land or pasture as a consequence of its destruction during the devastations of the Caesarian wars.

While the gifts and concessions which the Romans made to favoured elites as a reward for their allegiance, or as an inducement to obtain their support, will have been of considerable value to them in maintaining their position immediately after the Conquest, consolidation of their status as the rulers of nominally free or allied populations would have ultimately required more than the manipulation of structures of signification and the process of disposal of the dead to legitimate their rule. In particular, this required the mobilisation of the means to acquire a continuing supply of the very symbols that were central to the new processes of consumption, and could be substituted for traditional valuables in the spheres of elite circulation and display; Roman commodities such as wine, serving and drinking vessels, and fine tablewares. That some groups notably the *Remi* and the *Treveri* were clearly successful in obtaining these commodities through exchange, is clear from the concentration of later first century BC amphorae in the Aisne-Marne and Mosel regions respectively (Fig. 10.4 above), where they are found even on the rural settlement sites (Haselgrove 1983). Spanish fabrics now occur alongside those of Italian origin. The question of what was exchanged for these southern commodities must now be posed, assuming that they represent a scale of importation above the level of Roman diplomatic gifts.

The most obvious strategy available to the elite will have been the initiation of surplus production geared to exportable commodities. The classical texts mention three main categories of goods of Gaulish origin arriving in Italy; metals, products from herd-raising, notably wool and ham, and slaves (Tchernia 1983); each of these may be examined in turn.

Belgic Gaul is not noted in antiquity for its mineral resources. However, both copper and iron ores are found in the Middle Rhine and Saarland and it is possible that these resources were exploited for export by the *Treveri*, as well as, in the case of copper, for the production of post-Conquest bronze coinages. This does, however, assume that the exploitation of mineral resources was left to the free native populations. Unfortunately, we have no direct information on this problem, but it was the solution adopted for the iron and copper deposits of Macedonia (Livy XLV, 29.11), and appears perfectly plausible in the case of Gaul in the later first century BC, whatever the case after the Augustan reorganisation, and in other provinces. Another resource which was certainly prized in the Mediterranean and may have been exported, was salt, but there is no mention of Gaulish salt in the sources, and archaeological evidence is silent on the question. Its significance, if any, is more likely to have lain in the export of the next category to be considered, i.e., products from stock-raising.

Belgic Gaul was famous for its textiles and its salt pork, and there can be no doubt that these were amongst its exports from the earliest date. Indeed, this is confirmed by Strabo, writing at the end of the century: 'They have such enormous flocks of sheep and herds of swine that they afford a plenteous supply of *sagi* and of salt meat, not only to Rome, but to most parts of Italy' (*Geographica* IV, 4, 3, translation in Tierney 1960). However, as Tchernia (1983) has observed, it is difficult to believe that a country such as Italy where the raising of sheep and pigs was already well-developed should have imported commodities such as salt-pork and wool in quantities sufficient to have given them great commercial importance; they were clearly luxuries, and their reputation in Rome rested on their quality rather than their quantity. In any case, the existence of other sources for high-quality hams, such as the territory of the *Sequani* (Strabo *Geographica* IV, 3, 2) will have precluded the development of a monopoly, and kept their exchange-value low.

A commodity that would still have been quantitively important to the Roman world was slaves; even the large quantity of captives which would have come on to the market as a result of the Gallic Wars is unlikely to have satisfied the demand for more than a short time. Even so, slaves are unlikely to have been a major export from Belgic Gaul at this period. While it is true that even under the Empire, a number of slaves continued to be bought in the provinces in contravention of legal prohibitions, unrestricted trade of the dimensions that existed before the Conquest will no longer have been possible (cf. Tchernia 1983). In any case, the demographic consequences of the Gallic Wars were such as to render the existence of an exportable surplus highly unlikely; the remaining population will have been essential for productive labour. Similarly, predation on neighbouring groups for war captives was prevented by the *Pax Romana*, while the *civitas* regiments serving as auxiliary forces with the Romans are equally unlikely to have been a source of slaves; any captives arising from their activities during this period are likely to have been appro-

priated by their Roman commanders, or sold direct to merchants accompanying the army.

It would seem then that home-based exports are unlikely to have provided the ruling elites of Belgic Gaul who were successful in their trading with the Roman world with an adequate basis for their activities. This being the case, it seems that the elites, particularly of the *civitates* on the southern fringes of Belgic Gaul, will have taken advantage of their nominally free status and geographical location, and had recourse to the only strategy left open to them to produce an exportable surplus of commodities in demand in the Roman world. This will have been to revitalise the old alliances and marriage relations linking them with communities still beyond the nominal frontiers of the province, and thus to reactivate the dendritic networks which had been beginning to develop before the Roman Conquest, to channel the produce of Britain and Germany towards the commercial core to the south. They would, in effect, be taking a middleman position in procuring commodities in demand by Rome, but only available at a distance, and using their role to siphon surplus wealth from the network, which could then be reinvested in their own trade relations with the south. At first glance, their potential to exploit alliances and exchanges with the elites of Britain and Germany might seem weak on account of the survival of a far greater proportion of the traditional wealth forms for circulation in those areas. However, this was more than outweighed by the advantage of their access to Roman luxuries. Providing that the Belgic elites could exchange these with their external trading partners at a favourable rate – and it must be assumed that they could, as Roman merchants themselves had long since discovered (cf. above and Diodorus Siculus V, 27) – then it would be possible for them to

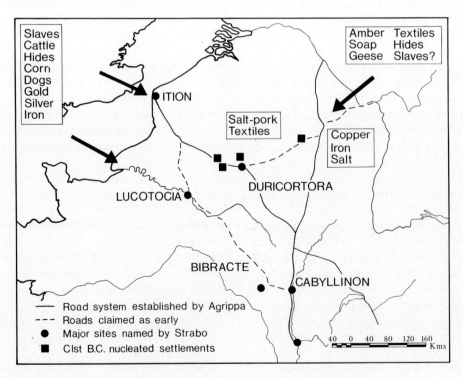

Fig. 10.8 Exports from southern England, northeast Gaul and Germany in the later first century BC.

obtain commodities which could be exchanged for further Roman goods in sufficient quantities to satisfy their own needs for objects of elite consumption as well as their partners' demands. A spiral of accumulation would thus be set in motion.

An attempt has been made to summarise some of the more important commodities which may have been channelled through this network to the advantage of the middleman communities such as the *Remi* and the *Treveri* (Fig. 10.8). The importance of exchange with Free Germany after the establishment of the *Limes* is well known and has been fully analysed on an archaeological and historical basis by Hedeager (1978a and this volume). Germany was a source of various luxuries, to which we might add products like furs or resins; slaves, it must be assumed, were also an important component. Fine tablewares and vessels would appear to be the most important export, with amphorae remarkably rare beyond the Rhine and Danube. The *Treveri* will have been excellently placed to exploit the potential of the North German region. For the *Remi*, and perhaps other southern Belgic groups such as the *Ambiani* and the *Bellovaci*, Britain will have provided the source for slaves, minerals, and other commodities with which to supplement those mobilised for export within Belgic Gaul through relations of dependence analogous to those hinted at by the later archdiocesan arrangements.

Precious metal coinage (cf. Kent 1981) and the texts leave us in no doubt of the close ties which had previously existed between Belgic Gaul and parts of southern England, notably the areas around the Thames estuary; the pattern of importation of post-Conquest Belgic coins (Fig. 10.9) suggests that it was much the same networks which continued to be exploited. The apparent clustering to the north of the River Thames of the Roman imports which we assume were used in these exchanges is largely due to their consumption in burials, and it has recently been suggested that the number of amphora finds from settlement sites south of the Thames compares favourably with the finds to the north of the river (Fitzpatrick, 1985). With warfare available as a means for acquiring an exportable surplus and additional productive land in an area which had escaped depopulation on the scale of Belgic Gaul, it is clear that the potential for elaboration of well-placed and successful elites would have been considerable and is perhaps mirrored by the appearance of the wealthy burials of the Welwyn group, a further case of developments of the kind discussed in the preceding section as the frontiers moved forward and the periphery continued its outward advance.

It has been argued that a substantial proportion of the Romanised commodities reaching Britain at the period were actually transported by means of a route along the Rhine (Partridge 1981; Williams 1981). However, recent research casts doubts on this proposition, with imported goods largely absent from the Rhineland until its conquest by the Roman army at the end of the first century BC (Fitzpatrick, Pers. Comm.) while Strabo (*Geographica* IV, 5.2) observes that those who made the journey to Britain from areas near the Rhine, did so not from its estuary, but from the coast in the territory of the *Morini*, where the port of *Ition* (Boulogne) was also situated.

Strabo also furnishes details of the route running from the

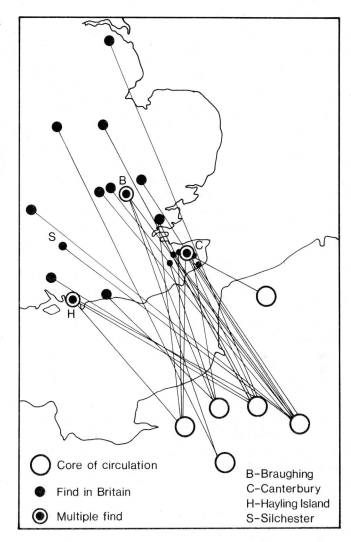

Fig. 10.9 Areas of origin of Belgic bronze and potin coins found in Britain.

Mediterranean all the way to the shores of Britain at this period, which would seem to offer further support for the concept of a dendritic network radiating out through Belgic Gaul (*Geographica* IV, 1.14). According to him, merchandise was carried up the rivers Rhone and Saône, and then overland between the Saône and Seine. It then moved by water again down the latter river to the groups occupying the territories flanking either side of its estuary; from there to Britain was less than a day's sailing. More circumstantial evidence for the network is provided by the road system based on Lyon which was founded by Agrippa during one or other of his governorships[27] (Strabo *Geographica* IV, 6.11).

Epilogue: Belgic Gaul under the early Empire
It must be assumed that the duration of this network in purely native hands was short, and was terminated by the commencement of the Roman campaigns against Free Germany in the penultimate decade of the first century BC. It seems likely that Rome took this opportunity to tighten control over Belgic Gaul (if this had not already occurred in the wake of Augustus'

reorganisation of the Province in 27 BC), and that Strabo's comment that its *civitates* were 'now for the most part subject to the commands of Rome' (*Geographica* IV, 4.3) is a thinly veiled 'apology' for its final annexation. Similarly, although Agrippa's primary consideration was presumably to facilitate troop movements into areas which had provided the obvious trouble spots of the post-Conquest period, it is possible that the foundation of his road system was also motivated by an early desire on the part of the Roman administration to impose a degree of direct control over the lucrative commercial networks radiating out to Britain and Germany, or, at least, to tap them effectively. Certainly, by the time Strabo wrote, heavy taxes were being imposed on British imports and exports at the Channel ports (*Geographica* IV, 5.3).

Assuming that the Belgic elites had thus far been relatively successful in maintaining their control of exchange beyond the frontiers, annexation of the region would have served the interests of Roman merchants and traders by undermining the ruling elites' middleman position. From this time on, the British trade (and presumably the German trade as well) must have been largely, if not entirely, in their own hands and they no longer had to overcome the problems of passage and transport through the territories of nominally allied or free populations, but were instead free to penetrate the source areas, subject only to Roman border controls. It is generally assumed that a significant increase in the volume of cross-Channel trade followed, and that this was a factor in the growth of an extensive state centred on Camulodunum (Colchester).[28] Whoever controlled the latter was able to take advantage of its location and establish a monopoly over the British end of the network (cf, Haselgrove 1982). This transformation appears to have had much in common with the development of the Central Gaulish states a century earlier. Similarly, trade beyond the Rhine appears to lie behind the differences which we can detect in the structuring principles articulating German-speaking populations in Caesar's time and in that of Tacitus (cf. Thompson 1965). In contrast to Britain, however, peripheral elaboration in Free Germany followed a path which resembled developments in an earlier phase of European prehistory, during the sixth century BC (cf. Rowlands 1980). Owing to the sheer length of the common frontier it was impossible for local groups to establish and hold on to monopolies over Roman trade, with a result that a 'buffer zone' some two hundred kilometres deep evolved. Only beyond this are more obviously hierarchical polities to be found, represented by the wealthy burials of the Lübsow group (Hedeager 1978a).

By interfering with the ruling elites' newly-evolved mechanisms for maintaining control over the accumulation of wealth and its circulation in their territories, the imposition of direct Roman rule might be assumed to have once again threatened their position, but there are no indications that this was in fact the case in Belgic Gaul, if our sources can be relied upon. If anything, the elites' position went from strength to strength, and in a short space of time the province emerged as one of the wealthiest in the Empire as a whole. Indeed, this was true of *Gallia Comata* in general (Drinkwater 1983; Duncan-Jones 1981), so much so that only a century after the Gallic War, Claudius was able to boast of

receiving gold crowns, weighing in all 9,000 lb, from its constituent provinces for the celebration of his British triumph (Pliny *Nat. Hist.* XXXIII, 54). This was 2,000 lb more than those contributed by *Hispania Citerior* with all its mineral wealth.[29]

According to the model advanced in this chapter and Hopkins' (1980) analysis of the Roman economy during the early Empire, the causes of this state of affairs, for Belgic Gaul at least, reside in a combination of circumstances: conditions in the province at the end of the Civil Wars in the Mediterranean, the initial Caesarian settlements with the Belgic elites, and the effect of stationing a large standing army along the German frontier. In the preceding section, it was argued that despite the problems they experienced, the ruling Belgic elites were in the end able to reassert their position thanks to a number of strategies, most obviously their commercialisation of the periphery, substituting traditional valuables with Roman imports, which they were able to draw into the region, presumably along with some currency, by virtue of the extra-territorial commodities they could procure for Roman merchants. As a result, they succeeded in maintaining the allegiance of their dependents and managed not just to hold on to their land, but quite possibly to strengthen their control over its disposition.

It is this success which I would see as a critical feature of later developments. In achieving it, the ruling elites were helped immensely by the weakness of the centre at this period, and by the very favourable terms they received at Caesar's hands, due to a large extent to the exigencies of impending civil war. In other circumstances, the burden imposed by state taxation might have been expected to have brought about something approaching the total disintegration of the indigenous social and tenurial structure; where tribute had previously circulated within the region, it would now be siphoned off as tax from a population which had already been relieved of most of its portable wealth in bullion. As a result, Roman money-lenders could move in, giving loans to oppressed landowners and then distraining upon their estates when they were unable to pay extortionate rates of interest (cf. Hopkins 1980). In the event, however, it seems that the Caesarian settlement enshrined genuine privileges (cf. Drinkwater 1983) and that 'allied' and 'free' *civitates* like the *Remi* and the *Treveri*, were exempted from the full rigours of taxation, responsible only for forwarding the tribute required of the 'stipendiary' client territories which had been attached to them.

In such circumstances, reinforced by the 'commercial' success of the ruling elites postulated earlier, land-grabbing in Belgic Gaul during the early post-war decades is likely to have been kept to small-scale proportions. Moreover, since the autonomy enjoyed by privileged groups like the *Remi* must have continued, through force of circumstances, to have been less fictional than in other newly annexed provinces, inroads by Roman manufacturers and traders will have been possible only on terms which were acceptable to the ruling elites.

In general, pressure on provincial land probably increased as, under Augustus, the Centre gradually reasserted control, and was further compounded by the efforts of those Romans attempting to enhance their status by converting into land wealth acquired by other means. For obvious reasons, much of the land taking which did occur, is likely to have been concentrated in the territories of the weakest and poorest client populations – Strabo, for instance, comments on the success of 'the Romans' in raising sheep in the most northerly parts of Belgic Gaul (*Geographica* IV, 4.3) – particularly after the Augustan reorganisation had detached them from groups such as the *Remi* and made them responsible for their own affairs as *civitates stipendariae*. In most *civitates*, however, landownership will still have been almost entirely in the hands of the indigenous elite, soon to emerge into history as wealthy landowners such as Julius Florus of the *Treveri* and Julius Sacrovir of the *Aedui* (Tacitus *Annales* III, 40).

The permanent presence of the Roman army in force from the penultimate decade of the first century BC, can only, according to Hopkins' thesis (1980), have transformed the situation still further to the advantage of the indigenous elite. The land on which the army was stationed, whether or not it was still under the technical jurisdiction of the Governor of Belgic Gaul (Drinkwater 1983) became in Hopkins' terms, a net tax-importing region. On account of its geographical proximity and riverine access, which kept transport costs to a minimum, this move was to open up immense commercial possibilities for the rest of Belgic Gaul. Crucially, the landowners who were able to maximise this opportunity by supplying the Roman army with their surplus agricultural produce and other necessities, were for the most part, still Gaulish.[30] In return, they acquired the means to pay their taxes – their circumstances may even have been compounded by any residual taxation privileges enjoyed by the region[31] – and thus to secure their position indefinitely, becoming in the process the immensely wealthy Gauls shown by literary sources to have been much talked about in Rome (Drinkwater 1983). Moreover, the Belgic landowning elite did not necessarily share their Roman counterparts' distaste for 'commercial' activities, and once deprived of their lucrative 'middleman' position, they may well have been among the leaders in intensifying productive activities in the province to supply the army with some of their other requirements. Among enterprises which may well have their origins in such an investment are the kilns of the so-called Gallo-Belgic pottery industry which made their appearance in the Mosel region and the vicinity of Reims at this period, and the production of textiles and wine for which the region was later noted.

For subsequent political developments, however, the formalisation of the Two Germanies as separate provinces seems to have been a decisive step. For groups like the *Remi*, this move effectively brought their influence to an end, if not their prestige – it was after all their chief settlements, *Duricortorum*, which continued to receive the Roman governors of *Gallia Belgica*; for the province of *Germania Inferior*, the move was to mark the beginning of the ascent of their chief settlement, *Augusta Treverorum*, to a position where it could claim to be one of the centres, if not the principal centre of the whole of the Western Empire.[32]

Conclusion

The primary argument of this chapter has been that many features of Late Iron Age society in Central and northeastern France, extending into Britain and Germany, are contingent on those areas' positions in a wider system of social reproduction, as a result of their incorporation into the economic networks which developed beyond the frontiers of the Roman world to effect the procurement of raw materials and other commodities consumed by the centre. In more general terms, we are looking at the material manifestations of periphery formation and the subsequent restructuring of centre–periphery relationships. In the case of Belgic Gaul in particular, the developmental cycle exhibits a number of distinct steps, each to a certain extent a consequence of the conditions created during the previous phase.

The forces which shaped the expansion of the periphery to include Belgic Gaul seem to have emanated from the zone of state formation around the boundaries of the Roman *Provincia* in southern Gaul, as much as from the Mediterranean world proper. By the middle of the first century BC, affairs in *Gallia Comata* necessitated direct Roman intervention (or at least afforded a plausible pretext in the context of Caesar's personal ambitions). Belgic Gaul's incorporation as a province was, however, long drawn-out and by no means free from problems, at a time when the centre was largely preoccupied with civil war, and was accompanied by further peripheral expansion as the process of acculturation spread to Britain. Reduction of Belgic Gaul to semi-peripheral status does not seem to have occurred until the centre reasserted itself under Augustus, and the state was drawn forward once more to intervene first in Germany, and then Britain. By then it is probable that the foundations for the eventual transformation of Belgic Gaul to the status of a centre in its own right had already been laid, although the respective roles of local forces, devolution within the larger system, and the presence of the frontier army on the boundary of the province, in subsequent developments, are not so easily ascertained.

Although it lies beyond the scope of this paper, this shift in centres though superficially short-lived in itself, was of longer-term significance in establishing a pattern, and a change of balance, which had lasting consequences and should probably be counted amongst the factors which eventually brought about the birth of Western capitalism. In this respect, the chapter stands in some contrast to the principles propounded by the historian, Henri Pirenne (1939) in relation to the formation of the Carolingian state, with its thesis that it was the impact of Islam on the Mediterranean world and its dislocation of that area's connections with northwest Europe that provided the necessary conditions. According to the views advanced here, these processes are of a far greater antiquity, 'the rupture of that unity' noted by Pirenne (1939) that 'had displaced the axis of the world', the case of a cyclical recurrence of the forces at work. It would indeed be as well to restate Pirenne's famous thesis 'without Mahommed', but only to reiterate it afresh, with different actors – not the least of them those ardent 'Republicans', Brutus and Cassius, whose assassination of Julius Caesar was to plunge the centre of the Roman world into a period of civil war and instability at a critical moment in the evolution of the newly annexed provinces of Gaul.

Acknowledgements
This paper was submitted in February 1984. The illustrations which accompany this text would not have been presentable but for the efforts of Yvonne Brown and Pamela Lowther. The paper has its origins in lectures to the Prehistoric Society and Welwyn Garden City Conferences on the later Iron Age in 1981. I owe much to Daphne Nash, Mike Rowlands, and Mansel Spratling and to discussions with Andrew Fitzpatrick and Martin Millet. It is hoped that a fuller discussion of the ideas presented here and supporting evidence will be published elsewhere.

Primary sources used
Athenaeus: *Deipnosophistae*
Caesar, Gaius Julius: *Commentariorum de Bello Gallico*
Diodorus Siculus: *Bibliotheca historica*
Livy (Titus Livius): *Epitome*
Livy (Titus Livius): *Historiae*
Plinius Secundus, Caius: *Naturalis Historia*
Polybius: *Historiae*
Strabo: *Geographica*
Suetonius Tranquillus, Gaius: *De vita Caesarium*
Tacitus, Publius Cornelius: *Annales*
Tacitus, Publius Cornelius: *Germania*

Notes

1 Belgic Gaul is taken here as the original Roman province of *Gallia Belgica*, i.e., most of the triangle of land between the rivers Rhine and Seine, including parts of Belgium, France, Holland, Luxembourg and West Germany. This area corresponds loosely to one of Caesar's three parts of *Gallia Comata* (*De Bello Gallico* I, 1); the provinces of Lower and Upper Germany were subsequently carved from its eastern limits (see Drinkwater 1983: maps 1–3).

2 The work of Wightman (e.g., 1975, 1978, 1985) is a notable exception.

3 Changes consequent on the introduction of the literary mode in a particular society introduce an additional stratum of problems (Goody 1977), which will not be pursued here. Classical sources (e.g., Caesar *BG* VI, 14) imply that parts of Gaul had achieved what Goody terms 'conditional literacy' before their annexation by Rome, though to what degree is less clear. Inscribed coinage was struck in both Britain and Gaul before the end of the first century BC.

4 There has been a great deal of discussion on whether the classical sources afford evidence of individual ownership of land in pre-Roman Gaul. On balance, most commentators are persuaded that they do (e.g., Crumley 1974; Wightman 1978), and in any case it is clear that the disposal of land was governed by the elite group as a whole.

5 As Middleton (1979) has pointed out, a comparable differentiation is found in Tacitus' account of Germanic society (*Germania* 5, 18, 21, etc.), where cattle are used in the internal network and in status competition, which appears to have been distinguished from gift exchanges between the elite, which are more frequently associated with such items as bracelets, torcs, slaves, and weaponry.

6 It has, in any case, been suggested that the units recognised and categorised by anthropologists as 'tribes' are to a large extent the product of the relatively recent pattern of contact between the European colonial powers and non-industrialised groups (cf, Fried 1968).

7 Nowhere in Caesar's narrative is there a better example of the competitive tendencies of the elite – uncurbed by the constitution of state government – and of the central role of wealth accumulation in the process, than in his account of the fortunes of the Aeduan brothers, Dumnorix and Diviciacus (*BG* I, 18–20). In this passage, Dumnorix is said to have made a fortune and amassed large resources to expend in bribery by buying the right of collecting river tolls and the other taxes of the *Aedui*, at a cheap price because no-one dared bid against him at the auction – no doubt because he maintained, at his own expense, a considerable force of cavalry. To increase his power, which extended over neighbouring territories, Dumnorix married his female relations to members of other *civitates*. Diviciacus complained that his brother was using these resources to undermine his own position and 'bring about his ruin'. Dumnorix's hatred of the Romans was attributable to their arrival having decreased his power and restored Diviciacus to his former position!

8 The forces at work in this process, and the balance between political and economic factors inherent in what *a priori* was an enormous and relatively sudden upturn in Roman involvement in the affairs of Gaul, would seem to be extremely complex (cf, Brunt 1971a; Crawford 1978; Hopkins 1980). Not least of these must have been the contradictory role of trade in the Roman economy, and the conflict of interests between the land-based elite who controlled the state and the merchants and producers of the private sector. The idea that Roman traders may have been drawn into external areas such as Gaul at this period, precisely because it allowed them to operate with a minimum of political constraints, is one for which I am indebted to Mike Rowlands, and numbers of them may even have settled there. Caesar's narrative implies that the colonies of Roman merchants he mentions at settlements such as *Cabyllinon* and *Cenabum* (Orléans) were already well established (*BG* VII, 3; 42), although the possibility of some or all of these having been established in the wake of the Roman army cannot be entirely discounted.

9 Although it could be argued that many of these commodities were imported by Roman merchants resident in Gaul for their own consumption, the textual evidence (e.g., Athenaeus IV 36; 40) and the discovery of items like amphorae on large numbers of rural sites in any area where intensive field surveys have been carried out, suggests that by far the greater proportion must have been trade goods.

10 Tchernia (1983) suggests that Gaul may have furnished some fifteen thousand slaves per year to meet the demands of the Italian markets.

11 Although Nash's model of state formation fits better with the principles of social reproduction postulated here, aspects of Crumley's (1974) interpretation clearly deserve serious attention, particularly her argument for the emergence of an autonomous intermediate stratum of producers and traders which is reminiscent of the process of peripheral commercialisation in the developmental sequence outlined above (cf Ekholm and Friedman 1980). The emergence of such a group would have presented a significant challenge to the land-owning elite, particularly under the conditions prevailing after the Conquest, a theme to which we shall return in the final section of this paper.

12 Extensive excavations at Condé and Villeneuve, both of which occupy a valley bottom location in contrast to the more usual elevated position, have revealed an orthogonal layout, functionally divided into living, workshop and agricultural zones, which would seem to indicate at least a quasi-urban organisation (Demoule and Ilett (1985). Against this, it has to be admitted that there are problems in demonstrating intensive activity on these sites until the Gallic War period; since there is disagreement about the dating of virtually every category of evidence which would normally be helpful (Buchsenschutz, 1981). At the Titelberg in Luxembourg, however, there is a more convincing stratified sequence and a complex of activities, including a mint, comparable to the other sites (Rowlett, Thomas and Rowlett 1976; 1982).

13 Tchernia (1983) calculates that the total of amphorae there was in excess of two hundred thousand. A full re-assessment of Dressel I

amphorae in northeastern Gaul is currently being undertaken by Fitzpatrick, whose preliminary results have been published (Fitzpatrick, 1985).

14 The Aeduan plea to Caesar that he should spare the Bellovaci, because by so doing he would enhance Aeduan prestige among the Belgic groups, which was a matter of some importance to them, not least because they relied on their clients for troops and resources in time of war (*BG* II, 14) should also be remarked upon.

15 In an earlier period, the booty in the triumph of P. Cornelius Scipio over the *Boii* in 191 BC included 1,471 gold torcs, 247 pounds of gold, 2,340 pounds of silver and 234,000 'Bigati' (Livy, *Historiae* XXXVI, 40). Even allowing for literary inaccuracy and exaggeration this is a phenomenal amount.

16 Not that many years after, Gaul was in a position to present a gold torc weighing one hundred pounds to Augustus (Quintilian, *Inst* VI, 3, 79). Jullian (1920–4) suggests that this decision may have been taken by the *Concilium Galliarum* held at the altar of Rome and Augustus at *Condate*. One may compare this with the treatment received by the East Anglian Client Kingdom of the *Iceni* who were left with wealth worth plundering (Tacitus *Annales*, XIV, 31) nearly twenty years after the Claudian Invasion of Britain.

17 That this is something of an exaggeration, as the revolt of the *Nervii* in 54 BC makes clear.

18 Besides the obvious motives of reward and the creation of territorial units to serve in the administrative framework of the future province, Caesar's intention may well have been to accentuate the divide between landowning elite and landless client, by increasing the lands of the former and the numbers of the latter. This would have brought Belgic Gaul more into line with the Central Gaulish states where this dichotomy was evidently well established, further binding the interests of its elite to those of the Roman state, synonymous, of course, with those of its own land-owning elite, the Senate.

19 Caesar (*BG* VI, 12) makes it clear that the *Remi*, through their alliance with Rome, acquired several other *civitates* as clients, to the extent that, since a group's power and importance was based on the number of its clients, they now ranked second only to the *Aedui* in the whole of *Gallia Comata*. As regards Fig. 10.5, the dependence of the pre-1790 diocese borders on the earlier *civitas* territories has long been recognised (cf. Rice Holmes 1911).

20 It is still a matter of contention to what extent Gaul was garrisoned between the close of Caesar's war and the opening of Augustus' campaigns against Germany. Initially the garrison will have been large, as befitted the power base at the rear of Caesar's advance into Italy, but as Drinkwater (1983) has suggested, it does seem likely that as the Civil Wars intensified, these troops will have been concentrated in the south, with only small forces, possibly mobile units rather than garrisons, available to control *Gallia comata*. Unfortunately, the archaeology and chronology of the early Roman military bases in Belgic Gaul has yet to be resolved satisfactorily (Agache 1978).

21 It can, of course, be argued that the degree of unrest was minimal in comparison to that in the more fluid context of the competing groups of the pre-Conquest period. Nor should it be taken for granted that unrest was invariably fuelled by anti-Roman sentiment; on the contrary, many of the problems are likely to have been internal to the Belgic groups.

22 It has been suggested that auxiliary service would be the context for the grant of Roman citizenship to many of the Julii, e.g., Julius Togirix (Drinkwater 1983), whose name appears on an extensive post-Conquest silver coinage, DLT 5546 (Scheers 1977). The number of 'Julii' among the Treveri gives further indication of their importance.

23 I owe this suggestion to Andrew Fitzpatrick.

24 Roman imports were presumably of central importance in this role, a matter which is dealt with further below.

25 According to Poseidonios, the treasure found at Toulouse amounted to fifteen thousand talents, part of it laid up in the Temple precinct, and part of it, as unworked gold and silver bullion in the sacred lakes; in general, the lakes provided inviolability for large quantities of precious metal (Strabo *Geographica* IV, 1.13).

26 Although Caesar describes Gallic funerals as splendid and costly (*BG* VI, 19) in Belgic Gaul at least, an archaeologically detectable wealth-consuming rite seems to be largely a post-Conquest phenomenon; even some of the burials shown as pre-Caesarian on Fig. 10.5, e.g., at Château Porcien and Hannogne (Flouset and Stead 1977), cannot be shown without a shadow of doubt to pre-date the Conquest. Britain, of course, was still outside the boundaries of the Empire, although after Caesar's invasions in 55 and 54 BC, some of its populations were technically in alliance with Rome and it was liable to tribute (*BG* V, 20).

27 Most authorities would now date the commencement of this enterprise to Agrippa's first governorship in 39–37 BC. However, it should be observed that there is a dendrochronological date of 17 BC for the construction of the Augustan bridge at Trier, which was presumably part of the road to the Rhine, and would fit Agrippa's second governorship in 19–17 BC (Hollstein 1980).

28 *Contra* Haselgrove 1982 and others, there is little evidence to suggest that even at this stage the Rhine estuary to Thames estuary crossing had become the major route it was to be at a later period. Roman imports in the Rhineland are restricted almost exclusively to military sites and appear to reflect no more than a product of the arrangements for army supply (Fitzpatrick, Pers. Comm.). It seems probable that the bulk of the imports and exports of Britain, even those commodities which travelled between Gaul and the region to the north of the Thames, continued to be shipped by the traditional cross-channel crossing, i.e., from the coastlands of Belgic Gaul, which lay at the end of the route to the Mediterranean documented by Strabo. The crucial differences at the end of the first century BC will have been more direct participation by Roman merchants and administrators in this trade, and the quantum leap in the volume of traffic which must have followed this move.

29 This emendation of codex B seems a better reading of the text: individual crowns weighing such amounts are improbable, while the figures of nine and seven in the other MSS appear far too low to have attracted comment.

30 Most important of all, the land remained in the hands of residents of the *civitas*, rather than being alienated, with its profits, to absentee landlords in the Centre.

31 If Tiberius did abolish these Gallic privileges, (Drinkwater 1983), the role of 'endless taxation' and 'crushing rates of interest' (Tacitus *Annales* III, 40) in inducing Roman citizens such as Florus and Sacrovir to revolt in AD 21 becomes clearer. Despite personal privileges, they could well have been adversely affected by their clients' debts and the confiscation of land they held in dependency. Only 'debtors and dependents' took up arms (*Ibid* 42), and the *civitates* as a body seem to have remained loyal, which suggests that the ruling elites can hardly have seen the rebellion as in their own interests. The *Treveri*, in particular, were quick to play an active part in crushing Florus, although the role of the *Aedui*, who are described as being richer, is open to more conjecture.

32 This section has benefited greatly from revision following comments on an earlier draft by Professor J. C. Mann, to whom I am extremely grateful. Needless to say, culpability for the views expressed here, and for any residual errors, is mine alone. It should be emphasised that although the model advocated for Belgic Gaul remains at variance with Professor Mann's perception of the Roman Empire and its anatomy, many of the difficulties revolve around the question of what to assume as normal in respect of certain phenomena and whether Belgic Gaul was in any way

exceptional – e.g., the scale of land-grabbing in a newly acquired province, or the level of support afforded to indigenous elites – all too often, the detailed evidence is lacking. The reality of a given situation is also frequently open to some doubt, e.g., although taxation was low, what was its real impact for a group who had lost a significant proportion of their portable wealth already as a result of defeat and conquest?

Chapter 11

Empire, frontier and the barbarian hinterland: Rome and northern Europe from AD 1–400

Lotte Hedeager

The genesis of the northern Roman frontier

When the Roman army and fleet under the command of Tiberius reached the mouth of the Elbe in AD 4, it was a provisional result of several centuries of Roman expansion to the west and north. It had been preceded by the conquest and subjugation of large parts of the Celtic world, *inter alia* the campaigns of Julius Caesar in Gaul in the mid-first century BC which pushed the Roman frontier forward to the Rhine. Half a century later Tiberius attempted to establish the frontier at the Elbe/Saale line following the defeat of the west German tribes in the area between the Rhine and the Elbe.

Furthermore, by AD 6 the intention was to extend the northern frontier of the Empire to the Elbe/Moldau line, one of the aims being to crush the strong tribal alliance under Maroboduus of Bohemia which covered extensive areas of east and central Germania. But this military operation had to be called off because its commander-in-chief, Tiberius, was summoned to Pannonia where the legions were in revolt.

These 'events' resulted in Rome giving up the attempt to annex Bohemia to the Empire. On the other hand, German territory in the north-west was already regarded as a Roman province and Colonia Agrippina its capital. The newly appointed procurator Varus Quinctilius acted accordingly: in the summer of AD 9 he penetrated deep into Upper Germany. Here, besides acting as adjudicator – on the basis of Roman law – in Germanic disputes, he also built roads, fortified new camps, and levied taxes (*i.a.*

Bolin 1927: 85; Rostovtzeff 1960: 150; Schlette 1972). However, while the Romans thought this territory to be under their control, a secret tribal alliance was being formed with the object of beating back the Roman army and liberating Upper Germany from Roman jurisdiction. And, as we know, at the battle of Teutoburg forest, the German army succeeded in surrounding and annihilating the greater part of Varus's field unit comprising three legions, some auxiliary cohorts and cavalry.

After the defeat of Varus, Augustus gave up holding the frontier along the Elbe, and Tiberius returned from the east to safeguard the frontier at the Rhine. When Augustus died in AD 14 Tiberius became the emperor, and the supreme command of the Roman armies passed to Germanicus. In the years which followed, Germanicus repeatedly launched campaigns against German tribes north of the Rhine, in some cases against the wishes of Tiberius. Spoils from these expeditions failed to outweigh the severe losses suffered by the Romans, and in AD 16 Roman policy towards Free Germany changed from one of military force to one of political intervention.

The first serious Roman setback in the north was the defeat of Varus, and it brought about the cessation of Roman advances into German territory once and for all. Instead, the reinforcement of the Empire's northern frontier along the Rhine was undertaken. Further to the east the Romans abandoned their attempts to conquer and annex the Marcomanni and the Quadi, two Celtic tribes with a well-developed political structure. The Romans chose to strengthen their frontier along the Danube, and the Marcomanni and the Quadi became vassal states under Rome.

Briefly, this was the position along the northern frontier of the Roman Empire in the decades round the beginning of the Christian era. The historical conclusion of Roman expansionism in northern Europe, however, was by no means fortuitous. It was largely determined by the structural genesis of Celtic and Germanic society which originated during the transition from the Bronze Age to the Iron Age, i.e. about 500 BC (Kristiansen 1980, and this volume). At this period the late Hallstatt culture developed a stratified and centralised political structure based on the trade of prestige goods in the Mediterranean region, especially with the Etruscans (Frankenstein and Rowlands 1978). It meant that trade relations with northern Europe were no longer important, and a devolutionary process based on local economic autonomy came to characterise early Iron Age Germanic society (see also Buch 1973 and Ostoja-Zagórski 1983). The evolutionary trajectories of central and northern Europe had bifurcated.

This structural divergence determined the course of Roman expansion. It generally stopped at the border between the more highly stratified Celtic society and the less stratified Germanic society. Certain Celtic areas were not incorporated and served as a buffer zone.

We thus distinguish between three structures:

1)   A Roman system on a Celtic base, the result of Roman expansion whereby former Celtic areas with a highly developed 'archaic civilisation' were incorporated into the Roman Empire.
2)   A former Celtic system with vassal kingdoms beyond the Roman frontier which acted as a buffer zone between the Roman Empire and German tribes.
3)   The Germanic system, based on an independent Germanic course of development mediated, particularly from c. 100 BC, through contact with the Celtic region.

The Roman frontier was well consolidated during the first centuries of *Pax Romana*. Then the Marcomannic Wars broke out, followed by centuries of strife and persistent German attacks on the *Limes* (*i.a.* Lüttwak 1976; *Die Germanen* 2, chs. III–IX). In the following, the effects of this development on Germanic society will be analysed, both at a regional and at a local level.

The formation of centre/periphery relations. A view from the periphery

Two structurally different systems existed on the northern periphery of the Roman Empire at the beginning of the imperial era, one with its roots in the Celtic world, and the other with its roots in the Germanic world. Whereas Roman expansion suffered a definitive defeat at the hands of Germanic tribal society, it succeeded in incorporating large areas of Celtic territory into the Empire (cf. Haselgrove and Nash, this volume). These ancient societies with their centralised political system corresponded far more closely to Roman perceptions of political organisation than the Germanic tribal societies, and were far easier for the Roman

state to incorporate (for a discussion of this contrast, see also Roymans 1983).

In the region north of the *Limes* the Romans used the remaining Celtic tribes as a means of establishing a buffer zone against the Germanic tribes further to the north, and they contributed actively by the forced removal and resettlement of several Celtic and Germanic tribes in an effort to ensure that there were areas under Roman dominance beyond the Roman frontier.

In this border area the Roman presence was permanent enough to have left direct archaeological evidence in the form of inscriptions and the remains of houses. Many of the Romans were probably merchants who traded at markets with the local population, and also presumably with itinerant Germans. Even though the border area did not have such a well-developed, independent money- and market economy as within the imperium, we may assume that there was a limited market economy with some money in circulation (Roman), and possibly too, a merchant class (cf. Schlette 1975, Kunow 1980, 1983 with others). The only places north of the *Limes* with a high concentration of copper coins are the border areas (Bolin 1926), and it testifies to the circulation of low value coins for the trade of everyday goods.

The two, structurally different political systems which together constituted the Roman periphery also had totally different economies:

(1)   The Roman Empire, characterised by a money- and market economy
(2)   The 'buffer zone', which lacked independent coinage, but maintained a limited money economy, perhaps including markets and a merchant class
(3)   Free Germany, which used money without a monetary economy and perhaps moneyless markets (Hedeager 1978a: 210).

Archaeological evidence for trade and exchange relations is found everywhere in the form of Roman drinking vessels of bronze, bowls of glass or silver, brooches and pottery, weapons and coins (*i.a.* Eggers 1951), but their distribution north of the *Limes* is neither uniform nor random (Hedeager 1978a). In the border country there is a preponderance of articles for everyday use such as pottery or various kinds and brooches, whereas the more luxurious Roman artefacts are found to a greater extent in the remoter German hinterland.

A quantitative analysis of the distributional pattern of each group shows that whereas brooches and pottery are most heavily represented in a zone of up to 200 km from the *Limes*, and diminish in number as the distance from the Roman border increases, so the reverse is the case for Roman luxury goods such as bronzes, glass, and silver bowls which grow in frequency, reaching their maximum number at a distance of 400–600 km from the frontier (Hedeager 1978a.).

On the other hand, the archaeological record remains silent on the question of what the Germans provided in return. Philological and written sources convey the impression that exchange might have been in commodities such as hides and grain

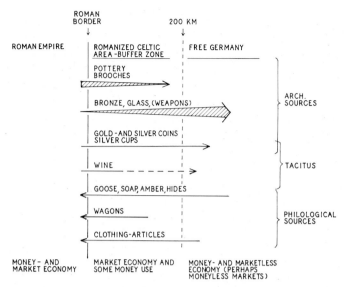

Fig. 11.1 Commodities exchanged between the Roman Empire, the 'buffer zone' and Free Germany. (Hedeager 1978a).

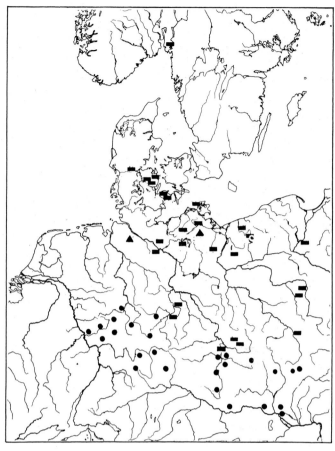

Fig. 11.2 The distribution of princely graves of the Lübsow group (after Eggers 1949/50, Fig. 11; 1951: map C) and late Celtic oppida north of the Roman border. (after Hedeager 1978a).
■ inhumation grave
△ cremation grave
● late Celtic oppida

presumably for the Roman army) as well as slaves (cf. Nash and Haselgrove, this volume) (Fig. 11.1).[1]

While the Roman motive for this exchange was a mixture of economic and political interests (peace along the frontier, economic gain), the Germanic tribes were principally concerned with the acquisition of Roman luxury goods, gold and silver (coins) because together with weapons they were important symbols of status in the Germanic social system.

The social implications of these Roman artefacts in the Germanic environment are most clearly expressed through their use as grave-goods, for example in graves from the so-called princely sphere of early Roman times (Eggers 1949/50). Spread throughout the Germanic region there are a number of exceptionally richly furnished male and female graves with Roman imports among their grave-goods. Yet these 'princely graves' are in the Germanic hinterland and are missing from the 200 km buffer zone along the *Limes*, precisely that area which had its own characteristic political and economic structure based on an earlier Celtic system. The distribution of princely graves is thus complementary to the former Celtic territory as demarcated by the great late Celtic *oppida* (Fig. 11.2). In the latter area the Roman imports did not serve as indications of status to any marked extent, either in 'princely' graves or in graves in general: Roman pottery, brooches, copper coins and inscriptions simply express the presence and proximity of the Romans.

As already mentioned, Roman influence was powerful enough in the border areas to control local tribal politics and chieftains, as in the case of, for example, the Marcomanni and the Quadi. On the other hand, the degree of Roman domination and control over the south-west German tribes north of the Rhine is more doubtful. For it was here that strong alliances developed and took up arms against the Roman army and prevented the Romans from securing the frontier along the Elbe/Saale at the beginning of the first century AD.[2]

From written sources, including Caesar's, we know that in

some of these areas trade in Roman luxury goods was thought to threaten the cultural barrier built up by Germanic – and one or two Gallic – tribes as protection against Roman influence. These records agree well with the archaeological evidence, in that Roman imports are virtually never recovered from graves in that part of the Germanic world (von Uslar 19038; Redlich 1980).

Conditions were different for the Germanic tribes not in direct contact with the Romans. Through written sources we know that the Romans tried to split alliances between Germanic tribes by means of bribery ('diplomatic gifts'), favouring of course those among the German leaders who were pro-Roman (Tacitus 5, Thompson 1965: 72–108). From among the archaeological material we may perhaps interpret 'princely graves' dated to the first century AD as direct evidence of this policy.

However, the periphery of the Empire not only comprised a buffer zone (strongest to the east) but also a generically homogeneous Germanic hinterland. Apart from discord between the Roman central government and the Germanic tribes, an equally important clash of interests arose at the same time between those Germans who supported Roman policy and those who were against it.

In the west this is most distinctly conveyed by the historical facts about Roman expansionism in the first decades AD. When the Roman military machine suffered defeat in AD 9 it was at the hands of Arminius, leader of the secret Germanic alliance and the German fighting forces. A 'Chieftain' of the Cherusci and himself a Roman citizen, Arminius had been trained in the Roman army where he reached the rank of *eques*. After the battle of Teutoburg, Arminius attempted to maintain his powerful position as leader of a west Germanic tribal alliance. On the other hand, Segeste his father-in-law stood for a policy of appeasement with the Romans, and he warned Varus of the plot in AD 9 but to no avail. We also find disagreements within the same tribe, inducing one group of leaders to enter into battle against another group – a trend which the Romans exploited and encouraged. The Romans may have been militarily unable to beat the Germans but they did their best to get them to exterminate each other (Bolin 1927: 90–100; Thompson 1965: 72–108).

Arminius tried to keep the western Germanic alliance together, and in Bohemia, Maroboduus, king of the Marcomanni, established an extensive alliance among tribes in eastern and central Germania, which included all the larger ethnic groups that had remained unaffected by the campaigns of Drusus and Tiberius to the west.

To the east Maroboduus ruled over the Marcomanni. He commanded a standing army said to number 75,000 men (undoubtedly a great exaggeration), organised after the Roman model. A great number of tribes took part in the Marcomannic alliance, and many had to pay tribute to Maroboduus (Schlette 1972: 26). In the west Arminius reached prominence through his campaigns against the Romans, but his leadership was restricted to times of war and other tribes never came to tributary terms with him (Wallace-Hadrill 1971: 3ff. For a general account of Germanic tribal organisation in the first and second centuries cf. *Die Germanen* I, ch. 12).

For a short time after AD 9 it seems as if the Germanic regions were about to be divided into two armies: one in the northwest, the other in the southeast, commanded respectively by Arminius and Maroboduus. But in AD 19 the latter was lured to Italy by Tiberius, and he was replaced by a Roman vassal king. In the year AD 21 Arminius was assassinated by political opponents among the Cherusci. Thereafter, the Romans succeeded in building up massive political control over large areas along the periphery of the Empire.

Although very different in character and of very limited duration the two alliances can perhaps be taken as exponents of a political development which started as a consequence of Roman expansion under Augustus, and which in the period leading up to the Marcomannic Wars (AD 161–180 AD) presumably influenced conditions in east and west Germania. The fundamental difference between these two regions lay in the degree of external control over other tribes, and in the nature of leadership. To the west no tribe ever ruled over another – be it the Cherusci, the Chatti or some other, nor did any political authority become permanent. To the east the position was different. The domination of Maroboduus at the head of the Marcomanni and the eastern tri-

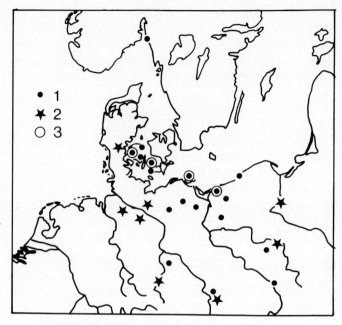

Fig. 11.3 Distribution of princely graves (after Eggers 1949/50 Fig. 11).
(1) Graves without sex-determining objects;
(2) graves with spurs (weapons) and
(3) with rich ornamental equipment.
(after Hedeager and Kristiansen 1981, Fig. 4.7).

bal alliance was more institutional, and not determined by periods of warfare (Hachmann *et al.* 1962: 67; Wallace-Hadrill 1971: 5–7). The divergences in the two political systems and their border areas also reflect a difference revealed archaeologically through the distribution and contents of 'princely graves'. Rich burials in the west are men's graves and they contain spurs (rarely weapons), yet in the east – to judge from ornaments and jewellery – it seems that these are usually women's graves. There are other princely burials in this area which cannot be classified according to sex (Fig. 11.3).

The social implications of horsemen, i.e. warriors, are thus particularly discernible in the areas where contact with the Roman armies occurred.[3] Geographically, then this group is connected with the areas of Free Germany lying to the west and south-west; in other words nearest the buffer zone bordering the Empire. The other group, women's graves and possibly men's graves without weapons occur in more distant Germanic territory to the northeast.[4]

From the function of military leaders in the west we gain the impression of a society in which war and conflict play a prominent part. Such societies are often strongly patrilineal – a fact which accords well with the general conception of the Germanic hereditary system (discussed e.g. in Much 1967: 297–8), and accentuated by the absence of social indicators relating to women of the group. In the east, on the other hand, Roman imports found in the furnishings of rich male and female graves (but never in those with weapons) may reflect a more bilateral hereditary system, where women are important links in political alliances although not incorporated in the ancestral line of their husband. Therefore, this group of women would have been able to transfer and preserve social symbols from one group of kindred to another. The number of rich female burials with fairly similar furnishings comprising locally made jewellery (and amulets) can perhaps be explained in this way (cf. Hedeager and Kristiansen 1981).

We may conclude that in the western areas, through greater contact with the Romans and their armies, a political structure developed in which military leadership became institutionalised. Roman imports played a less substantial role in the forming of internal alliances, and likewise as indicators of status. On the other hand, war and conflict in the north-eastern regions had neither the same dimension nor the same level of military organisation, and political leadership was not dominated by military leaders. This may mean either that armies were of a temporary nature (Thompson 1965: 65) or that they were completely subordinate to political authority (cf. Tacitus 44: 3, 'weapons are not as widespread here as among the other Germans because they are locked away and guarded by a slave'). Some women held high social status and political alliances were forged through dynastic marriages with tribal chiefs or arranged between small kingdoms. This system prevailed throughout the greater part of Germanic territory in the late Roman Iron Age, and Roman imports played an important part in the negotiations.

Therefore, we can associate three different geo-political structures with the spread of Roman imports, in which these imports represent varying degrees of social and political regeneration: (1) The buffer zone (Roman vassal states to the south, and areas with cultural barriers to the west); (2) The warrior-aristocracy of the south-west, and (3) The horizon of princely graves without weapons in the northeast.

Upon closer scrutiny it is as if the structural differentiation between the Roman Empire, its buffer zone and the outer periphery conceals a more complex system of political and social differences.

It is not improbable that here archaeological evidence reflects conditions along the border between the old northwest Germanic tribal alliance and non-member tribes which were targets for the Roman policy of appeasement, i.e. between enemies of the Romans and friends of the Romans. But it does not necessarily mean that historical constellations such as these decided the further course of social and political development in Germania as interpreted by the grave finds. The background lay in pre-existing regional, social and political differences rooted in the pre-Roman Iron Age which influenced alliances and wars between both the Romans and Germans, and between Germanic tribes. This provided the impetus for a more dynamic political and military development in Germanic areas, based for example on the control of trade in prestige goods, and thereby necessary control over the local economy. Permanent political leadership was established throughout large areas, and interaction through alliances and warfare (exemplified by the formation and dissolution of the Germanic alliance between east and west under Maroboduus and Arminius) caused a political system to evolve which we find reflected in the so-called 'horizon of princely graves'. It contained the seeds of the social upheaval and political centralisation which came about in the late Roman Iron Age.

In the first centuries AD, up to the Marcomannic Wars, the barbarian hinterlands constituted some sort of economic and political balance in relation to the Roman Empire. By exporting cheap surpluses – probably for the Roman army – the Germanic people helped to finance the defence system of the northern border, just at a time when Roman products filled an important niche in the social and political structure of the Germanic tribes. Romano-Germanic trade relations would seem to be in favour of the Romans, both economically and politically. Yet in the long run it was a policy with inherent risks as it accelerated the internal dynamics of Germanic society and, consequently, the demand for imports among Germanic tribes. In periods of crisis, perhaps themselves the outcome of imbalances in the more extended trade system, the area south of the border may well have become an attractive prize. In the following, we shall take a closer look at the social dynamics of the periphery.

The social dynamics of the periphery – power and prestige

It has been demonstrated that various regions in the northern Roman periphery and the barbarian hinterlands reacted very differently towards Roman values. The place occupied by Roman products in the internal development of Germanic societies throughout the period AD 1–400 deserves, therefore, to be discussed in greater detail. In what way did Roman prestige goods widen the scope of internal developments? Did they replace other prestige goods, or did they introduce a more elaborate symbolic and ideological set of Roman values? Values that could be used by a local elite to establish and consolidate political power and prestige?

Already at the close of the pre-Roman Iron Age (200 BC) the first exotic alien objects found their way to southern Scandinavia. They range from skilfully crafted swords and carts, to cauldrons and golden torcs, and their provenance is wide-ranging: Celtic, Etruscan, Greek and Roman. In Denmark they are recovered in ritual contexts and in votive deposits and only occasionally in burials. However, not until the early Roman Iron Age do foreign prestige goods appear in larger quantities. Gold rings, Roman bronze imports, silver brooches, pins, beakers, etc., are now a recurrent feature among grave furnishings of the period, whereas votive deposits are absent. Graves containing weapons are frequent but only in Jutland and Funen, not in eastern Denmark (which corresponds with the western and eastern groups, as described in the preceding section).[5] Likewise, in the late Roman Iron Age (third to fourth century) Roman imports are prominent among grave furnishings, whereas graves with weapons have by now almost entirely disappeared.

No other prehistoric period has yielded such an unlimited accumulation of imported objects and prestige wares as the Roman Iron Age. The objects are not part of a set, i.e. of jewellery or armour, as in the early Bronze Age for example, when the demonstration of wealth entailed making individual articles heavier and more elaborately ornamented, and possibly gilded (Randsborg 1974; Kristiansen 1984a). In the Roman Iron Age in

Denmark the combination of imports of gold and silver is evidently without any deeper significance – the decisive factor was quantity (cf. Hedeager 1980: Figs. 11–12). Prestige goods of the Roman Iron Age and those of the Bronze Age also differ in another respect, in that copies of Roman imports are never made locally, in spite of the highly developed skills of Germanic craftsmen, demonstrated for example in costume ornaments and jewellery of iron, as well as of bronze and precious metals.

It is surprising that no 'accumulation of capital' occurred in the form of hoards and deposits. For the nerve-centre of the system was a network of trade contacts throughout the Germanic world. The explanation must be that the Roman imports lacked purchasing power. They were a tangible, symbolic expression of alliances, both social and political, the significance of which was personally linked to the individual. Therefore it did not circulate by being 'bought and sold'. Such imports were not so much evidence of material wealth but primarily of exalted connections and political alliances, and indicative of some knowledge of the Roman way of life.

The earliest foreign prestige goods of the first century BC were sacrificed to the gods, and this reflects the communal and ritual control of such items. With the increasing influx of Roman prestige goods after the birth of Christ, they entered a sphere of individual consumption as grave-goods. It is most probably an indication that their distribution was under the control of certain families. Thus the objects became secularised and could be used in competition for power and prestige (a similar process took place during the early Bronze Age, Kristiansen 1984b).

From the above we venture two propositions. First, a process of this kind would be inflationary if the influx of imports (prestige goods) was not controlled. This implies that these quality imports will tend to occur in greater quantities in a larger proportion of rich burials. Second, it might be expected that this spiral would come to a halt when the elite had consolidated their position, as was the case in the Bronze Age (Kristiansen 1984a). Another implication is that prestige goods are most likely to occur in regions and at periods characterised by political expansion and centralisation, and would cease or take on new meanings in periods characterised by consolidation. This latter phenomenon, however, can be difficult to distinguish from periods of crisis, e.g. warfare and/or a decline in supplies of prestige goods.

With the above propositions in mind let us take a closer look at the employment of Roman prestige goods as burial furnishings during the preiod 1–400 AD. Our point of departure is a number of analyses of finds in various local regions (for the early Roman Iron Age, e.g. Gebühr 1974; Kunst 1978; Hedeager and Kristiansen 1981. For the late Roman Iron Age, e.g. Hedeager 1978b and 1980; Köhler 1975).

During the period AD 1–200 Roman prestige items are generally employed as grave-goods in a rather small proportion of the richest graves. The distributional pattern of these graves is rather uneven throughout the settlement areas of Free Germany. Certain graves are extraordinarily rich, the so-called 'princely graves', and they may reflect the ability of local leaders to create temporary positions of power. In general, however,

we are dealing with elite exchange between autonomous local chiefs.

On the basis of an analysis of large, well-excavated burial sites in north-western Europe, it has been possible to delineate and define both the demographic structure of the population, and the relationship between grave-goods, age, sex and rank (Gebühr 1975; Gebühr and Künow 1976; Kunst 1978; Gebühr et al. in press). Here, too, at a communal level we find the pattern of a single leading family, displaying extraordinary wealth and access to Roman prestige goods. The following trends emerge on the basis of male graves:

(1) Warriors are defined by age; older men are never buried with weapons. Thus weapons are related to the active function of a warrior.

(2) Spurs designate high and exclusive rank. They are combined with gold grave-goods and sometimes with Roman imports. Weapons are absent from this age group, but wealth and spurs are not.

(3) Both weapons and spurs are found in the burials of quite young males, indicating that the right to be a warrior and access to wealth are not achieved but inherited.

These burials with spurs reflect a powerful group of leading, often older men, who controlled warfare (as mounted commanders), and military leadership became unified as an inheritable office, linked to a small group of leading families. This interpretation is supported by a spatial analysis of chiefly warrior graves in a local area in east Jutland, dividing the area into a number of political modules of equal size, Hedeager and Kristiansen 1981: Fig. 4.6. It is this network of local elites which was able to mobilise military strength throughout large regions of north-western Europe at the time of Varus's defeat, and later during the Marcomannic Wars.

These periods of extensive alliances are probably reflected by the 'princely graves' (Gebühr 1974; most recently Steuer 1982).[6] However, it seems that local areas retained their autonomy throughout most of the period. Yet it does not imply that the time-span between AD 1–200 saw no change in social and political structures. Detailed chronological analyses have shown a significant increase in social stratification – more wealth being concentrated in relatively fewer burials (Gebühr 1970, 1976: 177ff; Kunst 1978; Pearson 1984). This process of centralisation has many causes, and these will be discussed more closely in the following pages. Contact with the Roman Empire caused a new, dynamic military organisation to develop and this process was strengthened by trade in and exchange of Roman prestige goods.

Consequently, after the Marcomannic Wars in the late Roman Iron Age, political centralisation had become an established fact. Large regions were now controlled politically and militarily from a single centre. In Free Germany this is reflected by a strong regional concentration of rich graves with Roman imports, as opposed to the even distributional pattern of the preceding period (e.g. Steuer 1982: Figs. 52 and 58). At the regional level the distribution would seem to suggest that Roman prestige

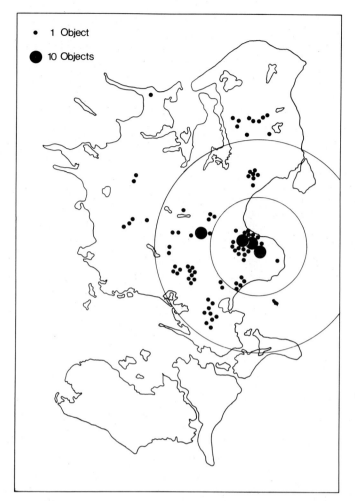

Fig. 11.4 The distribution of Roman imports (bronzes, glass and silver cups) from undisturbed grave finds in the Late Roman Period in ZEALAND (after Hedeager 1978b, Fig. 8).

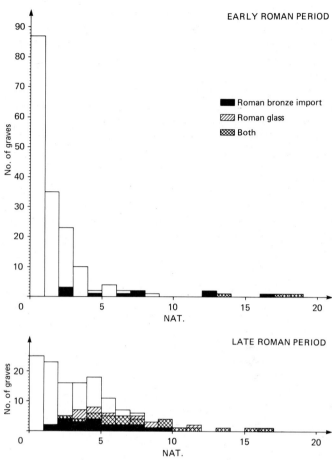

Fig. 11.5 Histograms showing the NAT (Number of Artifact Types) values of undisturbed grave finds from the Early Roman and the Late Roman periods in ZEALAND (after Hedeager 1978b, Fig. 1.2).

goods now circulated among the new elite in a regional system of redistribution. In other words, they are distributed to a wider range of petty chiefs by the paramount chief in exchange for goods and services. This new pattern of control over long distance exchange and in the local distribution of prestige goods is probably most clearly demonstrated in eastern Denmark (south-east Zealand and south-east Funen) (Fig. 11.4), and in Thüringen in southern Germany.

Moreover, there are significant similarities in burial ritual between south-east Denmark and Thüringen (Høj unpublished), and identical place-names occur in both areas, but not in the intermediate areas (Mildenberger 1959/60: map 1).[7] This is a general trend in Free Germany, although most clearly demonstrated in the above regions. Old tribal names are also replaced by new regional configurations: those of the Franks, Saxons and Frisians, which continued into the Middle Ages (*Die Germanen* 2: Fig. 1, also ch. VIII).

There is likewise evidence that after the initial phase of political and military expansion, centres in eastern Denmark were stabilised and prestige goods were no longer used as grave-goods. In northern Europe, Roman imports shift to a new elite in west-

ern Norway. However, the distribution of gold hoards shows that the centres in eastern Zealand and south-east Funen maintained their position throughout the following period, but a new pattern of wealth emerges (Geisslinger 1967; Fonnesbech-Sandberg 1985; Hedeager in preparation).[8]

This supports the hypothesis put forward at the beginning of this section. Roman prestige goods were part of a process in which power and influence were created and in combination with military and economic expansion, brought about significant changes to the social and political landscape of Free Germany in the four hundred years of the Roman Empire. During this period the role of Roman prestige goods underwent a change – from autonomous elite exchange towards regional redistribution. The contrast between the early and late phase is probably best illustrated by the example from Zealand (Fig. 11.5) showing the changing pattern of Roman prestige goods in burials: from the autonomous, chiefly elite to redistribution via chiefly centres to sub-centres. Thus prestige goods were used as a means of sustaining and legitimising new power structures that cut across earlier local social structures. Perhaps this process also brought about the final distortion of an earlier kinship-based system of ranking. This will be further discussed in the section on settlement and subsistence.

Warfare and Germanic military organisation

Already by the earliest period of the Empire it had been customary for Germanic chieftains – at any rate those in the frontier areas – to send off their sons to serve with the Roman armies. We know this in the case of Arminius, leader of the Cherusci; of his contemporary, Maroboduus of the Marcomanni, and also although less directly the chieftain from Hoby in Lolland (Hedeager and Kristiansen 1981). It was, on the whole, a small group of particularly prominent Germans that became acquainted with Roman culture and Roman military organisation. They learnt how to build up a professional army, and the necessary ingredients, e.g. a command hierarchy and a means of payment – a structure alien to earlier Germanic warrior culture. But in principle there were elements of these in the past, and the description by Tacitus at the close of the the first century AD reveals that a germ of this process existed then:

> On the field of battle it is a disgrace to a chief to be surpassed in courage by his followers, and to the follower not to equal the courage of their chief. And to leave a battle alive after the chief has fallen means lifelong infamy and shame. To defend and protect him, and to let him get the credit for their own acts of heroism, are the most solemn obligations of their allegiance. The chiefs fight for victory, the followers for their chief ... They are always making demands on the generosity of their chief, asking for a coveted warhorse or a spear stained with the blood of a defeated enemy. Their meals, for which plentiful if homely fare is provided, count in lieu of pay. The wherewithal for this openhandedness comes from war and plunder. (Tacitus 14; translation Handford 1970)

The account refers to both traditional and new elements. On the one hand, the concept of honour, and on the other, the question of payment in kind. The principle of 'the chiefs fight for victory, the followers for their chief' had succeeded the stage when each warrior fought for his family and for the honour of his family. Warriors now fought for the honour of their chieftain, and they did this for payment in provisions (daily meals) and in the form of presents. Loyalty was no longer to the family but the chieftain and his interests. The *hird* or following of warriors differed from the rest of society because they worked for pay, although not as explicitly as the professional soldiers of the Roman armies, who were in fact wage-earners with pension rights.

The archaeological evidence for warfare and military organisation in this period is largely supplied by grave-goods. Yet the description by Tacitus of the chieftain and his *hird* is derived from the Germanic tribes closest to the *Limes*, and it cannot be transported without further discussion to the north Germanic region, where finds in graves reveal some trends which cannot be dismissed.

At this period, graves with weapons form a striking contrast to the great number of graves which contain a wide range of artefacts. This is partly because the former rarely yield small functional objects (if that) besides weapons and also because the type and number of weapons in these graves reveal the outline of a hierarchical grouping. Only a relatively small number of graves share in the increasing amount of more lavish grave-goods (Gebühr 1970; Hedeager and Kristiansen 1981). Yet, although the grave-goods tell us nothing about the organisation of armies or

hirds, it is possible to deduce some significant points from them. Firstly, that a small group of warriors had special status, probably combining political and military leadership, and that this position was hereditary. Secondly, that a large number of 'ordinary' warriors were buried only with their weapons. As we are unlikely to be able to extend our knowledge in this sphere, or to gain greater insight into the relationship between these groups of armed men, the following description by Tacitus remains uncorroborated:

> Particularly noble birth, or great services rendered by their fathers, can obtain the rank of 'chief' for boys still in their teens. They are attached to others of more mature strength who have been approved some years before, and none of them blushes to be seen in a chief's retinue of followers. There are grades of rank even in these retinues, determined at the discretion of the chief whom they follow; and there is great rivalry, both among the followers to obtain the highest place in their leader's estimation and among the chiefs for the honour of having the biggest and most valiant retinue. Both prestige and power depend on being continually attended by a large train of picked young warriors, which is a distinction in peace and a protection in war. (Tacitus 13; translation Handford 1970)

On the other hand, the big votive weapon deposits, particularly those recovered from Danish bogs, supplement the grave finds. Although these votive deposits are slightly later, the oldest among them date from the close of the second century AD – with one exception (Hjortspring third to second century BC) – they confirm nevertheless that the military organisation of the Germanic tribes near the *Limes*, as described by Tacitus, also spread further to the north. These bog finds are the arms and equipment of large *hirds* – even of entire armies – which have been mutilated and destroyed before being deposited as votive offerings after the defeat of the enemy (Engelhardt 1863, 1865, 1867; Ørsnes 1963, 1968; Ilkjaer and Lønstrup 1983).

The total excavation of a votive weapon deposit in Ejsbøl Mose in south Jutland (Ørsnes 1964, 1984) sheds light on the size and nature of the armed force whose weapons were destroyed and sacrificed sometime during the third century. It had consisted of two hundred men armed with spears, lances and shields; at least sixty also carried a sword and a knife. In addition, there were an unknown number of archers (675 arrowheads have been excavated), as well as between twelve and fifteen men with more exclusive equipment than the rest, nine of which were mounted.

The combination of weapons at Ejsbøl suggests a *hird* or army with ranks and a command hierarchy, specialised arms, and mounted commanders. Its striking power is based on the strategic deployment of various weapons, infantry and horsemen: close-range weapons for hand to hand fighting combined with attack from a distance by arrow and spear.

Large armies (often considerably larger than Ejsbøl's two hundred men) with a variety of weapons imply well-trained warriors and an extremely effective command structure unlikely to have been drawn from local peasant communities. Here, perhaps more clearly than anywhere else, we see the material results of contact with the Roman Empire, especially its armies, which the Germanic peoples had become well acquainted with in the course of centuries of warfare on both sides of the frontier.

The votive weapon deposits from the close of the second century AD are the earliest complete evidence of indigenous military specialisation on Roman lines and with Roman types of weapons. Military leaders now clearly appear from the testimony of richer equipment, including decorative details on accoutrements such as buckles, strap-ends, etc. In the graves of prominent warriors dating from the first and second centuries AD, rank is denoted by Roman imports, gold finger-rings, spurs, and the like. In battle these warriors were distinguished from other warriors by being mounted. On the other hand, the quality of weapons and equipment begin to vary in the late Roman Iron Age, i.e. sometimes weapons and accessories are elaborate, sometimes plain. A high standard of craftsmanship and the use of precious metals now distinguish the weapons and equipment of military leaders: to be mistaken by neither friend nor foe. Prior to this, finely executed artefacts, jewellery etc. had been associated with civilian life.

Whereas in the first and second centuries AD the Germans faced an unbroken frontier across Europe, and a well-organised Roman army into which some of them were recruited, the third century AD was marked by unrest, anarchy and disintegration. On the northern frontier it began with the Marcommanic Wars (AD 160–188), and there can be little doubt that these lengthy wars were of great importance – militarily, politically, and probably also psychologically – to the Germanic tribes. They helped to unite and mobilise fighting forces (Raddatz 1967, 1976; Gebühr 1980), and to demonstrate that the Roman army was not invincible. In addition, the spoils of war circulated further northwards in considerable quantities, illustrated for example by the distribution of ring swords from Bohemia to Denmark (Raddatz 1959/61: 53, map 13).

The effects were also far-reaching. In the third century onwards the Franks, Alemanni, Thüringii, and Burgundians emerge as large tribal confederations, later to become the first ancient states in Barbarian Europe. They grew out of the tensions between the Roman Empire, now weakened by the turmoil of its western reaches, and the strong partly Romanised warrior societies of the Germanic world.

A contributory factor to this process was undoubtedly that the structure of the Roman army had remained in principle the same since the time of Marius (beginning of the first century BC), but in the course of the third century it wholly changed character. Soldiers and officers were increasingly recruited from the most distant and least Romanised areas of the Empire, and even from beyond the frontier, and Germans were the most highly prized of all. The defence of the Empire's northern borders was more frequently entrusted to Germanic tribes (*gentes foederatae*) who helped, in return for payment, to defend the frontier while living outside it themselves. It was also from these areas that the Romans recruited soldiers for their expeditionary forces and the praetorian guard. The rank of officer also underwent a complete change in the course of the third century in that every soldier (including the Germans) was able to make a career in the army

and reach the highest commands. The only requirements were intelligence, courage, loyalty to the emperor and, to some extent, the right connections. Professional soldiers turned into the new aristocracy of warriors, and the Germans made up the larger part of it (Rostovtzeff 1960).

The frontier between the Roman and Germanic worlds was in this way gradually erased, and in the course of a few centuries new German tribal confederations had become established on west Roman ground. This process was partly due to the economic crisis which had in particular struck the western Roman provinces and Italy. Towns and cities declined because trade and craft production stagnated, and the economy became increasingly based on exchange in kind (Hopkins 1980; Whittaker 1983). The surplus necessary to maintain a growing army and expanding bureaucracy had to be collected by tax in kind. The economic burdens shouldered by the population increased sharply, and peasants were bound to the land in order to ensure that sufficient taxes were collected. The most badly affected areas were the western provinces, where agriculture was based on great estates worked by tenants, who had to pay taxes to the state and to their lord (Jones 1966).

This system of taxation was assimilated by the German warrior-aristocracy, and it later laid the economic foundations for the feudal structure of land tenure in the Frankish Empire (Whittaker 1983). Undoubtedly it was also imitated by other Germanic tribes. Land took on a new significance. And territorial control through conquest became the motive behind the violent local and regional battles which ensued in the Germanic world. It is reflected not only in the evolution of military equipment and military organisation from the close of the second century, but also by the appearance of contemporary linear earthworks (e.g. *Olgerdiget* in southern Jutland: Neumann 1977, 1982) and blockaded waterways (Crumlin-Pedersen 1975). Votive weapon deposits in bogs are the concrete proof of a highly specialised form of warfare, which presupposes centralised political organisation based on a band of followers or a *hird*, i.e. fighting men bound to their lord by oath of allegiance and tribute, not by kinship.[9]

War, pillage and robbery were necessary measures to sustain the system and to provide the elite with a necessary surplus. Even though the territorial definition of this political system first fully developed in the course of the late Iron Age, we may assume that it is rooted in the late Roman Iron Age (third to fourth century AD). The question of military organisation and the development of the *hird* are therefore crucial to the interpretation of the processes of political centralisation in Free Germany (see also Herrmann 1982).

Settlement and subsistence

The changes observed in political, social and military organisation during the period AD 1–400 were accompanied by a profound change in the pattern of settlement and production throughout northern Europe.

Over large areas in the pre-Roman Iron Age (500–1 BC), agriculture was based on the Celtic field-system, viz. rectangular plots bounded by low banks (lynchets) of stones and soil (cf.

Kossack *et al.* 1984: 246ff). Networks of these fields covered extensive areas (more than 100 hectares). They presumably represent a form of systematised extensive agriculture whereby periods of cultivation alternated with long periods in which these fields lay fallow (Müller-Wille 1965; Lindquist 1974; Myhre 1978; Windelhed 1984). However this method of farming was abandoned everywhere in the course of the Roman Iron Age (evidence seems concentrated on the first and second centuries AD), in favour of more intensive agriculture (Myhre 1978; Bradley 1978; Windelhed 1984). Investigations in central Sweden and Gotland have shown that the infield system became established over the same period, and this represents the earliest integration of arable farming and stock breeding. The hay harvest from meadowland provided winter fodder for livestock which supplied manure for the infields (Widgren 1983, 1984; Windelhed 1984 Fig. 7). The production system was now based on the combined productivity of field, meadow and pasture in relation to livestock.

This transition from extensive agriculture to a more intensive kind of farming did not necessarily occur everywhere in the same span of time. Due to the lack of adequate dating it is impossible to determine, for example, whether it was adopted earlier in the marginal areas with a lower production potential, or in the central regions where the effect of population growth was probably greater. Nor has it yet been decided whether it happened concurrently in the lowlands of north-western Europe.

It is implicitly accepted that the change-over in farming methods developed because of a steadily increasing demand for a surplus product.[10] This had been preceded by the expansion of settlements and rising pressure on natural resources, as revealed by pollen analyses (e.g. Iversen 1960; Berglund 1969; Lang 1971; Andersen 1976; Påhlsson 1977; Andersen *et al.* 1984). Deforestation and the spread of commons had already begun in the pre-Roman Iron Age, and agriculture steadily gained ground. This trend was encouraged by a change in the climate which had turned dryer and warmer in the last centuries BC (Aaby 1976; Willerding 1977). But it caused, among other things, a reduction in the yield, which would have had to be compensated for by some means, e.g. more intensive arable farming needing larger quantities of manure, and consequently more stock rearing, winter fodder and labour. This process would be further exacerbated by clearing steadily larger tracts of land for basic production, resulting in more open country at the expense of forests. Such a tendency would have easily resulted in over-exploitation and, on light soils, the collapse of agricultural production, such as occurred in west and north-west Jutland (Glob 1951).

A logical consequence of this development would have been to make a radical change and emphasise intensive farming. Throughout the Roman Iron Age, this is precisely what characterised the cultural landscape of northern Europe. At the same time territorial – and social – organisation underwent a profound change (Widgren 1984; Hedeager in preparation). The effect on the vegetation can to some extent be read from the pollen diagrams, and the plans of both the homestead and the village enters a new phase. Unfortunately not nearly enough is known as yet

about their contemporary field-systems, forms of cultivation and agricultural technology (cf. Kossack *et al.* 1984).

In those parts of north-western Europe where they have been localised, early Iron-Age settlements (from 500 BC onwards) seem generally to have averaged between five and fifteen homesteads within the framework of a village (Fig. 11.6).[11] Each homestead consisted of a long-house with dwelling and byre under the same roof, and occasionally a separate building with some other function (for recent surveys cf. Jankuhn 1976; Steuer 1982, Kossack *et al.* 1984).

In one or two places it has been possible to establish that desertion and resettlement occurred within a limited area, for example in west Jutland from the fifth to the third and second centuries BC (Becker 1971). On the whole, villages from the later pre-Roman Iron Age and the early Roman Iron Age were more permanent; at all events those with good soil conditions. This would perhaps suggest more intensive agriculture (Myhre 1978: 238). The functional organisation of the homestead unit divides in that several other buildings or huts now belong to the individual long-house. The first true smithies are known from this period, even though iron-working pre-dates this by several centuries (e.g. Fig. 11.6 (Hodde); Jacobsen 1979). The expanded farmstead with several outbuildings and greater byre-capacity is now part of a large, well organised village.

The change which takes place in settlements during the later Roman Iron Age (in most areas from the second to third and fourth centuries) reflects this organisation of production, and likewise of farming land, the village and the farmstead. The average size of the latter increases and its layout is more functional. More livestock and larger granaries indicate greater productivity, due to a number of technological innovations (e.g. new querns, new weaving techniques, improved iron-smelting furnaces, as well as rye, though not yet a widespread crop), as well as another agricultural strategy (Fig. 11.7). Settlements seem to become increasingly enduring and permanent throughout the whole region (Myhre 1978: 234; Windelhed 1984). Farming based on the Celtic field-system is abandoned and replaced by the infield and outfield system with more intensive cultivation and shorter fallow periods (e.g. Sporrong 1971; Widgren 1984) as revealed in Sweden, in the form of new fields enclosed by dry stone walling. Individual farmsteads now function more independently, with rights of some sort to the infield. Two-course rotation may have been introduced, not only on the Continent but also in Denmark and Sweden (Myhre 1978: 235; Sporrong 1971: 197).

More people than before lived and worked under the same roof. In the lowland areas of northern Europe the enclosed village is succeeded by single, large enclosed farmsteads (corresponding to the walled infields in Sweden). They appear often to have stood in a row, farm house after farm house, as found for example at a number of Iron-Age villages in Jutland (e.g. Fig. 11.8 (Vorbasse); Hvass 1983; Nr. Snede: Hansen 1982); single farmsteads are also known. We may assume land is no longer redistributed, either in reality or symbolically, but that it is the property of individual farmsteads, although reverting to village common land between harvest and sowing (Widgren 1984: 121). The means of

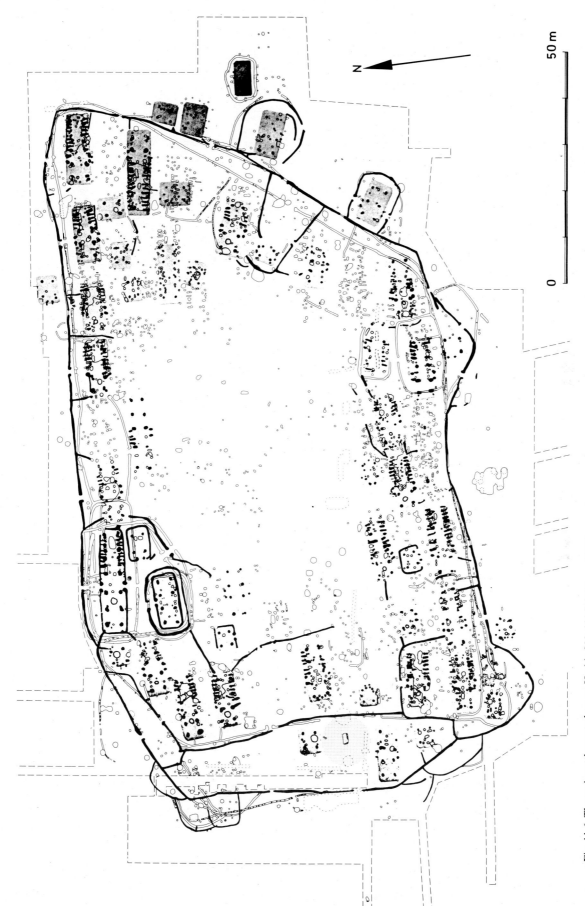

Fig. 11.6 The main settlement phase at Hodde 200–100 BC (Hvass 1975).

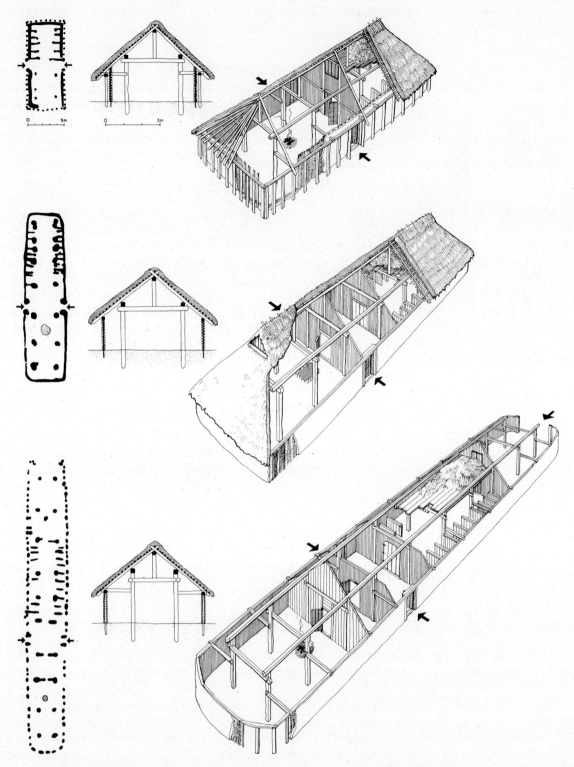

Fig. 11.7 The evolution of the Danish Iron Age house, ground plan and reconstruction. At the top 500–300 BC, in the middle from 100 BC and at the bottom AD 200–500 (revised drawing of Flemming Bau, after the illustration in L. Hvass, Jernalderen, Copenhagen 1980).

subsistence are far more differentiated than before, and part of the population probably no longer participated in the basic mode of production. Among these would have been chieftains and members of the *hird*. Land was held in fewer hands, and we may assume that more people had become landless serfs because a reduced

number of large farmsteads took the place of the many small homesteads and dwellings of the earlier Iron Age. This is especially evident if we compare the villages of the pre-Christian era with those of the third and fourth centuries AD (Fig. 11.8).

The structural reorganisation of the village, farmstead and

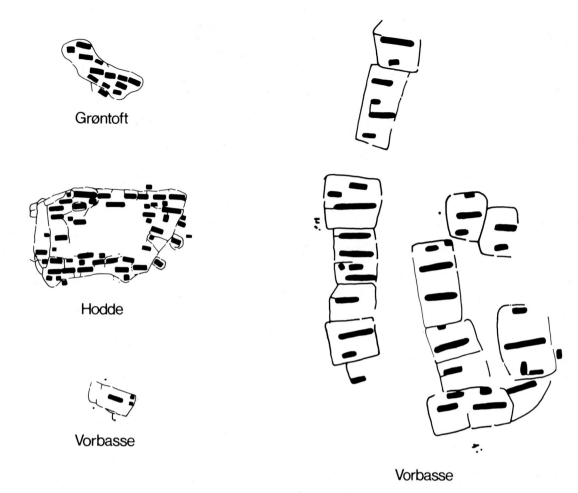

Fig. 11.8. The evolution of the Danish Iron Age village. Grøntoft from 300–150 BC, Hodde about 100 BC, Vorbasse, single farm from the birth of Christ and the village Vorbasse from AD 300–400. The village-areas are respectively 2,700 m^2, 15,000 m^2 and 135,000 m^2 (after Flemming Bau in L. Hvass, *Jernalderen*, Copenhagen 1980).

field-system which took place everywhere in Free Germany during the Roman Iron Age has been interpreted as an expression of a profound change in access to and control of land. Limited opportunities for expansion and territorial growth are perceived as causative factors. The disappearance of grazing forest and an increase of common land continued at greater speed. With the result that open country spread throughout the course of the third century, to an extent not reached again (according to pollen analyses) until about one thousand years later.[12] Thus, more effective farming could only be achieved through a more effective exploitation of decreasing natural resources: meadow, grazing forest, common and arable land. As demonstrated, the changes resulted in (or depended on) a new social and territorial organisation.

It is difficult, however, to decide whether the primary cause of the changes in agricultural strategy and village organisation between the first and fourth centuries AD was demographic or socio-political. Yet to try to pinpoint cause and effect in an evolutionary process by concentrating alone on one or two trends cannot and should not be done. Therefore the complex interaction of political, military, economic and social factors will be briefly touched upon in the conclusion.[13]

Conclusion

In the four centuries which saw the expansion, consolidation, decline and division of the Roman Empire, the rest of Europe underwent changes which ensured that after the demise of the Empire, the areas close to it were on the threshold of a new era: the Middle Ages. Communities further to the north in the Germanic hinterland experienced a decisive change. The old tribal structure based on ties of kinship and alliance transformed gradually into permanently class-divided states.

This development, however, was not exclusively determined by the influence of the Roman Empire, because already before the expansion of the Empire it is evident that the Germanic tribes of northern Europe were structurally peripheral in relation to the archaic Celtic state system. The completion of Roman expansion in Europe took place in accordance with their pre-existing framework. But the Germanic periphery was also characterised by regional variations in social structure as reflected by differences in the distribution of Roman prestige goods in burials.

Indeed, the periphery and the hinterland beyond together formed quite a complex regional system. Its development during the first and second centuries had been primarily determined by the evolutionary potential inherent in this structure. For although the formal establishment of centre–periphery relations amplified the processes of stratification and centralisation, it took place within the framework of existing social structures. Yet there can be little doubt that the establishment of a political and military border zone between centre and periphery, as well as an explicit Roman policy towards the periphery in the period AD 1–200 tended to balance differences in the social evolution of the periphery. In the long run it meant that the Germanic world became more homogeneous, and in periods of conflict it would have represented a greater political and military threat. Tensions and contradictions between centre and periphery now assumed larger proportions on a regional scale. This is what happened during the late Roman Iron Age and the ensuing period of decline of the Western Empire.

In general, a structural transformation of Free Germany did not take place until the third century, viz. the period after the Marcomannic Wars. During the latter large contingents of Germanic mercenaries were on both sides of the border, and large sums of money were paid to Germanic troops in an attempt to secure peace along the northern frontier. During the same period Germanic societies underwent drastic social and political changes which resulted in political centralisation on a scale never seen before in this area. None of the tribal names of the Early Roman period survived as political entities as they had been replaced by much larger tribal confederations; for example the Franks, Saxons, Frisians, Thüringii, all later to become the first ancient states of the early medieval period.

It is tempting to imagine that an empire on the defensive opened up new and hitherto inconceivable opportunities of accumulation to be seized by those areas still within its political sphere but beyond imperial frontiers. It would provide them not only with material gain in the form of booty, but also with experience in military systems, discipline, money wages, command hierarchies, advanced fighting techniques, etc. It is hard to see how the ancient tribal societies, based on the seniority of age, could withstand such influences. Political autonomy, military discipline and good pay were innovations which could be assimilated by local chiefs and powerful men as long as local conditions were under control. Spoils of war and a chiefly retinue (housecarls) were part of the process sparked off by the Romano-Germanic wars, especially the Marcomannic Wars, and by mercenaries returning home. Internal raids took over on an increasing scale in order to keep the system going: at first these were probably intended to secure booty, and prisoners of war for sale as slaves; later, probably embarked on to maintain territorial control in order to establish a more permanent claim to payments of tribute. It could be suggested that the reorganisation of settlement represented an adjustment to a more elaborate system of tribute payments. However, all that we know at present about a system of taxation in the North is the one introduced when the Church became established in the Viking period. Yet even without a system of this kind it could be maintained that political and military relations with the Roman Empire triggered off the development of a new chiefly elite, based on a retinue of warriors that could be used on trading expeditions or for raids. Territorial control and tribute payments

may have fitted into this pattern. After AD 200 the increasing intensity of raids and pillaging would have accelerated existing trends in social differentiation and political centralisation.

But the question remains whether contact with the Roman Empire and Roman armies is a sufficient explanation for the evidently profound changes which took place in the barbarian homelands during the late Roman Iron Age. Perhaps we ought rather to imagine that Roman influences acted as a catalyst in a process which had already begun. To determine whether this is indeed the case, we have to consider the relation between the internal factor: levels of subsistence, and the external factor: trade in prestige goods.

The community-based village organisation of the early Iron Age with farmsteads as individual production units in a common field system disappears in the late Roman Iron Age. This change in the organisation of the village as revealed by evidence of differentiation in the size of dwellings, stalls, and village plan, would seem also to apply to its productive basis of field and grazing land. The individual right to cultivate the common fields of the village is superseded by either rights of individual ownership or of tenure. The redistribution of land no longer takes place; owners' and users' rights are now established.

The emergence of a landowning/controlling class is unlikely to have occurred through military dominance alone. The means would rather have been a massive legitimisation of the ideology of certain groups of people. And in this context Roman imports fulfilled the functions necessary if prestige and status had to be emphasised.[14] They indicated participation in the wide network of political alliances and trade links which, in turn, represented contact with the Roman Empire, the Roman life-style, and Roman norms – no doubt with some knowledge of Roman rights of ownership and Roman agricultural technology. Apart from enhancing the social position of the owner, the most important function of prestige goods is their employment in social reproduction. They could circulate as dowry, as tribute, and other forms of payment. Control over prestige goods thus implies social and political power (Ekholm 1977; Friedman and Rowlands 1977: 224f), useful in the negotiation of alliances (possibly in conjunction with armed force), thereby expanding the political and economic power base of a chieftain. Regionally, it would be done by establishing political and military dependence in the form of 'protection' offered in return for tribute such as, for example, military service, slaves or wares, *the payment of which had to be in prestige goods* (cf. Fig. 11.4). Locally, in the villages, prestige goods may have been used as a means of creating economic and social dependence gradually leading to the surrender of land and livestock, and to the status of slave/serf. If the process was intensified it could cause the system to break down and be a contributory factor in the reorganisation of land tenure and the village. The decrease after the change in the number of farmsteads in a village would be explained by a process such as this. Although fewer in number, farmsteads became larger with more room for people and livestock – which leads us to production.

To underpin the system, a surplus in production was a necessity, and likewise the control of land and of those producing the crops. It has already been shown how the exploitation of land increased throughout northern Europe in the early and late Roman Iron Age, with steadily increasing deforestation and extension of common land. The oldest Danish place-names indicate a tremendous increase in settlements in eastern Denmark (*i.a.* Clausen 1916; Hald 1950 and 1966; Søndergaard 1972).

There is also evidence of a sharp rise in population. Women appear to have married late, and this may have been one of the mechanisms that controlled population growth (Gebühr *et al.* in press). The expanding population combined with the high marriageable age of women (and thereby the need of bigger dowries), also suggests that many young men looked upon military service not only as a source of prestige and riches,[15] but as an attractive alternative to life at home in the village.

Thus, Germanic societies in the period AD 1–400 experienced population growth, expanding settlement, and an increasing demand for surplus production in order to feed their populations and as payments of tribute, which were channelled further into alliances and long-distance trade in Roman prestige goods. To meet these pressures intensive agriculture was developed throught the infield/outfield system, the redistribution of land took place, as well as the replanning of the village. These processes were accompanied by more successful, centrally organised trading and raiding expeditions, possibly territorial conquest, based on a following of warriors (*hird*/housecarls).

The circle is closed. We are able to describe the processes of change and to point out clarifying factors, but not one solitary factor determines since we are dealing with the interaction of many. The strongest influence was undoubtedly social processes resulting from the conversion of prestige goods into political and economic power; these processes were related to the organisation of production. It was the changes in the organisation of production which gave the system a new basis for expansion. When land became a commodity to be exchanged the conditions were established for the formation of a landed aristocracy. Therefore the transformation of the social organisation of production after AD 200 was of paramount importance for the evolution of a class-based society and the state. Considered in a long-term evolutionary perspective, however, the formation and expansion of the Western Empire did not alter the trajectory of these processes but responded to them. The foundations had already been laid in the centuries around 500 BC. Yet Roman expansion in the west amplified the evolutionary potential of the periphery, so that in the short term, it tipped the balance of power in its favour. The social landscape in Europe after AD 400 was largely determined by this process. With the decline and disintegration of the Roman Empire, a transitional evolutionary phase prevailed in northern Europe – a cyclical process of political centralisation and disintegration. This evolutionary structure[16] reached a new climax during the Viking Period which finally led to its transformation, with the formation of centralised states in Scandinavia by about AD 1000.

Notes

This article is based on previous research (Hedeager 1978 a and b, 1980; Hedeager and Kristiensen 1981), supplemented by some material from a comprehensive analysis of the evolution of Iron Age societies in Denmark between 500 BC and AD 700 entitled 'From Tribe to State' (in preparation). I refer the general reader to the exhaustive and useful selection of descriptive syntheses of Germanic societies in the Iron Age, published in two volumes: *Die Germanen*, 1–2, J. Herrmann (ed.) 1976 and 1983. I am also grateful to Mike Rowlands for his helpful comments. Translation by Jean Olsen.

1 Strabo (IV: 5, 2) refers to trade between England and Gaul during the first century BC. England exported corn, cattle, gold, silver, iron, hides, slaves and hunting dogs. Roman products from Gaul comprised ropes of ivory beads, bracelets, amber, glass bowls, and other 'beautiful objects'. The Romans therefore imported raw materials or primary produce for a consumer market in exchange for manufactured 'luxury' goods for the local upper class (Cunliffe 1984).

2 The acculturation of the Low Countries during the Roman period is excellently analysed and discussed from a more theoretical viewpoint in a number of recent articles (Brandt and Slofstra 1983).

3 Graves with weapons in the Germanic areas south of the Baltic are treated collectively by Weski (1982). It has been established that graves with weapons are found throughout the Germanic region with the exception of the eastern buffer zone along the Danube, as well as in Pomerania and Prussia, i.e. the Baltic area east of the Oder. As might be expected, the biggest concentration of graves with weapons is found in the Germanic area of the Elbe basin, with its focal point in the Lower Elbe area where they begin shortly before B1, i.e. contemporaneously with Roman expansion into the northern areas (Weski 1982, map I).

4 We also find that the distribution of east and west Germanic brooches throughout the Germanic world in the early Roman Iron Age coincides with a characteristic difference between princely graves in the east and west respectively (Almgren 1897, map II).

5 The east Danish islands of Zealand, Lolland and Falster are therefore linked with the north-east German area, not only through the absence of graves with weapons (cf. note 3), but also through the occurrence of 'east German' princely graves and 'east German' types of brooch (cf. note 4).

6 Warrior graves are absent in the north-eastern part of Free Germany (Weski 1982), whereas rich female burials with rather standardised grave-goods predominate. This indicates a social and symbolic uniformity which linked the chiefly elite of this area through regular ties of exchange/marriage into an ideological and political network. Roman prestige goods are employed in the same manner as in the north-west, although no political modules seem detectable. Here, the distribution of rich graves is more irregular and over greater distances, which may suggest a more centralised structure.

7 This connection has been disputed (Søndergaard 1972) although no alternatives are offered to explain the evidence.

8 This contradicts my previous interpretation (Hedeager 1978 a and b, 1980) omitting the late Iron Age. In other areas, like eastern Jutland, it seems that the disappearance of Roman imports among grave-goods may also be linked with extensive warfare. This is reflected by the huge weapon deposits in moorland (discussed in the following section).

9 It is tempting to interpret the large votive weapon deposits, earthworks and the blockading of navigable channels as the result of an (easterly?) expanding power attempting to subjugate eastern Jutland, which appears to have fairly large regional divisions. This assumption is based on the interpretation that votive weapon deposits in bogs represent ritual centres for given areas. Their geographical distribution down the east coast of Jutland and in Funen is at regular intervals of between 30 and 40 km, which seems to suggest that a political unit now covered an area of that size. It more

or less corresponds to the area of the Stevns territory and its sub-centres.

10 Close to the *Limes*, however, a direct Roman influence on production has to be reckoned with, see Groenman-van Waateringe 1983.

11 Hodde should not be considered representative of the villages of the late pre-Roman period, its plan and organisation is different to the other villages known from this period.

12 This picture of a densely settled and thickly populated region is documented by the results of intensive local investigations (e.g. Hvass, pers. comm.; Myhre 1983; Albrectsen 1970; Kossack *et al.* 1974 and 1984; Hinz *et al.* 1974, 1978, 1979; Reichstein *et al.* 1981; Edgren and Herschend 1982).

13 In an inspiring article Parker Pearson (1984) discusses, *inter alia*, the economic changes which occurred during the course of the Iron Age in an area which included south and central Jutland. However, the interpretation of changes in productivity is founded on doubtful premises. The earliest Iron Age is exemplified by the village of Grøntoft in west Jutland which, until recently, was the only Danish settlement from the early Pre-Roman Iron Age. Generalisations on the basis of one village are subject to some uncertainty. The example of settlement from the close of the Pre-Roman Iron Age is based solely on an analysis of Hodde. Yet among the innumerable investigated villages from this period, Hodde is unique. It is considerably larger and better organised than the others, and as such cannot be taken as the basis for general conclusions about the productive capacity of Jutland. The example used to illustrate the late Iron Age (including the late Roman Iron Age) is again one village, namely Vorbasse. Its plan and organisation recur in other contemporary villages, although the size of farm varies. Until a few years ago it was thought that settlement declined from *c*. fifth to

sixth centuries. Therefore, because the farms in Vorbasse decrease in average size from the fourth to the fifth centuries, Parker Pearson interprets it as a symptom of general economic crisis and decline in the productive capacity of Jutland. Yet investigations carried out more recently both at Vorbasse and other villages show that the settlements continue to grow (Hvass 1983). At the same time as the farms in Vorbasse decrease slightly in size over a period, the farms in other villages in the same area become slightly larger. A generalisation on the basis of Vorbasse is deceptive. It must be added, however, that the results of the latest investigations in which the continuity of villages throughout the late Iron Age has been confirmed post-date Parker Pearson's article.

14 That this legitimation of socio-political rank could also include the legitimation of a military function is not tantamount to saying that military power was the basis and prerequisite for internal political control. Ideological legitimation was rather the result of the prestige latent in the military function.

15 Changes in the right of inheritance in connection with the reorganisation of land may also have encouraged sons with no hereditary rights to seek their fortune as warriors.

16 The processes which characterise the development and changes within Germanic society in this period contain elements of what has been termed a prestige-goods economy. There are also some elements summed up by Fried in the term 'stratified society'. Marx and especially Engels termed the Germanic social structure a 'military democracy'. In a revaluation of this stage of social development, Joachim Herrmann has described it more generally as 'the transition to class society' (Hermann 1982). His dynamic characteristics correspond by and large to that phase in the development of Germanic society which has been described in this article.

BIBLIOGRAPHY

Aaby, B. 1976 'Cyclical climatic variations in climate over the past 5,500 years reflected in raised bogs', *Nature* 263 no. 5575

 1985 'Norddjurslands landskabsudvikling gennem 7000 år. Belyst ved pollenanalyse gennem bestemmelse af støvindhold i højmosetørv', *Fortidsminder 1985. Antikvariske Studier* 7: 60–84

Adams, R. McC. 1966 *The Evolution of Urban Society* Chicago

 1974 'Anthropological Perspectives on Ancient Trade', *Current Anthropology* 15: 239–58

 1979 'Late prehispanic empires in the New World' in M. Larsen (ed.) *Power and Propaganda* Akademisk Verlag, Copenhagen

 1981 *Heartland of Cities* University of Chicago Press

Agache, R. 1978 *La Somme pre-Romaine et Romaine* Mémoires de la Société des Antiquaires de Picardie 24). Amiens

Aharoni, Y. 1947 *The settlement of the Israelite Tribes in Upper Galilee*, Jerusalem

 1967 *The Land of the Bible*, London

Albrectsen, E. 1970 'Den ældre jernalders bebyggelse på Fyn' *Kuml*

Albright, W. F. 1931 *The Archaeology of Palestine and the Bible*, New York

Alföldy, G. 1974 *Noricum*, London

Allchin, B. and Allchin, R. 1982 *The Rise of Civilisation in India and Pakistan* Cambridge University Press

Allen, D. F. and Nash D. 1980 *The Coins of the Ancient Celts*, Edinburgh

Almgren, O. 1897 *Studien über nordeuropäische Fibelformen*. Stockholm (Manus–Bibl. 32, Leipzig 1923)

 1905 *Kung Björns Hög och andra forn-lämningar vid Häga*, Stockholm

Alt, A. 1959 (1925) 'Die Landnahme der Israelites im Palastina', *Kleine Schriften* I, Munich, pp. 89–125

Amiet, P. 1957 'Glyptique susienne archaique', *Revue d'Assyriologie* 51: 121ff

 1971 'La glyptique de l'Acropole (1969–1971)' *Cahiers de la Délégation archéologique Française en Iran*, I: 217ff

 1972 *Glyptique susienne des origines à l'époque des Perses Achéménides* Paris

 1977 'La Bactriane proto-historique', *Syria* LIV (1–2): 89–121

 1978 'Antiquités de Bactriane', *La Revue du Louvre et des Musées de France* XXXVIII 30: 153–64

 1980 *La Glyptique Mésopotamienne archaique* Paris; 2nd ed.

Amin, S. 1974 *Accumulation on a World Scale* New York: Monthly Review Press

Amiran, R. (*et al.*) 1970 'The beginnings of urbanization in Canaan': in J. Sanders (ed.), *Near Eastern Archaeology in the 20th Century*. Garden City: Doubleday. pp. 83–100

 1973 'The interrelationship between Arad and sites in southern Sinai in the Early Bronze II', *Israel Exploration Journal* 23: 193–7

 1974 'An Egyptian jar fragment with the name of Narmer from Arad' *Israel Exploration Journal* 24: 4–12

 1978 *Early Arad* Jerusalem: Israel Exploration Society.

 1980 'The Arad countryside', *Levant* 12: 22–9

Andersen, S. Th. 1976 'Local and regional vegetational development in eastern Denmark in Holocene', *Danmarks Geologiske undersøgelser, Årbog 1976*. Copenhagen

Andersen, S. Th., Aaby, B. and Odgaard, B. V. 1984 'Environment and man. Current studies in vegetational history at the geological survey of Denmark', *Journal of Danish Archaeology* 2: 184–96

Askarov, A. 1973 *Sapallitepa* Tashkent: FAN

 1977 *Drevnezemledel'cheskaya Kultura epokhi bronzi iuga Uzbekistana* Tashkent: FAN

Asselberghs, H. 1961 *Chaos en beheersing: documenten uit aeneolithisch Egypte* Leiden

Badian, E. 1972 *Publicans and Sinners*, New York

Baer, K. 1960 *Rank and Title in the Old Kingdom* University of Chicago Press

Bakka, E. 1973 'Om aldren på veideristningene', *Viking* 37

1976 *Arktisk og nordisk i bronsealderen i Nordskandinavia* Det kgl. norske videnskabers selskab, Museet. Miscellanea 25. Trondheim

Bar-Adon, P. 1980 *The Cave of the Treasure* Jerusalem

Baudou, E. 1960 *Die regionale und chronologische Einteilung der jüngeren Bronze-zeit im Nordischen kreis* Studies in North-European Arch. I. Stockholm

1977 'Den förhistoriska fångstkulturen i Västernorrland' in E. Baudou and K. G. Selinge, *Västernorrlands förhistoria* p. 11–135, Motala

1982 'Det förhistoriska Jordbruket i Norrland: Bakgrunden i det arkeologiska fyndmaterialet' in Sjövold (ed.) *Introduksjonen av jordbruk i Norden* p. 163–73, Oslo

Baumgartel, E. 1947/60 *The Cultures of Prehistoric Egypt*, 2 vols., Oxford. 1970 *Cambridge 'Ancient' History* I(I): 463ff

Beale, T. W. 1973 'Early trade in highland Iran: a view from a source area', *World Archaeology* 5: 133ff

Becker, C. J. 1971 'Früheisenzeitliche Dörfer bei Grøntoft, Westjütland', *Acta Archaeologia* 39

Berglund, B. 1969 'Vegetation and human influence in South Scandinavia during prehistoric time', *Oikos* supp. 12. Copenhagen 9–28

Berman, M. 1970 *The Politics of Authenticity* Heineman, London

Bertilssom, U. 1981 What do the cairns mean? In Moberg (ed.): *Similar finds? Similar Interpretations?* (pp. G–C19) Gothenburg

Biga, M. G. and Milano, L. 1984 'Testi amministrativi: Assegnazioni di tessuti'. *Archivi reali di Ebla. Testi* IV. Roma

Binford, L. 1962 'Archaeology as anthropology', *American Antiquity* 28: 217

Biscione, R. 1977 'The Crisis of Central Asian Urbanism in II n.d. Millennium B.C. and Villages as an Alternative System' in J. Deshayes (ed.) *Le Plateau Iranien et L'Asie Centrale dès Origines à la Conquête Islamique* Paris: CNRS, pp. 113–27

Biscione, R. and Tosi, M. 1979 *Protostoria degli Stati Turanici*. Supplemento n. 20 ogli Annali Dell' Istituto Universitario Orientale, XXXIX, 3 Naples

Bloch, M. 1977 'The disconnection between power and rank' in J. Friedman and M. Rowlands (eds) *The Evolution of Social Systems* pp. 279–340, Duckworth

Bloch, M. and Parry, J. 1982 *Death and the Regeneration of Life* Cambridge University Press

Boehmer, R. M. 1974a 'Das Rollsiegel im Prädynastischen Agypten', *Archäologischer Anzeiger* (Beiblatt zum Jahrbuch de Deutschen Archäologischen Instituts) 89: 495ff

1974b 'Orientalische Einflusse auf vierzierten Messergriffen aus dem Prädynastischen Agypten', *Archäologischen Mitteilungen aus Iran*, 7: 15ff

Bolin, S. 1926 *Fynden av romerska mynt i det fria Germanien*, Lund. 1927 *Romare och Germaner*, Stockholm

Bradley, R. 1978 'Prehistoric field systems in Britain and north-west Europe – a review of some recent work', *World Archaeology* 9 no. 3

Braidwood, R. J. and Braidwood, L. 1960 *Excavations in the Plain of Antioch I* OIP 61. Chicago: University of Chicago

Brandt, R. and Slofstra, J. (eds). 1983 *Roman and Native in the Low Countries* BAR Intern. Ser. 184, Oxford

Braudel, F. 1972 *The Mediterranean and the Mediterranean World in the Age of Philip II*. 2 Vols 2nd Ed. New York: Harper and Row

1949 *The Mediterranean World* Collins, London

1978 'History and the social sciences' in P. Burke (ed.) *Economy and Society in Early Modern Europe*, Cambridge University Press

Braudel, F. and Spooner, K. 1967 *Prices in Europe from 1450 to 1750*. *Cambridge Economic History of Europe* IV, 374–486. Cambridge University Press

Brenner, R. 1977 'The origins of capitalist development: a critique of neo-Smithian Marxism', *New Left Review* 104: 25–93

Brentjes, B. 1971 'Ein Elamitischer Streufund aus Soch, Fergana (Usbekistan)', *Iran* IX: 155

Briant, P. 1982 *Etat et pasteurs au Moyen-Orient ancien*, Cambridge and Paris

Brinkman, J. A. 1972 'Foreign relations of Babylonia from 1600–625 B.C.: the documentary evidence' *American Journal of Archaeology* 76: 271ff

Broadbent, N. D. 1983 'Too many chiefs and not enough indians. A peripheral view of Nordic Bronze Age society', in B. Stjernquist (ed.) *Struktur och förändring in bronsåldrens samhälle* p. 7–23, University of Lund

Brogan, O. 1974 'The coming of Rome and the establishment of Roman Gaul' in S. Piggott, G. Daniel and C. McBurney (eds). *France before the Romans*, 192–219. London

Broholm, H. C. and Hald, M. 1940 *Costumes of the Bronze Age in Denmark*, Copenhagen

Broughton, T. R. S. 1952 *The Magistrates of the Roman Republic*, Ohio, reprinting Michigan 1968

Brumfiel, E. 1983 'Aztec state making: ecology, structure and the origin of the State, *American Anthropologist* 85, 2: 261–84

n.d. 'Specialisation and exchange in the development of the Aztec State, XI Congress Anth. and Ethn. Sciences, Vancouver, Canada

Brunt, P. A, 1971a *Social Conflicts in the Roman Republic*, London

1971b *Italian Manpower 225 BC–AD 14*, Oxford

Brunt, P. A., and Moore, J. M. (eds.) 1967 *Res Gestae Divi Augusti*, Oxford

Brunton, G. 1948 *Matmar*, London

Brunton, G. and Caton-Thompson, G. 1928 *The Badarian Civilisation and Prehistoric Remains near Badari*, London

Buch, D. W. 1973 'Siedlungswesen und gesellschaftliche Verhältnisse bei den Stämmen der früheisenzeitlichen Billendorfer Gruppe', *Etnographisch-Archäologische Zeitschrift*. Berlin

Buchanan, B. W. 1967 'The Prehistoric stamp seal, a reconsideration of some old excavations', *Journal of the American Oriental Society* 87: 265ff.; 525ff

Buchsenschuts, O. 1981 'L'apport des habitats à l'étude chronologique du premier siècle avant J–C' *Mémoires de la Société Archéologique Champenoise* 2: 331–8

Burenhult, G. 1973 *The Rock Carvings of Götaland*, Acta Archaeologia Lundensia, Series in 40 no. 8

Burke, M. L. 1964 'Lettres de Numusda-nahrari et de trois autres correspondants a Idiniatum', *Syria* 41: 67–103

Burney, C. 1980 'Aspects of the excavations in the Altinova, Elazig', *Anatolian Studies* 30: 157–67

Butz, K. 1979 'Ur in altbabylonischer Zeit als Wirtschaftsfaktor', in E. Lipinski (ed.) *State and Temple Economy in the Ancient Near East*, Leuven, 257–409

Butzer, K. W. 1976 *Early Hydraulic Civilization in Egypt: A Study in Cultural Ecology*, Chicago

Cameron, R. 1973 'The logistics of European economic growth: a note on historical periodisation', *Journal Economic History* II, 1: 145–8

Canby, J. V. 1976 'The sculptors of the Hittite capital', *Oriens Antiqvus* 15: 33–42

Carlsson, D. 1982 'Bronsåldern – Tiden för kultur-landskapets territoriella framväxt och etablering på Gotland', in B. Stjernquist (edl) *Struktur och förändring i Bronsåldrens Samhälle*, pp. 23–37, University of Lund

Carneiro, R. L. 1970 'A theory of the origin of the state', *Science* 169: 733ff

Carpelan, C. 1982 'Om bronsåldrens jordbrukssamhälle i Finland', in Th. Sjøvold (ed.) *Introduksjonen av jorbruk i Norden* p. 267–79, Oslo

Case, H. J. and Payne, J. C. 1962 'Tomb 100 – the decorated tomb at Hierakonpolis', *Journal of Egyptian Archaeology* 48: 5ff

Casson, J. M. 1966 'Canaanite maritime involvement in the 2nd millennium B.C.', *Journal of the American Oriental Society 86: 126–38*

Cerny, J. 1954 'Prices and wages in the Ramesside period', *Journal of World History* 1: 903–21

Champion, T. C. 1980 'Mass migration in later prehistoric Europe' in P. Sorböm (ed.) *Transport technology and Social Change*, 32–42. Stockholm

Charpin, D. 1982 'Marchands du palais et marchands du temple à la fin de la Ire dynastie en Babylone', *Journal asiatique* 270: 25–65

Chehab, M. 1969 'Noms de personalités égyptiennes découvertes au Liban', *Bulletin du Musée de Beyrouth 22: 1–47*

Childe, V. G. 1957 'The Bronze Age', *Past and Present* 12: 2–15

Christiansson, G. and Broadbent, N. 1975 'Prehistoric coastal settlement on the upper Bothnian coast of Northern Sweden', in W. Fitzhugh (ed.) *Prehistoric Maritime Adaptions in the Circumpolar Zone*. The Hague

Cipolla, C. M. 1976 *Before the Industrial Revolution*, London

Claessen, H. T. and Skalnik, P. 1978 *The Early State*, The Hague

Clausen, H. V. 1916 'Studier over Danmarks Oldtidsbebyggelse', *Årbøger for nordisk Oldkyndighed og Historie*

Cleuziou, S. 1980 'Three seasons at Hili: toward a chronology and cultural history of the Oman Peninsula in the 3rd Millennium B.C.', *Proceedings of the Seminar for Arabian Studies* 10: 19–32

　n.d. 'Oman Peninsula and Western Pakistan during the 3rd millennium, B.C.'

Cleuziou, S. and Berthoud, T. 1982 'Early tin in the Near East: a reassessment in the light of new evidence from Western Afghanistan', *Expedition* 25(1): 14–25

Collis, J. R. 1975 *Defended sites of the Late La Tène in Central and Western Europe*, BAR Series 2, Oxford

　1977 'Pre-Roman burial rites in North-west Europe'. In R. Reece (ed.) *Burial in the Roman World*: 1–12, CBA Research Reports, London

　1982 'Gradual growth and sudden change – urbanisation in temperate Europe'. In C. Renfrew and S. Shennan (eds) *Ranking Resource and Exchange*, 73–78. Cambridge

Crawford, H. E. W. 1973 'Mesopotamia's invisible exports in the third millennium B.C.'. *World Archaeology* 5: 232–41

Crawford, M. H. 1973 *Roman Republican Coinage*, Cambridge

　1977 'Republican denarii in Romania: the suppression of piracy and the slave trade', *Journal of Roman Studies* 1977: 117–24

　1978 *The Roman Republic*, Cambridge University Press.

Crumley, C. 1974 *Celtic Social Structure*. (Anthropological Papers, Museum of Anthropology, University of Michigan 54). Michigan

Crumlin-Pedersen, O. 1975 'Ae Lei' og 'Margrethes bro', *Nordslesvig Museer* 2

Cunliffe, B. 1984 'Relations between Britain and Gaul in the first century B.C. and early first century A.D.', *Cross-Channel trade between Gaul and Britain in the pre-Roman Iron Age*. S. Macready & F. H. Thompson (eds). Society of Antiquaries Occasional Paper IV London

Curtin, P. 1984 *Cross Cultural Trade in World History* Cambridge University Press

Curtis, J. and Hallo, W. 1959 'Money and merchants in Ur III', *Hebrew Union College annual* 30: 103–39

Dales, G. F. 1977 'Shifting trade patterns between the Iranian Plateau and the Indus Valley in the third millennium B.C.' ... in J. Deshayes (ed.) *Le Plateau Iranien et L'Asie Centrale dès Origines à la Conquête Islamique*, Paris: CNRS

Damon, F. 1980 'The Kula and generalised exchange', MAN 15, 2: 267–93.

D'Arms, J. H. 1977 Rostovtzeff, M. I. and Finley, M. I: The status of traders in the Roman World, in D'Arms and Eadie (eds) *Ancient and Modern*, Ann Arbor

　1981 *Commerce and Social Standing in Ancient Rome* Cambridge, Mass

Davis, R. 1967 *Aleppo and Devonshire Square*, London

Déchelette, J. 1914 *Manuel d'archéologie préhistorique celtique et Gallo-Romaine II. 3: Second Age du Fer ou Epoque de La Tène*, Paris

Delougaz, P. 1952 *Pottery from the Diyala Region* O.I.P. LXIII, Chicago

Demoule, J. P. and Ilett, M. 1985 'First Millennium Settlement and Society in Northern France: a case study from the Aisne Valley'. In T. C. Champion and J. V. S. Megaw (eds) *Settlement and Society: aspects of Western European prehistory in the First Millennium B.C.*

　pp. 193–221, Leicester University Press.

Digerfildt, G. S. and Welinder, S. 1985 'An example of the Bronze Age cultural landscape in SW Scandinavia', *Norwegian Archaeological Review* 18, no. 1–2: 000

Dolukhanov, P. M. 1981 'The Ecological Prerequisites for Early Farming in P. L. Kohl (ed.) *The Bronze Age Civilization of Central Asia: Recent Soviet Discoveries*, Armonk, NY: M. E. Sharpe, pp. 359–85

Dossin, G. 1964a 'A propos de la tablette administrative de A.R.M.T., No 1', *Syria* XLI: 21–4

　1964b 'Tablette administrative', *Archives royales de Mari* XIII. *Textes divers*. 1–14

　1970 'La route de l'étain en Mesopotamie au temps de Zimri-Lim', *Revue d'Assyriologie 64: 97–106*

Drinkwater, J. F., 1983 *Roman Gaul*, London

Dunand, M. 1950 'Chronologie des plus anciennes installations de Byblos', *Revue Biblique* 57: 583–603

　1973 *Fouilles de Byblos V*. Paris: Librarie d'Amérique et d'Orient

Duncan-Jones, R. P. 1974 *The Economy of the Roman Empire*, Cambridge

　1980 'Demographic change and economic progress under the Roman empire', in *Tecnologia, economia e società nel mondo romano, atti del convegno di Como, 27–29 Settembre 1979*, pp. 67–80

　1981 'The wealth of Gaul', *Chiron* 11: 217–20

Eaton, R. and McKerrell, H. 1976 'Near Eastern alloying and some textual evidence for the early use of arsenical copper', *World Archaeology* 8: 169–191

Ebel, C. 1976 *Transalpine Gaul: the Emergence of a Roman Province*, Leiden

Ebeling, Erich 1938 *Bruchstücke eins politischen Propagandadichtes aus einer assyrischen Kanzlei*, Leipzig

Edel, E. 1974 'Zwei Originalbriefe der Königsmutter Tuja in Keilschrift', *Studien zur altägyptischen Kultur* 1: 105–46

　1976 *Ägyptische Ärtzte und ägyptische Medizin am hethitischen Königshof*, Opladen

Edgren, B. and Herschend, F. 'Arkeologisk ekonomi och ekonomisk arkeologi. Et försök till beskrivning av det öländska jordbrukets förudsättningar under áldre järnålder', *Fornvännen Årg.* 77

Edgren, T. 1984 'On the economy and subsistence of the Battle Axe culture in Finland', *Iskos* 4: 9–16, Helsinki

Edwards, I. E. S. 1971 'The Early Dynastic Period in Egypt', *Revised Cambridge Ancient History*, 1(2); 1ff

Edzard, D. O. 1957 *Die 'Zweite Zwischenzeit' Babyloniens*. Wiesbaden

　1960 'Die Beziehungen Babyloniens und Aegyptens in der mittelbabylonischen Zeit und des Gold', *Journal of the Economic and Social History of the Orient* 3: 18–40

Eggers, H. J. 1949/50 'Lüsow, ein germanischer Fürstensitz der älteren Kaiserzeit', *Praehistorische Zeitschrift* 34/35

　1951 *Der römische Import im freien Germanien*, Hamburg

　1955 'Zur absoluten Chronologie der römischen Kaiserzeit im freien Germanien', *Jahrbuch des Römisch-Germanischen Zentral museums, Mainz*, 2

Eidem, J. 1983 'Turukkum and its Neighbours. A study of the Western Zagros in the early 2nd Millennium B.C.', Unpublished dissertation. Copenhagen University,

Ekholm, K. 1977 'External exchange and the transformation of central African Social Systems' in J. Friedman and M. Rowlands (eds) *The Evolution of Social Systems* Duckworth, London

Ekholm, K. and Friedman, J. 1979 '"Capital", imperialism and exploitation in ancient world systems' in M. Larsen (ed.) *Power and Propaganda*, Akademisk verlag, Copenhagen

　1980 'Towards a global anthropology' in L. Blusse, H. Wesseling and G. Winius (eds) *History and Underdevelopment* Leiden Centre for the History of European Expansion

　1985 'Towards a global anthropology', *Critique of Anthropology* V, no. 1: 97–119

Eliade, M. 1959 *The Sacred and the Profound* Harcourt and Brace, N. York

Emery, W. B. 1949 *Great Tombs of the First Dynasty* Vol. 1. Cairo.

Emmanuel, A. 1972 *Unequal Exchange: a Study of the Imperialism of Trade* New Left Books, London

Engelbach, R. 1923 *Harageh* London

Engelhardt, C. 1863 *Thorsbjerg fundet. Sønderjyske Mosefund I* Copenhagen

1865 *Nydam fundet. Sønderjyske Mosefund II*, Copenhagen

1867 *Kragehul Fundet. Fynske Mosefund I*, Copenhagen

1869 *Vimose Fundet. Fynske Mosefund II*, Copenhagen

Engelmark, R. 1976 'The vegetational history of the Umeå during the past 4000 years', in *Early Norrland*, vol. 9 (pp. 73–113), Kungl. Vitterhets Historie och Antikvitets Akademien, Stockholm

1982 'Dkologiska Synspunkter på jordbrukets spridning och etablering i Norrland', in the Sjovold (ed.) *Introduksjonen av jordbruk i Norden* pp. 153–61, Oslo

Engelmayer, R. 1965 *Die Felsgravierungen im Distrikt Sayala-Nubien*, Vienna

Erichsen, E. 1933 *Papyrus Harris I*, Bruxelles

Fales, F. M. 1979 'Kilamuwa and the foreign kings: propaganda vs. power', *Welt des Orients* 10: 6–22

1974 'L' ''ideologo'' Adad-šuma-Usur, *Rendiconti del'Accademia nazionale dei Lincei*, series VIII, 29: 453–96

1982 'The enemy in the Neo-Assyrian royal inscriptions: the ''moral'' judgement', *Acts of the XXV Rencontre assyriologique internationale*, Berlin

Faulkner, R. 1940 'Egyptian seagoing ships', *Journal of Egyptian Archaeology* 26: 3–9

Fett, E. and Fett, P. 1941 *Sydvestnorske helleristninger*, Rogaland og Lista Stavanger Museum

Fieldman, K. 1981 'A Late Uruk pottery group from Tell Brak, 1978', *Iraq* 43: 157–66

Finet, A. 1977 'Le Vin a Mari', *Archiv für Orientforschung* 25 (1974–77): 122–31

Finley, M. 1973 *The Ancient Economy* Chatto & Windus, London

Firth, R. 1939 *Primitive Polynesian Economy* RKP, London

Fitzpatrick, A., 1985 'Dressel I wine amphorae in North-west Europe', *Oxford Journal of Archaeology* 4, 305–40

Flouest, J.-L. and Stead, I. M. 1977 'Une Tombe de la Tène III à Hannogne, Ardennes' *Mémoires de la Société D'Agriculture, Commerce, Sciences, Arts de la Marne* 92: 55–72

Fonnesbech-Sandberg, E. 1985 'Hoard finds from the Early Germanic Iron Age – a study of their general representativity', in K. Kristiansen (ed.) *The Representativity of Archaeological Remains from Danish Prehistory*, Copenhagen

Francfort, H. -P. and Pottier, M. -H. 1978 'Sondage préliminaire sur l'établissement protohistorique Harapéen et post-Harapéen de Shortugai (Afghanistan du N. -E.)', *Arts Asiatiques* XXXIV: 29–79

Frank, A. G. 1966 'The Development of Underdevelopment', *Monthly Review* 18: 17–31

Frank, A. G. 1967 *Capitalism and Underdevelopment in Latin America: Historical Studies of Chile and Brazil* New York: Monthly Review Press

1969 *Capitalism and Underdevelopment in Latin America* Monthly Review Press, New York

Frank, T. (ed.) 1938–41 *An Economic Survey of Ancient Rome*, 5 vols., Baltimore

Frankenstein, S. 1979 'The Phoenicians in the Far West: a function of Assyrian imperialism' in M. T. Larsen (ed.) *Power and Propaganda* Akademisk Verlag, Copenhagen

Frankenstein, S. and Rowlands, M. 1978 'The internal structure and regional context of early Iron Age society in southwest Germany', *Bulletin of the Institute of Archaeology of London* 15: 73–112

Frankfort, H. 1939 *Cylinder Seals*, London

1941 'The origins of monumental architecture in Egypt', *American Journal of Semitic Languages and Literature*, 58: 329ff.

1951 *The Birth of Civilization in the Near East*, London

Freud, S. 1909 'Notes upon a case of obsessive neurosis', *Standard Edition of the Works of Sigmund Freud*, London, vol. 10, pp. 153–318

Fried, M. 1968 'On the concept of the Tribe' in *Essays on the Problem of the Tribe*: 3–22. *American Ethnological Society*. New York

Friedman, J. 1975 'Tribes, states and transformations' in Bloch M. (ed.) *Marxist Analyses and Social Anthropology* Malaby, London

1979 *System, Structure and Contradiction* National Museum, Copenhagen

1982 'Catastrophe and Continuity in Social Evolution' in A. C. Renfrew *et al.* (eds.) *Theory and Explanation in Archaeology* Academic Press, New York

1984 'Civilisation cycles and the history of primitivism', *Social Analysis* 14: 31–52

Friedman, J. and Rowlands, M. J. 1977 'Notes towards an epigenetic model of the evolution of ''civilization''' in J. Friedman and M. J. Rowlands (eds.) *The Evolution of Social Systems*: 201–78. London

Frifelt, K. 1976 'Evidence of a third millennium B.C. town in Oman', *Journal of Oman Studies* 2: 57–73

Frobel, F. 1980 *The New International Division of Labour*, Cambridge University press

Furingsten, A. 1984 'Västsvensk arkeologi och pollen-analys', in A. Furingsten, M. Jonsäter and E. Weiler (eds.) *Från flintverkstad till processindustri* pp. 159–80, Kungälv 1984

Galliou, P. 1984 'Days of wine and roses? Early Armorica and the Atlantic wine trade' in S. Macready and F. H. Thompson (eds.), *Cross-Channel Trade between Gaul and Britain in the pre-Roman Iron Age*, London, 24–36

Gardiner, A. and Peet, T. E. 1955 *The Inscriptions of Sinai* P. II. London: Egyptian Exploration Fund

Garelli, P. 1963 *Les Assyriens en Cappadoce*, Paris

Garnsey, P. 1983 'Grain for Rome', in P. Garnsey, K. Hopkins, C. R. Whittaker (eds.), *Trade in the Ancient Economy*, London, 118–30

Garnsey, P., Hopkins, K. and Whittaker, C. R. 1983 *Trade in the Ancient Economy* Chatto and Windus, London

Gebühr, M. 1970 'Beigabenvergesellschaftungen in mecklenburgischen Gräberfeldern der älteren römischen Kaiserzeit', *Neue Ausgrabungen und Forschungen in Niedersachsen* 6

1974 'Zur Definition älterkaiserzeitlicher Fürstengräber vom Lübsow-Typ', *Praehistorische Zeitschrift* 49

1975 'Versuch einer statistischen Auswertung von Grabfunden der römischen Kaiserzeit am Beispiel der Gräberfelder von Hamfelde und Kemnitz', *Zeitschrift für Ostforschung* 1975, 24. Jahr. 3

1976 *Der Trachtschmuck der älteren römischen Kaiserzeit im Gebiet zwischen unterer Elbe und Oder und auf den westlichen dänischen Inseln*, Neumünster

1980 'Kampfspuren an Waffen des Nydam-Fundes', *Materialheft zur Ur- und Frühgeschichte Niedersachsen* 16

Gebühr, M. and Kunow, J. 1976 'Der Urnenfriedhof von Kemnitz, Kr. Potsdam-Land', *Zeitschrift für Archäologie* 10

Gebühr, M., Hartung, U. and Meier, H. in press 'Das Gräberfeld von Neubrandenburg. Beobachtungen zum anthropologischen und archäologischen Befund', *Zeitschrift für Archäologie*

Geertz, C. 1982 *Negara* Princeton University Press, New Jersey

Gelb, I. J. 1969 'On the alleged temple and state economies in Ancient Mesopotamia', in *Studi in Onore di Edoardo Volterra*, Vol. 6. pp. 137–54 Rome: Giuffre Editore

1979 'Household and Family in Early Mesopotamia' in E. Lipinski (ed.) *State and Temple Economy in the Ancient Near East* (Leuven), pp. 1H

1980 'Comparative Method in the Study of the Society and Economy of the Ancient Near East' *Rocznik Orientalistyczny* 41, 29ff.

Geisslinger, H. 1967 *Horte als Geschichtsguelle*, Offa-Bücher vol. 19. Neumünster *Germann, Die vols. 1, 2.* cf. Herrmann 1976, 1983

de Geus, C. H. J. 1975 'The importance of archaeological research into the Palestinian agricultural terraces', *Palestine Exploration Quarterly* 65–74

Gibbon, E. 1896 *The History of the Decline and Fall of the Roman Empire* (ed. J. B. Bury). Sixth edition. London

Giddens, A. 1979 *Central Problems in Social Theory*, London

Gilbert, A. 1982 'The introduction of the horse into Mesopotamia', Paper presented at the Symposium of the Upper Pleistocene and Holocene Distribution and Discrimination of Equids in the Palearctic Region with Special Emphasis on the Middle East. Tübingen 1982

Gledhill, J. 1978 'Formative development in the North American Southwest' in D. Green, C. Haselgrove, M. Spriggs (eds.) *Social Organisation and Settlement* BAR Oxford, pp. 241–90

Gledhill, J. and Larsen, M. 1982 'The Polanyi paradigm and a dynamic analysis of archaic states' in A. C. Renfrew *et al.* (eds.) *Theory and Explanation in Archaeology* Academic Press, New York

Glob, P. V. 1951 Jyllands øde agre. *Kuml*

Godelier, M. 1972 *Rationality and Irrationality in the Economy* NLB, London.

1977 *Perspectives in Marxist Anthropology* Cambridge University Press

Godelier, M. 1980 'The emergence and development of Marxism in anthropology in France', in E. Gellner (ed.) 1980 *Soviet and Western Anthropology*. London.

Gödecken, K. B. 1976 *Eine Betrachtung der Inschriften des Meten in Rahmen der sozialen und rechtlichen Stellung von Priviatleuten im Ägyptischen Alten Reich.* ÄA 29. Wiesbaden: Harrassowitz.

Goldman, I. 1984 *The Mouth of Heaven* Honolulu

Goldmann, I. 1970 *Ancient Polynesian society*, London

Goldstein, L. 1981 'One-dimensional archaeology and multi-dimensional people: spatial organisation and mortuary analysis' in R. W. Chapman, I. Kinnes and K. Randsborg (eds.) *The Archaeology of Death*: 53–70. Cambridge

Goodman, D. and Redclift, M. 1983 *From Peasant to Proletarian* Longman, London

Goody, J. 1962 *Death, Property and the Ancestors* Cambridge University Press

1977 *The Domestication of the Savage Mind* London, Weidenfeld

Gophna, R. 1976 'Egyptian immigration into southern Canaan during the First Dynasty?' *Tel Aviv* 3: 33–6

Gottwald, N. K. 1979 *The Tribes of Yahweh. A sociology of the Religion of Liberated Israel 1250–1050 B.C.E.*, New York

Goudineau, C. 1983 'Marseilles, Rome and Gaul from the third to the first century BC', in P. Garnsey, K. Hopkins, C. R. Whittaker (eds.), *Trade in the Roman Economy* London, 76–86

Gräslund, B. 1981 'Climatic fluctuations in the early Subboreal period. A preliminary discussion', *Striae* 14: 13–22

Green, M. W. 1980 'Animal husbandry at Uruk in the Archaic Period', *Journal of Near Eastern Studies* 39, pp. 1ff

Greenidge, A. H. J., and Clay, A. M. (eds.) 1960 *Sources for Roman History 133–70 BC*, Oxford, 2nd edn.

Gregory, C. 1982 *Gifts and Commodities* Academic Press, London

Groenman-van Waateringe 1983 'The disastrous effect of the Roman occupation' in R. Brandt and J. Slofstra (eds.) *Roman and Native in the Low Countries.* BAR Int. Ser. 184. Oxford

Gruen, E. 1968 *Roman Politics and the Criminal Courts 149–78 BC*, Harvard

Hachmann, R. 1976 'The problem of the *Belgae* seen from the Continent', *Bulletin of the Institute of Archaeology of London* 13: 117–37

Hachmann, R., Kossack, G. and Kuhn, H. 1962 *Völker zwischen Germanen und Kelten*, Neumünster

Hafsten, U. 1958 Jordbrukskulturens historie i Oslo – og Mjøstrakten belyst ved pollen-analytiske undersøgelser. *Viking* 21/22: 51–74

Hagen, A. 1969 *Studier i vestnorsk bergkunst*, Årbok for Univ. i Bergen. Hum. Ser. No 3.

Hakemi, A. 1972 *Catalogue de l'exposition Lut-Xabis (Shahdad)* Teheran

Hald, K. 1950 *Vore Stednavne* Copenhagen

1966 *Stednavne og kulturhistorie*, Copenhagen

Hall J. A. 1985 *Powers and Liberties; the causes and consequences of the rise of the West*. Oxford: Blackwell

Hallo, W. W. 1964 'The road to Emar', *Journal of Cuneiform Studies* 18: 57–88

Handford, S. A. 1970 *Tacitus: The Agricola and The Germania*. Revised translation. Original translation by H. Mattingly. Penguin, Harmondsworth

Hansen, T. Egeberg 1982 'En landsby fra uldhorneses tid', *Vejle amts Årbog*

Haselgrove, C, 1982 'Wealth prestige and power: the dynamics of political centralisation in South-east England'. In C. Renfrew and S. Shennan (eds.) *Ranking, resource and exchange*: 79–88. Cambridge

1983 *La Vallée de l'Aisne, 1983: Excavations and Fieldwork by the University of Durham*, Durham

1984 'Warfare and its aftermath as reflected in the precious metal coinage of Belgic Gaul', *Oxford Journal of Archaeology* 3, 81–105.

Haselgrove, S. 1979 'Romano-Saxon attitudes', in P. J. Casey (ed.) *The End of Roman Britain*: 4–13, BAR 71, Oxford

Hawkes, C. F. C. 1968 'New thoughts on the Belgae', *Antiquity* 42: 6–16

Hawkins, J. D. (ed.) 1977 *Trade in the Ancient Near East*. XXIII RAI. London: British School of Archaeology in Iraq

Hauptmann, A. and Weisgerber, G. 1980 'Third millennium B.C. copper production in Oman', *Revue D'Archéometrie, Actes Du XX Symposium International D'Archéometrie* vol. III: 131–9

1979 'The origins and development of writing in Western Asia' in P. R. S. Moorey (ed.) *The Origins of Civilization*, Oxford, pp. 128ff

Hechter, M. 1975 *Internal Colonialism: the Celtic Fringe in British National Development, 1536–1966* Berkeley: University of California

Hedeager, L. 1978a 'A quantitative analysis of Roman imports in Europe north of the limes (0–400 AD), and the question of Roman-Germanic exchange', in K. Kristiansen & C. Paluden-Müller *New Directions in Scandinavian Archaeology* The National Museum. Denmark

1978b Processes towards state formation in Early Iron Age Denmark. in K. Kristiansen and C. Paludan-Müller (eds.) *New Directions in Scandinavian Archaeology* The National Museum. Denmark

1980 'Besiedlung, sociale Struktur und politische Organisation in der älteren und jüngeren römischen Kaiserzeit Ostdänemarks', *Praehistorische Zeitschrift* 55, 1

in preparation *From Tribe to State. The evolution of Iron Age societies in Denmark 500 B.C.–700 A.D.*

Hedeager, L. and Kristiansen, K. 1981 'Bendstrup – en frystegrav fra eldre romersk jernalder, dens sociale og historiske miljø. (Bendstrup – a princely grave from the Early Roman Iron Age: Its social and historical context). *Kuml*.

Helck, W. 1962 *Die Beziehungen Aegyptens zu Vorderasien in 3. und 2. jahrtensend v. Chr.*, Wiesbaden

1971 *Die Beziehungen Ägyptens zur Vorderasien im 3 und 4 Jahrtausend v. Chr.*, 2nd. Ed., Wiesbaden

Helms, M. W. 1979 *Ancient Panama. Chiefs in search of power*, University of Texas Press

Helskog, K. 1985 'Boats and meaning. A study of change and continuity in the Alta Fjord, Arctic Norway, from 4200 to 500 years B.C.', *Journal of Anthropological Archaeology* 4, no. 3: 177–205

Heltzer, M. 1978 *Goods, Prices and the Organization of Trade in Ugarit*, Wiesbaden

Hennessy, B. J. 1967 *The Foreign Relations of Palestine during the Early Bronze Age*, London

Herrmann, G. 1968 'Lapis lazuli: the early phases of its trade', *Iraq* 30: 21–57

Herrmann, J. (ed.) 1976 *Die Germanen* vol. I, Berlin.

1982 'Tendenzen und Grundlinien der Produktivkraftentwicklung an der Wende von der Antike zum Mittelalter', in J. Herrmann and I. Sellnow (eds.) *Produktivkräfte und Gesellschaftsformationen in vorkapitalistischer Zeit*. Berlin

1983 *Die Germanen* vol. II. Berlin

Hinz, H. 1974 *Bosau I. Untersuchung einer Siedlungskammer in Osthol-stein*. Offa-Bücher vol. 31

Hinz, H. (ed.) 1978 *Bosau II. Untersuchung einer Siedlungskammer in Ostholstein*. Offa-Bücher vol. 37

Hinz, H. and Kiefmann, H. M. 1979 *Bosau III. Historische-Geographische Untersuchungen zur älteren Kulturlandschaftsentwicklung*. Offa-Bücher vol. 39

Hodder, I. 1982 *Symbols in Action*. Cambridge University Press

Hoffman, M. A. 1980 *Egypt before the Pharaohs: The Prehistoric Foundation of Egyptian Civilization*, London

Hofseth, E. H. 1980 'Bronsedolken fra Lesjafjell', in *Festskrift til Sverre Marstrander på 70–årsdagen* pp. 131–7, Oslo

Høj, G. Unpublished [1980] *Undersøgelser over den gravfundne keramik i yngre romertid fra Danmark*. Unpubliceret speciale. Copenhagen

Hollstein, E. 1980 *Europäische Eichenchronologie*, Trier

Holmes, T. Rice 1911 *Caesar's Conquest of Gaul*, Oxford

Hopkins, K. 1978 *Conquerors and Slaves* Cambridge University Press

1980 'Taxes and Trade in the Roman Empire (200 B.C.–A.D. 400)', *Journal of Roman Studies*, vol. LXX

1983 Introduction to Garnsey *et al.* 1983

Howard, A. and Skinner, D. 1984 'Networks and power in 19th century Sierra Leone', *Africa* 54, 2: 2–28

Humphreys, S. 1969 'History, economics and anthropology: the work of Karl Polanyi', *History and Theory* 8: 165–212

Hunt, V. 1978 The rise of feudalism in Eastern Europe: a critical appraisal of the Wallerstein World System thesis', *Science and Society* XLII 1: 43–61

Huttunen, P. and Tolonen, M. 1972 'Pollen-analytical studies of prehistoric agriculture in Northern Ångermanland', in *Early Norrland* 1: 9–34, Stockholm

Hvass, S. 1975 'Das eisenzeitliche Dorf bei Hodde, Westjütland', *Acta Archaeologia* 46

1983 Vorbasse. The development of a settlement through the first millennium AD. *Journal of Danish Archaeology* 2

Hvass, S. 1980 *Danmarkshistorien*, Jernalderen, Copenhagen

Hyenstrand, Å. 1968 'Skärvstenshögar och bronsåldersmiljøer', *Tor* XII p. 61–80, Uppsala

1979 *Ancient monuments and prehistoric Society*, Central Board of National Antiquities, Stockholm

1984a *Bronsåldersforskning – kring aktuella projekt*, Stockholm

1984b *Fasta fornlämningar och arkeologiska regioner*, RAÄ no. 7, Stockholm

Ilkjær, J. and Lønstrup, J. 1983 'Der Moorfund im Tal der Illerup-Å bei Skanderborg im Ostjütland' *Germania* 61

Iversen, J. 1960 *Problems of the early post-glacial forest development in Denmark*. Danmarks Geologiske undersøgelser (DGU). IV. rk. 4. Copenhagen

Jaanusson, H. 1981 *Hallunda. A study of pottery from a Late Bronze Age settlement in Central Sweden*, The Museum of National Antiquities Stockholm, Studies 1

Jacob-Friesen, G. 1967 *Bronzezeitliche Lanzenspitzen Norddeutschlands und Skandinaviens*, Hildesheim

Jacobsen, J. A. 1979 'Bruneborg, en tidlig førromersk boplads med jernudvinding', *Fra Jernalder til Middelalder. Skrifter fra Historisk Institut, Odense Universitet* 27

Jacobsen, T. 1970 'On the textile industry at Ur under Ibbi-Sin', in W. Moran (ed.), *Toward the Image of Tammuz*, pp. 216–29. Cambridge: Harvard

Jankuhn, H. 1976 'Siedlung, Wirtschaft und Gesellschaftsordnung der germanischen Stämme in der Zeit der römischen Angriffskriege', in H. Temporini and W. Haase (eds.) *Aufstieg und Niedergang der römischen West II*, Berlin, New York

Janssen, J. 1975 *Commodity Prices from the Ramessid Period* Leiden: Brill

Jarrige, J. -F. 1982 'Syvazi Beludzhistana v Srednei Azii vo vtoroi polovine III tis, do n.e. v svete novikh rabot v raione Mergara (Les rapports du Baluchistan avec l'Asie Centrale méridionale dans la deuxieme moitié d 3 ème millenaire à la lumière de travaux récents (dans la fgion de Mehrgarh)', in R. M. Munchaev, V. M. Masson, N. N. Negmatov, and V. A. Ranov (eds.) *Drevneishie' Kul'turi Baktrii: Sreda, Razvitie, Svyazi*.

Jarrige, J. -F. and Santoni, M. 1979 *Fouilles de Pirak*, vols I and II. Paris: Diffusion de Boccard

Jay, M. 1977 'The concept of totality in Lukacs and Adorno' *Telos* 32: 117–37.

1984 *Marxism and Totality* Polity Press, Oxford

Jenkins, N. 1980 *The Boat beneath the Pyramid: King Cheops' Royal Ship*, London

Jensen, J. 1981 'Et rigdomscenter fra yngre bronzealder på sjælland', *Årbøger for Nord. Oldkyndighed og Historie*, pp. 48–96

Jidedjian, N. 1971 *Byblos Through the Ages* Beirut: Dar el-Machreq.

Johansen, O. Sverre 1979 'Early farming north of the arctic circle', *Norwegian Archaeological Review* 12, no. 1: 22–35

1982 'Det eldste jordbruk i Nord-Norge, en arkeologisk oversikt', in Th. Sjøvold (ed.) *Introduksjon av jordbruk i Norden*, p. 195–208, Oslo

Johansen, Ø. 1981 *Metallfunnene i Østnorsk bronse alder*. Kulturtilknytning of forutsetninger for en marginalekspansjon. Universitetets Oldsakssamlings skrifter. Ny rekke nr. 4, Oslo

1983 'Bronsealderproblemer – en teori om mellomhandlervirksomhet', in Marstrander (ed.) *Varia 9*. Foredrag ved det 1. nordiske bronsealdersymposium på Isegran (p. 3–6) Oktober 1977, Oslo

Johnson, G. A. 1975 'Locational analysis and the investigation of Uruk local exchange systems' in J. A. Sabloff and C. C. Lamberg-Karlovsky (eds.) *Ancient Civilization and Trade* Albuquerque, pp. 285ff

Johnstone, P. 1980 *The Sea-Craft of Prehistory*, London

Jones, A. H. M. 1966 *The Decline of the Ancient World*, London

Jullian, C. 1920–4 *Histoire de la Gaule* Vols I–III. Paris. Fourth edition

Kaiser, W. 1957 'Zur inneren Chronologie der Naqadakultur', *Archaeologia Geographica* VI: 69ff

1964 'Einige Bemerkungen zur ägyptischen Frühzeit' III, *Zeitschrift für Ägyptische Sprache* 91: 86ff

Kanawati, N. 1977 *The Egyptian Administration in the Old Kingdom*. Warminster: Aris and Phillips

Kantor, H. 1944 'The final phase of predynastic Culture: Gerzean or Semainean?' *Journal of Near Eastern Studies* 3: 110ff

1965 'The chronology of Egypt and its correlation with that of other parts of the Near East . . .' in R. W. Ehrich (ed.) *Chronologies in Old World Archaeology* Chicago, 2nd ed., pp. 1ff

1972 'New evidence for the prehistoric and protoliterate culture development of Khuzestan', *The Memorial Volume, the Vth. International Congress of Iranian Art and Archaeology* I, Tehran, pp. 26ff

Kay, G. 1975 *Development and Underdevelopment* Macmillan, London

Kemp, B. J. 1973 'Photographs of the decorated tomb, Hierakonpolis', *Journal of Egyptian Archaeology* 59: 36ff

1977 'The early development of towns in Egypt', *Antiquity* 51: 185ff

Kempinski, A. 1978 *The Rise of an Urban Culture. The Urbanization of Palestine in the Early Bronze Age* Jerusalem: Israel Exploration Society

Kent, J. P. C. 1981 'The origins of coinage in Britain' in B. W. Cunliffe (ed.) *Coinage and Society in Britain and Gaul: 40–42 CBA Research Reports* 38, London

Kestemont, G. 1976 Review of Zaccagnini 1973 *Bibliotheca Orientalis* 33: 162–4

Kitchen, K. 1973 *Ramesside Inscription. Historical and Biographical 1/3*, Oxford

Kjellén, E. and Hyenstrand, Å. 1977 *Hällristringar och bronsålderssamhälle i sydöstra Uppland*, Upplands Fornminnesförenings Tidskrift 49

Klapinsky, R. 1984 *Automation: the Technology and Society* Longman, London

Klengel, H. 1979 *Handel und Händler im alten Orient*. Leipzig

Klengel, H. 1980. 'Mord und Bussleistung in Spätbronzezeitlichen Syrien', in B. Alster, *Death in Mesopotamia*, Mesopotamia 8, Copenhagen, 189–97

Knapp, A. B. 'KBOI 26: Alašiya and Hatti', *Journal of Cuneiform Studies* 32: 43–7

Knudtzen, J. A. 1915 *Die el-Amarna – Tafeln I*, Leigzig

Kohl, P. L. 1975 'The archaeology of trade', *Dialectical Anthropology* I: 43ff

1977 'The "world economy" of West Asia in the third millennium BC' in *Papers of 4th International Conf. Sth. Asian Archs. Naples*

1978 'The balance of trade in southwestern Asia in the mid-third millennium B.C.', *Current Anthropology* 19: 463–92

1979 'The "world-economy" of West Asia in the third millennium BC', *South Asian Archaeology, 1977*. Naples, 55–85

1981 'The Namazga Civilization: An Overview' in P. L. Kohl (ed.) *The Bronze Age Civilization of Central Asia: Recent Soviet Discoveries*, Armonk, NY: M. E. Sharpe, pp. vii–xxxviii

1983 *L'Asie Centrale: dès origines à l'âge du Fer (Central Asia: Palaeolithic Beginnings to the Iron Age)*. Synthèse 8, Editions Recherche sur les Civilizations. Paris

Kohl, P. L. and Wright, R. 1977 'Stateless cities: the differentiation of Societies in the Neolithic in the Near East', *Dialectical Anthropology* 2: 271–83

Köhler, R. 1975 *Untersuchungen zu Grabkomplexen der älteren römischen Kaiserzeit in Böhmen unter Aspekten der religiösen und sozialen Gliederung*, Neumünster

Kondratieff, N. D. 1979 'The long waves of economic life', *Review* 11, 4: 519–62

Kossack, G., Harck, O. and Reichstein, J. 1974 'Zehn Jahre Siedlungsforschung in Archum auf Sylt', *Bericht der römisch-germanischen Kommission* vol. 55: II

Kossack, G., Behre, K. E. and Schmid, P. (eds.) 1984 *Archäologiesche und naturwissenschaftliche Untersuchungen an ländlichen und frühstädtischen Siedlungen in deutschen Küsten gebiet vom 5. Jahr. v. Chr. bis zum ll. Jahrh. n. Chr*, Acta Humaniora. Weinheim

Kraus, F. R. 1958 'Ein Edikt des Königs Ammi-saduqa von Babylon', *Studia et documenta ad iura orientis pertinentia* 5 Leiden

1984 'Konigliche Verfügungen in altbabylonischer Zeit', *Studia et documenta ad iura orientis pertinentia* 11, Leiden

Kristiansen, K. 1978 'The consumption of wealth in Bronze Age Denmark. A study in the dynamics of economic processes in tribal societies', in K. Kristiansen and C. Paludan-Müller (eds.): *New directions in Scandinavian Archaeology* pp. 158–91, Copenhagen

1980 'Besiedlung, Wirtschaftsstrategie und Bodennutzung in der Bronzezeit Dänemarks', *Praehistorische Zeitschrift* vol. 55.

1981 'Economic models for Bronze age Scandinavia – towards an integrated approach', in A. Sheridan and G. Barley (eds.) *Economic Archaeology*, pp. 239–303, BAR International Series 96, Oxford

1982 'The formation of tribal systems in later European prehistory: Northern Europe, 4000–500 B.C.' in A. C. Renfrew, M. Rowlands and B. A. Segraves (eds.) *Theory and Explanation in Archaeology*, pp. 241–80, Academic Press

1984a 'Krieger und Häptlinge in der Bronzezeit Dänemarks', *Jahrbuch des Römische-Germanischen Zentralmuseums Mainz 31. Jahrg*

1984b *Value, ranking and consumption in the Bronze Age*. Paper presented at the 1984 TAG conference in Cambridge

1984c 'Ideology and material culture: An archaeological perspective', in M. Spriggs (ed.) *Marxist Perspectives in Archaeology*, pp. 72–100, Cambridge University Press.

1987 'From stone to bronze. An essay on the evolution of social complexity in Northern Europe 2300–1200 B.C.', in Brumfiel and Earle (eds.) *Specialization and exchange in Complex Societies*, Cambridge University Press

Kuftin, B. A. 1956 'Polevoi otchet: o rabote XIV otrade luTAKE po izucheniiu kul'turi pervobitno-oshchinikh osedlozemledel'cheskikh poselenii epokhu medui bronzi v 1952 g.', *Trudi Iu.T.A.K.E.* VII: 260–90

Kühne, C. and Otten H. 1971 *Der Šaušgamuwa-Vertrag*, Wiesbaden

Kula, W. 1976 *An Economic Theory of the Feudal System* NLB. London

Kunow, J. 1980 *Negotiator et Vectura. Händler und Transport im freien Germanien*. Kleine Schriften aus den Vorgeschichtliche Seminar. Marburg Hf. 6. O. H. Frey & H. Roth (eds.) Marburg

1983 *Der römische Import in der Germania libera bis zu den Marcomannerkriegen*. Neumünster

Kunst, M. 1978 'Arm und Reich – Jung und Alt', *Offa* vol. 35

Kuzmina, E. E. 1980 'Etapi razvitiya kolesnogo transporta Sredne Asii v epokhu eneolita i bronzi', *Vestnik Drevnei Istorii* (4): 11–35

Laclau, E. 1971 'Feudalism and Capitalism in Latin America', *New Left Review* 67

Laessoe, J. 1959 *The Shemshara Tablets, A Preliminary Report*, Copenhagen

Lamberg-Karlovsky, C. C. 1972 'Trade mechanisms in Indus-Mesopotamian interrelations', *JAOS* 92: 222–9

n.d. 'Caste or Class Formation within the Indus Civilization' to appear in E. C. L. During-Caspers (ed.) *A Felicitation Volume for Beatrice de Cardi on the Occasion of Her 70th Birthday* Academic Publishers Association

Lambert, M. 1953 'Textes commerciaux de Lagash (époque présargonique)', *Revue d'Assyriologie* 47: 57–69, 105–20

Landström, B. 1970 *Ships of the Pharaohs*, London

Lane, F. C. 1973 *Venice. A Maritime Republic*. Baltimore

Lange, E. 1971 *Botanische Beiträge zur mitteleuropäischen Siedlungsgeschicht* Schriften zur Ur- und Frühgeschichte 27. Berlin

Larsen, M. T. 1972 'The city and its king. On the Old Assyrian notion of kingship', in P. Garelli (ed.). *Le palais et la royauté*, Paris, 285–300

1976 'The Old Assyrian city-State and its colonies', *Mesopotamia* 4 Copenhagen

1977 'Partnerships in the Old Assyrian trade', *Iraq* 39: 119–45

1979 *Power and Propaganda* Akademisk Verlag, Copehhagen

1982, 'Your money or your life! a portrait of an Assyrian businessman', *Societies and Languages of the Ancient Near East. Studies in honour of I. M. Diakonoff*, Warminster, 214–45

Larsson, T. B. 1984 'Multi-level exchange and cultural interaction in Late Scandinavian Bronze Age', in K. Kristiansen (ed.) *Settlement and Economy in later Scandinavian Prehistory*, pp. 63–84, BAR international series 211, Oxford

Le Brun 1978 'La Glyptique de Niveau 17B de l'Acropole' *Cahiers de la Délégation Archéologique Française en Iran* 8: 61ff

Le Brun, A. and Vallat, F. 1978 'L'Origine de l'écriture à Suse', *Cahiers de la Délégation Archéologique Française en Iran*, 8: 11ff

Leemans, W. F. 1950, 'The Old Babylonian merchant. His business and his social position', *Studia et documenta ad iura orientis pertinentia* 3 Leiden

1960, 'Foreign trade in the Old Babylonian Period as revealed by texts from Southern Mesopotamia', *Studia et documenta ad iura orientis pertinentia* 6. Leiden

1968, 'Old Babylonian letters and economic history, *Journal of the Economic and Social History of the Orient*11: 171–226

1971 'Gold', *Reallexikon der Assyriologie* III: 504–15

Leube, A. 1976 'Probleme germanischer Adelsentwicklung im 1. und 2. Jh. unter dem Aspekt der römischen Beeinflussung', in H. Grünert and H. J. Döller (eds.) *Römer und Germanen in Mitteleuropa*. Berlin

Levick, B. 1971 'Cicero, Brutus and the foundation of Narbo Martius', *Classical Quarterly* XXI, 1971: 171–9

Lévi-Strauss, C. 1966 *The Savage Mind* Weidenfeld, London

Levy, J. 1982 *Social and religious organization in Bronze Age Denmark. An analysis of ritual hoard finds*, BAR international series 124. Oxford

Lewis, N., and Reinhold, M. (eds.) 1966 *Roman Civilization Sourcebook 1: The Republic*, New York

Lieberman, S. J. 1980 'Of clay, pebbles, hollow clay balls, and writing: a Sumerian view', *American Journal of Archaeology* 84: 339ff

Limet, H. 1960 *Le travail du metal au pays de Sumer au temps de la IIIe dynastie d'Ur*. Paris: Société d'Edition

1972 'Les metaux a l'époque d'Agade', *Journal of the Economic and Social History of the Orient* 15: 3–33

Linder, E. 1981 Ugarit: a Canaanite Thalassocracy, in G. D. Young (ed) *Ugarit in Retrospect*. Winona Lake

Lindquist, S. -O. 1974 'The development of the agrarian landscape on Gotland during the Early Iron Age', *Norwegian Archaeological Review* 7 no. 1

Lipiński, E. (ed.) 1979 *State and Temple Economy in the Ancient Near East* 1–2. Leuven

1985, 'Products and Brokers of Tyre according to Ezekiel 27', *Studia Phoenicia*, III, 213–20, Leuven

Lisitsina, G. N. 1978 *Stanovlenie i razvitie oroshaemogo zemledeliya v iuzhnoi Turkmenii* Moscow: Nauka

Liverani, M. 1962 *Storia di Ugarit nell'eta degli archivi politici*, Roma

1965 'Il fusruscitismo in Siria nella tarda età del bronzo', in *Rivista Storica Italiana*, 77, pp. 315–36

1971a 'Le lettere del Faraone a Rib-Adda' *Oriens Antiqvus* 10: 253–68

1971b *Sydyke Misor*, in 'Studi in onore di E. Volterra', IV, Milano, pp. 55–74

1972a 'Elementi "irrazionali" nel commercial amarniano', *Oriens Antiquus* 11: 297–317

1972b 'Partire sul carro, per il deserto' *Annali dell'Istituto Orientale di Napoli* 22: 403–15

1973a 'Storiografia politica hittita – I. Šunaššure, ovvero: della reciprocita', *Oriens Antiquus* 12: 267–97

1973b 'Memorandum on the approach to historiographic texts' *Orientalia* 42: 178–94

1974a 'L'histoire de Joas' *Vetus Testamentum* 24: 438–53

1974b 'Rib-Adda, giusto sofferente', *Altorientalische Forschungen* 1: 175–205

1974c 'La royauté Syrienne de l'âge du bronze récent', in M. Liverani, *Le palais et la royauté*, Paris

1975 'Communautés de village et palais royal dans la Syria IIème millenaire', *Journal of the Economic and Social History of the Orient* 18: 146–64

1977 'Storiografia politica hittita – II. Telepinu, ovvero: della solidarieta', *Oriens Antiquus* 16: 105–31

1978 'Non slave labour in Syria (Bronze Age)', in *7th International Economic History Congress*, Edinburgh

1979a 'Three Amarna Essays' *Monographs on the Ancient Near East* 1/5 Malibu

1979b 'La dotazione dei mercanti di Ugarit', *Ugarit forschungen* 11: 495–503

1979c 'Dono, tributo, commercio: idologia dello scambio nella tarde et del bronzo', *Annali dell'Istituto Italiano di Numismatica* 26: 9–28

1979d 'The ideology of the Assyrian empire' M. T. Larsen (ed.) *Power and Propaganda. A Symposium on Ancient Empires* Copenhagen 297–317

1979e 'Messaggi, donne, ospitalita. Comunicazione intertribale in Giud. 19–21', *Studi storico religiosi* 3: 303–41

1979f 'Ras Shamra histoire', *Supplement au Dictionnaire de la Bible*, IX, Coll. 1343–1348, Paris

1980 'Le "origini" d'Israele. Progetto irrealizabile di ricerca etnogenetica', *Rivista Biblica Italiana* 28: 9–31

1983 'Aziru, servo di due padrone' in O. Carruba, M. Liverani and C. Zaccagnini (eds.), *Studi F. Pintore*, Pavia 93–121

Lopez, R., Miskimin, H. and Udovitch, A. 1970, 'England to Egypt, 1350–1500: long-term trends and long-distance trade', M. A. Cook (ed.). *Studies in the Economic History of the Middle East*, London, 93–128

Lucas, A. 1962 *Ancient Egyptian Materials and Industries* 4th edition, revised by J. R. Harris, London

Lukacs, G. 1968 *History and Class Consciousness* Merlin Press, London

Lundmark, H. 1984 'The identification of tribal hierarchies', in K. Kristiansen (ed.) *Settlement and Economy in later Scandinavian Prehistory* pp. 43–62, BAR international series, 211, Oxford

Lüttwak, E. N. 1976 *The Grand Strategy of the Roman Empire: From the First Century AD to the Third* (John Hopkins University Press) Baltimore

Luxemburg, R. 1951 *The Accumulation of Capital* RKP, London

Lythoe, A. M. and Dunham, D. 1965 *Naga-ed-Deir 4: The predynastic cemetery N. 7000*, Berkeley, California

McCaslin, D. 1980 *Stone anchors in Antiquity: coastal settlement and maritime trade routes in the Eastern Mediterranean ca. 1600–1050 B.C.*, Goteborg

McKerrell, H. 1977, 'Non-dispersive XRF applied to ancient Metalworking in copper and tin bronze', *Journal of the European Study Group on Physical, Chemical and Mathematical Techniques Applied to Archaeology (PACT)*, Strassbourg; 1: 138–73

Magie, D. M. 1950 *Roman Rule in Asia Minor to the End of the Third Century after Christ*, Princeton

Magnus, B. and Myhre, B. 1976 *Norges Historie*, vol. 1, Forhistorien, Cappelans forlag

Maidman, M. P. 1980 Review of *Trade in the Ancient Near East*. XXIII Recontre Assyriologique International *Bibliotheca Orientalis* 37: 187–9

Malamat, A. 1971, 'Syro-Palestinian destinations in a Mari tin inventor', *Israel Exploration Journal* 21: 31–8

Malmer, M. P. 1975 'The rock carvings at Nämforsen, Ångermanland as a problem of maritime adaption and circumpolar interrelations', in *Prehistoric Maritime Adaptions of the Circumpolar Zone*, pp. 41–6, Chicago

1981 *A Chorological study in North European Rock Art*, Antikvariska Serien 32, Stockholm

Mandel, E. 1975 *Late Capitalism* NLB. London

Mandt, G. 1972 *Bergbilder in Hordaland. En undersøkelse av bildenes sammensætning, deres naturmiljø og kulturmiljø* Bergen

Marcus, J. 1976 *Emblem and State in the Classic Maya Lowlands* Dumbarton Oaks, Washington

1984 'Lowland Maya archaeology at the crossroads', *American Antiquity 48, 3*: 454–88

Marfoe, L. 1978 'Between Qadesh and Kumidi', PhD. Dissertation, University of Chicago

1979 'The Intergrative Transformation', *Bulletin of the American Schools of Oriental Research* 234: 1–42

1980 Review of A. Kempinski (1978) and R. Amiran (1978). *Journal of Near Eastern Studies* 39: 315–22

Margueron, J.-Cl. 1980 *Le moyen Euphrate*. Leiden: Brill

Marstrander, S. 1963 *Østfolds Jordbruksristninger*, Institut for sammenlignende kulturforskning, serie B. Skrifter LIII, Oslo

1983 'Porfyr- og nakkebøyde økser som indikatorer for bosetning og sociale strukturer i Norges yngre bronsealder', in S. Marstrander (ed.) Foredrag ved det l. nordiske Bronzealder-symposium på Isegran 3.–6. okt. 1977 *Varia 9*, pp. 52–147, Oslo

Masson, V. M. 1956 'Raspisnaya keramika iuzhnoi Turkmenii po raskopkam B. A. Kuftina', *Trudi Iu. T.A.K.E.* VII: 291–373

1968 'Urban revolution in southern Turkmenia', *Antiquity* XLII: 178–87

1981 *Altyn-depe. Trudi Iu.T.A.K.E.* vol. XVIII. Leningrad: Nauka

Matthiae, P. 1981 *Ebla*. Garden City: Doubleday

Mauss, M. 1923–4 'Essai sur le don', *L'Année Sociologique*, II Ser., 1, pp. 30–186, republished in M. Mauss, *Sociologie et anthropologie*, Paris 1950, pp. 143–279

1954 *The Gift*. Cohen, London

Meeks, N. D. and Tite, M. S. 1980 'The analysis of platinum-group element inclusions in gold antiquities', *Journal of Archaeological Science* 7: 267ff

Meillassoux, C. 1971 *Trade and Indigenous Markets in West Africa* IAI, Oxford

Meinander, C. F. 1954 *Die Bronzezeit in Finland*, Finska Fornminnesföreningens Tideskrift, 54, Helsinki

Mellaart, J. 1975 *The Neolithic of the Near East*. New York: Scribner's

Mendenhall, G. E. 1962 'The Hebrew conquest of Palestine', *Biblical Archaeologist* 25: 66–87

Merquior, J. 1979 *The Veil and the Mask* RKP, London

Merrillees, R. S. 1968 *The Cypriote B.A. pottery found in Egypt*, Lund METU See Middle East Technical University. 1970–9 *Keban Project Activities 1968–73*. Ankara

Middleton, P., 1979 'Free Germans and Lineage Slaves', MA Dissertation, University of London

Mikkelsen, E. 1980 'Sporaneset – en bronsealders "utpost" i Telemark', in *Festskrift til Sverre Marstrander på 70-årsdagen*, Universitetets Oldsakssamlings Skrifter, Ny rekke no. 3, pp. 35–41, Oslo

Mikkelsen, E. and Høeg, H. J. 1979 'A reconsideration of neolithic agriculture in Eastern Norway', *Norwegian Archaeological Review* 12, no. 1: pp. 33–48

Milano, L. 1978 'KLY nel lessico amministrativo del Semitico di Nord-Ouest', *Vicino Oriente* 1: 83–97

Mildenberger, G. 1959/60 'Archäologische Betrachtungen zu den Ortsnamen auf"-leben".',*Archaeol. Geographica* 8/9

Miller, D. 1985 'Ideology and the Harappan Civilisation', *Journal of Anthropological Archaeology* 4: 34–71

Miller, D. and Tilley, C. 1984 *Ideology, power and prehistory*. Cambridge University Press

Moberg, C. -A. 1970 'Regionalt och globalt syn på hällristningar', *Kuml* pp. 223–32

Møllerop, O. 1962 'Fra Rogalands eldre bronsealder', *Stavanger Museum*, 72. årg pp. 5–59

Mommsen, T. 1909 *The Provinces of the Roman Empire from Caesar to Diocletian* (trans. W. P. Dickson). London

Montet, P. 1928 *Byblos et l'Egypte*. Paris: Paul Ceuthner

Moorey, P. R. S. 1982 'The archaeological evidence for metallurgy and related techniques in Mesopotamia, c. 5500–2100 B.C.' *Iraq* 44: 13–38

Moortgat, A. 1957–78 *Tell Chera in Nordost-Syrien*. 8 Vols. Wiesbaden

Much, R. 1967 *Die Germania des Tacitus*. 3. Auf. Unter mitarbeit von H. Jankuhn. Heidelberg

Muhly, J. D. 1973 'Copper and tin. The distribution of mineral resources and the nature of the metals trade in the Bronze Age', *Transactions of the Connecticut Academy of Arts and Sciences* 43: New Haven 155–535

1976 'Supplement to copper and tin', *Transactions of the Connecticut Academy of Arts and Sciences* 46: 77–136

Müller-Wille, M. 1965 *Eisenzeitliche Fluren in den festlandischen Nordseegebieten* (Siedlung und Landschafte in Westfalen 5). Münster

Myhre, B. 1978 'Agrarian development, settlement history and social organization in Southwest Norway in the Iron Age', in K. Kristiansen and C. Paluden-Müller (eds) *New Directions in Scandinavian Archaeology*, The National Museum, Denmark

1983 'Beregning av folketall på Jæren i yngre romertid og folkevandringstid', *Hus, Gård och Bebyggelse*. Foredrag från det XVI. nordiska arkeologmötet, Island 1982. G. Olafsson (ed.)

Myhre, B. 1980 *Sola og mMadla i førhistorisk tid*, AmS – Småtryk 10, Stavanger

Nash, D. 1975 'Foreign trade and the development of the state in pre-Roman Gaul'. Paper read at the University of Sussex

1976 'The growth of Urban Society in France' in B. W. Cunliffe and R. T. Rowley (eds.) *Oppida*: 95–134 BAR series 11, Oxford

1978a *Settlement and Coinage in Central Gaul c. 200–50 BC*, Oxford, BAR Series 39

1978b 'Plus ça change …; currency in Central Gaul from Julius Caesar to Nero', in R. A. G. Carson and C. M. Kraay (eds), *Scripta Nummaria Romana, Essays presented to Humphrey Sutherland* London, 12–31

1978c 'Territory and state formation in Central Gaul' in D. Green, C. Haselgrove and M. Spriggs (eds) *Social Organisation and Settlement*: 455–76 BAR Series 47, Oxford

1985 'Celtic territorial expansion and the Mediterranean World', in

T. C. Champion and J. V. S. Megaw (eds), *Settlement and Society; aspects of Western European Prehistory in the First Millennium BC*, Leicester, 45–68

1981 'Coinage and state development in Central Gaul', in B. W. Cunliffe (ed.) *Coinage and Society in Britain and Gaul*: 10–17, *CBA Research Reports* 38, London

Näsman, U. 1978 'Öland, Eketorp and the transition between Montelii periods VI and VII', *Tor* 1975–77

Naville, E. 1898 *The Temple of Deir el Bahari*, Vol. III, London

Needler, W. 1980 'Two important predynastic graves from Henri de Morgan's excavations' *Association Internationale pour l'Étude de la Préhistoire égyptienne, Bulletin*, I (read in a manuscript provided by Mrs J. C. Payne)

Neumann, H. 1977 'Die Befestigungsanlage olgerdige und der jütischen Heerweg', *Studien zur Sachsenforschung* 1

1982 *Olgerdige – et bidrag til Danmarks tidligste historie*, Haderslev

Newberry, P. 1913 'Some cults of prehistoric Egypt' *Liverpool Annals of Archaeology and Anthropology* 5: 132ff

1938 'Three Old Kingdom travellers to Byblos and Pwenet', *Journal of Egyptian Archaeology* 24: 182–84

Nibbi, A. 1981 *Ancient Egypt and some Eastern Neighbours* (Noyes Press, New Jersey)

Nordbladh, J. 1980 *Glyfer och rum kring hällristningar i Kville*, University of Gothenburg

Norden, A. 1925 *Ostergötlands bronsålder*, Linköping

Oates, D. 1968 *Studies in the Ancient History of Northern Iraq*, London

Oates, J. *et al.* 1977 'Seafaring merchants of Ur?' *Antiquity* 51: 221–34

Odgaard, B. 1985 'Kulturlandskabets historie i Vestjylland. Foeløbige resultater af nye pollenanalytiske undersøgelser', *Fortidsminder 1985*, Antikvariske Studier 7, pp. 48–60

Odner, K. 1969 *Ullshelleren i Valldalen Røldal* Univ. i Bergen, Humanistisk Serie, no. 1

O'Laughlan, 1975 'Marxist anthropology', *Annual Review of Anthropology*, 5

Oldeberg, A. 1974–6 *Die ältere Metalzeit in Schweden* I–II, Stockholm

Oppenheim, A. Leo 1954, 'The seafaring merchants of Ur', *Journal of the American Oriental Society* 74: 6–17

Oren, E. 1973 'The overland route between Egypt and Canaan in the Early Bronze Age', *Israel Exploration Journal* 23: 198–205

Ørsnes, M. 1963 'The weapon find in Ejsbøl Mose at Haderslev', *Acta Archaeologica* 34

1964 'Mosefund – stratigrafi og kronologi', *Tor* 10

1968 'Der Moorfund von Ejsbøl bei Hadersleben. Deutungsprobleme der grossen nordgermanischen Waffenopferfunde', *Abhandlung der Akademie der Wissenschaft in Göttingen*

1984 *Sejrens Pris*, Haderslev museum

Ostoja-Zagórski, J. 1983 'An attempt at the reconstruction of economic transformations in the Hallstatt period in the north and west zone of the Oder and Vistula River Basin', *Unconventional Archaeology V–5*

Påhlsson, I. 1977 'A standard pollen diagram from the Lojsta Area of Central Gotland', *Striae* 3. Uppsala

Palmieri, A. 1973 'Scavi nell'area Sud-Occidentale di Arslantepe', *Origini* VII: 55–215

1981. 'Excavations at Arslan tepe (malatya)', *Anatolian Studies* 31: 101–19

Parker Pearson, M. 1984 'Economic and ideological change: cyclical growth in the pre-state societies of Jutland; in D. Miller and C. Tilley (eds.) *Ideology, Power and Prehistory*. New Directions in Archaeology. Cambridge

1984 'Social change, ideology and the archaeological record', in M. Spriggs (ed.) *Marxist Perspectives in Archaeology* Cambridge University Press

Parpola, S., Parpola A. and Brunswig, R. H. 1977 'The Meluhha village: evidence of acculturation of Harappan traders in late third millennium Mesopotamia?' *Journal of the Economic and Social History of the Orient* XX(2): 129–65

Parry, J. 1986 The gift, the Indian gift and the 'Indian gift', *Man* n.s. vol. 21, 3: 453–73

Partridge, C. 1981 *Skeleton Green. (Britannia Monograph Series* 2). London.

Payne, J. C. 1968 'Lapis lazuli in early Egypt', *Iraq* 30: 58ff

Peacock, D. P. S. 1971 'Roman amphorae in pre-Roman Britain' in D. Hill and M. Jesson (eds) *The Iron Age and its Hillforts*: 161–88. Southampton

1984 'Amphorae in Iron Age Britain: a reassessment', in S. Macready and F. H. Thompson (eds), *Cross-Channel Trade between Gaul and Britain in the pre-Roman Iron Age*, London, 37–42

Pearson, H. W. 1957 'The secular debate on economic primitivism' in K. Polanyi, C. M. Arensberg, and H. W. Pearson (eds) *Trade and Market in the Early Empires* Chicago: Free Press, pp. 3–11

Peet, T. 1935–8 'The unit of value s^{c}ty in Papyrus Bulaq 11', in *Melanges Maspero* I, 1. pp. 185–99 MIFAOC 66. Cairo

Petrie, W. M. F. 1939 *The Making of Egypt*, London

Petrie, W. M. F. and Quibell, J. E. 1896 *Naqada and Ballas*, London

Pettinato, G. 1979 'Il Commercia Internazionale di Ebla', in E. Lipinski (ed.), *State and Temple Economy in the Ancient Near East* I. pp. 171–231 Leuven: Department of Orientalistiek.

1981 *The Archives of Ebla: An Empire Inscribed in Clay* New York: Doubleday

Pettinato, G. and Matthiae, P. 1976 'Aspetti administrative e topografici de Ebla nel III millennio av. Cr.', *Revista degli Studi Orientali* 50: 1–30

Piggott, S. 1965 *Ancient Europe*, Edinburgh

Pintore, F. 1978 *Il matrimonio interdinastico nel Vicino Oriente durante i secoli XV–XIII* Rome

Pintore, F. 1983 Osservazioni sulle vie el'orientamento dei commerci nella Siria-Palestina meridionale, in *Studia orientalistici in ricordo di F. Pintore*, 223–57. Pavia

Pirenne, H. 1939 *Mohammed and Charlemange*, London

Polanyi, K. 1957 *Trade and Markets in the Early Empires* Chicago University Press

1978 *The Livelihood of Man* Harvard University Press

Pottier, M. -H. 1981 *Matériel Funéraire de la Bactriane méridionale de l'Age de Bronze*, vols. I and II, Thèse pour le Doctorat de IIIe Cycle. Université de Lille III. Unpublished

Potts, D. n.d. 'On Salt and Salt Gathering in Ancient Mesopotamia' to appear in *Journal of the Economic and Social History of the Orient*

Powell, M. A. 1977 'Sumerian merchants and the problem of profit', *Iraq* 39: 23–9

Prag, K. 1978 'Silver in the Levant in the fourth millennium B.C.' in R. Moorey and P. J. Parr, (eds) *Archaeology in the Levant: Essays for Kathleen Kenyon* Warminster, England, pp. 36ff

Pritchard, J. (Ed.) 1969 *Ancient Near Eastern Texts Relating to the Old Testament*. 3rd Ed. with supplement. Princeton: Princeton

Raddatz, K. 1959/61 'Ringknaufschwerter aus germanischen Kriegergräber', *Offa* 17/18

1967 *Die Bewaffnung der Germanen in der jüngeren römischen Kaiserzeit*. Nachrichten der Akademie der Wissenschaften in Göttingen 1967 nr. 1

1976 *Bewaffnung* in J. Hoops *Reallexikon der germanischen altertumskunde* II. Berlin, New York

Randsborg, K. 1974 'Social stratification in Early Bronze Age Denmark: a study in the regulation of cultural systems', *Praehistorische Zeitschrift* vol. 49

Redlich, C. 1980 'Politische und wirtschaftliche Bedeutung der Bronzegefässe an Unterelbe und Saale zu Zeit der Römerkriefe', *Studien zur Sachsenforschung* vol. 2

Redman, C. 1978 *The Rise of Civilization*. San Francisco: W. H. Freeman

Reichstein, H. *et al.* 1981 *Bosau IV. Untersuchung einer Siedlungskammer in Ostholstein*. Offa-Bücher vol 42

Reineke, W. F. 1979 Waren die *Šwtjw* wirklich Kaufleute? in *Altorientalische Forschungen*, 6: 5–14

Renfrew, A. C. 1972 *The Emergence of Civilisation* Methuen, London

Rice Holmes, T. 1911 *Caesar's conquest of Gaul,* Oxford Second edition

Richards, J., and Mazzaoui, M. n.d. 'Precious metals and the pattern of commerce in the late medieval world economy, 1200–1500 A.D.' in *idem, Precious Metals in the Later Medieval and Early Modern World 1200–1800 A.D.* Forthcoming

Roover, R. de 1965, 'The organization of trade', *The Cambridge Economic History of Europe* III. chapter 2. Cambridge, 42–118

1966 *The Rise and Decline of the Medici Bank 1397–1494* New York

Rostovtzeff, M. 1957 *Social and economic history of the Roman Empire.* Second edition, Oxford

1960 *Rome* Oxford (Copenhagen 1966)

Rothenberg, B. 1972a 'Sinai explorations 1967–72', *Bulletin Museum Haaretz* 14: 31–42

1972b *Timna*, London

Rouault, O. 1977 'Mukannisum. L'administration et l'économie palatiales à mari', *Archives royales de Mari* XVIII. Paris

Rowlands, M. 1979 'Local and Long distance trade and incipient state formation on the Bamenda Plateau' *Paideuma* 15: 1–15

1980 'Kinship, alliance and exchange in the European Bronze Age' in J. C. Barrett and R. Bradley (eds) *Settlement and Society in the British Later Bronze Age*: 15–56 BAR 83, Oxford

1984a 'Conceptualising the European Bronze and Iron Age' in J. Bintliffe (ed.) *European Social Evolution* Bradford University Press

1984b 'Objectivity and subjectivity in archaeology', in M. Spriggs (ed) *Marxist perspectives in archaeology*. Cambridge University Press

Rowlett, R. M., Thomas, H. L. and Rowlett, E. 1976 'Excavations on the Titelberg. Luxembourg', *Journal of Field Archaeology* 3: 241–59

1982 'Stratified Iron Age House Floors on the Titelberg. Luxembourg', *Journal of Field Archaeology* 9: 301–12

Rowton, M. B. 1965 'The topological factor in the hapiru problem', in *Studies B. Landsberger*, Chicago, pp. 375–88

1967 'The woodlands of Ancient Western Asia', *Journal of Near Eastern Studies* 261–77

Roymans, N. 1983 'The North Belgic tribes in the 1st century B.C.: an historical-anthropological perspective', in R. Brandt and J. Slofstra (eds.) *Roman and Native in the Low Countries*. BAR Intern. Ser. 184. Oxford

Sahlins, M. 1974 *Stone Age Economics* Tavistock. London

1981 *Historical Metaphors and Mythical Realities* Chicago University Press

Salo, U. 1983 'Bronseåldersamhället vid Satakuntakysten: Käller och tolkningsforsök', in S. Marstrander (ed.) Foredrag ved det 1. nordiske Bronzealdersymposium på Isegran 3.–6. okt, 1977 *Varia 9*, pp. 1–15, Oslo

Sarianidi, V. I. 1977 *Drevnie Zemledeltsi Afganistana* Moscow: Nauka

Sarianidi, V. I. 1981 'Margiana in the Bronze Age', in P. L. Kohl (ed.) *The Bronze Age Civilization of Central Asia* pp. 165–93

Sasson, J. 1966 'A Sketch of North Syrian economic relations in the Middle Bronze Age', *Journal of the Economic and Social History of the Orient* 9: 161–81

Scheers, S. 1977 *Traité de Numismatique Celtique II: La Gaule Belgique* (*Annales Littéraires de l'Université de Besançon* 1950). Paris

Schlette, F. 1972 *Germanen zwischen Thorsberg und Ravenna*. Leipzig, Berlin.

1975 'Formen des römisch-germanischen Handels', in H. Grünert and H. J. Döller (eds) *Römer und Germanen in Mitteleuropa*. Berlin

Schmandt-Besserat, D. 1980 'The envelopes that bear the first writing', *Technology and Culture* 21: 357ff

Schneider, J. 1977 'Was there a pre-capitalist world system?' *Peasant Studies*, vol. VI, no. 1: 20–9

Scullard, H. H. 1963 *From the Gracchi to Nero*, London

Seger, T. 1983 'On the structure and emergence of Bronze Age society in coastal Finland: a systems approach', *Suomen Museo* pp. 31–45, Helsinki.

Selinge, K. G. 1979 *Agrarian Settlement and Hunting Grounds. A study of the prehistoric culture systems in a North Swedish Valley*. Theses and papers in North-European Archaeology 8, Stockholm

Sethe, K. 1961 (1927) *Urkunden der 18. Dynastie*, Vol. 2, Berlin

Shaffer, J. 1982 'Harappan culture: a reconsideration'. In G. L. Possehl (ed.) *The Harappan Civilization: A Contemporary Perspective*, New Delhi: Oxford and ISB Publishers, American Institute of Indian Studies, pp. 41–50

Shennan, S, 1982 'Ideology, change and the European Early Bronze Age' in I. R. Hodder (ed.) *Symbolic and Structural Archaeology*: 155–61. Cambridge

Sherwin-White, A. N. 1973 *The Roman Citizenship*, Oxford, Second Edn.

Siiriäinen, A. 1980 'On the culture ecology of the Finnish Stone Age', *Suomi Museo*, pp. 5–40, Helsinki

1982 'Jordbruket i Finland under stenåldern – en arkeologisk kommentar', in Sjøvold (ed.) *Introduksjonen av jordbruk i Norden* pp. 215–29, Oslo-Bergen-Tromsø

Simiand, F. 1932 *Recherches anciennes et nouvelles sur le mouvement generale des prix au XVIe au XIXe siècles* Lib. F. Alcan, Paris

Simonsen, A. 1975 'Nye bidrag til Rogalands landskapshistorie', *Fra Heid on Haug* 1975, no. 1, pp. 231–4

Sjøvold, Th. (ed.) 1982 *Introduksjonen av jordbruk i Norden*, Universitetsforlaget 1982

Skjøsvold, A. 1978 *Slettabø. Et bidrag til diskusjonen om forholdet mellem fangst – og bondesamfundet i yngre steinalder og bronsealder*. Ark. Mus. Stavanger Skrifter 2

Snell, D. C. 1982 'Ledgers and prices. Early Mesopotamian merchant accounts', *Yale Near Eastern Researchers* 8. New Haven

Søndergaard, B. 1972 *Indledende studier over den nordiske stednavnetype lev (löv)*, Copenhagen

Speiser, E. A. 1961 'The verb SHR in Genesis and early Hebrew movements', *Bulletin of the American Schools of Oriental Research* 164: 23–8

Sporrong, U. 1971 *Kolonisation, bebyggelsesutveckling och administration*, Lund

Spratling, M. G. 1976 'Currency, systems of weight, and trade in the La Tène Iron Age and beyond', paper read to the Prehistoric Society London

Stager, L. E. 1975 *Ancient Agriculture in the Judaean Desert: a Case Study of the Bugeʿah Valley*. Ph.D. Diss. Harvard

n.d. 'The first fruits of civilization', in J. Tubb (ed.), *Olga Tufnell Festschrift*. Institute of Archaeology Occasional Papers. London: University of London, forthcoming

Stech Wheeler, T., Muhly, J. D. and Maddin, R. 1979 'Mediterranean trade in copper and tin in the late Bronze Age', *Annali dell'Instituto Italiano di Numismatica* 26: 49–70

Stech Wheeler, T., Muhly, J. D., Maxwell Hyslop, K. R. and Maddin, R. 1981 'Iron at Taanach and early iron technology in the Eastern Mediterranean', 85: 245–68

Stein, A. 1931 *An Archaeological Tour in Gedrosia* (Memoires of the Archaeological Survey of India no. 43)

Steuer, H. 1982 *Frühgeschichtlich Sozialstrukturen Mitteleuropa*, Öttingen

Stevens, C. E. 1951 'The "Bellum Gallicum" as a work of propaganda', *Latomus* 11: 3–18, 165–79

1980 'North-West Europe and Roman politics (125–118)', in C. Deroux (ed), *Studies in Latin Literature and Roman History II (Collection Latomus vol. 168)*, Brussels 1980, 71–97

Stevenson Smith W. 1962 'The Land of Punt', *Journal of the American Research Center in Egypt* I

Steward, J. 1949 'Cultural causality and Law: a trial formulation of the development of early civilisations' in J. Steward *Theory of Culture Change* Illinois University Press

Stol, M. 1982 'State and private business in the land of Larsa', *Journal of Cuneiform Studies* 34: 127–230

Stolper, M. W. 1982 'On the dynasty of Simaski and the early Sukkalmahs', *Zeitschrift für Assyriologie* 72: 42–67

Stos-Gale, Z. A. and Gale, N. H. 1981a 'Sources of galena, lead and silver in predynastic Egypt', *Revue d'Archéométrie: Supplement*, pp. 285ff

1981b 'Ancient Egyptian silver' *Journal of Egyptian Archaeology* 67: 103ff

Strathern, A. 1971 *The Rope of Moka* Cambridge University Press

1982 'Death as exchange: two Melanesian cases' in S. Humphreys and H. King (eds) *Mortality and Immortality* Academic Press, London

Strathern, M. 1985 'Kinship and Economy: constitutive orders of a provisional kind', *American Ethnologist* 12: 191–209

Strommenger, E. 1980a 'The chronological division of the Archaic levels of Uruk-Eanna VI – III/II: Past and Present', *American Journal of Archaeology* 84: 479ff

1980b *Habuba Kabira*. Mainz: Philipp von Zabern

Struve, K. W. 1979 *Geschichte Schleswig-Holsteins Die jünger Bronzezeit* Neumünster

Sürenhagen, D. 1974–5 'Untersuchungen zur Keramikproduktion innerhalb der Spät-Urukzeitlichen Siedlung habuba kabira-Süd in Nordsyrien', *Acta Praehistorica et Archaeologica* 5/6: 43ff

Tadmon, H. 1979 'The decline of empires in W. Asia ca. 1200 B.C.E.', in F. M. Cross (ed.) *Symposia celebrating the 75th Anniversary of the American Schools of Oriental research*, Cambridge, Mass.

Tchernia, A. 1983 'Italian wine in Gaul at the end of the Republic', in P. Garnsey, K. Hopkins, C. R. Whittaker (eds), *Trade in the Ancient Economy*, London, 87–104

Thill, G. 1967 'Ausgrabungen bei Goeblingen-Nospelt', *Hémecht* 1967: 483–91

Thompson, E. A. 1965 *The Early Germans*, Oxford

Thrane, H. 1974 'Hundredevis af energikilder fra yngre broncealder' *Fynske Minder*. (p. 96–115) Festskrift for E. Albrechtsen

1982 'Indledende overvejelser af strukturudviklingen i Sydskandinaviens broncealder', in B. Stjernqvist (ed.) *Struktur och förändring i Bronsåldrens samhälle*, p. 151–66, University of Lund

Tierney, J. J., 1960 'The Celtic ethnography of Posidonius' *Proceedings of the Royal Irish Academy* 60: 189–275

Tilly, C. 1977 *The Formation of Nation States in Western Europe* Princeton University Press New Jersey

Tolonen, M. 1981 'An absolute and relative pollen analytic study on prehistoric Agriculture in South Finland', *Ann. Bot. Fennia* 18: 213–20

1982 'Om de första tecknena på odling i några pollendiagram från södra Finland', in Th. Sjøvold (ed.) *Introduksjonon av Jordbruk i Norden*, pp. 241–52, Oslo

Topperwein, E. 1973 'Habuba Kabira zur Zeit der Frühesten Schriftkulturen: Kleinfunde', *Mitteilungen der Deutschen Orient-Gesellschaft* 105: 20ff

Tosi, M. 1970 'A tomb from Damin and the problem of the Bampur sequence in the third millennium B.C.', *East and West* 20(1–2): 9–50

1973 'Early urban evolution and settlement patterns in the Indo-Iranian Borderlands', in C. Renfrew (ed.) *The Explanation of Culture Change: Models in Prehistory*, London: Duckworth

1973 'The northeastern frontier of the Ancient Near East', *Mesopotamia* VIII–IX: 21–76

Trigger, B. 1976 *Nubia under the Pharaohs*. Boulder: Westview.

Upham, S. 1982 *Politics and Power: an Economic and Political History of the Western Pueblo* Academic Press, New York

Uslar, R. von 1983 *Westermanische Bodenfunde der ersten bis dritten Jahrhunderte nach Chr. aus Mittel- und Westdeutschland*, Berlin

Vaiman, A. A. 1972 'A comparative study of the proto-Elamite and proto-Sumerian scripts', *Vestnik Drevnei Istorii* 121 (3): 124ff. (in Russian, English summary)

van Dijk, H. J. 1968 *Ezekiel's prophecy in Tyre*, Rome

van Driel, G. and van Driel-Murray, C. 1979. 'Jebel Aruda 1977–78', *Akkadica* 12: 2–28

van Loon, M. N. 1977 'Archaeological evidence of trade in Western Asia: problems and perspectives', *Ex Horreo* (ed. B. L. van Beek *et al.*) Amsterdam, pp. 1ff

van Loon, M. 1978 *Korucutepe II*. Amsterdam: North Holland/Elseivier.

Veenhof, K. R. 1972 *Aspects of Old Assyrian Trade and its Terminology*. Leiden

Veenhof, K. R. 1977 'Some social effects of Old Assyrian trade', *Iraq* 39: 109–18

Vercoulter, J. 1959 'The gold of Kush', *Kush* 7: 120–53

Vincentelli, I. 1971 'Alleanze o paragoni?' *Rivista degli studi orientali* 46: 143–6

    1976 'Alasia: per una storia di Cipronell ita del bronzo', *Studi Ciprioti e Rapporti di Scavo* 2: 20–2

Vinogradov, A. V. 1979 'Issledovaniya pamyatnikov kammenogo veka v severnom Afganistane', *Drevnaya Baktriya* 2: 7–62

Vinogradov, A. V. and Mamedov, E. D. 1975 *Pervobitnii Lyavlyakan* (materiali Khorezmskoi Ekspeditsii, no. 10). Moscow: Nauka

Vorren, K. D. 1979 'Anthropogenic influence on the natural vegetation in coastal North Norway', *Norwegian Archaeological Review* 12, 1: 1–21

Vorren, K. D. and Nilssen, E. 1982 'Det eldste jordbruk i Nord-Norge, en palæo-økologisk oversikt', in Sjøvold (ed.) *Introduksjonen av jordbruk i Norden*, pp. 173–93

Vuorela, J. 1981 'The vegetational and settlement history in Sysmä, Central South Finland, interpreted on the basis of two pollen diagrams', *Bulletin of the Geological Society of Finland* 53, 1: 47–61

Vuorela, J. 1982 'Tidigt jordbruk in S–SW Finland enlight pollenanalys och C14-dateringer', in Sjøvold (ed.) *Indroduksjonen av jordbruk i Norden*, pp. 253–67, Oslo

Waetzoldt, H. 1972 'Untersuchungen zur neusumerischen Textilindustrie', *Studi economici e technologici* 1. Rome

Waldbaum, J. C. 1978 *From Bronze to Iron. The Transition from the Bronze Age to the Iron Age in the Eastern Mediterranean*, Goteborg

Walker, C. 1980 'Some Assyrians at Sippar in the Old Babylonian Period', *Anatolian Studies* XXX: 15–22

Wallace-Hadrill, J. M. 1971 *Early Germanic Kingship in England and on the Continent*, Oxford

Wallerstein, I. 1974 *The Modern World-System: Capitalist Agriculture and the Origins of the European World-Economy in the Sixteenth Century* vol. 1, New York: Academic Press

    1979a *The Capitalist World Economy* Cambridge University Press

    1979b 'The rise and demise of the world capitalist economy: concepts for comparative analysis' in Wallerstein 1979a

    1979c 'Krondratieff up or Krondratieff down', *Review* II, 4: 663–73

    1980 *The Modern World System* Vol. 2 Academic Press, London

Webb, M. C. 1975 'The flag follows trade: an essay on the necessary interaction of military and commercial factors in state formation' in J. A. Sabloff and C. C. Lamberg-Karlovsky *Ancient Civilization and Trade* Albuquerque, pp. 155ff

Weber, M. 1976 *The Agrarian Sociology of Ancient Civilisations* NLB, London

Weeks, K. R. 1971–2 'Preliminary report on the first two seasons at Hierakonpolis: the Early Dynastic palace', *Journal of the American Research Centre in Cairo* IX: 29ff

Weidner, E. F. 1923 *Politische Dokumente aus Kleinasien*, Leipzig

Weigend, P., Harbottle, G., and Sayre, E. 1977 'Turquoise sources and source analysis' in T. Earle and J. Ericson *Exchange System in Prehistory* Academic Press, New York

Weiner, A. 1985 'Inalienable Wealth', *American Ethnologist* 12, 2: 210–27

Weisgerber, G. 1980 '. . . und Kupfer in Oman', *Der Anschnitt-Zeitschrift für Kunst und Kultur im Bergbau* 32(2–3): 62–110

    1981 'Mehr als Kupfer in Oman – Ergebnisse der Expedition 1981', *Der Anschnitt-Zeitschrift für Kunst und Kulturim Bergbau* 33:5–6): 174–263

    n.d. 'Makan and Meluhha-3rd millennium B.C. copper production in Oman and the evidence of contact with the Indus Valley'

Weiss, H. 1977 'Early state formation in Khuzistan' in L. D. Levine and T. Cuyler Young, Jr., (eds) *Mountains and Lowlands* Malibu, pp. 247ff

Weiss, H. and Cuyler Young, T. Jr., 1975 'The merchants of Susa; Godin V and the plateau–lowland relations in the late fourth millennium B.C.', *Iran* 13: 1ff

Welinder, S. 1974 *Kulturlandskabet i Mälarområdet*, University of Lund. Dept of Quarterinary Geology, Report 6

Welinder, S. *Ekonomiska processer i förhistorisk expansion* (Prehistoric economy during an expansion stage) Acta arck. Lundensia. Series in 8, Minore no. 7

Welinder, S. 'The ecology of the Bronze Age landscape in Central Sweden', in B. Stjernquist (ed.) *Structur och förändring i Bronsåldrens samhälle*, pp. 166–83, University of Lund

Wertime, T. A. and Muhly, J. D. (eds.) 1980 *The Coming of the Age of Iron*, New Haven

Weski, T. 1982 *Waffen in germanischen Gräbern der älteren römischen Kaiserzeit südlich der Ostee*. BAR Intern. Ser. 147. Oxford

Whallon, R. 1979 *An Archaeological Survey of the Keban Reservoir Area of East-Central Turkey*. Memoirs of the Museum of Anthropology II. Ann Arbor: University of Michigan

Whallon, R. and Kantmann, S. 1967 'Early Bronze Age development in the Keban reservoir, east-central Turkey', *Current Anthropology* 10: 128–33

Wheatley, P. 1971 *The Pivot of the Four Quarters* Chicago University Press

    1975 'Satyarvta in Sinvarnadvipa: from reciprocity to redistribution in Ancient S.E. Asia' in J. Sabloff and C. C. Lamberg Karlovsky (eds) *Ancient Civilization and Trade* New Mexico University Press, Albuquerque

Wheeler, R. E. M. and Richardson, K. M. 1957 *The Hillforts of Northern France (Research Reports of the Society of Antiquaries of London* 19). London

Whimster, R. 1981 *Burial Practices in Iron Age Britain* BAR 90, Oxford

Whittaker, C. R. 1983 'Late Roman Trade and Traders', in P. Garnsey, K. Hopkins and C. R. Whittaker (eds) *Trade in the Ancient Economy*. University of California Press

Widgren, M. 1983 *Settlement and Farming Systems in the Early Iron Age*, Stockholm

    1984 'The settlement and farming system in Ostergötland Sweden 1 to AD 500' in K. Kristiansen (ed.) *Settlement and Economy in Later Scandinavian Prehistory* BAR Interm. Ser. 211. Oxford

Wightman, E. M. 1975 'The pattern of Rural Settlement in Roman Gaul' in H. Temporini, W. Haase (eds) *Aufstieg und Niedergang der römischen Welt*: 2.4 584–657. Berlin

Wightman, E. M. 1978 'Peasants and potentates', *American Journal of Ancient History* 3: 97–128

    1985 *Gallia Belgica*. London, Batsford

Will, E. 1954 'Trois quarts de siècle de recherches sur l'économie grècque antique', *Annales E.S.C.* 9: 7–22

Willcox, G. H. 1974 'A history of deforestation as indicated by charcoal analysis of four sites in eastern Anatolia', *Anatolian Studies* 24: 117–33

Willerding, U. 1977 'Über Klima-Entwicklung und Vegetationsverhältnisse im Zeitraum Eisenqeit bis Mittelalter', in H. Jankuhn *et al.* (eds.) *Das Dorf der Eisenzeit und des frühen Mittelalter*, Göttingen

Williams, D. 1981 'The Roman amphorae trade with later Iron Age Britain'. In H. Howard and E. L. Morris, *Production and distribution: a ceramic viewpoint*: 123–32, BAR 5–120 Oxford

Wilson, J. A. 1951 *The Burden of Egypt*, Chicago

Windelhed, B. 1984 '"Celtic fields" and prehistoric agrarian landscapes', in K. Kristiansen (ed.) *Settlement and Economy in the Later Scandinavian Prehistory*. BAR Inter. Ser. 211. Oxford

Winkler, H. A. 1938 *Rock Drawings of Southern Upper Egypt*, I, London

Winter, I. J. 1977 'Perspective on the "local style" of Hasanlu IVb: a study of receptivity' in L. D. Levine and T. Cuyler Young Jr. (eds) *Mountains and Lowlands* Malibu, pp. 371ff

Wittfogel, K. 1957 *Oriental Despotism: A Comparative Study of total power*, New Haven

Wolf, E. R. 1982 *Europe and the People Without History* Berkeley: Univ. of California Press

Wright, H. T. 1977 'Recent research on the origin of the state', *Annual Review of Anthropology* 6: 379ff

Wright, H. T. and Johnson, G. A. 1975 'Population, exchange and early state formation in southwestern Iran' *American Anthropologist* 77: 269ff

Yeivin, S. 1960 'Early contacts between Canaan and Egypt, *Israel Exploration Journal* 10: 193–203

Yoffee, N. 1979 'The decline and rise of Mesopotamia civilization: an ethnoarchaeological perspective on the evolution of Social Complexity', *American Antiquity* 44: 5–35

1981 'Explaining trade in Ancient Western Asia', *Monographs on the Ancient Near East* Volume 2. fascicle 2. Malibu

Zaccagnini, C. 1970 'KBO I 14e il "Monopolio" hittita del ferro'. *Rivista degli studi orientali* 45: 11–20

1973 *Lo scambio dei doni nel Vicino Oriente durante i secoli XV–XIII*, Rome

1976 'La circolazione dei beni' in M. Liverani (ed.), *L'Alba della civilta* II Torino, 423–582

1977 'The merchant at Nuzi', *Iraq* 39: 171–89

1979a 'Materiali per una discussione sulla "moneta primitiva": le coppe d'oro e d'argento nel Vicino Oriente durante il II millennio', *Annali dell'Istituto Italiano di Numismatica* 26

1979b *Bullettino del'Istituto di Diritto Romano Vittorio Scialoja* 82: 203–21

1981 'An Uratrean royal inscription in the report of Sargon's eighth campaign' in F. M. Fales (ed.), *Assyrian Royal Inscriptions: New Horizons* Rome 259–62

1982 'The enemy in the Neo-Assyrian royal inscriptions: the "ethnographical" description' in Hans-jörg Nissen and Johannes Renger (editors), *Mesopotamien und seine Nachbarn, Berliner Beiträge zum Vorderen Orient* Band 1, Teil 1, 409–424, Berlin

1983a 'On gift exchange in the Old Babylonian Period', in O. Carruba, M. Liverani, C. Zaccagnini (eds), *Studi F. Pintore* Pavia

1983b 'Patterns of mobility among Ancient Near Eastern craftsmen', *Journal of Near Eastern Studies* 42: 245–64

1984 'Patterns of mobility among Ancient Near Eastern craftsmen', *Journal of Near Eastern Studies* 43: 20–32

in press a 'Transfers of movable property in Nuzi private transactions' *Acts of the Symposium on Non-Palatine Circulation of Goods in the Ancient Near East*

Zarins, J. 1978 'The domesticated equidae of third millennium B.C. Mesopotamia', *Journal of Cuneiform Studies* 30: 3–17

Zvelebil, M. S. and Rowley-Conwy, P. 1985 'Transition to farming in Northern Europe: a hunter-gatherer perspective', *Norwegian Archaeological Review* 17, no. 2: 104–28

INDEX

Page numbers in *italics* refer to illustrations or their captions